Washington
Bedtime Stories

Washington Bedtime Stories

The Politics of Money and Jobs

Herbert Stein

THE FREE PRESS
A Division of Macmillan, Inc.
NEW YORK

The Free Press
A Division of Macmillan, Inc.
866 Third Avenue, New York, N.Y. 10022

Collier Macmillan Canada, Inc.

Printed in the United States of America

printing number

1 2 3 4 5 6 7 8 9 10

Library of Congress Cataloging-in-Publication Data

Stein, Herbert.
  Washington bedtime stories.

  Includes index.
    1. United States—Economic policy—1981–
2. Finance, Public—United States.   3. Economists—
United States.   4. Economics—United States.   I. Title.
HC106.8.S742   1986   330′.0973   86–14290
ISBN 0–02–930870–4

For Mildred

Contents

Preface

The essays included in this volume are the reflections of an economist who has spent almost fifty years in Washington as a bureaucrat, researcher, presidential adviser, observer, and commentator. Two main lessons derived from this experience are the themes of these essays:

1. Economists do not know very much.
2. Other people, including the politicians who make economic policy, know even less about economics than economists do.

These beliefs do not provide a platform from which to make strong pronouncements about economics or economic policy. But they do suggest one important conclusion. We should be grateful that we have a private economic system that is considerably resistant to the errors of economists and politicians and a political tradition that limits the scope of such errors by limiting the power of politicians and their advisers. If these safeguards are recognized, the pretensions of both economists and politicians can be taken in better humor than would otherwise be possible.

Much of what passes for discussion of national economic policy these days consists of bedtime stories made up to amuse or frighten the citizenry. Much of my writing included here is a commentary of these stories, although some of it is stories of my own.

Most of the essays in this volume were published between 1980 and 1985, although a few go back earlier. On page xiii I acknowledge my debt to publications that permitted me to reprint these articles here. I want especially to thank the *Wall Street Journal*, which tolerated on its editorial page an irreverent attitude toward economic policy, including the economic policy it was advocating. Most of all I thank the American Enterprise Institute for maintaining an attitude of serious but not somber discussion of economic policy which encouraged the kind of writing included here.

Acknowledgments

I wish to thank the following for permission to reprint articles originally published by them:

The *American Economic Review*
The American Enterprise Institute
Business Economics
Commentary
Contemporary Policy Issues
Fortune
Klewer-Nijhoff Publishing
Newsweek
The *New York Times*
Southern Economic Journal
The *Wall Street Journal*

The source of each article is indicated in the text.

I am indebted to Gretchen Chellson and Kenneth Couch for help in preparing this volume for publication.

HERBERT STEIN

PART 1

A Washington Economist Looks at Economics

The Washington Economics Industry

Richard T. Ely Lecture
Delivered at the Annual Meeting of the
American Economic Association
New York, December 28, 1985

W HEN Alice Rivlin invited me to give the Ely Lecture I was, of course, honored; I was also puzzled. What could I talk about that most of the audience would not know as well as I, or better? I decided that the answer is the Washington economics industry. I have been working in, living in and observing that industry for more than forty-seven years. Probably there are not over ten people who can say that. I was going to say that the other nine are in Palm Springs, but I see that Walter Salant is here. He nearly qualifies, so I will say that the other eight are in Palm Springs. Also, the one-hundredth anniversary of the Association seems an appropriate occasion for a little nostalgia. Moreover, Richard Ely, for whom this lecture series is named, had an interesting association with Washington economics. In fact, he seriously considered running for Congress in 1912 but was dissuaded by the president of the University of Wisconsin, who didn't think that was an appropriate job for a professor.

In the Ely lecture last year Sir Alec Cairncross referred to economics having become an industry. That is a term that economists do not usually apply to themselves. Probably few economists know that in the Standard Industrial Classification there is an industry called "Economic Research". It is a six-digit industry, 739210. We don't even know how many economists there are in the United States. The Bureau of Labor Statistics has estimated that there were 110,000 economists in 1984. Every economist to whom I have mentioned this figure has been amazed at it. Of course, the BLS statistic comes from the Current Population Survey, in which people classify themselves by occupation. That introduces the possibility of bias. But why should anyone say that he is an economist if he is not?

If we start with the exceedingly rough estimate that there are about 100,000 economists in the country, variously employed, we can make an even rougher estimate of the income originating in the industry. According to the National Science Foundation the average annual salary of economists in 1982 was $35,000. Probably each of these economists had on the average one secretary or other assistant not counted as an economist, with an average salary of $15,000. On the reasonable assumption that the amount of physical capital involved is negligible, that means an income originating in the industry of $50,000 per economist. Thus we have a 5 billion dollar industry. That is about the same size as the motion picture industry, which is, like economics, involved in producing a combination of information and entertainment.

I propose, however, to concentrate on the Washington branch of the industry. And I shall rely heavily on my own observations and impressions rather than on statistical data. This is partly because the statistical data are meager. Also, my advantage in telling the story is that I was there, not that I had any special access to statistics, although I have collected some statistics for this occasion. You will recognize the inevitable subjectivity of my observations. Especially, what I report as the difference between 1938 and 1985 may be only the forty-seven-year difference in the age of the observer and not the difference in the things being observed.

Let me assure you that I am not going to give a memoir of an ex-chairman of the Council of Economic Advisers. That has become a boring literary genre, filled with episodes like this:

"And then I said to the president, 'You should cut taxes,' or 'You should roll back steel prices,' or whatever."

"And the president said to me, 'You're a smart fellow, Tom,' or Dick, or whatever the name was, 'Not like that dumb Treasury secretary I've got.' "

"And that showed that although he had no formal training the president had a good intuitive understanding of economics and appreciation of economists, especially me . . ."

My story begins, then, in 1938, when I came to Washington.

Thinking back at that now, I am surprised to realize that by then the executive branch of the federal government was already pretty well infiltrated by economists. Every agency for which it was at all relevant had a staff of economists. I worked for one of the smallest agencies, the Federal Deposit Insurance Corporation, and we had at least six economists.

According to a survey taken by the Bureau of Labor Statistics and the Civil Service Commission there were 5050 economists employed by the federal government at the end of 1938, not including home economists. Probably the most realistic figure for the present is the 16,000 economists in the federal government estimated by the National Science Foundation for 1982. That would mean that the number of economists had roughly tripled, which is about what has happened to the total federal civilian work force. Of course, not all of those government economists worked in Washington and its environs, but about two-thirds of them do now and probably the same proportion did then.

The number of economists in the federal government had increased greatly in the years before 1938. In a paper given at the meeting of the American Economic Association in December 1936 Leonard White, chairman of the Civil Service Commission, estimated that the size of the federal economics and statistical services had doubled within the previous two years. He also re-ferred to a study estimating that in 1931 there had been 742 posi-tions in economics and statistics, not including home economists. White said: "This may or may not correspond to the accepted defi-nition of a professional economist. The figure doubtless repre-sents a maximum if we are thinking of 'genuine' economists." White put the word "genuine" in quotation marks. What he meant by that, or by the accepted definition of professional econo-mists, I do not know. It is not a distinction I intend to make.

Pushing the history back before 1930 in statistical terms is difficult. In 1896, according to White, there had been 87 people in the government with the title of "statistician." But there was only one with the word "economic" in his title, and he was an "economic ornithologist." That only shows how unreliable these classifications are. Many economists had worked for the federal government, not only before 1930 but also before 1900. Francis Amasa Walker, the first president of this association, had been director of the Census in 1880 and 1890. In fact, half of the men who were presidents of the AEA during the first fifty years of its existence had some experience working for the federal government. The Census Bureau and the Interstate Commerce Commission were favorite places.

Richard Ely did not work for the federal government, although he held several positions for the State of Wisconsin in Madison. He was, however, much interested in the employment of economists in the federal government and seems to have been uncommonly diligent in promoting his students and colleagues for federal jobs. He apparently thought that there was a given number of University of Wisconsin slots in the federal service. (The following facts about Ely and his contemporaries of the years before 1920 are derived from a fascinating dissertation "Professors and Public Service, 1885–1925" by David M. Grossman.)

When Walter Willcox, later to be president of the AEA, was appointed as chief statistician of the Census, in 1899, he wrote to Ely as follows:

"It may conduce to a better understanding of the situation if I explain that the selection of a college teacher for one of the positions was not intended as a compliment to the University he represented. . . ."

Ely and others of his time did not regard Washington as a useful place for a career; it was a place for temporary exposure to the real world before returning to the serious business of the University. In 1906 Ely wrote to John R. Commons about government service:

"I believe that very generally it is felt that two or three years of that sort of work is about as much as a man can safely undertake."

These economists before World War I were generally involved in technical positions in Washington, often as statisticians. During World War I some economists came to Washington in positions with more policy responsibility—Frank W. Taussig at the Price Fixing Commission, Wesley Mitchell with the War Industries Board, and Edwin Gay with the War Shipping Board. Wars have played a major part in the development of the Washington economics industry.

These early notables, although they spent some time in Washington, were not what we would call today Washington economists. That is, their careers were not made in Washington. An interesting case is that of Henry Carter Adams, who, when he accepted a post with the Interstate Commerce Commission, insisted on the creation of a field office in Ann Arbor which would allow him to devote most of his time and energy to the university.

Let me now return to 1938. Opportunities for the employment of economists in the academic world or in business were not good. Fellowships for remaining in graduate student status for years and years were not available. Economists turned to the federal government because that was where the jobs were. Many came to Washington expecting to earn a living while they finished their theses, which some did and some found, many years later, they had not done. To some extent the increase of employment of economists in the federal government was supply-driven. The federal government was in the business of providing jobs for all kinds of people—artists, actors, writers, for example. Some of the employment of economists came about in this permissive atmosphere.

But also the economists, mostly young, who came to the federal government fifty years ago found it an interesting, satisfying place to work—beyond the satisfaction of having a job and an income. It is not that we thought ourselves to play important roles in great revolutionary decisions. When I came to study the period later, to write *The Fiscal Revolution in America,* I was surprised at how little I had known of what was going on although I was there. That was not a time when every whisper of a hint of a thought about economic policy was reported in the Washington press and mulled over at lunch by every economist in town. But there was a certain freshness and interest in the tasks that we were doing, even though they were small tasks. We were working in new agencies or on new assignments of old agencies, and we were bringing to many of these tasks for the first time the economics we had just learned. Much of what we were doing would now be regarded as drudgery. Work that took me months at the FDIC would now be done by a computer in minutes. But at least I thought I understood why I was doing it.

One might think that although economists were spread widely through the executive branch by 1938 they were not as influential as they later became. But I am not sure that was true. People like Harry White at Treasury, Isadore Lubin at Labor, and Herbert Feis at State were important. In fact, they were probably more important than any subsequent economist in those departments until an economist became secretary in each of them. And but for the accident that George Shultz is an economist it might still be true that those people in the 1930s were the most influential economists those departments ever had.

There was no President's Council of Economic Advisers, of course. But the president did talk to some economists—Lauchlin Currie, Isadore Lubin, Leon Henderson for example. Whether their influence was as great as that of later Councils of Economic Advisers over their presidents is uncertain. Probably the difference was not dramatic. Roosevelt got all the advice of economists he wanted, which is about as much as any President gets.

In one respect at least the late 1930s was the golden age for government economists. That was in the development of economic statistics. This was the period when scientific sampling was introduced into federal statistical methods. The chief product of that was the Current Population Survey, which yields the employment and unemployment figures and much else. It is of some interest that the Current Population Survey was initiated by the WPA, which existed primarily to provide jobs. Also in this period the official national income statistics were initiated and developed most of the way to their present condition. A large part of the statistics upon which economists rely heavily today originated in the years 1935–1940.

These years, just before World War II, were not a period of sharp division among Washington economists on grounds of theory or ideology. We were all Keynesians in a loose, eclectic, pragmatic sense. We thought that the immediate economic problem was inadequacy of total demand and that the long-run problem was instability of total demand. We thought that a flexible fiscal policy was a useful and possibly essential means for correcting these problems. By 1938 interest in structural or micro issues, the kind of interest that had given rise to the National Recovery Administration, had faded among economists. There was a view in Washington that industrial monopoly was a major source of our economic problems, but that view was largely confined to lawyers. The attention of economists was focused on macroeconomics. It was not until Alvin Hansen revealed his version of Keynesian economics, in 1941, and Henry Simons replied to it in 1942, that I realized that I was not the same kind of Keynesian as everyone else.

A little nest of dissent existed at the Brookings Institution. Brookings was then the only nongovernment research institute, the term "think-tank" not yet having been invented. It was a prod-

uct of World War I, when Robert Brookings, a St. Louis businessman serving in wartime economic agencies, became convinced
of the need to apply social science to government. I worked for
a man who had been a Fellow at Brookings and we went there
frequently for lunch. The stalwarts of the institution, who only
a few years earlier had been in the front line of economic discussion, now seemed to talk an archaic language and to be completely
out of the picture. They worried about the federal debt, and were
either ten years behind the times or forty years ahead.

I do not think of the Washington economists of 1938 as being
identifiably Democrats or Republicans, as would be true of many
today. Perhaps that is because they were all Democrats. But I
don't think that is the whole explanation. Certainly the upper
level of government economists were devoted to Roosevelt and
the New Deal. But that was not the same as being a Democrat.
For many economists serving in the government during the New
Deal was a nonpartisan activity, like serving during a war.

World War II was a watershed in the history of Washington
economics. The first World War had established the fact that
economists could be useful in the operation of a war economy.
But the infusion of economists was much greater in World War
II. Of course, the second war was much bigger and longer and
had much more extensive economic controls. But also, the second
war came to a Washington that already had a large number of
government economists, they were naturally drawn to the early
stages of economic planning for the war and they naturally re-
cruited other economists as the control activities expanded.

The most important contribution of economists to the war
effort was not in the management of the price and production
controls, which was probably as well done by lawyers, accountants,
businessmen, and engineers. It came in the big decisions about
the overall size of the effort. The economist who made this contribution was Robert Nathan, who turns out in my story to be one
of the outstanding figures in five decades of Washington economics. He had been one of the pioneers in the development of the
national income accounts at the Department of Commerce. After
the war he would pioneer the movement of Washington economists into the world of profit by establishing one of the first private
consulting firms. In the early days of the war, before the United
States entered, there was substantial disagreement about how
much military buildup the economy could afford. Using the na-

tional income statistics, Nathan made an effective argument that we could afford a much bigger buildup than the War and Navy Departments were planning. After Pearl Harbor the situation was reversed. The services wanted everything. Nathan by then was director of the Planning Division of the War Production Board. He showed that the combined requirements could not be met and that the attempt to meet them all would result in unbalanced forces, uncompleted weapons systems, and wasteful production.

Macroeconomists can feel confident in wartime, because in wartime they deal with large numbers—large enough to override the noise in the data and the conditionality of the analysis. We may not predict very well the consequences of the difference between federal spending of 20 or 25 percent of GNP, or of a deficit of 2 or 3 percent of GNP. But we can give a useful, if rough, estimate of the consequences of raising federal spending from 10 to 50 percent of GNP or of raising the deficit from 3 to 25 percent of GNP.

The war years were the time of the closest connection between Washington economics and the rest of the economics industry. One evidence of that is the frequency of publications in economic journals by government economists. George Stigler once made a tabulation of the sources of articles in four general economics journals at ten year intervals from 1882–83 to 1962–63. With the help of my secretary, I have repeated that for 1972–73 and 1982–83. In the years 1942–43, 17 percent of the articles came from economists in government. The average of all the other years was only 5.5 percent and the highest figure aside from the war years was 9.4 percent in 1912–13. It was not only that more economists were in government during the war. It was also that a large proportion of the articles in the journals were related to war or postwar problems. The program of the 1944 annual meetings of the American Economic Association was almost entirely filled with papers on such subjects. As a further contribution of the profession to the war effort, the meetings were canceled at the request of the Office of Defense Transportation in order to save transportation.

By the end of the war it was clear that a large role for the federal government in the economy was here to stay. The 1930s fight about the New Deal was over. For one thing, scores of businessmen, the chief recalcitrants about the New Deal, had spent the war in Washington and learned that they could live with it.

And it was also clear that the language in which this activity would be conducted was economics. It was almost as if someone had suddenly decreed that the language of the government would be Latin. There would be a great demand for people who could speak Latin. So there was a great demand in Washington for people who could speak economics. There was also a large supply of them, who had come for the war and didn't want to go home again.

The growth of the Washington economics industry proceeds largely by competition and emulation. Washington is an arena of competition—the White House against the Departments, the Executive Branch against the Congress, the regulated against the regulators. If one team has economists the other team must respond by having economists. Much, of course not all, of what has happened in the past forty years can be explained by this process.

I shall not try to unravel the tangled web of statistics about the size and growth of the Washington economics industry. About all one can say with confidence is that there are lots of economists in Washington, that their numbers have increased substantially, and that the growth of Washington economics outside the government since before the war has been much greater than the growth inside the government. For those who insist on numbers I will offer the following guesses. I think that there are about 15,000 economists in the Washington area, excluding academics, compared to about 3000 in 1938. Of those 15,000 about 11,000 are in the federal government, including about 500 in the legislative branch, where there were probably none in 1938. The 4000 outside the federal government are divided in about equal thirds among international institutions—the International Monetary Fund, the World Bank, and their smaller brothers—nonprofit research institutions, think tanks—and representatives of the private profit sector, including consultancies. Almost all of this is new since World War II. In 1938 there were only eight economists listed in the yellow pages of the Washington phone book. I should add to the category of the Washington economics industry a handful of people who will be forever identified with Washington, whether they live in Minneapolis, Ann Arbor, St. Louis, or wherever.

One real statistic I cannot forebear to mention. According to the National Science Foundation the number of economists in the federal government increased by about 60 percent from 1980 to 1983. I wonder whether President Reagan knows that.

If my estimate is anywhere near correct there are about two-thirds as many economists in the Washington economics industry as on all the college and university faculties in the country, and about three-fourths as many as belong to the AEA. Also, clearly the Washington economics industry is much more than the fifteen or so people who appear on television all the time. The fifteen are to the Washington economics industry what Lee Iacocca is to the automobile industry.

As far as the executive branch is concerned, the main development of the postwar years is not the increase in the number of economists. The increase has apparently been large, but that is a continuation of the trend noticed before the war. The main development in the executive branch was the change in the level of economists. Starting with the Council of Economic Advisers we got an increasing number of economists of cabinet or sub-cabinet rank, appointed by the president, confirmed by the Senate and serving at the president's pleasure. Even the leading members of the Roosevelt Brain Trust did not have such status. That had a number of implications that I will point out later.

What are all of these economists doing in the Washington economics industry? Broadly, their functions can be divided into three—research, advocacy, and decision making. This does not mean that the individual economists can be segregated into these three boxes. Many do two or three of these things, although I suppose most Washington economists could be identified as being primarily engaged in one.

I shall have little to say about the advocacy function. It comes in two parts—micro, that is, advocacy before a limited audience such as a regulatory agency or a congressional committee, for a specific purpose such as a rate increase or a desired tax treatment, and macroadvocacy, that is, trying to appeal to a broader audience, ultimately the public. I have little experience with micro advocacy, except to observe that its practitioners eat lunch at the expensive K Street restaurants and smoke big cigars. Most of my life in Washington was spent in a combination of research and macroad-vocacy, at the Committee for Economic Development. This function is commonly misunderstood, even by those who participate in it, and perhaps especially by them. They believe, and tell their supporters, that they are having a great influence on public policy by talking to decision makers in Washington and appearing before Congressional committees. The fallacy of that became clear to me when I was later in the government. The self-appointed outside advisers to government do not function quickly enough, or with enough information, to have much direct influence on the government decision-making process. Where they do have an influence, and I believe it is a real influence, is in gradually affecting the climate of public opinion within which government officials feel they have to operate.

According to the National Science Foundation, 80 percent of all federal government economists in 1982 reported that their primary work activity was research and development, the management of R&D and reporting and statistical activity. Two questions come to my mind about this. The first is whether government economists, presumably engaged in research of some kind, are keeping up with developments in the academic side of the industry. I am led to this question by observing that when I came to Washington I could read and reasonably understand almost everything in the economic journals. Today I can read hardly any of it. Also, I observe that although government economists are about 15 percent of all economists and about two-thirds as numerous as the economics teachers, they contribute only 3 or 4 percent of the articles in economic journals. This is a smaller percentage than at the turn of the century.

Further reflection and observation lead to more reassurance. When I recall the economists with whom I worked at the Council of Economic Advisers and solicit the experience of my colleagues at the American Enterprise Institute, I am persuaded that while economics has left me behind it has not left the Washington economics community behind. I often think of the occasion at the Council of Economic Advisers in 1969 when we were asked what the effect of repealing the investment tax credit would be on economic growth. One of the young members of the staff, drawing on the latest journal articles, produced the answer overnight, to two decimal places. It may not have been the right answer, but it was the best economics had to offer.

As for why government economists do not write more for economic journals, I am reminded of the answer the woman gave when asked why her twenty-year-old son was carried from the car to the apartment house by the chauffeur. "Of course he can walk, but thank God he doesn't have to."

The second question about the research activities of the Washington economists is whether they are adequately serving their function of providing the rest of the profession with the data, mainly statistical, that it needs. If, for example, you compare the statistical appendices to the CEA's economic reports for 1960 and 1985 you will find some increase of detail in the later year but hardly any new subjects covered except for the poverty and productivity statistics. Perhaps that is not a sufficient sample, but still I think it is clear that the pace of advance in supplying new data has slowed down from the 1930s and the first postwar decade. It may be that we have measured everything that could or should be measured, but I doubt that. I have the fear that unless some new data are turned up soon the econometricians will be unemployed for lack of inputs, having exhaustively analyzed all the existing information. Of course, Washington does provide occasional revisions of the old data, which provides some new work to do.

Let me turn now to the part of the Washington economics industry that is in or near the policy-making process, or aspires to be. That is certainly a small part of the industry, and may not be the most important, but is certainly the most conspicuous. Three things strike me about this part of the industry, especially as compared with my impression of the situation in the 1930s. These things are all related. The participants are more political; they are more divided, in talk although not in action, into different schools of economics; and they get much more publicity.

I have said elsewhere that the Employment Act of 1946 may or may not have succeeded in its goal of introducing economics into politics but it certainly succeeded in introducing politics into economics. This would have happened anyway, in time, even if there had been no Council of Economic Advisers. Once Presidents and Cabinet members get to appointing economists who will be close to them, speak for them and, on occasion, act for them, they look naturally for sympathy and loyalty, and they are likely to take party affiliation as evidence of that. Even where economists are not chosen on that basis, they tend to acquire a feeling of membership in the political team if they have been treated as members of it, and few who have had that experience ever regain their virginity. And economists who aspire to such positions, or who only enjoy the excitement of involvement in the political process, take on political coloration and offer themselves to candidates who all now want economists on their campaign planes along with the make-up men and the TV producers.

So we have developed a cadre of economists who are identifiably Republican or Democrat. Even beyond that we are developing coteries that are particular kinds of Republicans or Democrats—Kemp followers or Bush beaters or what not.

Connected with their partisan identification is an increasing tendency to differentiate the product that economists have to offer, as far as talk is concerned. If you are the adviser to a Republican candidate or incumbent you tend even in your own mind to magnify your differences from the advisers of the Democrats. So you get little schools of economists who cling together, help each other and talk as if they had serious ideological or theoretical differences with the others, about incomes policy, or monetary rules, or the natural rate of unemployment, or other things. But the relations among these political, ideological schools have been amicable, with some exceptions. The participants seem to recognize that although they are on different teams they are in the same game and that they need each other.

Moreover, when these people get into positions of responsibility their differences fade. I think that a study of the recommendations and reports of the Council of Economic Advisers during the twenty-eight years from 1953 to 1981—sixteen Republican years and twelve Democratic—would reveal little durable difference among them. Each team comes into office with a grand manifesto emphasizing its fundamental differences from its predecessors. Within a year or two that is all submerged in the attempt to wrestle with the same problems with the same inadequate instruments and knowledge. The Reagan team of economists entered office with exceptionally large differences from all of their predecessors, Republican as well as Democratic. But by now the sharp edges of those differences have worn away. The most devoted supporters of what was peculiarly Reagan economics have left the team and accuse those who remain of infidelity. To some on the outside this tendency towards an eclectic, mainstream position looks like weakness and political compromise. In my opinion, it is compromise all right, but with reality, with the reality of the limitations of economics and with the intractability of the economy. Just as there are no atheists in foxholes there are no dogmatists at the Council of Economic Advisers, and for similar reasons. The risks are too great.

The greatly increased publicity of Washington economists in the popular media since the end of the war is connected with their politicization. The media are interested in economics mainly as a branch of politics. What they want to know about the tax bill is not what it means for the economy but what it means for President Reagan or Congressman Rostenkowski. They look to economics as a window for observing politics and they are attracted to economists with political connections.

As an attempt to measure the publicity given to Washington economists, with the help of my wife, my only research assistant, I have counted up the number of times the *New York Times* index referred to what I considered the most conspicuous Washington economists at intervals beginning in 1938. In 1938 there were eleven, or twenty-three if one includes Leon Henderson who was an economist not functioning as an economist. In 1948 and in 1953 there were thirty-four. In 1984 there were seventy-four. 1972 was off the trend with 132, because that was a year of great excitement about price controls as well as about a presidential election.

I have also counted the number of appearances by economists on "Meet the Press" in the thirty-seven years of its weekly programming. There have been fifty-seven such appearances, far more than for any other group of people other than full-time politicians. (I exclude people like George Shultz and James Schlesinger who are economists but not being interviewed as economists.) Almost all of these appearances were by Washington economists, except for the occasional appearance by a newly crowned Nobel laureate. And when the little red light went on and the camera was rolling, the Nobel laureates all sounded like Washington economists anyway—just as partisan and just as willing to give easy answers to hard questions. Twelve of these appearances were by Walter Heller who, although he no longer lives in Washington, will always be the Washington economist par excellence. Heller even appeared more often than King Hussein. The only three people who had more appearances than he were Henry Cabot Lodge, Hubert Humphrey, and Nelson Rockefeller—all of whom had been vice-presidents or candidates for the vice-presidency.

This increased public exposure is gratifying to a degree, but also worrisome. It is largely confined to the more political members of our profession, who are not always the most candid or best informed. These people tend to emphasize controversy. Frequently the TV producer will call up to ask what answers you would give to certain questions if invited to appear on the program, and this usually sounds like the try-out for a combat. Frank Knight liked to repeat the saying that the trouble was not what people didn't know but what they knew that wasn't so. I am not sure whether our public appearances are reducing what people don't know more than they are increasing what people know that isn't so. But I am reassured when I consider the alternatives. The TV time must be filled, and the FCC requires that a certain amount of it be filled with talk. If someone is going to talk about economics on TV it is probably better done by economists than by politicians, columnists, sociologists, or clergymen—who seem the most likely alternatives.

Probably that applies to much of what the Washington economics industry does. We may not do very well what we do, but if it has to be done it is better done by us than by the alternatives.

I observe that most articles in the *American Economic Review* have a conclusion. I have always supposed that this was because the body of the article is so impenetrable that one last-gasp effort had to be made to explain what it all means. And I suppose I should have a conclusion evaluating the Washington economics industry. But how does an economist evaluate an industry? We are not Ralph Naders, asking whether the industry causes cancer or highway fatalities, or even whether it is good or true. We may ask whether the industry is profitable, but that is not measurable for most of the Washington economics industry.

Probably the best standard for evaluating this industry is the quality of life experienced by the people who participate in it. By this standard the statistics are ambiguous. The average salary of a government economist was almost twelve times as high in 1983 as in 1938. Deflated by the Consumer Price Index, the real increase was almost 70 percent. But in the same period real annual wages and salaries per full-time equivalent employee in the economy as a whole increased by 120 percent.

Even this computed 70 percent increase in the real incomes of government economists does not seem realistic to me. I feel like the housewives I am always meeting who tell me that their cost of living has gone up more than the CPI. But when we came to Washington in 1938 we could rent an apartment four blocks from the White House for $50 a month and hire a maid for twenty-five cents an hour. There is no comparable rent today and the maid's wage would be at least twenty times higher. As I think of the living standards of people in comparable positions today and in 1938 it seems to me that the main differences are that today's economists have color televisions and trips to Europe, with which they are getting bored, and less domestic service, if any.

But still, the Washington economist leads a comfortable life in the dimensions measured by income statistics. The average salary of a Washington economist is about twice as high as the salary of the average American worker. It is a little less than the salary of the average Washington lawyer, but not enough less to be irritating. And there is more to life than can be measured by income statistics. The Washington economist is likely to have a job with some intellectual challenge. He faces a certain amount of competitiveness or rivalry in his professional life, enough to make the game interesting, but the game is played with civility—more civility than I understand is found on many college campuses. This civility is, I believe, derived from the style of politicans, who may be ruthless but are also in the business of being nice to people. The Washington economist, if he has even a little imagination, gets an occasional thrill out of feeling that he lives in the shadow of history. He gets a kick out of being connected, even in a small way, with events that are part of the daily news not only of the city but also of the nation and the world. Of course, there is a certain repetitiveness in the news—the new tax simplification plan, the new plan for balancing the budget, the new turn of monetary policy. After forty-seven years one has the sense of having gone around this track many times. But after forty-seven years that happens everywhere. Even the pilot of the space shuttle must say, after the forty-seventh orbit, "Gee, here comes that old Great Wall of China again." But for the first forty-five orbits it is all very exciting.

I hope you will not think it too prosaic or even belittling that I have summed up my observations on the Washington economics industry by appraising the lives of those who work in it instead of by judging how the industry has changed the world for good or ill. Even though we are economists we like to think that we have not only a price but also a value, which is presumably greater. I do not want to deny that there may be another standard for judging the industry. But that will have to wait for another occasion and another judge.

Bricks Without Straw

Remarks of Herbert Stein
Western Economic Association
Las Vegas, Nevada, June 27, 1984

I AM honored to be invited to address the Western Economic Association, and especially honored to be introduced by Milton Friedman. My speech is really inspired by Professor Friedman. I am going to talk about some of the things economists don't know. The way I learn what we don't know is this: If I observe that 99 percent of all economists say one thing and Milton Friedman says another, I conclude that the economic profession is evenly divided and we don't know what is true.

When Professor Friedman invited me to give this lecture I accepted without hesitation. That was out of respect and admiration for him and not out of love for Las Vegas. I told him that I thought some subject to talk about would occur to me before the scheduled date arrived. In any case, I would not talk about the budget deficit, because I was sick of that subject.

Since then, of course, I have been like the small boy whose mother told him not to put a bean up his nose. I have been unable to think of anything else. My bean, which I cannot get out of my mind, is the budget deficit.

But still I was struggling to think of something else to talk about until I received an announcement informing me that the general theme of this conference would be "Bridging the Gap between Theory and Decision." It seemed to me irresistibly appropriate that I should talk about this general theme and that I should also talk about the budget deficit because the question of deficit policy illustrated well what I think about the decision-making process.

It is appropriate for me to talk about the general theme of

the conference because I have spent all of my professional life in the gap that lies between theory and decision. I have been neither a theory maker nor a decision maker, but I have been part of the transmission belt which lies between them and have had an opportunity to observe both ends of the belt and the movement between them.

I realize that there is a theory of decision making that has achieved a certain degree of sophistication, but I am not a student of that. I have looked into the literature of that subject a little in the thought that it might help to prepare me for this lecture. I read enough to learn that if I was a prisoner locked in one cell and my colleague was locked in the next cell I should confess. That has some relevance to my theme today, because I am making a confession. But I did not find this a fruitful line of study, because the policy maker I am concerned with knows less than the prisoner in his cell. So I am not offering you a systematic analysis of decision making but only some casual empiricism. I present some observations in ichthyology from the standpoint of the fish rather than the ichthyologist.

My basic point is that on many questions of economic policy there is no bridge between theory and decision. Travel between theory and decision is not by a bridge but by a flight of fancy. The knowledge of economists is far short of what would be reasonably needed for making a decision. I refer here to matters of fact, about the consequences of possible courses of action, and not to value judgments about the desirability of the consequences, a subject on which economists have no special competence. That economists do not know enough should be obvious and require no demonstration. But when I raise this thought with my economist friends at lunch at the American Enterprise Institute—which is my usual way of doing research—they resist, and try to convince me that even I, despite my demurrers, know enough. That is where the deficit comes in, because it is a leading example of how much or little we know.

Before going further I want to try to guard against misinterpretation. I do not want to give comfort to the view that because economists do not know enough everything is possible, indeed that everything is equally probable and that one can say anything one wants without fear of contradiction. I especially want to reject the view that because economists do not know enough politicians, newspaper columnists, and all-purpose intellectuals know better. That is not what I am saying.

Even though we don't know enough, different economists do assert different propositions with apparently much confidence, and it is of some interest to ask why different economists believe and say such different things. And despite the limitations of our knowledge, decision makers must make decisions and do. We have to ask how they do that.

Let me now turn to topic A, the overmasticated subject of the budget deficit, and discuss what we would like to know as a basis for making a decision about that.

Ten or fifteen years ago a discussion of the consequence of a large budget deficit would have started with a consideration of the size of its effect in stimulating total demand, and the consequences of that effect for output, employment, and prices. This aspect of the matter seems to have been subordinated in recent discussion of the deficit. For example, the most recent report of the Council of Economic Advisers does not mention this kind of consequence except for a half sentence which warns that a very large, sudden reduction of the deficit might have a temporarily retarding effect on the recovery, which seems more like a bow to an ancient superstition than a realistic worry. This is partly because we are now talking about deficits stretching out as far as the eye can see, which diverts attention from the shorter-run demand-stimulating effect. But it is also because we have become uncertain about the stimulating effect. The present state of thinking was well summarized in the remark of a leading government economist that we know there is a deficit multiplier but we don't know whether it is positive or negative.

We used to have two theories, one that said deficits, or increases of deficits, were stimulating and one that said they weren't. Now for the first time in fifty years we have had a revival of the idea that deficits are depressing. This idea is embodied in the most common economic forecasts. Despite the failure of the deficit to abort the recovery it remains a standard view that the duration of the recovery is threatened by the size of the deficit. The theories by which this conclusion is justified range from incredibly naive to incredibly sophisticated. I do not find any of this argument convincing and I do not think that this stimulating or depressing effect should be a main consideration in decisions about the budget deficit. But we should recognize that there is a greater range of disagreement in the profession about this effect than there has been in a long time.

Current attention on the consequences of deficits focuses

on longer run effects, properly, in my opinion. Many of these effects are supposed to operate through interest rates. Ordinary analysis would say that an increase in the government deficit is an increase in the demand for loanable funds which should have the effect of increasing the price of loanable funds, or interest rates. But current discussion makes clear that this conclusion is not obvious or firmly demonstrable. There have been many efforts to discover the relationship between deficits and interest rates econometrically. These attempts have been inconclusive. That surely does not mean that no relationship exists. It only means that some studies have found a relationship and others have not and we cannot be sure that there is such a relationship.

There are several possible explanations for the failure to find the conventional relationship. One is that there are many factors influencing interest rates and that the variations in the size of the cyclically adjusted deficit relative to saving that we are able to observe in the postwar period have been too small to permit isolation of the effect of the deficit. We can observe a very large deficit during World War II, and interest rates remained low then. But that was also a period of price control, consumer rationing, and restriction of private investment, so the free-market relations between deficits and interest rates cannot be deduced from that experience.

Other explanations would imply that either the private demand for savings or the private supply of savings is perfectly elastic with respect to interest rates, so that an increase in the budget deficit either displaces an equal amount of private investment or induces an equal amount of private saving without an increase of interest rates. The classic explanation is that the supply of private saving is very elastic, not to interest rates but to the deficit itself, so that an increase in the demand for saving to finance the deficit will induce a corresponding increase in the supply of saving without an increase of interest rates. The presumed mechanism is that taxpayers recognize that the deficit implies higher taxes in the future and save more in order to prepare for paying for those taxes.

I am not aware of any evidence that this process works. One might have thought that at the end of World War II, when the depression and the war had increased federal debt enormously, people would save more to prepare for the higher taxes, but there is no sign of that. I have never met anyone who claims that he personally reacts to deficits in the way stipulated. I have examined the one person whose behavior I am able to examine, namely myself, and I do not find such a reaction. Indeed, I have recently become aware of a paradoxical possibility. As I near retirement I become more sensitive to the possible implications of future taxes on my present saving. The higher I think future taxes will be the more I will save today. But when I ask myself what I expect future taxes to be, the answer I get is that I expect them to be what they are today. This has the result that if taxes are raised today to reduce the deficit my expectation of future taxes is raised and I save more. That is, a lower deficit induces more saving.

This may be a particularly slovenly attitude on my part, but I do have a lawyer, an accountant, and an actuary and no one of them has ever suggested that I should save more because of the deficit, and when they think of future taxes they simply extrapolate present taxes.

I am not trying to prove that deficits do not increase saving by an equal amount, but only trying to illustrate the easier point that we really do not know that they do.

The concern about the effect of deficits on interest rates is largely due to concern about the crowding-out effects of deficits. Presumably if deficits raise interest rates they crowd out private investment and if they don't they don't. This is not an airtight proposition, because if the demand for investment is infinitely elastic it might be crowded out without any increase of interest rates.

Some of you may find it difficult to accept the idea that we don't know whether deficits raise interest rates or whether they crowd out private investment. But you may agree that a priori reasoning certainly does not tell us anything about the magnitude of this effect, which is surely something one would want to know in order to make a decision about the deficit.

But the problem becomes even worse as we go on. Presumably one reason for our concern about the crowding out of private investment is concern about the growth rates of total output and productivity. So we have to ask by how much a specified reduction of the rate of private investment will reduce the rate of economic growth. We do not know the answer to that within a wide margin. This has been the subject of much study in the past thirty years and one can find competent research that says that reducing the rate of private investment by one percent of GNP will reduce

the rate of growth by one-tenth of one percentage point and
other competent research that says the growth rate will be reduced
by one-half of one percentage point. The two people whose studies have most influenced me, Edward Denison and William Fellner,
came to greatly different conclusions. There is surely enough uncertainty about the magnitude to leave a decision maker quite
perplexed.

My conclusion from this kind of argument is that even if
we feel confident that reduction of the deficit will reduce interest
rates, increase private investment, and increase economic
growth—none of which we can be really sure of—we are far from
answering the significant question, which is "How much?"

I will now turn to another aspect of the subject. A key issue
is whether increasing tax rates will reduce the deficit. I do not
refer here to the argument that increasing tax rates will reduce
the revenue. I have so many commitments in that argument that
even I am reluctant to say that we don't know, although there
are still people who maintain that an increase of tax rates will
not raise the revenue. I am concerned here with the proposition
that an increase of revenue will lead to an equal increase of expenditures so that the deficit will not be reduced. This would seem
to be a subject for political scientists, rather than for economists,
but political scientists do not seem to have much interest in it,
except for C. Northcote Parkinson, whose law it is. The law that
expenditures rise to equal the revenue is one of those statements,
like Murphy's law and the Peter principle (should I add the Laffer
curve?) that are appealing because they are paradoxical, amusing,
and reflect a certain aspect of life, but that no one takes to be
literally true. If I propound the proposition that the politicians
will spend all the revenue they have, you will all nod in world-
weary agreement. If I offer the Law that politicians will always
spend all of the revenue plus 5 percent of GNP, that will not
strike you as a perpetual law. You will ask, "Why five percent?"

It might be argued that although the size of the deficit is
not constant over time at any moment there is a fixed size of
deficit that the political process will generate. In this decade it
is 5 percent of GNP and in the 1970s it was 2 percent of GNP
and in earlier periods it was zero. This progression might be
explained by historical processes, including the spread of economic sophistication. That would lead to the conclusion that a
revenue increase would not reduce the deficit. It would also lead

to the surprising conclusion that an expenditure reduction would not reduce the deficit but would only lead to an equal revenue decrease. Pursuing this line of reasoning should lead to some inquiry into what determines the size of the deficit that at any moment is taken to be immutable, and whether an effort to reduce the deficit by increasing the revenue would change the immutable size in the future.

In considering this question it is necessary to be clear about what the question is. It is one thing to ask what the politicians will do with the revenue if it floats down upon them like manna from heaven. It is another thing to ask what they will do if, worried by fear of deficits, they reluctantly decide to do something they much dislike to do, which is to raise tax rates.

I do not intend to pursue this question further but hope that enough has been said to indicate that the question of the size of the response of government spending to an increase in the revenue falls into the category of questions we cannot confidently answer.

But let us suppose that an increase of the revenues leads to an increase of expenditure in some proportion that we do not know. What will be the consequence of the increase of expenditure? To some people the serious consequence of increasing expenditure is the potential loss of personal freedom. But the evidence on that is also quite slim. One could surely argue that personal freedom in America today is greater than it was fifty or a hundred years ago, when government expenditures were relatively much lower. That, of course, doesn't prove that increasing expenditures increases freedom, but the contrary is not evident. One would at least have to distinguish among types of expenditure. As I understand it, the traditional route by which high government expenditures were supposed to impair freedom was that the government would be able to coerce or direct people's behavior by threatening to withhold payments, benefits, employment, or contracts from certain individuals, groups, or regions—or offering to grant such benefits. So what we should be concerned about is the category of expenditures over which the government can exercise that kind of discretion, which is by and large the purchase of goods and services, as distinct from transfer payments and interest payments. The federal purchases of goods and services are rather small, about 8 percent of GNP. The overwhelming bulk of that is for national defense, which is regarded as more a protector of freedom that a threat to it. Non-defense federal purchases are only 2 percent of GNP. This figure is not on a rising trend. In 1949 it was almost 3 percent.

Some people see a threat to our freedom in the rise of the number of federal civil employees. They see them as a new class aspiring to take power over the rest of us. But federal civilian employment today is 2.6 percent of total civilian employment, compared to 3.3 percent in 1949. Perhaps it is the result of living too long in Washington, but as I watch the civil servants driving slowly to work in the morning and rapidly home in the afternoon, I have difficulty visualizing them seizing power. I can more easily imagine a man or woman on horseback riding into power from Moscow, Idaho than from Bethesda, Maryland.

So, despite the attractiveness of the argument, I must say that the negative effect of government spending on freedom is uncertain. The case for saying that an increase in government expenditures in general is harmful to economic growth would seem easier to demonstrate. But the simplest evidence is not helpful. Real output per capita has grown almost exactly as fast in the United States since World War II as in the forty years before 1929, although government expenditures have been enormously higher in the more recent period. This is not proof, but it is a question mark, which is all I am trying to generate.

The questions are also obvious if we turn to the consequences of specific expenditures. Do we know whether an increase of defense spending increases the national security? There are people who say it does not. I find that hard to swallow. But there is little one can say about *how much* an increase of $10 or $20 billion in defense expenditures adds to our national security at all. Does an increase of expenditures for aid to dependent children increase the number of dependent children? To make a long list of such questions is not difficult.

The situation is similar on the other side of the budget— the revenue side. A good deal of work has been done lately in estimating the effects of tax rate changes on the labor supply, or saving and investment. But still the estimates are far apart and in a state of flux.

I hope that I have said enough to show that we are far from knowing with confidence the kinds of factual things that one should know to make a sound decision about the budget deficit. I certainly hope that you will not regard this as a confession of my private ignorance but will accept it as describing the condition of the economics profession at large. Perhaps in talking about the deficit I have chosen an exceptionally easy case for my point. I don't deny that there are things we know. But there also are other subjects in which the catalogue of our ignorance would be about as compelling.

Of course, I have opinions on all of the uncertain points I have listed. So do we all. That is precisely the matter I want to discuss next. Why have we taken the firm opinions we do have and why do we have the particular opinions that we do, given that the scientific basis is so weak?

One might argue that it is of no interest why we believe what we do and that what is significant is only whether what we believe is true or not. But in cases where it is so hard to know what the truth is, it is useful to know the motivation of the talker. If someone tells me that this used car was owned by a little old lady who only took it out of the garage on Easter Sunday I would like to know whether I am being told that by a used car dealer who is trying to sell it to me or by her minister. Also, a reminder of how we got our opinions may stimulate us to keep trying to learn more.

On the subject of why we have such firm opinions, economists have an all-purpose answer. We have such opinions because there is a market for them—because it pays to have such opinions. That covers a great deal of ground, if one is not too simple-minded about what the payment is. The payment is not only money.

Economists who are selling consulting, lectures, and writing undoubtedly find that the market wants clear, firm opinions. True, the market is large and diversified and there is a niche in it for economists who reveal uncertainty, because some audiences find candor refreshing, once in a while. But on the whole, certitude pays money. (I call your attention to William Safire's column in the *New York Times* of June 24, 1984 in which he explains the difference between "certitude," which is the psychological quality of the person who holds the opinion, and "certainty," which is a quality of the opinion itself.)

But it also pays other things economists want. It pays in attention. There are few economists who will not respond if invited to appear on the MacNeil-Lehrer show, or who will not answer the phone if called by a reporter from the *New York Times* or the *Wall Street Journal*. On these occasions there is a tremendous temptation to shake off the pale cast of thought and take a position that can be explained in fifteen seconds or thirty words.

Of course, there is a selective process at work here. The media will only quote the economists who have unequivocal opinions. If you tell the reporter that you don't know he won't quote you. So whatever may be the distribution of uncertainty among economists, the public only gets to hear from those who have certain opinions. There is a further bias in the reporting process. The media rely heavily on the opinions of economists with political identification—which warps both the degree of certitude and the content of the opinions.

Economists want not only money and attention but also influence. That payment also goes to the advocates of clear, firm opinions. I try all the time to explain to people that Harry Truman was wrong in wanting a one-armed economist who would not say on the one hand and on the other hand. But most people seem to sympathize with Truman and being a one-armed economist seems to be the way to influence. At least, many economists are trying that way.

Another thing economists want is the comfort of belonging to a group, and they get that by representing clearly the distinguishing creeds or signals of their group. If you want to be accepted as a Keynesian or monetarist or rational expectationist or supply-sider, there are certain things you have to believe and say. There is no "don't know" school to which you can belong.

Another explanation of the certitude of economists about the truly uncertain is in the field of psychology or temperament. One could also force that into the mold of economizing or maximizing, but I won't try to do that. George Stigler, usually most consistent in using only economistic arguments, explains John Stuart Mill's softness on socialism in part by Mill's "remarkable propensity to understand and state fairly almost any view." It isn't clear whether Professor Stigler considers that a deficiency or not. In any case, if John Stuart Mill could have that propensity, we lesser mortals can have the opposite propensity of being able to see only one side of a question and having a strong aversion to uncertainty.

If we can agree that many economists, especially the most conspicuous ones, have more certain opinions on many matters of fact than the evidence will suggest, we can turn to the question why economists assert and believe the particular things they do. This has not been the subject of much study but I will offer some hunches and personal observations about it.

Personal history must be terribly important. One aspect that we all observe is the tendency for economists who have been trained at a particular school to have the beliefs that are character-istics of that school. There are exceptions, of course, and we would still have to ask what determined the character of the school. But still the positions of a great many economists can be explained by such an influence. Even where a university department of eco-nomics does not have an single dominant intellectual outlook, individual students become attached to individual professors, for nonscientific reasons, and that attachment influences them for the remainder of their careers.

Economists who may now have given up other Keynesian ideas love his sentence that says: "Practical men, who believe themselves to be exempt from any intellectual influences, are usu-ally the slaves of some defunct economists." But it is even truer that economists who believe themselves rigorous sifters of the evidence are slaves of some defunct or not-so-defunct economist.

But there is more to personal history than graduate school. Not much has been revealed about that, but I will give some examples from the only economist whose personal history I know much about—namely, me.

One constant in my policy outlook has been the belief that we should spend more for defense. I believe that there are objec-tive reasons for that but the intensity and persistence of my feeling goes back to my early days in Washington, in 1939 to 1941. The point is not simply that I, like many others, was frightened by the Nazis. Washington in those days was divided between people who pushed for a very rapid increase of defense spending and people who warned against that on the ground that it could be economically disruptive or unfeasible. I was a very junior member of the big spending team—and I use the word team because there is a phenomenon of team spirit, and the implication of being involved in a contest. The sense of belonging to a team and of being loyal to it has influenced my belief ever since.

In that same period, 1940 and 1941, Mr. Leon Henderson, who was in charge of price stabilization, had two research staffs, or teams. One team was for price control and one team was against price control. I was on the team against price control—again for what I still believe are good objective reasons. Participation in that contest, which we lost, contributed to the intensity of my feeling on this subject, which persisted even through my service in the 1971–1974 price control program. This is an intensity of belief about what might be called questions of fact—do price controls work, how much do they impair efficiency, and so on.

I seem for some years to have been less able than most of my friends to see the adverse economic consequences of taxes. I attribute this in part to my own history. When some young journalists and economists won the hearts and minds of the Republican party with the notion that reducing tax rates would increase the revenue I was affronted by the flimsiness of the evidence and even more by the fact that greybeards like me were displaced on such flimsy evidence.

I do not recite this personal history because there is anything special about it but precisely because I think it is not special. If we knew enough we would find a great deal of such nonscientific influence in what economists believe. In fact, I am thinking of applying to the National Science Foundation for a grant to study identical twin economists who are separated at birth and sent to different graduate schools. I want to see if monetarism, Keynesianism, and the like are genetic traits.

Another important determinant of what economists believe about the theory and the facts is what they believe policy should be. The theme of this conference is "Bridging the Gap from Theory to Decisions." This implies that the traffic is in one direction—from theory to decisions. But there is at least as much traffic in the other direction—from decision to theory. Some people believe that a tax rate cut would raise the revenue because they had decided they were for a tax rate cut.

You can see this process at work all the time. For example, last week there was a story in the newspaper about the allegation that the proportion of the population in the middle income brackets had declined. That would seem to be a question of nonideological fact. But all the economists typically identified as liberals asserted that the allegation was correct and those identified as conservatives denied it. In my opinion the explanation is that people who are ideologically eager for government to do things are quick to see conditions that might call for doing things and vice versa.

I will refer to only one other reason why some economists

believe some things and others believe other things. That is the aesthetic factor, commonly overlooked. Some economists simply find one view of the world attractive or lovely and others find a different view aesthetically pleasing.

An example of this aesthetic reaction may be found in the following paragraph from my book, *The Fiscal Revolution in America:*

> Professor Paul Samuelson, one of the leading expositors of Keynes, describes the reaction of his contemporaries as graduate students of economics in 1936 when they first encountered the General Theory. "Bliss was it in that dawn to be alive, but to be young was very heaven!" Samuelson did not immediately share this rapture, which he describes further in reporting his initial abstention: "I must confess that my own first reaction to the General Theory was not at all like that of Keats first looking into Chapman's Homer. No silent watcher I, upon a peak in Darien." It was not only in the General Theory that Keynes could rouse Wordsworthian or Keatsian emotions in the breasts of young economists. Another distinguished economist, Professor Kenneth Boulding, reported the effect upon him of Keynes' earlier work as follows: "I shall never forget the excitement, as an undergraduate, of reading Keynes' Treatise on Money in 1931. It is a clumsy, hastily written book and much of its theoretical apparatus has now been discarded. But to its youthful readers it was a peak in Darien, opening up vistas of uncharted seas—Great [sic] was it in that dawn to be alive, and [sic] to be young was very heaven!" [1]

What all these people with their poetry are reflecting is an aesthetic emotional kick, which is different from and in this case prior to analysis or evidence. I must say that, recalling my school days, I am amazed at anyone getting this kind of kick out of the Treatise on Money. But that is just the point. Different people get their aesthetic satisfaction from different ideas. I was a student at Chicago when the General Theory came out and I don't remember any of my colleagues getting the feeling that they were first looking into Chapman's Homer. Perhaps that is because we were getting our aesthetic joys out of contemplating the self-regulating system—Professor Viner's balanced aquarium. We absorbed that because it was so neat, not because of any evidence that it described the real world. Such evidence as there is came later.

[1] Herbert Stein, *The Fiscal Revolution in America* (Chicago: University of Chicago Press, 1969), p. 162

Why economists think what they do on subjects where the evidence is inconclusive is an interesting question on which I hope someone will do some research. I will not speculate on it further, however. It is only a way station on the path from theory to decision. What we are aiming to reach is why decision makers do what they do, especially given the uncertainty of economists.

There are people who believe that there is no connection between what economists think—however good the evidence— and what decision makers do, at least in government. The explanation of the behavior of the decision makers is said to be in politics—the process by which the government decision makers try to maximize their chance of reelection, or their power, or their campaign contributions, or whatever private goals they have.

I do not believe that this exclusion of economics from the decision-making process is justified. For one thing, in many cases it is impossible to tell what is good policy from the political standpoint without knowing the economic consequences of the policy. Probably it would be good politics for the administration if interest rates would decline before the election. But what kind of policy, if any, would bring that about is a question of economics. Also, there are issues in which the political consequences are so unclear that economic considerations can be allowed to dominate. The issue of closing or not closing the gold window in 1971 was such a one. No one could detect any important constituency on either side of that. In some circumstances the decision maker feels rather independent of political necessities and gives more weight to economic arguments. I suppose that was true of Eisenhower facing the recession of 1960, although ironically until recently the standard view of Eisenhower's policy for that period was that it was bad economics.

Despite the scorn that many public figures express for economists, I think that they feel disadvantaged in public discourse unless they have in their entourage at least a few professional economists to certify to the validity of their ideas. For example, although the idea that tax cuts increase the revenue was standard Republican congressional doctrine from 1947 on, and possibly earlier, it did not become Republican Presidential doctrine until 1976, when some Ph.D.'s came forward to attest to it. This is not a very demanding requirement, but it is something. Finally, one should not neglect the fact that one of the things politicians, especially Presidents, want to maximize is their place in history, and that gives them reason to pay attention to what economists have to say.

So it would be wrong to think of government decision making as an efficient political-gain maximizing machine in which the role of economics is only epiphenomenal. But if we admit economic theory and evidence into the process we have to ask how political decision makers cope with the uncertainties of the economics and the disagreements among economists. How do they select from the menu of possible beliefs offered to them by economics in instances where political advantage does not give an obvious answer?

A few things can be said about this.

Politicians, like economists and other people, have personal histories that help to explain their views. President Nixon, like me and unlike Kenneth Galbraith, had an unhappy experience working on price control during World War II and acquired a dislike for the controls which he retained even while he was running them. Politicians also take on with their party labels a body of ideas on many subjects that have a historic origin and which they live with unless there is a serious challenge.

Politicians tend to be very distrustful of ideas that do not come from people they consider to be on their side. I cannot conceive of President Reagan taking an economic idea from Robert Reich any more than he would take a rum drink from Fidel Castro, unless it had first been tasted by a Republican loyalist. Of course, that still leaves a considerable range of ideas to choose from, but it narrows the possibilities somewhat.

There is a saying among politicians that you should not propose any policy that cannot be explained on a bumper sticker. That is probably a little extreme, but explainability is certainly a limit on the ideas that a politician will entertain. For example, a major factor in President Nixon's initial hesitance about closing the gold window hung on his ability to explain such a step on national television. Once he figured out how to do that he was prepared to go ahead.

An important determinant of the behavior of politicians is the images they have of themselves, as they are, or as they would like to be. I think the policies of Lyndon Johnson, for example, become more understandable if you realize that he was trying to emulate or surpass Franklin Roosevelt. The case I know best is Richard Nixon. In my opinion, he wanted to be a daring, innovative person, contrary to his usual image, and to be accepted or at least respected by the eastern intellectual establishment (a condition he is only now approaching). Ruefully he would describe the suggestion of his conventional economic advisers as a strategy of "three yards in a cloud of dust." He would have liked to throw the long bomb. (For the benefit of any nuclear freezers here, let me explain that the President was using a football metaphor.) When he found another long-bomb player for his team—John Connally—he imposed comprehensive, mandatory price and wage controls.

In addition to these idiosyncrasies, there are general laws that influence how political decision makers react to economic conditions. One is Bert Lance's law: If it ain't broke don't fix it. I observe a corollary of that law, which is: If it might break, don't go near it. This is known as preserving deniability. The third is: If it does break, change something. This might be called Demosthenes' law, because he said "Some people think they can stump the man who mounts the tribune by asking him what is to be done. To those I will give what I believe to be the fairest and truest answer: don't do what you are doing now."

These are all somewhat Delphic laws, particularly because they are vague about what constitutes being broken or not being broken. In application they have a terribly short-run bias, because being broke is interpreted as meaning obviously and immediately painful to a lot of people, not being on a trend which if continued will lead to worsening of conditions.

These "laws," or "rules of thumb," are aspects of the process known as "using judgment." What this seems to mean, as I have seen it practiced by experts in using judgment, is to list pros and cons on two sides of a sheet of yellow lined paper, the pros and cons being immeasurable and incompatible, and staring at the list until a decision is reached.

I can see that I have drawn a picture of economists not knowing all they would like to know or claim to know and politicians not making very good use of what economists do know. But I cannot leave the picture like that because the picture raises an obvious question. Crudely put, the question is, "If we are so dumb why are we so well off?"

The basic fact is that the U.S. economy works very well by all historical standards. There are, in my opinion, two reasons why this is so despite the limitations of economists and politicians.

The first is that while I have been pointing to individual decisions made by individual people, mainly Presidents, policy is the outcome of a group process in which there are checks and balances and a continuous opportunity for revision. The checks and balances are a restraint against extreme changes of policy to which the economy cannot adapt. Moreover, if there are such changes there is a strong tendency for subsequent moderation. Thus, we had a radical change of policy between 1933 and 1940, but some of that was discarded early, some was subsequently revised, and some we just grew up to or grew around between 1940 and 1960. The Nixon price and wage controls were a radical change but they did not constitute a step towards permanent controls; instead they disappeared without a trace. The 1981 tax cuts were, in my opinion, extreme but we have since been undoing some of the revenue effects of those cuts and will probably undo more.

There seems to be an anti-immune system in the political economy that causes it to reject elements that are incompatible with its effective functioning. Our follies have been remediable. In fact, it is hard for me to think of an error that would not be remediable except failure to provide adequately for the national defense.

The more important reason for the nation's economic success is that economics and economic policy are not as important as many of us, at least many of us Washington economists think. A few weeks ago I had a revelation and told my secretary that I could give him a synthesis of forty-six years of living with economic policy. It is: "Economic policy is random with respect to the performance of the American economy but, thank God, there isn't much of it." What makes the economy function well is that a hundred million people get up every morning and go to work, doing the best for themselves that they can. As long as that happens the economy will be strong enough to resist policy errors, within a considerable range, and provide time for corrections.

The key thing is to preserve the freedom of those hundred million people to get up every morning and do their own thing. This has been preserved. Economists deserve some credit for that, which is probably the main thing for which they deserve credit.

Ten years ago, when I became a professor at the University of Virginia, I thought I should have a quotation from Mr. Jefferson. So I went around saying: "If a nation expects to be ignorant and free, in a state of civilization, it expects what never was and never will be." I used that as an argument for the need to struggle against ignorance. I now see that in a more mature way. If 168 years after Mr. Jefferson said that, we are both more free and more civilized than we were, we must not be very ignorant.

Are Economists Getting a Bum Rap?

Presidential Address
Delivered to the fifty-fourth
annual meeting of the
Southern Economic Association
Atlanta, Georgia, November 1984

T HERE has been a lot of disparaging talk about economists lately. My good and respected friend, Irving Kristol, wrote an article in the *Wall Street Journal* entitled, "Most Economists Ignore Reality." A little later the same newspaper ran a front page story about the inadequacy of economists and the declining reliance that businessmen place on them. *Time* magazine on August 27, 1984 carried a feature article headlined "The Forecasters Flunk." The subhead was "Poor predictions give once prestigious pundits a dismal reputation." A leading journalist for the *Washington Post*, most of whose writing consists of retelling what economists said to him, wrote an Op-Ed piece entitled, "The Economists Are Guessing Again." During his first debate with Walter Mondale, when he was asked why his 1980 promise of a balanced budget by 1983 had not come true the President blamed the failure on poor forecasts by economists. The President seems to like economics jokes—that is, jokes about economists, not by them. Murray Weidenbaum, the first Chairman of President Reagan's Council of Economic Advisers quotes the President as wondering whether he needs a Council of Economic Advisers. Lester Thurow has said that "the public esteem of economists is lower than at any time since World War II." My statistical abstract contains no series on the public esteem of economists, and Professor Thurow is too young to remember back to World War II, so I wonder how he knows that, but I will take his word for it.

All of this gives one to think, as Hercule Poirot says. That is why I have taken as title for this talk, "Are Economists Getting a Bum Rap?" For the benefit of those who have to leave early to catch a plane I will summarize the answer. The answer is "Yes and no." That is the kind of answer economists are accused of always giving. In fact, they don't give it often enough.

I believe that I can evaluate these charges with objectivity, and not only because I am nearing the stage of retirement from the economics business. I have always been quite aware of the limitations of my own knowledge, limitations that I did not think were much more severe than those of the rest of the profession. A good deal of my career as an economist for twenty-two years at the Committee for Economic Development was devoted to developing and explaining a strategy for managing fiscal policy that had as its basic premise that neither economists nor politicians could forecast the movements of the economy very well. In 1969, when Paul McCracken came into office as Chairman of the Council of Economic Advisers, and Hendrik Houthakker and I were members, the *New York Times* said that the distinguishing feature of the new Council was humility. That was accurate. As compared with our predecessors, and probably compared with most economists, we had a low estimate of what economists knew. As things turned out, we were probably not as humble as we should have been, but we were on the modest side of the profession. During my service on the Council of Economic Advisers I frequently found myself making forecasts of the short-run behavior of the economy. That was not because I had come to believe that I had a great ability to do that. It was only because I had learned that my ability in the field, when fortified by the Council staff, was not significantly less than the ability of other people who did it all the time. After I left the Council I returned to my stance of eschewing short-run forecasting and of emphasizing the limitations of the knowledge claimed by economists, which is a full-time occupation. Earlier this year I gave a lecture at the annual meeting of the Western Economic Association entitled "Bricks Without Straw," which was mainly a demonstration that economists do not know many of the things they say, together with some speculations on why they say them anyway and on how the economy nevertheless prospers.

So I do not feel personally aggrieved by all the recent criticism of the economics profession. But I do believe that much of this criticism rests on little information and less analysis.

For one thing, most of the criticism relates to errors in short-term forecasts of economic aggregates like GNP, unemployment, and inflation. As I shall explain at greater length below, that is too narrow a standard by which to evaluate the work of economists. But even on that standard the criticism rests on little information. In the articles about the errors of economic forecasts written by journalists and other noneconomists, I never see any factual information on the record of economic forecasting. It is as if a sports reporter were to appraise Ted Williams as a batter without giving his batting average but only giving an anecdote about the day he struck out three times. In fact, there is a good deal of work on the record of economic forecasting, all of it done by economists rather than by their critics. I think of the work done by Victor Zarnowitz [7] and Stephen K. McNees [5].

In a survey of forecasts done a year ago, McNees reported the following results for the median forecasts of five prominent forecasters for the period 1971 to 1983 [5, p.10]: The average absolute errors of the forecast of the change of nominal GNP made four quarters earlier was 2.2 percent. This was for a period in which the average annual change of nominal GNP was 9.7 percent. For the change in real GNP the average absolute error was 1.6 percent when the average actual change was 3.3 percent. The error in forecasting the change in the implicit price deflator for GNP was 1.4 percent when the average change was 6.8 percent, and the average error in forecasting the level of the unemployment rate was 0.7 percent when its average level was 7 percent. Forecasting the figure for a particular quarter four quarters ahead is harder than forecasting the figure for a year, which allows for compensating errors in the quarters. The average error of the consensus of the Blue Chip panel in forecasting the next year's change of real GNP was 1.1 percent for the past seven years, when the actual changes averaged 3.6 percent [1, p.8].

Are these errors large or small? I will turn to that question in a moment, but first I want to emphasize that the usual critics of economists' forecasts are not looking at this information at all, as one would expect from a serious appraisal.

One way in which economists have sought to measure the validity of these forecasts is to compare their results with the results of using some naive hypothesis, such as the extrapolation of last year's change. The usual finding is that the sophisticated forecasts come out better than the naive ones, although there may be some variables for which that is not true. But still this kind of comparison does not provide a satisfactory explanation of the contribution of economists to our knowledge of the future. For even a naive process like extrapolation is the extrapolation of a quantity that was conceptualized and measured by economists, without whose work the naive process would have been impossible. It's like criticizing Christopher Columbus for not knowing where Columbus, Ohio would be. It is relevant that two economists, Simon Kuznets and Richard Stone, have received the Nobel Prize for work in the definition and measurement of national income. That was considered sufficient contribution without the further requirement of ability to forecast it. But now people who would never have imagined the GNP without the prior work of economists criticize economists for errors in forecasting it.

Another question that might be asked about economists' forecasts is whether they are inferior to the forecasts of the same variables made by noneconomists. This is hard to answer with confidence, because as far as I know no systematic records have been kept of the forecasts of noneconomists. I suppose that every year there is some noneconomist who makes a better forecast than the median of economists. If there were some one noneconomist who had a long-term batting average better than the median of economists, I am sure we would have heard of him, but we have not. If we had heard of him we would, of course, declare him to be an economist, because the requirements for that designation are quite flexible. In any case it is inconceivable that this unknown forecaster did not use information provided by economists. And I am sure that the average forecast of all noneconomists is not as good as the average forecast of all economists. I do not think we need to feel depressed about the possibility that someone else is forecasting the economy better than we are.

It would be interesting to compare the accuracy with which economists forecast the near-term behavior of the economic aggregates with the accuracy of other scientists in estimating their variables. That is not, however, possible in a meaningful way, because the difficulty of the forecasts varies enormously among subjects. It is obviously easier to forecast the time of tomorrow's sunrise than to forecast the GNP for the next quarter. I see no way to discount the accuracy of the forecasts for the degree of difficulty, except by assuming that economists are as smart as astronomers and the relative accuracy of their forecasts measures the difficulty of the subject. But that would beg the question.

I tried to raise this issue with a friend who is the president of the National Academy of Sciences. When I was unable to make the question clear in general terms I asked him whether he could compare the accuracy of economists' forecasts with the accuracy of physicians' forecasts. He replied that he did not consider medicine a science. I came away from that conversation only slightly consoled by the knowledge that physicians are in great demand and earn high incomes. I have always been impressed by the fact that engineers do not know with great precision what is the load that a steel beam will bear. They guard against the collapse of bridges by using much more steel than their most probable estimate of the requirements. They are able to do that because the cost of steel is low compared to the probable cost of a bridge collapsing. That is much harder to do with economic policy, but it does point to the need to consider how we can most efficiently hedge against the consequences of the limitation of our knowledge.

Having found no better way to evaluate the degree of our ignorance I fall back on the market test. The premise of much writing about the decline of economists is that the users of economists have become disillusioned and no longer rely upon them or employ them. One aspect of that question was examined in a recent address on a subject like mine by A. Nicholas Filippello of the Monsanto Company and president of the National Association of Business Economists [3]. He pointed out that the number of members of the National Association of Business Economists increased from 322 in 1959 to 2200 in 1974 and to about 4000 in 1984. Moreover, according to salary surveys conducted by the NABE, the compensation of business economists is still rising. Also, short-run predictions are a more important part of the job of business economists than of other economists.

The job market for college and university economists is not booming, but that is due to the leveling out of the college population, not to disaffection with economists and economics. The demand for economists on the lecture circuit seems to continue strong, and what the audiences on this circuit most want to hear from an economist is a short-run prediction. I have pointed out elsewhere that the demand for economist lecturers is motivated by the desire of business organizations to make weekends at golf resorts tax deductible. But the recent reduction of marginal tax rates does not seem to have reduced the demand. Also, the employment of professional economists in writing for newspapers and magazines is flourishing. The number of best-seller books about economics, even excluding self-help books, is large. And hardly a day passes without some economist appearing on national television.

Even the present administration, not notoriously enamored of economists, contains an impressive number. The secretary of state, the chairman of the Federal Reserve, the undersecretaries of Treasury and Commerce, the chairman of the Federal Trade Commission, and undoubtedly other high officials of whom I do not now think, are economists. The White House keeps two of the three members it is authorized to have on the President's Council of Economic Advisers. We even have a president who was an economics major in college.

So I find little basis for criticizing the short-run forecasting of economists, except to say that it is not as good as we would like—but then, few things are. Neither is there much evidence that, despite the complaints, the customers have stopped buying the product.

But the most important point, in my mind, is that economists should not be judged by the forecasts of next year's GNP or price level. I am prepared to stipulate that the value of economics should be judged by forecasts of some kind. I will confess that there are moments when I think that economics is a branch of literature, or entertainment, or show business, which can have value even if it cannot forecast. But economics would not rank very high in that category, and I will not press the matter. The main thing to say is that short-run aggregate forecasts are not the most significant forecasts that economists make or the ones they do best.

Economists have made a major contribution to the world's thinking by predicting some general consequences of the way the world is organized. The most important of these predictions was that an economy organized by voluntary exchange would be more satisfactory to its participants than one organized by command. That prediction has turned out to be correct. It was made a little over two hundred years ago, and some might ask whether that justifies the presence of about 20,000 economists in the United States today. But everyone does not yet know about that prediction, and most economists are still engaged in reminding people of it, just as most physicists are engaged in teaching about predictions that Isaac Newton made centuries ago.

There is a less grand level of prediction that is nevertheless very useful. Thus, in an illuminating essay on Friedrich Hayek, Samuel Brittan said:

> . . . even before the fashion for forecasting models had fully developed, Hayek wrote a shrewd critique of bogus quantification based on the complexity of the phenomena studied. His essential point is that we cannot count on the good fortune of being able to discover by direct observation simple quantitative regularities between economic variables—but it is still possible and worthwhile to formulate general rules. For instance, economic theory can tell us that we cannot maintain a fixed rate of exchange and at the same time maintain an independent financial policy with a national price level objective; but this does not mean that we can predict where the exchange rate will go if the latter option is chosen. [2, p.58]

What Brittan here calls a general rule is a prediction—a prediction that if a country maintains an independent financial policy with a national price level objective its exchange rate will not remain fixed. That is a useful prediction, and one that could only have been made by economists.

Even in the area of quantitative forecasts, where we have been most criticized, we have allowed ourselves to be too much measured by unrealistic expectations to which we have contributed. I believe that one of the best-established findings of economics is the relation between the money supply and the price level. This relation is commonly belittled these days because we cannot tell how much difference it will make for next year's price level whether the money supply grows by 5 percent or 6 percent. But the prediction that if there is a very high rate of monetary growth for a very long time there will be much inflation is valid and useful. Such a prediction may seem so obvious today that one doesn't have to be an economist to make it. But it was not made, however, without the work of economists. And one has only to look at Israel and Argentina, for example, to see that the prediction has not been obvious to everyone.

Whether or not economists make predictions about the economy, many other people will do so. Economists serve a useful function as critics of these predictions, helping to cast light on their probable validity. As one example, for a long time there has been a popular prediction that a general reduction of tax rates would, within a short period, raise the revenues. This predic-

tion has been mainly the property of old Republican war horses—
Andrew Mellon, Harold Knutson, Daniel Reed—and others not
so old. Although some economists have recently supported the
proposition, on the whole economics has been skeptical of it.
The basic contribution of economics to this issue has been to
analyze the proposition into the parts that would have to be true
if the conclusion were to be true. If the tax cut were to raise
the revenue the elasticities of supply of labor and of savings and
of tax shelters would have to be not only in the right direction
but also of at least a certain magnitude. Then it would be possible
to speculate about or try to measure the relevant magnitudes.
The measurements, admittedly inconclusive, at least suggested
that the prediction of more revenue from lower taxes was very
doubtful.

There was another kind of valuable contribution to this question. That came from the attention economics pays to indirect
effects usually overlooked by noneconomists. In the case under
consideration, if the tax cut did not raise the revenue, there would
be, under reasonable assumptions, an increase in the deficit, and
the effects of that would have to be considered. Thus there was
at least a possibility that the tax cut would not only not raise
the revenue but would actually depress rather than raise the long-
run rate of growth through the adverse effect of the deficit.

These warnings of mainstream economics may have been un-
justified, although nothing that has happened in the past three
years has suggested that. But whatever may yet turn out to be
true in that case, consideration of the kinds of analysis that economists use will, on the average, yield better results than the intuition
and wishful thinking commonly applied.

I was struck recently by a tribute to economics from what
would be universally considered a "real scientist." Edward O.
Wilson, a noted biographer, was discussing with a colleague, Robert MacArthur, the problem of determining how many species
would exist in a certain piece of territory, such as an island. Mac-
Arthur said:

> Here's how a physicist or economist would represent the situation.
> As the island fills up, the rate of extinction goes up and the rate
> of immigration goes down, until the two processes reach the same
> level. So by definition you have dynamic equilibrium. When extinc-
> tion equals immigration, the *number* of species stays the same, even

though there may be a steady change in the particular species making up the fauna. [6, p.456]

Economists will recognize the economists' kind of reasoning
in these remarks.

Economists can contribute to improving the general run of
predictions on which the citizens base their ideas of public policy
by dispensing even the simplest kind of information. I have recently participated in a number of radio and TV shows in which
the audience calls in to express its thoughts. I have been staggered
by the ignorance that is out there and that must influence what
policy makers feel they can do. Callers insist that the budget could
be balanced by cutting out foreign aid or by recapturing the interest the Federal Reserve earns on the federal debt it holds. A
recent poll showed that a large proportion of the population thinks
that defense expenditures absorb about 40 percent of GNP and
only 6 percent of the respondents believe, correctly, that it is
less than 10 percent. Can you imagine trying to make reasonable
decisions about the defense budget in a country like that? Can
you imagine trying to make reasonable decisions about tax policy
in a country where the common belief is that corporate profits
equal 40 percent of corporate sales. Economists know better than
that.

At the man-in-the-street level, among callers-in to radio and
TV shows, there is a mass of economic information that just isn't
so. At a somewhat more sophisticated level, among politicians
and journalists, there is a body of influential beliefs that if not
certainly wrong are highly improbable and where facts readily
available to economists will reveal their improbability. I think of
the common prediction that the economy can or will grow by
5½ percent per annum for the next five years, instead of the
3½ percent projected by the Congressional Budget Office or the
4 percent projected by the Office of Management and Budget,
and that this higher rate of growth will bring the budget into
balance without other measures being taken. But I look at the
thirty-three overlapping five-year periods since World War II (that
is, 1946 to 1951, 1947 to 1952, and so on) and see that the
average annual rate of growth in those periods was 3.4 percent,
that the standard deviation around the average was 1.0 percent,
that there was only one period in which the rate was over 5 percent
and that the trend of the growth rates has been declining. None

of this means that the economy cannot grow by 5½ percent per annum in the next five years. It does mean that a plausible forecast of such a growth rate requires a good reason for thinking that the economy has changed substantially. I bring this up to illustrate the point that the simple facts with which economists are all familiar can make a useful contribution to the consideration of economic policy that is carried on continuously by noneconomists.

The claims that economists can legitimately make for themselves are modest ones. There are a great many decisions that people must make, or at least do make, in their private and public lives, to which the information, analysis, and way of thinking of economists can make a useful if not conclusive or infallible contribution. That should be enough. I said at the outset of these remarks that I would answer the question, "Are Economists Getting a Bum Rap?" by "Yes and no." I have talked so far about the yes side. I will turn now to the other side.

Our problem is not so much that the world thinks too little of us. It is more that we have allowed the world to think too much of us. We have allowed the world to think that we know more than we do, or that we know what we know with more certainty than we do. We have *allowed* the world to think that; we have not *made* the world think that. We have not insisted on how much we know, but we have not insisted on telling the world about all the limitations of our knowledge.

We are led into this behavior because that is what the world seems to want, and we supply it. If they want to know what percent of the nation's poverty is due to President Reagan's budget cuts, we tell them—down to two decimal places. If they want to know how much the deficit will raise interest rates, we tell them, to at least one decimal place. If they want to know next year's inflation rate, we tell them. There are exceptions—economists who emphasize that they don't know or at least indicate the range of possible answers and what can be said about their probabilities. But, unfortunately, even when that happens only the unqualified guesses make the editorial pages of the newspapers.

Still, economists have a share of the responsibility. Partly it is because they seek the attention and other rewards that come from clear, unqualified statements. But it is also partly because they are so fascinated by their econometric finger exercises that they mistake them for revelation. They are like pharmaceutical companies that rush to try their new medicines on humans before testing them on rabbits.

In his excellent book, *Knowledge and Ignorance in Economics,* T. W. Hutchinson delivers a forceful admonition to economists:

> No kind of ignorance can be more dangerous than ignorance regarding the limits and limitations of one's knowledge. Insofar as he may be able to combat and reduce this kind of ignorance, the student of the methodology and history of economics has a task which is of considerable social and political importance, as well as a worthy scholarly and philosophically interesting pursuit. In fact, to promote clarification of the extent and limits of economic knowledge and ignorance may well do much more to reduce dissatisfaction with current economic policies and their results, than do many or most of the contributions to confused and undisciplined wrangles and debates on particular policy problems. [4, p.5]

Hutchinson then goes on to quote Keynes saying that he looked forward to the day when economists would be regarded as modest, useful people, like dentists—which is ironic, because there has probably been no economist less like a dentist than Keynes was.

The exaggerated view of what we know leads to occasional spasms of public disappointment and annoyance when the exaggeration is discovered, as must happen from time to time. There is, however, a more serious consequence. Because we think, erroneously, that we know so much we fail to give the necessary attention to developing policies to cope with our ignorance. This takes me back to the work we were doing at the Committee for Economic Development almost forty years ago. Being greatly impressed with the unreliability of short-run forecasts, we tried to formulate a fiscal policy that did not depend on such forecasts. That was the origin of the idea of setting the budget to balance at high employment. Subsequently, especially after inflation became a major factor in our lives, inadequacies of this strategy appeared. But I believe that we were making a step in the necessary direction. Similarly, proposals for stable rules of monetary policy, like the rule of a constant rate of growth of the money supply, are efforts to cope with the policy consequences of our ignorance and inability to forecast changes in velocity. But on the whole the profession seems too confident of what it already knows, or is about to learn, to be much interested in policies that start from the proposition that we do not know very much.

We have immediately before us an example of neglect of the basic fact that we do not know what we pretend to know.

Contending parties in the debate over tax and budget policy rest their case on projections of the economic growth rate for the next five years. But the basic fact is that neither Donald Regan, nor Rudolph Penner nor I knows what this growth rate will be. We should not simply insist on a policy that is consistent with what we now believe to be the most probable growth rate. Since the probability of making an error is high, we should be asking ourselves which error—assuming too high or too low a growth rate—will be less costly. We should be deciding what we will do if the initial assumption, whatever it is, turns out to be incorrect, and how we will recognize that it has been incorrect. We should be exploring what advance preparations we can make for the adaptation of policy when the error of the initial assumption appears. Those would be more useful reactions to the limited state of our knowledge than repeated assertions that growth will be 3½ percent or 5½ percent.

So I conclude where I began. We should not be bowed down by the complaints of our vulgar critics, but we should try to adapt intelligently to the fact of our ignorance.

I will close with one last reminiscence. When I was a student at Chicago almost fifty years ago, Professor Frank Knight used to ask medical doctors how many years they thought it would be before they cured more people than they killed. I used to think that was a terribly cynical remark, and I also thought that he had economics in the back of his mind as being even more primitive than medicine. But I later came to see the hopeful side of Knight's question. He was assuming that the time *would* come when medicine cured more people than it killed. Indeed, fifty years later it may have already come. The same may be true of economics. We *will* pass the cost/benefit test, and may already be doing so.

References

1. *Blue Chip Economic Indicators,* February 10, 1984.
2. Brittan, Samuel. *The Role of Government: Essays in Political Economy.* Minneapolis: University of Minnesota Press, 1983.
3. Filippello, A. Nicholas. "Where Do Business Economists Go From Here?" Presidential Address to the National Association of Business Economists, Atlanta, Georgia, 1984.

4. Hutchinson, T. W. *Knowledge and Ignorance in Economics.* Chicago: University of Chicago Press, 1977.

5. McNees, Stephen K., and John Ries. "The Track Record of Macroeconomic Forecasts." *New England Economic Review,* November-December 1983, pp. 5–13.

6. Wilson, Edward O. "The Drive to Discovery." *American Scholar,* Autumn 1984, pp. 447–464.

7. Zarnowitz, Victor. *An Appraisal of Short-term Economic Forecasts.* New York: National Bureau of Economic Research, 1967.

Conservatives, Economists, and Neckties

The First Adam Smith Address
to the National Association of
Business Economists
Seattle, Washington,
September 23, 1982

I AM honored to be invited by the National Association of Business Economists to deliver the first Adam Smith address. I hope that the series will be long and successful.

It seems to me highly appropriate that the Association of Business Economists should give this series the name of Adam Smith. It was Adam Smith two centuries ago who attested to the intelligence and effectiveness of businessmen in utilizing the nation's economic resources to meet the desires of the population. And if we can assume, as I suppose we can, that business economists supply the intelligence of business then Adam Smith's tribute to businessmen is also a tribute to business economists. Of course, Adam Smith did not think that everyone who aspired to be a businessman or, by association, a business economist, was a person of great capability. He relied upon the market to weed out the ones who were not, so that survival would be a certificate of quality. Since you are all survivors here you can regard yourselves as certified by Adam Smith.

It is well known that Adam Smith was suspicious of meetings of businessmen, and, if he had ever heard of a business economist he would have been suspicious of their meetings also. He thought that they never got together for lunch or other social occasions without conspiring to raise prices or otherwise defraud the consumer. But Adam Smith wrote that before he knew about the income tax. He didn't know that businessmen and business economists get together now not to do business but to enjoy a deductible lunch or golf weekend.

I do not, however, intend to say much about Adam Smith today. Instead my talk today is inspired by the Adam Smith necktie. I do not want to talk about how they are made or about their commercial success. I want to talk about who wears them and why.

One might expect Adam Smith to be the patron saint of economists of all ideologies. He was the father not only of a particular idea of how the economy works but also of the idea that there is an economic system. Moreover, some of his ideas about how the system works are incorporated in all kinds of economics, from extreme left to extreme right. Any economist teaching the history of economic thought would start with Adam Smith. But the wearing of the Adam Smith necktie is not uniformly or randomly distributed among economists. Only economists who are, loosely, called conservatives wear it. For example, Milton Friedman wears it but Paul Samuelson does not.

Adam Smith would also have a claim to be one of the patron saints of conservatives. At least as commonly viewed today one of the main elements in conservative doctrine is the need to minimize the power and responsibility of the state. Certainly Adam Smith did more than any other person to demonstrate the folly of state intervention in economic life. So one would expect other conservatives, and not only economists, to wear the Adam Smith tie. But in my observation they do not.

There are exceptions. Edwin Meese, counselor to President Reagan, is not an economist but he does wear the Adam Smith tie. In fact, it is reported that he has cushions in his office made of the Adam Smith necktie material. I have sometimes wondered what it is about Adam Smith that endears him to Mr. Meese. Perhaps it is Smith's statement that there is a great deal of ruin in a nation, which must certainly be a comfort to a counselor to a president.

So what I want to talk about is why conservative economists wear the Adam Smith tie but other conservatives and other economists do not. That is, I want to talk, first, about the differences between conservative economists and other conservatives and then, about the differences between conservative economists and other economists—other than wearing the tie, of course.

The relation between conservative economists and non-economist intellectual conservatives ranges from indifference to hostility. In fact, until recently the typical American intellectual conservative ignored economics. If you read the writings of the leading people, like Russell Kirk or Peter Viereck, you will have difficulty in learning what they thought about any of the issues that engage economists.

Clinton Rossiter's excellent study of conservatism in America[1] contains in its index thirty-seven references to Edmund Burke and two to Adam Smith, twenty-three references to Russell Kirk and one each to Frank H. Knight, Henry Simons, and Milton Friedman. It contains no reference to inflation, unemployment, taxes, or budgets.

That was written in 1962. Since then conservative intellectuals, perhaps because they feel themselves closer to power, have become more interested in economic policy, but no less disdainful of conservative economics and economists. I will give three examples.

The first is George F. Will, who is my ideal and with whom I agree 99 percent of the time. Yet he has a suspicious attitude toward economists and specifically toward Adam Smith. In one of the columns reprinted in his recent book, *The Pursuit of Virtue and Other Tory Notions,* [2] Will tells the story of Adam Smith going out for a walk in his garden in his dressing gown and absent-mindedly ambling fifteen miles away. A student of Adam Smith assures me that the story is apocryphal, but Will's telling it reveals his belief that there was something not quite right with Adam Smith. And what was wrong with Adam Smith was that "he assumed that the aim of social life is to increase the consumption of goods and services." "He argued that individual self-interestedness, when given ample scope, can produce this result and guarantee social harmony." Again quoting, "The theory makes government seem merely coercive and barely necessary."

In other words, Adam Smith and the generations of economists descended from him, and especially those who now wear his necktie, have a materialistic and vulgar view of society. They

[1] Clinton Rossiter, *Conservatism in America* (New York: Knopf, 1962).
[2] George F. Will, *The Pursuit of Virtue and Other Tory Notions* (New York: Simon and Schuster, 1982).

think that the objective of society is to serve the desires of individuals, whatever they are, all desires being equally worthy. This objective is most efficiently met by the unhampered play of self-interest in a free market. To paraphrase, economists see no need for anything but the free market because they do not appreciate the higher things of life.

A similar position is taken by my friend, the Godfather of the neo-conservatives, Irving Kristol. His reservations are already apparent in the title of his collected essays, *Two Cheers for Capitalism.*[3] Perhaps oversimplifying a little, capitalism gets only two cheers, and not three, because it is only efficient, and not good, or noble, or beautiful, or something else. Kristol also finds the root of the problem in Adam Smith. He quotes Smith asking, "What can be added to the happiness of man who is in health, who is out of debt, and has a clear conscience?" And Kristol answers: "But if you believe that a comfortable life is not necessarily the same thing as a good life, or even a meaningful life, then it will occur to you that efficiency is a means, not an end in itself. Capitalist efficiency may then be regarded as a most useful precondition for a good life in a good society. But one has to go beyond Adam Smith, or capitalism itself, to discover the other elements that are wanted."

My third example is George Gilder, whose *Wealth and Poverty*[4] was for at least a year the conservative politician's bible. In a way he takes up Kristol's challenge, and gives capitalism not two cheers, but four. Like Kristol he finds the conventional economists' justification for capitalism, that it is efficient, inadequate. But he believes that there is much more to be said for capitalism and especially for capitalists. The capitalist in Gilder is not a pawn in the invisible hand, doing good to others unknowingly and unintentionally. Instead he is an active, purposeful, and therefore moral doer-of-good. The evidence of this is that the capitalist puts forth his resources for the sake of an uncertain future return. By this test, of course, the bettors at Las Vegas get high marks also. In any case, Gilder rescues capitalism from the charge of immorality by also rejecting the defense of the free market made by Adam Smith and the economists who followed him.

More generally, the intellectual conservatives reject the think-

[3] Irving Kristol, *Two Cheers for Capitalism* (New York: Basic Books, 1978).
[4] George Gilder, *Wealth and Poverty* (New York: Basic Books, 1981).

ing of conservative economists as being inadequate on the moral, ethical, or cultural scale. We—for I consider myself to be one of those benighted creatures—regard all wants as equal, not recognizing some to be better or more valuable than others. We are like Oscar Wilde's cynic, who knows the price of everything and the value of nothing. Being satisfied with the preferences of individuals, we extol a system which meets those preferences.

Moreover, the system we extol is worse than indifferent to the relative qualities of values. It rewards and encourages certain base values—material consumption—and certain rather pedestrian or even low personality traits—prudence, calculation, competitiveness, and selfishness. The intellectual conservatives start with the proposition that some values are more valuable than others and therefore better deserve being met. They go beyond that; at least they frequently do. They think they know what the better values are. They think that the quality of these values is revealed by tradition. And they believe that some authority is needed to promote these values and see to it that they are served.

It is precisely at this point—the identification of the hierarchy of values and the need for an authority to effectuate them—that conservative economists find themselves most in disagreement with other conservatives. Some economists in their enthusiasm for the neatly ordered economic model they have constructed may have gone too far in talking as if economics is the end of life. But more serious economists have not. This is especially clear in the writings of Frank H. Knight. Since Knight was the teacher of Milton Friedman, George Stigler, and Allen Wallis, one can validly regard him as the father of modern conservative American economics. Knight emphasized that economics, like other sciences or would-be sciences, has to abstract from some aspects of the real world and concentrate on others. Economics assumes that wants, resources, and technology are given and it studies how the economy works and how it should be organized on that assumption. Economists do not believe that wants are really given, either in the sense that they are unchangeable or in the sense that all wants are to be considered equally valuable. How wants are changed, and which wants are most valuable, are legitimate subjects for inquiry. They are not the subjects of economics. The conclusions of economics, whether positive or normative, are contingent upon this condition. Despite this self-imposed limitation, economics has proved to be useful, both as description and as guide.

Economics does not deny the point of its conservative critics that consumers' preferences are not the final determinant of what is good, true, or beautiful. But conservative economists tend to be very skeptical about the claim of anyone, including conservatives, to be the arbiter of what is good. And most of all, they resist the notion that cultural or moral values, however well recommended they come, should be imposed by coercion.

The classic statement of this position of economists is found in an essay by Friedrich Hayek, the Nobel Prize winning economist. Professor Hayek does not call himself a conservative. Indeed, the essay I am about to quote is called "Why I Am Not a Conservative." Yet there is no doubt that within the spectrum of economists he is a conservative. By all the tests of positions on economic policy that conventionally distinguish liberals from conservatives Hayek is one of the most conservative. I do not know whether he wears the Adam Smith tie. But I was present when he laid a wreath on the tomb of Adam Smith. (This was, of course, some years after Smith died.) It is a sign of the depth of their difference from other conservatives that Hayek and other economists whom we all call conservative, like Milton Friedman, insist on calling themselves liberals, or "old-fashioned liberals," or libertarians.

The quotation I want to read from Hayek is this:

> There are many values of the conservative which appeal to me more than those of the socialists; yet for a liberal the importance he personally attaches to specific goals is no sufficient justification for forcing others to serve them. To live and work successfully with others requires an intellectual commitment to a type of order in which, even on issues which to one are fundamental, others are allowed to pursue different ends.
>
> It is for this reason that to the liberal neither moral nor religious ideals are proper objects of coercion, while both conservatives and socialists recognize no such limits. I sometimes feel that the most conspicuous attribute of liberalism that distinguishes it as much from conservatism as from socialism is the view that moral beliefs concerning matters of conduct which do not directly interfere with the protected sphere of other persons do not justify coercion. This

may also explain why it seems to be so much easier for the repentant
socialist to find a new spiritual home in the conservative fold than
in the liberal.[5]

The key words here are "proper objects of coercion." What
Hayek calls the liberal and I call the conservative economist does
not deny that moral, religious, or cultural values are proper objects
of concern. He denies that they are proper objects of coercion.
He does not deny the right of anyone to try to influence others
to his own view of these matters. And of course there are elabo-
rately developed processes of communication—through education, literature, art, religion—by which some people are always
trying to influence the values of others. But he is deeply suspicious
of efforts to coerce individuals into the observance of principles
of conduct except, as Hayek says, where necessary to safeguard
"the protected sphere of other persons."

This matter on which the conservative economists and other
conservatives differ is highly conspicuous and serious today. The
prominence of social issues in the national discourse and political
struggle—issues like abortion, pornography, prayer, sexual practice—is evidence of division within the nation about acceptable
models of behavior in areas usually considered private. It is also
evidence of the desire or willingness of many conservatives to
invoke the authority of the state to "correct" this behavior. Even
from the standpoint of what Hayek calls the liberal and what I
call the conservative economist, these are hard issues. It is hard
to tell where Hayek's exception for interference with the rights
of others applies. And in a society where government does so
much, it is hard to tell what coercion is. For example, is the government's refusal to pay for something coercion? But despite these
difficulties of interpretation a difference of leaning between conservative economists and many other conservatives on this issue
is clear.

I would hope that discussion would narrow this difference.
Economists could be more explicit in recognizing the limitations
of their discipline and accepting the relative worth of different
goals and values as legitimate objects of concern, even if they
are not the concerns of economics. Other conservatives could
be more cautions about asserting their claim to be the final arbiters

[5] Friedrich Hayek, "Why I Am Not a Conservative," in *The Constitution of
Liberty* (Chicago: The University of Chicago Press, 1960), p. 402.

of values and especially about the role of the state in determining and enforcing values.

I want to turn now from the distinction between conservative economists and other conservatives to the distinction between conservative economists and other economists. I confine myself to economists within what I call the mainstream. The mainstream dominates the economics profession and also, although not quite to the same extent, nonprofessional discussion of economic issues. The views of the mainstream include the largest part of the range of economic policy options among which choices will be made in, say, the next ten or twenty years, although that is not necessarily true if we look fifty years ahead.

The limits of the mainstream are not precisely definable. I think of it as ranging from, say, Friedman to, say, Tobin. It excludes Marxists and Anarcho-libertarians. It includes all past presidents of the American Economic Association, with the possible exception of Galbraith, who would not thank me if I did include him in the mainstream. It includes all members of the President's Council of Economic Advisers of the past thirty years. Although there has been no census taken, I would be surprised if the mainstream did not include 95 percent of all economists.

Reading the popular press makes it clear that each economist, like every child who's born alive, is either a little liberal or else a little conservative. The press knows, for example, that the American Enterprise Institute is a conservative think-tank and the Brookings Institution is a liberal think-tank. Some economists think of themselves as difficult to classify, but popular opinion finds few economists difficult to classify, even when they are not wearing neckties.

The positions that distinguish these mainstream conservative economists from the mainstream liberal economists are well known. By and large, conservatives are suspicious of government intervention in the market, they are opposed to what they call fine tuning, they are particularly averse to what are commonly called incomes policies, they place relatively more emphasis on price stability and relatively less on unemployment, relatively more on efficiency and growth and relatively less on income redistribution. Anyone can expand or elaborate this list.

These differences in practical terms—in terms of what is actually being proposed—are so much smaller than the differences that noneconomists associate with the words liberals and conservatives that they seem to be of an entirely different kind. They are not the differences between the Gulag Archipelago and anarchy. They are differences of degree within a fairly narrow range.

The differences are not mainly the result of differences of economic analysis. Conservatives do not differ from liberals because they have different estimates of the interest elasticity of the demand for money or of the tax rate elasticity of the supply of savings. The reverse is more likely to be true. They have the elasticity estimates they do because they are conservatives or liberals.

To some extent the differences are aesthetic. There are some economists who are fascinated by the beauty of the picture of an economic system endowed by nature and running optimally down the groove of time as long as it is untouched by human hands. Others love the idea of the sophisticated and compassionate government planner playing the instruments of economic policy to produce a harmony of growth, stability, and equity. They especially love it if they dream of themselves as the organist.

There is some narrow political element in the differences. Economists like to participate in the political process. To participate it is necessary to join. And once joined the economist becomes committed to a line of policy and especially policy argument—not insincerely but naturally. They are liberals because they are Democrats and not Democrats because they are liberals.

How much do these differences within the present range of policy discussion matter? How much difference does it make whether federal government spending as a percentage of GNP rises to 25 percent or falls to 21 percent, whether the budget is balanced or runs deficits equal to 2 percent of GNP, whether the nation's water is 99 percent pure or 98 percent pure, whether Social Security is indexed to wages or prices, whether the inflation rate is stabilized at 10 percent, 6 percent, or 2 percent, whether the standard deviation of the quarterly money supply around its average path is 1 percent or 5 percent? The simplest answer is that we do not know for sure. Probably these are important but not critical differences. They do not entail radical differences in our social system or way of life. They are important—worth the attention that the country, including economists—pay to them. But they are not the differences between disaster and utopia.

There is, however, another, more apocalyptic, way of looking at all this. Today's policy issues are not the end of the road. They are part of an historical process in which one argument, one way of thinking, and one decision leads to another. What we have to be concerned with is where the current steps lead us in the end. This is a way of looking at the matter which is especially impressive to conservatives and which is best suggested by the title of Hayek's book, *The Road to Serfdom.* [6] Each step towards more government control, however apparently innocuous in itself, reinforces a trend which makes further steps more probable, if not inevitable. Little by little, without any decision to change the system, we have gone in about fifty years from a federal government spending 3 percent of GNP to one spending 24 percent. We have increased the number of major federal regulatory agencies from fifteen to fifty-five in the same period. Eisenhower's gentle exhortation to labor unions to restrain wage increases led, in about thirteen years, to Nixon's mandatory, comprehensive wage-price freeze. Each step must be resisted and if possible repulsed before the process reaches a point at which it is irreversible and irresistible.

There are, of course, replies to this argument. Although government is bigger than ever the private sector is also bigger than ever and the American people on the whole are freer than ever. We are not necessarily on a straight road to serfdom or anywhere else. As Colin Clark said in another connection, every pig that grows up to be a hog does not grow up to be an elephant. The expansion of government that began with F. D. Roosevelt was slowed down and absorbed in a growing private economy in the time of Eisenhower. The expansion that began with Kennedy is being slowed and digested within the free system in the regime of Reagan.

In fact, liberals have their own version of the road to serfdom, which is different from Hayek's. In their version the failure of government to try actively to meet the public's demands for stability, security, and equity leads finally to popular revulsion against the system and a flight to Big Brother. In this view, for example, Franklin Roosevelt was the savior of the free system, not its enemy.

Which of these scenarios for the road to serfdom is more

---

[6] Friedrich Hayek, *The Road to Serfdom* (Chicago: University of Chicago Press, 1944).

realistic or probable is hard to say. There is, in my opinion, force to both of them. Careless acceptance of the growth of government by an indifferent public led by power-seeking politicians and alienated intellectuals is a danger. But so is popular resentment against the neglect of real problems out of subservience to doctrinal purity. Each of these dangers may be more real at one time and less real at another. In my opinion, the danger of excessive government has in recent years been the more serious, and the reaction now under way in the Reagan administration is proper. But it is important that the other danger be kept in mind.

There is much room for constructive cooperation between those economists who wear the Adam Smith tie and those other mainstream economists who do not. They have a common interest in trying to find ways to solve the nation's real economic problems that do not threaten freedom. Although the tendency on both sides to promise a free lunch—policies that are all benefits and no costs—is unfortunate, I do not believe that economic policy is a zero-sum game. In other words, I believe it is possible to find policies that both sides would recognize as yielding a net benefit from their standpoint. We will have a better chance of finding those policies and getting them adopted if those who wear the tie and those who do not will try to listen to each other rather than concentrate on leading cheers for their own team.

How to Introduce an Economist

Fortune, November 30, 1981

S UMMER is over, and the season of the business convention is upon us again. From White Sulphur Springs to Palm Springs, resorts will be filled with meetings of trade associations and corporations, each featuring a well-balanced program of golf and lectures. The presence of an economist on these programs is obligatory, because the Internal Revenue Service believes that a conference including a lecture by an economist cannot be for the purpose of pleasure and therefore must be a deductible expense.

As a result, hundreds of corporate executives and trade association presidents are going to face the problem of introducing an economist. It is a good bet that over half of them will use one, two, or even three of the following lines:

1. "Economics is the dismal science." That was a favorite line of President Nixon's early in his administration, perhaps because that was the only thing his speechwriter on economics, William Safire, knew about the subject. As time passed, both the president and his speechwriter learned more and gave up the cliché.

It is not an apt remark. Economics as a science is dismal only in the sense that it recognizes the existence of limits. But so do all sciences. Geometry is not called dismal because it says that the square of the hypotenuse cannot exceed the sum of the squares of the other two sides. Chemistry is not called dismal because two units of hydrogen have to be combined with one unit of oxygen to make water. No one goes around saying that these limits could be escaped by cutting marginal tax rates.

Now it is true that economists do not know where their limits are as well as other scientists know their limits. At times, economists have been too pessimistic in their judgments about the location of the limits. This was surely true of Malthus and his followers, who argued that laws of economics and nature destined man to live at the level of subsistence. But such pessimism is not an inherent feature of the science. In our time, the prevailing error has probably been to be excessively optimistic—to overestimate the productive capacity of the system—and that has led to inflationary policy.

2. "As President Truman said, 'I wish that I had a one-armed economist, so that he wouldn't say on the one hand and on the other hand.'" If that was what Mr. Truman wanted, he was wrong. Economics is an uncertain science. To all the questions difficult enough to reach the president, the answers are uncertain. If the answers could be given with 100 percent confidence, the decisions could be made by a lesser official. It is the president's role to decide what to do when no one "knows" what to do. It is the role of the president's economic advisers to tell him of his options and of the *possible* consequences of his decision. It is their role to tell him that on the one hand this might happen and on the other hand that might happen. If the president isn't told that, he doesn't have the information he needs.

3. "Economists never agree." This is sometimes buttressed with a quotation attributed to George Bernard Shaw that if all the economists were laid end to end, they would not reach a conclusion.

That is, in fact, not true. Economists agree on many things—probably on most things. It has been observed that if almost any economic subject is discussed in a group including economists and noneconomists, the economists are likely to agree with each other and to disagree with the consensus of the noneconomists. The contrary impression results in part from the fact that noneconomists look to economists mainly for answers to the questions on which economics is most uncertain—notably the short-run forecast for the economy. Even on that subject there is usually not much disagreement. For example, in the October (1981) *Blue Chip* survey of economic forecasters, thirty out of forty-four said that the real increase of the GNP between 1981 and 1982 would be between 1.2% and 2.9%. That is *too much* agreement. The true range of probability is greater than that. On such matters the profession is divided into two groups. Most fall in the category of sheep who cluster together to reduce the danger of an exceptional error. A few are contrarians, who exploit the sheepishness of the rest to distinguish themselves and hope for an exceptional success.

If it is necessary to tell a joke in introducing an economist, the best one goes like this:

President Ford and Secretary Brezhnev were negotiating in the Kremlin. Throughout several days of discussion, Ford had on the table next to his place a bulging black briefcase, which he never opened. When the negotiations were satisfactorily concluded, Brezhnev asked Ford what was in the briefcase. Ford said that it was full of Colorado black beetles, and if the Russians had not agreed to his desires he would have released the beetles and they would have destroyed Soviet agriculture.

The following year negotiations were held in the White House. Brezhnev had alongside his chair a large wooden box, which he never opened. At the end of the talks, in similar circumstances, Brezhnev explained that if the outcome had not been satisfactory he would have opened the box and released its contents, a Hungarian economist, who would have destroyed the U.S. economy.

That story is, of course, most suitable for the introduction of a Hungarian economist, an occasion that arises only rarely in the United States. Moreover, it is quite unfair, because the economists who have come to the United States from Hungary have been quite constructive.

In any case, there is no need to introduce an economist with a joke. It is done, presumably, to put the audience in a tolerant frame of mind, but that doesn't last. It only succeeds in irritating the economist, who then feels obliged to continue with other jokes. If the convention wants jokes, it should engage Art Buchwald. Economists should not be expected to tell jokes for one-fourth of Buchwald's fee.

A sufficient introduction of an economist might be the following:

We will now hear from Mr._____, professor of economics at _____. He has spent his working life studying, teaching, and practicing economics. He is not a fortuneteller. He does not know when interest rates are going to go down. If he knew that, he would already have told the public and it would be too late for you to profit from the information. But he knows things about the future of interest rates that fortunetellers do not know. He knows what seems to have made interest rates fluctuate in the past and what may influence them in the future. I use interest rates, of course, only as an example of the many aspects of the economic present and future with which we are concerned.

Professor _____ has in the past served as a government official. But he is not a political partisan, and we have invited him here not to present the views of any political party but to tell us what economics has to say, as well as he can. We have abandoned our past practice of inviting two economists, one Republican and one Democrat, with the thought that we could distill the truth from their competing statements. We found that this only gave us a cat-and-dog fight, which showed only who was the better debater—probably meaning the less honest.

Professor _____ has been a teacher and an adviser to government officials. We have asked him to take a similar role with us, and not to seek the role of salesman or entertainer.

Since many of you are already wearing your golf shoes, I may illustrate the role of the economist by comparison with the role of the teaching golf pro. He can instruct you in the rules of the game and he can explain to you what techniques tend to make for success and what do not. Where there are differences of opinion about that among qualified people, he can tell you what they are. But he cannot play the game for you. He cannot give you the physical equipment, the coordination, the judgment that make a good golfer. Some of you may become better golfers than the pro. Many of you will never break a hundred. But you will all learn from him. So the economist cannot tell you what is going to happen or what you should do, but he can supply you with some of the information and ways of thinking that will be helpful to you in making up your own minds. He is worth listening to.

Verbal Windfall

The New York Times Magazine,
September 9, 1979

REPORTING of economics in the press has greatly increased in volume and sophistication, but the economic literacy of readers, even of the *New York Times,* has not kept pace. Therefore the public may not be getting the full benefit of the economic wisdom being spread before it. As a contribution to remedying this situation, I present here definitions of some words and terms most commonly encountered in current discussions.

Balanced Budget Amendment: An amendment to the Constitution proposed by politicians who have never balanced the budget, requiring their successors to achieve and maintain equality between two undefined conditions for undefined periods subject to undefined penalties, unless they decide to do otherwise.

Consumer: A person who is capable of choosing a president but incapable of choosing a bicycle without help from a government agency.

Consumerism: A policy of imposing regulatory burdens on production which hold down the incomes of workers, thereby keeping them from buying things they want that aren't good for them.

Demand Management: A ritual practice of governments, after 1936, in which they sought, by manipulating taxes, government spending, and money supply, to propitiate the gods and achieve full employment, efficiency, and economic growth. This last came to be regarded as a twentieth-century superstition.

Deregulation: A process of restoring free markets by eliminating the old, small regulations we are used to, as in the case of airline fares, and imposing big new regulations—as in the case of who can use how much energy of what kind for what purpose—

65

with the result that the total number of regulations becomes larger and stranger.

Energy Program: A plan under which low-cost energy will be taxed and high-cost energy will be subsidized, thus discouraging production of low cost energy and encouraging production of high-cost energy, and assuring that energy is produced at unnecessarily high cost. A variant of this is known as "The Nation's First Comprehensive Energy Program," which means the president's latest rendition of an oft-told story.

Eurodollar: A word used to indicate that economic discussion has reached its most rarefied level and amateurs should now leave the room.

Keynesian: An all-purpose pejorative used by editorial writers and politicians for economic policies they don't like. The origins of the term are obscure, but it probably derives from a British economist, John Maynard Keynes, whose economic writing is no longer read and who is best known as a member of the Bloomsbury set, a friend of Virginia Woolf, and husband of Lydia Lopokova, a famous ballerina.

Monetarism: The theory that there is a stable and predictable relation between the price level as effect and the supply of money as cause. This theory has firm empirical support if the definition of the money supply is allowed to vary in an unstable and unpredictable way.

Neo-conservatism: Old wine drunk by new winos, who have discovered the philosophy of Lady Marchmain: "I realize that it is possible for the rich to sin by coveting the privileges of the poor. The poor have always been the favorites of God and His saints, but I believe that it is one of the special achievements of Grace to sanctify the whole of life, riches included."

Obscene: A word formerly applied to books but now obsolete in that context and routinely applied to profits. This has given rise to a revision of Jimmy Walker's statement that he never knew a girl to be ruined by a book—to the effect that many, however, have been ruined by profits.

Quick Fix: Always used in the sentence "There is no quick fix." That should be interpreted to mean that the speaker is doubtful whether there is a long-run solution to the problem in question.

Rational Expectations: This is the hottest thing in economics in 1979. It seems that people cannot rationally expect the success of a policy whose success depends on the people's not understanding the policy. The lady in the box cannot be fooled by the illusionist who pretends to saw her in half.

Rationing by Price: A system in which economic goods go to the people who are most willing to pay for them. This is the normal way of distributing goods in capitalist countries, and is increasingly used in Communist countries. Economists generally consider it an efficient system, but some politicians consider it immoral and prefer a system of rationing by political pull.

Recession: Formerly a term of scientific analysis, this has now lost all meaning. It was briefly revived in 1979 by Alfred Kahn, an economist who was appointed President Carter's chief inflation fighter and after a few months of notoriety was never heard from again. When the White House staff complained that Kahn was tarnishing the president's image by constantly saying, "Yes, we have no bananas," Kahn cleverly substituted the word "recession" for "banana."

Supply Side: A theory which became popular in the late 1970s and which held that big effects could be produced by small actions. For example, a tax cut of $1 billion would raise the national income by $5 billion, increase the government revenue by $2 billion, reduce unemployment, and restrain inflation. This theorem was discovered written on the back of a napkin in a McDonald's restaurant. That gave rise to the axiom "There ain't no such thing as a free lunch, but there is a cheap one."

Underlying Inflation Rate: This is the inflation rate that would exist in the absence of special factors and to which the inflation rate will tend to return when the special factors have disappeared. These special factors include everything having to do with the prices of energy, food, housing, and medical care. The underlying rate of inflation is always below this year's actual rate and above last year's actual rate.

Wage-Price Guidelines: (Also known as guideposts or standards.) Wage-price controls imposed by a president who says that he will never impose wage-price controls. The repeated use of wage-price guidelines as a way of trying to control inflation is the leading example in economic policy of the triumph of hope over experience.

Windfall Profits: Profits earned by people who invested their money in developing a resource, such as oil, which later turns out to be of great value to other people who were not sufficiently foresighted or venturesome to invest their own money. For example, the grasshopper said to the ant, "What big windfall profits you have there, friend!"

Doctor, Am I Really a Keynesian?

The *Wall Street Journal*,
April 13, 1981

I KEEP having this terrible dream, Doctor. I dream that I have been hauled up for interrogation by the HKAC."

"HKAC? What's that?"

"It's the House Keynesian Activities Committee."

"Is there really such a committee?"

"There sure is in my dream. I expect there will soon be one in what is sometimes called real life too. 'Keynesian' has become a term of disrepute again. It has taken on a meaning like 'humanist' or 'permissive' or 'Darwinian.' That is, people who have no clear idea of its meaning nevertheless think of it as suggesting something un-American and subversive."

"You say it has become a term of disrepute again. When did that happen before?"

"Well, for ten or twelve years after Keynes made his big splash, in 1936, lots of people were frightened by him. You might call that the shock of the new. But that passed, as Keynesianism became modified and domesticated and people became used to it. But the hostile attitude is rising again, although from another direction. Now what we have is not shock of the new but disdain for the old, from people who claim to be the new wave."

"But what has that all got to do with you? Why do you think you are dreaming about it?"

"The thing is, more and more people are referring to me as a Keynesian, and not in a flattering way. Just the other day I saw an article which called me a Ford Keynesian."

69

"What does that mean?"

"At first I thought it was one of those new front-wheel-drive cars, but I guess it means a person who is either too dumb to know he is a Keynesian or too devious to admit it."

"Still, that dream doesn't sound too terrifying. What makes it seem so bad to you?"

"I'm afraid I might be blacklisted by the University of Virginia and the American Enterprise Institute and the *Wall Street Journal* if the HKAC gets after me. I might also be forced to denounce any Keynesians I know."

"But you're innocent, aren't you? You're not a Keynesian?"

"Well, . . . no."

"You hesitate. Are you guilty, or unsure?"

"I guess that's it, Doctor. That's what's worrying me. I never thought I was a Keynesian, but now I'm not sure. I might be a Keynesian. I just don't know what it is."

"You mean to tell me that you've been studying and practicing economics for almost fifty years and you don't know what a Keynesian is? That's not credible. You have to dig deeper."

"That's what the chairman of the HKAC said in my dream. But the fact is that Keynes said many things. His critics attributed many other things to him. I simply don't know which of these things make you a Keynesian.

"In my dream the counsel of the HKAC read me a list of propositions, and asked me about each one, 'Do I now, or did I ever, believe it?' There were propositions like—

That income and expenditures are equal,

That savings and investment are equal,

That unemployment can last for a long time and not be curable by monetary means alone,

That the United States is in a condition of secular stagnation,

That taxes should be low enough to prevent unemployment and high enough to prevent inflation,

That we don't have to worry about the debt because we owe it to ourselves,

That the government should fine-tune the economy by continuous manipulation of fiscal policy,

That monetary policy doesn't matter,

That the potential output of the economy is a given,

That the price level is a given,

That inflation doesn't matter,

That a low rate of unemployment can be obtained forever by running a high rate of inflation,

That a reduction in the rate of growth of demand will during a transitional period of uncertain duration increase the rate of unemployment."

"I'm afraid that I don't get the significance of these questions."

"Well, those are all ideas associated at one time or another with the name of Keynes, although only a few were ideas of Keynes himself and the rest were ideas of his more far-out followers. I tried to explain that most of these propositions I had never believed, some I had once believed but no longer did, and a few I still believed. And the Grand Inquisitor never said yes or no. He never blinked. I got no clue to which of my answers was a confession of guilt and which was a denial. The whole thing made me pretty nervous.

"Then the chairman took up the questioning. He said: 'I have in my hand a newspaper clipping which reports that in January 1971 you taught President Nixon to say that we are all Keynesians now. How do you answer?'

" 'In the first place,' I answered, 'I never taught President Nixon to say anything about Keynes and the word never passed between us. Second, he never said that we are all Keynesians now. He said, 'Now I am a Keynesian.' And he meant only that he had entered the modern world of economics and left behind what Dwight Eisenhower had called the fetish of the annually balanced budget.'

"Then I probably made a mistake. I said that it was Milton Friedman who said that we are all Keynesians now. He said that in 1965. And he also said that there are no longer any Keynesians. I told the chairman that I had thought at the time that would lay to rest forever any arguments about who was and who was not guilty of Keynesianism."

"And how did the chairman react to that?"

"He said that he was going to cite me for contempt. Whereupon I bit my tongue so hard that I woke up."

"Somehow, this story doesn't satisfy me. I don't understand why this whole fuss arises at this time or why they're picking on you. Are you maybe holding something back?"

"Well, Doctor, I think it may have something to do with the supply side. Sometimes I wish I hadn't invented that term. It all goes back to my childhood. My childhood as an economist in the 1930s, I mean. Twenty-five percent of the labor force was unemployed and there were idle factories all over. It seemed clear to us that the big economic problem was to find jobs for those workers and markets for those factories. Our problem was to increase the demand for the supply we already could produce.

"That was basic premise of Keynes. To criticize him now for that is like criticizing Noah for building an ark instead of a swimming pool. Moreover, it was not a particularly Keynesian idea. This view of the Depression problem was held then and later, and is still held, by many economists who never considered themselves Keynesians.

"That traumatic experience never left the minds of us economists who grew up in the 1930s. But we did gradually learn that demand management wasn't all or even most of economic policy. We learned that pumping up demand could be overdone and cause inflation, and we saw that happening. We learned that demand expansion was at best only a short-run solution for deficiencies of production and employment. And we learned that a satisfactory rate of growth of potential output in the United States could not be taken for granted but had to be protected and promoted by appropriate policy measures, including tax policy.

"But for the younger people who had never experienced the Depression this evolution of thinking was intellectually insufficient. More important, it was not psychologically sufficient. It did not get them enough attention. They had an Oedipal urge to run around to the head of the procession, to bang the drums more loudly, and to outshine and outshout their intellectual fathers. So they had to exaggerate the developing trend. While mainstream economists were saying that changes in the growth of nominal demand would at the end, after an uncertain period, affect only prices and not production, these new ones said that the whole effect would be on prices immediately, and there would be no effect on output, even for an instant. And while the rest of us were saying that some kinds of measures would have a gradual and limited effect in increasing the supply of output, they were maintaining that this effect would be immediate and enormous.

"This was, ironically, a Keynesian tactic. Keynes was frustrated by his inability to get the world's attention, and so he deliberately described his theory in extreme terms. This new wave has employed another Keynesian tactic, also. In order to demonstrate his own originality Keynes lumped all of his predecessors into a category which he called 'classical' and attributed to them naive and inane views, by contrast with which his looked very wise. Similarly the present new wave has lumped its predecessors into a category labeled 'Keynesian.' It is an epithet used instead of argument about the real issues. And now the epithet is being thrown around by people who never read a word of Keynes but want to identify with Conservative Chic."

"But why do they pin it on you?"

"Oh, Doctor, I hoped you would tell me that."

Professor Knight's Law of Talk

The *Wall Street Journal*,
October 14, 1981

THE late great economist Frank H. Knight propounded the law that bad talk drives out good. As soon as he said it everyone recognized that it was true. Perhaps for that reason little attention has been paid to explaining why it is true.

Of course, the law does not say that all bad talk drives out good, it is only some bad talk drives out good. So part of the question is what are the characteristics of the bad talk that drives out good.

My thoughts were led in this direction by two recent outstanding examples of Knight's law. They are punk supply-sidism and the gold craze. (I borrow the term "punk" from Denis Healey, who characterized Mrs. Thatcher's economics as punk monetarism, meaning extreme to the point of being bizarre. This meaning of punk derives, I believe, from punk rock.)

Until about 1979 or 1980 we were having a serious, active, professional discussion of the problems on the supply side of the American economy. A marked slowdown of the growth of total output and of productivity had been recognized. Work was going on to discover the causes of that slowdown—work associated with the names Denison, Kendrick, Nosworthy, Jorgensen, and others. This work had not yet led to final, agreed conclusions. At the same time it was pointing tentatively to partial solutions. Some policy steps, including limited tax reductions, were being proposed.

Suddenly, all of that was swept to the sidelines—punk supply-sidism took center stage. It offered a universal explanation for the slowdown: Tax rates (or government expenditures) were too high. It offered a universal solution: Cut tax rates (or government expenditures). This became the focus of discussion of the supply side of the economy.

In its most extreme form supply-sidism is no longer considered a serious contribution to policy. For example in the recent budget crunch no one suggested that there should be another cut of tax rates in order to increase revenue. Nevertheless there is still considered to be a supply-side school of thought which has superseded more conventional economics or at least deserves equal billing with it.

There has been a similar development about gold. For the past thirty years or so there has been intense discussion of monetary theory and policy, which in the past fifteen years has focused on the relation between money and inflation. The names of Friedman, Fellner, Tobin, Meltzer, Okun, and many others come to mind as participants in this discussion. Progress was being made. It was agreed that inflation would not permanently reduce unemployment. It was agreed that slowing and stabilizing the growth of the quantity of money was essential. It was agreed that the credibility of the monetary authority in adhering to its announced policy needed to be established. Federal Reserve policy seemed to be turning significantly in the direction indicated by the trend of economic thinking. Many questions remained, but there had been real advance.

But again, suddenly, all this train of thought was short-circuited. Gold is the answer. We don't have to wrestle with the hard questions that occupy the economists. Only go "back to gold" and the price level will be stable, interest rates will be low, budgets will be balanced, and harmony abroad and confidence at home will be restored. This is asserted without even as much evidence as would pass muster in a sophomore term paper. Nevertheless this becomes *the* subject of discussion. The media devote columns of type to it. Sages hem and haw and stroke their beards and ponder whether there may not be something to it. A National Commission is established to consider not what is the best monetary system and policy for the United States but gold versus paper. Meanwhile, serious discussion of monetary policy suffers.

Why does this happen? Why is Knight's law true?

I suppose that 90 percent of the explanation is in the "wouldn't it be nice to think so" syndrome. A usually sensible old woman gives her life's savings in one-dollar bills to a stranger who promises to return her an equal number of hundred-dollar bills. Greed, anxiety, a feverish desire to believe, stupefy her. So there is a strong wish to believe that economic problems can be quickly and painlessly solved. Politicians have an especially strong wish to believe it, because if true it would greatly ease their problems of getting elected and of governing.

The bad talk is believed because it would yield various benefits—price stability, growth, and so on—if it were true. One of the main benefits it would yield is understanding, or at least the feeling of understanding. Such ideas as that if you want more of something you should tax it less, or that the way to stabilize the price level is to make the dollar as good as gold, are easy to grasp when first encountered. They are the ketchup of economics—appetizing but not nutritious.

There seems to be an especially great appeal in ideas that contradict the beliefs of experts. Many people resent the fact that there are experts who claim to know things the common folk don't. *Épater les savants* is a stronger drive than *épater la bourgeoisie.* But there is still a certain hankering for "scientific" verification. So the idea most likely to succeed is one that goes against the expert consensus but has the endorsement of at least one Ph.D.

I have been speculating about why bad talk is bought. But bad talk has its supply side as well as its demand side. It is sold as well as bought. And the selling of it seems to be more energetic and effective than the selling of the good talk. There is something about the simple and extreme character of the bad talk which appeals to zealots, and they tend to be good salesmen. Also there are strong incentives to be on the side of the bad talk while it is displacing the good.

Dozens of conventions will now think they need to be enlightened by a debate about the gold standard. They will be able to choose from among hundreds of opponents but from only a handful of supporters. If you are one of that handful you will get many more invitations and much more attention than if you are one of the conventional crowd. And in our celebrity culture if you once become a celebrity by advocating an attractive idea, you will remain a celebrity long after the idea has been discredited and you will appear regularly on talk shows selling your books.

The selling of bad talk is sometimes assisted by the sporadic efforts of the media at evenhandedness. Fifteen thousand economists, including all living ex-presidents of the American Economic Association, may say they don't think the gold standard is a good idea. Six people, including two economists, may say they think it is a wonderful idea. Then the press reports that the experts are uncertain and divided, and editorial writers begin proposing we should try a little of it.

All of this is pretty discouraging, or even infuriating. But there is some good news too. Knight's law is disturbing to people who care about the talk. Most people don't. A majority of the people in my neighborhood supermarket think that supply side is a defensive football formation and the gold standard is a light beer.

And, after all, it is only talk. It isn't action or policy. Somehow, our policy is better than our talk. As I used to say about Kemp-Roth, there was nothing so bad about it as the arguments used in its favor. There must be some inertia, some competition among bad ideas as well as among different interests, some general ineffectiveness of government, that keeps extremely bad talk from leading to extremely bad policy. As I remember, Professor Knight was calm and good-humored about his discovery.

Economics at the New Yorker

The *Wall Street Journal*,
November 12, 1979

W HAT'S so funny?" asked my wife, diverted by my guffaws from her examination of the daily paper.

"It's this thing here in the *New Yorker*." I explained. "Listen to this. 'Worry is the prevailing state of mind in a market system.' "

"Oh, that must be the new story by Woody Allen. He's wonderful! I can just hear him walking up Madison Avenue with Diane Keaton and telling her that worry is the prevailing state of mind in the market system."

"Well," I said, "the pages of the *New Yorker* are the next best thing to Madison Avenue. Here is this story, sandwiched in between an ad for fine Scottish knitwear or the Welsh dragon tie, whether to take the trip to Greece or go to Bermuda. You long for the carefree times when all you had to worry about was the saber-toothed tiger, famine, the Black Death, being incinerated by the Inquisition in this world or burned by hell-fire in the next, or being awakened in the middle of the night by the knock on the door from the Gestapo or the KGB."

"The funny thing," I continued, "is that it's not meant to be funny. It's meant to be serious."

"How do you know?" she asked.

"Well, it's in the back of the magazine. All the stuff that's meant to be funny in the *New Yorker* is in the front, and all the stuff in the back is meant to be serious. Anyway, it's by an economist, Robert Heilbroner."

This conjugal banter was inspired by a gallimaufry in the October 8 issue entitled "Inflationary Capitalism." As soon as you saw the devilishly clever title you knew that you were in the hands of a Deep Thinker, an economist perhaps, but no "mere" economist. Linking capitalism to inflation assures us that we are going to get beneath such superficialities as money, oil, or wage rates to the real truth at last. And linking inflation to capitalism breathes a new spark of relevance to the old Marxian devil, which had been getting a little musty.

The theme of this pastiche is that as capitalism develops it reveals successively different aspects, all evil. First there was a period of general impoverishment, then a period of monopolistic concentration of power, then a period of Great Depression, and, now, the period of inflation. Professor Heilbroner adamantly resists the notion of calling these evils "diseases" of capitalism, because that would suggest the possibility of a healthy capitalism which did not suffer these ills. It is essential to the argument that these ills are parts of the thing itself, and not removable blotches on it.

Our author makes his task of supporting this argument easier than it would otherwise have been by omitting to define capitalism. True, this small lack does make the reader's task a little more difficult. But the slick paper, the perfume ads and the condescendingly superior *New Yorker* literary style combine to induce a suspension of disbelief in all but the most dyspeptic reader.

What we get instead of a definition of capitalism is an identification of its "*élan vital,*" its "peculiar property." To Heilbroner the élan vital of capitalism is the "universal drive for betterment," and he quotes Adam Smith's reference to "the desire for bettering our condition" as a motivation that is present with each of us from the womb to the grave.

But to describe the individual's drive for bettering his conditions as a peculiar property of capitalism is itself most peculiar.

As far as an outsider can tell, that drive is as powerful in the Kremlin or in the College of Cardinals as in the board room of General Motors. Certainly, Adam Smith did not think that the desire to better one's condition was confined to capitalism. In fact, he never heard the word "capitalism." He considered the desire to be universal. What he considered to be unique about the economic system he described, and from which he expected so much progress, was that freedom to use one's resources to better one's condition would be universal, and not confined to a few.

Freedom is the "peculiar property" of the economies that

Heilbroner is writing about, and much of the argument would be clearer if he used the term "freedom" instead of "capitalism." But that would not do, of course. The readers of the *New Yorker* are not yet accustomed to interpreting "freedom" as a pejorative, the way such sophisticated people now interpret "capitalism."

Mr. Heilbroner is reluctant to recognize the most obvious fact about the economic system that he calls capitalism and that I call freedom, which is the enormous improvement in the condition of life of the average man which it has produced. He says: "Ideologists of capitalism have always protested against the idea that capitalism creates poverty, insisting that just the contrary is the case—that capitalism is the greatest creator of wealth the world has ever known. But the truth of the latter contention does not vitiate the former. Capitalism has indeed produced wealth, but wealth of a particular kind—not the wealth of cathedrals or pyramids but that of commodities, objects made for sale."

That is one way of looking at the matter. But it would be more accurate to say: "Not only ideologists of capitalism but also economic historians and statisticians have shown that capitalism is the greatest creator of wealth the world has ever known. This wealth was not devoted, as in earlier times, to the glorification of pharaohs or bishops, but to satisfying the needs and wishes of the ordinary man by producing the things he wanted to buy. In the course of their economic development some people were injured, but their numbers were small compared to the numbers who were rescued from the misery in which their forebears had lived for centuries."

Mr. Heilbroner's authorities for "the tendency of capitalism to create a great mass of squalor and poverty" are Hogarth, Daumier, Dickens, and Zola. Probably the professor thought that these are names recognizable to readers of the *New Yorker*, but they are not names he would accept as citations in a Ph.D. thesis on economic history. I have encountered such a use of authority before. In 1960 I was traveling in the Soviet Union with a delegation of economists and we met a young man in the Tashkent market who would not believe that we were Americans because we did not look or act like the people in "The Book." It turned out that the book from which he derived his image of Americans was *Uncle Tom's Cabin*.

Space does not permit us to follow Professor Heilbroner on his tour of the back alleys of capitalism. We must hurry on to

Topic A, which is inflation, and why inflation is the normal way in which capitalism works. Mr. Heilbroner's explanation of inflation is rather commonplace, and has an element of truth in it. In the United States today and in many other countries people have high demands and expectations with respect to their incomes, employment, and security. In an effort to satisfy these demands and expectations the government maintains a pumped-up state of the economy which leads to inflation.

But it is odd to describe inflation as an inevitable aspect of "capitalism" when it is so clearly the government that is doing the inflating. To get around this difficulty Mr. Heilbroner describes our present era as one of "monopolistic governmental capitalism." The word "monopolistic" is thrown in here for auld lang syne, being irrelevant to the argument. The operative word is "governmental," and it is Orwellian to call this governmental policy the normal way in which capitalism works.

If the inflationary policy of government was necessary to the operation of the economic system, if it met the demands of the participants in the economic system for high real incomes, high employment, and security, one might consider the inflation to be part of the normal operation of the system. But this view is not supported by analysis or by experience. We see now that inflation has not reduced unemployment, speeded up the growth of real incomes or moderated insecurity. In fact, its result has been negative on all these scores.

Having dismissed or ignored almost all the explanations of inflation advanced by economists in the past two hundred years in favor of a more "fundamental" theory, Professor Heilbroner offers his own cure—or, since he insists there is no disease, his prediction of the next phase of capitalist development. That turns out, only a little surprisingly, to be the favorite anti-inflation medicine of the booboisie, of those ignorant of both history and economics, namely permanent price and wage control. This is a little surprising because his trail leads to the government as the source of the difficulty from which we are now suffering, and one would not expect him to propose or predict as the next step that a still larger share of our economic lives should be turned over to the institution which has done so miserably up to now.

If inflation meets any need, it is the need of the political system, not of the economic system. The interesting question raised by Mr. Heilbroner's essay is not whether inflation is the normal working of capitalism but whether it is the normal working of democracy. That is much the same as asking whether ignorance, shortsightedness, and parochialism are inevitable parts of the normal working of democracy. There is no reason to be a defeatist about this and certainly a professor should not be.

Baying at Economists

The *Wall Street Journal*,
June 15, 1976

W E have been flooded this spring with decline-and-fall books about the American economic system. These books remind me of all the babies born in New York City nine months after the November 1965 power failure. They are a lagged response to a shocking but transitory disturbance.

The disturbance which stimulated the cataclysmic writing about the economy was the combination of deep recession with high inflation in the winter of 1974–75, plus the uprising of the OPEC cartel, plus the trauma of Watergate and the ignominious end of the Vietnam war. Taken together, these events encouraged Götterdammerung watchers to believe that G-Day was here, or just around the corner.

The books appear in an environment different from that in which I assume them to have been conceived. Unemployment and inflation have both fallen more than almost anyone forecast a year ago. OPEC seems to have exhausted its capacity to exploit us, and other less-developed countries have not found the means to imitate OPEC. Most important, the disturbing economic and political events we have been living through have not sent the American people rushing to the barricades. On the contrary, the presidential primaries this year suggest that the American people want nothing else so much as a "return to normalcy."

However, the timing of the conception and birth of these books is accidental and superficial from the standpoint of their central purposes. The economic and political ups and downs of the last two or three years are ripples on the historical tides with which our authors are concerned. Delay of a year or two in the decline and fall of a socio-politico-economic system which is now about two hundred years old would not affect their message.

The books I have in mind are:

Robert Lekachman, *Economists at Bay—Why the Experts Will Never Solve Your Problems*
Robert Heilbroner, *Business Civilization in Decline*
Michael Harrington, *The Twilight of Capitalism*
Barry Commoner, *The Poverty of Power—Energy and the Economic Crisis*

I concentrate on Mr. Lekachman's book because it is the most comprehensive representation of the radical chic view of our economic condition and prospect. This view is that for a number of reasons the free market no longer serves, if it ever did serve, the needs of the people, and that therefore the system will be and should be radically changed. The nature of the change is unclear except that there will be a great increase in the role of the government in managing the economy.

The high ethical standards of this newspaper require that I reveal a personal interest in Mr. Lekachman's book. Its dust jacket is illustrated by pictures of nine economists: Adam Smith, John S. Mill, Karl Marx, John M. Keynes, Arthur F. Burns, Milton Friedman, J. K. Galbraith, Walter W. Heller, and me. Naturally I am flattered to be in such company. If I say anything kind about the book, the reader may make the appropriate discount.

I suspect that the cover picture is not meant to be entirely flattering. Smith, Mill, Marx, and Keynes are shown as noble busts on pedestals, whereas the rest of us are caricatured looking like the Tweed Ring in Nast's cartoon. Even so, I am proud to be in that company.

Several strands run through Lekachman's book, and other fashionable writing these days:

1. The world is getting richer less rapidly than it used to, and will begin getting poorer. This is primarily because we are running out of things, including clean air and water into which to dump our wastes. For the industrial world the slower rise of income, or actual decline of income, will be intensified by the demands of the underdeveloped world, enforced by cartels on the model of OPEC.

2. With per-capita incomes growing more slowly, or declin-

ing, the demand of the majority of the population for a more nearly equal distribution of income will become irresistible. The majority will no longer be bought off by the fact and hope of rising average incomes, but will insist on a larger share of the total.

3. More government management of the economy will be required, to cope with our straitened circumstances and to engineer the redistribution of income.

This is the kind of plausible argument which reads as well backwards as forward.

Whether the world will be getting poorer, or even getting rich less rapidly, is unclear. Surely we have been running out of things since the Year One, whenever that was. But investment in all forms, tangible and intangible, has far exceeded the depletion of man's initial stock of resources so that our productive capacity is now larger than ever before.

There is no general reason why investment must exceed depletion, and there have been long periods in which that did not happen. Perhaps we are going to enter another such. Whether we are or not is a matter of quantities and cannot be foretold by a priori reasoning. On this subject the conclusion of a review of the work of Professor Jay Forrester, one of the leading prophets of our impoverishment, is pertinent, especially since it sweeps in three of the deities in Mr. Lekachman's Pantheon. The review is by Professor William Nordhaus:

"Can we treat seriously Forrester's (or anybody's) predictions in economic and social science for the next 130 years? Long-run economic forecasts have generally fared quite poorly. Marx predicted the immiseration of the working class under capitalism; Keynes guessed that capital could have no net productivity in the present year (1973); Galbraith assured us that scarcity is obsolete. And now, without the scantest reference to economic theory or empirical data, Forrester predicts that the world's material standard of living will peak in 1990 and then decline. *Sic transit gloria.*"[1]

But suppose it should be true that at least in the United States, economic growth will come more slowly. Would that show the need for more government "planning" and for greater equality

---

[1] William Nordhaus, "World Dynamics: Measurement without Data," *Economic Journal,* December 1973, p. 1183.

in the distribution of income? One could argue, on the contrary, that if we are going to have less growth, growth will become more valuable. We should be more careful to maintain the conditions that contribute to an increase of output. Rich societies can afford waste; poor ones cannot. This is an argument for less government intervention and "planning" rather than for more.

Of course, I assume that the market is the route to efficiency and growth. Mr. Lekachman presumably would not accept this, but he makes no serious attack on the theoretical analysis and historical evidence in its favor. He does offer the Galbraithian proposition that the market is not efficient because it is not competitive and because it serves consumers' demands that are fabricated by producers. However, much time has passed since Galbraith, and Veblen and others before him, advanced these propositions and the evidence for them is still flimsy.

I was struck by the banality of these arguments while attending meetings of the National Restaurant Association and of the American Iron and Steel Institute on successive days recently. Many economists think of steel as the typical American industry and are ready to assume, with or without facts, that the industry works in a noncompetitive way. But the restaurant industry is enormously larger, in value added and in employment, and more typical of the American economy. It and the industries that supply it are obviously competitive, but it is not part of that backward economic subculture that Galbraith labels the market sector. It is efficient and progressive. And if any economist thinks that the growing American preference for eating out has been fabricated by advertising, he should spend more time doing the dishes.

The heart of Lekachman's argument has to do with equality. Since we are not going to become richer, he argues, we must become more nearly equal. But the connection between growth and equality could just as well, or better, be argued in the other direction. If, as seems likely, redistributive measures impair efficiency and slow down growth, we can afford less redistribution when conditions are making efficiency and growth harder to achieve.

Mr. Lekachman's main complaint against economists is that they have not made the case for income redistribution with enough passion. He blames the criticism of economists for the failure of the American people to buy George McGovern's $1000 per person grant program in 1972. He cannot understand why else a proposal to take from 49 percent of the people and give to 51 percent would not be a sure winner. But he gives economists too much credit. McGovern's Demogrant was rejected because it violated the belief of a great majority of Americans that a person should earn his own way, and not be dependent on the government, except in extreme circumstances. People have many other beliefs not entirely consistent with this one, but this is a real one, and it limits the degree of the redistributive measures that will be supported—regardless of what economists say.

In my opinion, we need a more reliable and efficient way to assure that people in this country do not fall into poverty. But this would be a long way from the general redistribution that Mr. Lekachman seeks, and would involve no radical change in the economic system. Indeed, a more reliable and efficient anti-poverty program would be consistent with, and would contribute to, reduction of the heavy burden of transfer payments and interferences the economy now bears in the name of equality.

It is symptomatic that the word "freedom" does not appear in the index of Mr. Lekachman's book except as part of the title of a work by Milton Friedman; I do not think the word appears in the text at all. Similarly, although there is admiring exposition of Marx's vision, there is no reference to the Soviet Union, the living embodiment of that vision, except as a country to which Richard Nixon sold wheat. An evaluation of our present condition and future prospects which gives no weight to freedom as a value to be cherished or to the Soviet Union as an example to be avoided will surely reach peculiar conclusions.

It is fair to say, as Mr. Heilbroner does, that social and economic systems do not last forever, and it is reasonable to contemplate the end of this one. Mr. Heilbroner cites Schumpeter as an admirer of capitalism who nevertheless foresaw its end. But he does not explain that a key factor in Schumpeter's view of the ending of capitalism was the increasing hostility of the intellectuals, in spite of, and even because of, the success of capitalism in improving the conditions of the people. For the modern intellectual to "predict" the end of capitalism is like Typhoid Mary predicting an epidemic.

Galbraith According to Galbraith

Fortune, July 27, 1981

R EVIEWERS of the works of J. K. Galbraith make a common mistake. They think they are dealing with an economist trying to do what other economists do. That is an understandable mistake, since he was, after all, once president of the American Economic Association.

Reviewers who are not economists are impressed because Galbraith doesn't use the statistics, charts, algebra, or long words that other economists use. They say, "What a wonderful writer he is for an economist!" Such reviewers are also flattered into thinking that because they understand Galbraith they understand economics.

Reviewers who are economists generally dislike Galbraith's writings. There is a large measure of envy in this, which they don't feel for other best-selling authors who write about economics because they don't think of these authors as economists, but which they do feel for Galbraith because he is playing in their league.

The difference between Galbraith and other economists is that he describes things as being just as they seem, whereas other economists are looking for an explanation behind what is superficially apparent. If you ask Galbraith why the price of gasoline is $1.30 a gallon, he will tell you that Exxon set the price there. If you ask other economists the same question, they will say something about supply and demand, not only for gasoline but also for other types of energy, and possibly something about production costs and about the time preference of Arab potentates compared with the marginal efficiency of capital, and that could go on and on. Galbraith's version is much easier for a writer to handle and is much closer to the way most readers look at the matter. It also, however, has much less explanatory power.

Galbraith says in his new memoir, *A Life in Our Times,*[1] that there is no idea associated with economics "that cannot, with sufficient effort, be stated in clear English." The true meaning of Galbraith's proposition is that he will not admit into his writing any ideas that he cannot state in clear English. He confirms this when he explains that he abandoned the idea of writing something in the style of a textbook because he "could not enlarge on the established truth in clear, straightforward English. It was a bore." What he can't enliven he excludes.

To understand and appraise Galbraith, one must start with the fact that he is first and foremost a writer who happens also to be an economist, a politician, a diplomat, a world traveler, an expert in Indian art, and a Scot, and he is prepared to write in any of those capacities insofar as he thinks he can do so entertainingly.

He is therefore to be judged in the class of amateur writers on economic, social, and political affairs who have a strong interest in good writing. I think, to name only those of high quality, of Joan Didion, Tom Wolfe, John Gregory Dunne, William Safire, George Will, Jimmy Breslin, Art Buchwald, and Russell Baker. In that class Galbraith is one of the better economists, not an outstanding writer.

Galbraith's literary style has become more and more irritating as he has become more determined to be a good writer, and is most irritating in these memoirs. I begin with minor irritants. He loves to startle the reader by putting words in an unnatural order, and misses no opportunity so to do—rather than to do so. He also has a fondness for ending paragraphs with short declarative sentences, usually of about six words, which leave you feeling that you have been sitting for a long time with a storyteller who keeps punching you in the ribs to make sure you get the joke.

Two other characteristics of the writing are more serious. One is the endless name dropping. Page after page reads like

---

[1] John Kenneth Galbraith, *A Life in Our Times* (Boston: Houghton Mifflin, 1981).

those "People" columns in the newspapers which report non-events because they are associated with some celebrity. Thus: "At one party I encountered Mrs. Vijaya Lakshmi Pandit, sister of Jawaharlal Nehru, former Indian ambassador to Washington and Moscow and former President of the General Assembly of the United Nations. She asked if she could accompany me that evening. So did Natacha Stewart Ullman of *The New Yorker* and also Princess Irene of the Netherlands, although she later defected to a Nixon rally at Madison Square Garden." By this time the reader can only say, "Who cares!"

And then there are the anecdotes. The book is full of stories that would probably make a grade-hungry student giggle when they are told by the professor but that do not deserve preservation between hard covers. The quintessential Galbraith style is most visible in the agricultural-economics story. Galbraith was a protégé of an agricultural economist, John D. Black, who described one of his contemporaries, George F. Warren, as the leader of the "retarded" school of agricultural economics. "When Warren retired, the nearly undisputed leader of the retarded school was Earl Butz at Purdue, who was joined by another distinguished member of the same school, Professor Joe Carroll Bottum. Butz and Bottum made a formidable team on the other side. Butz went on to be secretary of agriculture under Richard Nixon and to fall sadly afoul of John Dean, who told in the newspapers one of Earl's highly unappropriate stories." There you have a Galbraithian masterpiece. In three sentences he has four new names to be included in the index. He has the schoolboy thrill of juxtaposing Butz and Bottum. He has the sly reference to a salacious story by Butz. And he reminds the reader of the Nixon-Dean connection, with the inevitable memories of Watergate. In fact, the name of Nixon is dropped or dragged into this book on every twentieth page, on the average, which is well calculated to keep the *New York Review of Books* crowd salivating.

Galbraith's memoir, like all memoirs, is about its author. But memoirs differ in the degree to which they place their author in the context of his time. Kissinger's memoir is about Kissinger, but it is also a history of foreign policy in a certain period. Galbraith's memoir is about Galbraith. It is not also a history of economics or of economic policy except insofar as they happen to cross the narrow spotlight that is on him.

The picture of Galbraith that emerges from the book is puzzling. We know that he has made close and lasting friendships. I have myself had some personal contact with him and have found him generous, considerate, even a little sympathetic to someone who disagreed with him. But the Galbraith that Galbraith portrays in his own memoir is insufferable. It is as if he had decided to create this character and give him his own name in order to make the book more interesting.

The Galbraith in the book is extremely insensitive. I give one example. In 1936, having worked for the U.S. government and participated in U.S. politics, he was advised to become a citizen of this country. In 1937 he did so, and he says of taking the oath of allegiance, "No one in history has done so with so small a sense of emotion." He was giving up his citizenship in a country where his family had lived for over a hundred years and taking on new obligations to a new country, and yet he felt no emotion. I suppose I could come to understand this attitude, but I do not think I could understand this attitude being reported so casually, with no feeling of a need to explain it.

The arrogance of the public Galbraith is well known. He jokes about it slightly but does not recognize it as a fault. Among hundreds of examples in the book, one sticks in my mind. In the summer of 1942, when he was OPA administrator, Galbraith spent a little time in Puerto Rico. After that, "I returned to Washington to the bitterest and . . . most interesting months of the war." Now, I thought, we are going to get the stories of Guadalcanal and North Africa and Stalingrad, or at least of how those events were received in Washington, or of the efforts to mobilize the economy. But that was not what Galbraith meant. He meant his struggles to hold down the price of canned peas.

Arrogance is a charming quality in a heavyweight champion. It is not a good quality for a memoirist. It makes him think that everything that happened to him is interesting. It makes his reporting untrustworthy, because the point of view is too narrow. And it relieves him of any inclination to reflect on his life.

Galbraith played an active role in the great wave of American history that began in 1933. He promoted, and in some cases originated, many of the ideas which guided that wave until recently: that fiscal policy should be used to achieve economic stability and high employment; that price control is an efficient way to prevent inflation; that the market doesn't work; that businesses choose to produce and make the consumers want the product;

that corporations are run by a bureaucracy rather than by directors, stockholders, or the market; that the country is run by a consortium of corporate bureaucrats and government bureaucrats; that America places too much emphasis on economic growth; that America suffers from too little public expenditure and regulation; that capitalism and communism are converging; that U.S. defense forces are a menace.

These ideas have recently come under severe attack. Some hold them largely responsible for the high American inflation, the slow growth of output, and the weakened position of the United States in the world. The 1980 election can be interpreted as a rejection of these once-popular ideas, and the Democrats in Congress seem to accept that interpretation.

It would be interesting to know what Galbraith thinks about all this. Does he consider the possibility that he might have been wrong, or that he went too far, or that he may have stimulated forces which went too far? I did not expect a confession from Galbraith. I did think that there might have been some explanation, or some recognition of the need to explain. Their absence is a disappointment.

At seventy-two, Galbraith has reached an age where still to be an enfant terrible is to be childish. He has shown that he can write best-sellers. This would be the time for him to write a book that does not merely entertain but reveals the wisdom, and uncertainty, that must have accumulated in his unique career.

Industrial Policy, à la Reich

Fortune, June 13, 1983

*An influential academic is overstating our economic problems
and offering heavy-handed solutions.*

I F for no other reason, *The Next American Frontier*[1] will receive
attention because its author, Robert Reich, is an adviser to several
Democratic candidates for the 1984 presidential nomination. The
book is already endorsed by Senators Mondale and Hart. I would
worry about this if I did not think about politicians what Jimmy
Walker thought about girls. He never knew one to be ruined by
a book.

This book has three elements: a description of the terrible
present state and future prospects of the American economy, a
theory of the causes of that dreadful condition, and a prescription
for rescuing us. The description of our condition is grossly exaggerated. The theory of the causes of the alleged condition is inadequately supported. The prescription is, with some exceptions,
unpersuasive. If I thought there was any likelihood of its being
implemented, I would call it frightening.

The basic premise of the book is that the U.S. economy is
failing. Its failures are not temporary or marginal but durable
and major. Reich says, for example, that "the U.S. economy is
grinding to a slow, painful halt." So we require a new theory of
economic history to explain what's happening to us and a new
economic and social policy to cure it.

[1] Robert Reich, *The Next American Frontier* (New York: Times Books, 1983).

The main evidence of the alleged failure is the performance of total output per capita, compared with our own past experience and with the recent achievement of others, notably Japan and Western Europe. The years 1920 to 1970 were the years of America's great economic success. The failure, it is said, began in 1970. One would expect this turn to failure to be reflected in the statistics. But the facts, not included in the book, do not support this analysis. From 1929 (we have no good statistics before then) to 1970 real GNP in the United States rose at an average annual rate of 3.06 percent; between 1970 and 1980 GNP rose at a 3.10 percent rate. Between 1929 and 1970 real GNP per capita rose at a 1.76 percent rate; between 1970 and 1980 the comparable figure was 2.03 percent. Reich warns of the time, still to come, "when the standard of living falls even more precipitously than it is now falling." The best measure of the U.S. standard of living is real per capita income after taxes. From 1929 to 1970 it rose at a 1.66 percent rate; from 1970 to 1980 it rose at a 1.93 percent rate. (I have not carried these comparisons beyond 1980 because Reich's argument is not about the special effects of recessions.)

There was indeed a problem about the performance of the American economy in the 1970s. Output per hour of work during the decade rose at an annual rate of only 1.38 percent, compared with about 3 percent earlier in the postwar period. This needs explanation and I will return it to later. But the slippage in productivity is a long way from the economy grinding to a halt or a precipitous fall in the standard of living. Much of Reich's case concerns the decline, as he sees it, of the American economy relative to that of other countries. He says that several industrial countries have now surpassed the United States in gross domestic product (GDP) per capita. His main evidence here is a table showing per capita GDP in fourteen developed countries as a percentage of the U.S. figure in 1979 with the currencies in each country converted into U.S. dollars at 1979 exchange rates. He acknowledges that such comparisons can be somewhat flimsy because the exchange rate in any given year may not reflect the relative prices of all the output in that year; however, Reich doesn't attempt to deal with this difficulty and ends up offering comparisons in which nine of the countries do better than the United States. I have reworked the figures for 1982 and find that this time only two of the fourteen do better.

Reich further supports his contention about the relative decline of the U.S. economy with three tables showing the records of several countries with respect to growth rates, unemployment rates, and GNP per capita based on actual prices (rather than exchange rates). To my surprise, I discovered that these tables were taken from an article that I wrote in the May 1982 *AEI Economist,* although that source was not mentioned. Perhaps he did not want to acknowledge the source of the tables because my article was entitled "The Industrial Economies: We Are Not Alone." That is, my conclusion was quite different from Reich's. I saw the evidence as saying that what has been happening to the United States—the slowdown in growth of output and productivity and the rise of unemployment—had been happening in the other industrial countries as well. Reich sees the same evidence as showing that we, along with Great Britain, are experiencing a unique failure.

Reich uses the figures from my article to show that "other nations are gaining at a rapid clip." But the rate at which other countries are gaining on us is also declining rapidly. Take Japan. Between 1960 and 1979 Japanese real per capita output rose from 31.5 percent of ours to 70.2 percent. But the rate of gain on us fell sharply. If it continues to fall at the same pace, Japan's real per capita GNP would still be only about 74 percent of ours in 2083.

Reich does not make it easy to check the barrage of data with which he supports the picture of an American economy in a state of terrible decline. Some of his "facts" are stated in a way that defies verification, such as: "In any given year, 1 American family in 6 is temporarily impoverished." Where sources are cited at all they are often cited too vaguely to be found. What one can say with confidence is that the picture given is highly exaggerated and sensationalized.

But still, there is something to explain, namely that slowdown in the growth of U.S. productivity after 1973. One can generously interpret Reich's book as an effort to explain it. His explanation asks us to begin by contemplating three stages of economic development. The Era of Mobilization, 1870 to 1920, was a period in which the vast resources of America, the land and mines, the immigrant labor force, the flow of savings, were married to British and American technology by venturesome entrepreneurs. This was on the whole a period of great economic success, although tailing off at its end.

It was followed by the Era of Management, 1920 to 1970, in which business organized mass-production operations in an extremely efficient way. This was the era of autos, steel, rubber tires, electric appliances, and so on.

As rendered by Reich, this era had two features that were important for what followed. First, government agencies cooperated with the oligopolies in the mass-production industries to stabilize markets and prevent overinvestment, thereby making possible continuous, efficient production. It is important for Reich to demonstrate that government has always been involved in running the economy, and that his own prescriptions, which feature a major role for government, are not new in this regard but are only attempting to redirect this traditional involvement in ways that serve the national interest better. The lengths to which Reich goes to discover government participation in the planning done by American industries is amazing. Every government agency with a title suggesting any connection with any industry is imagined to be playing a significant role. The most laughable example is the Business and Defense Services Administration, an obscure agency in the Department of Commerce that couldn't plan its way out of a paper bag.

The second key feature of the Era of Management, as Reich elaborates it, is that organization is hierarchical. Companies are run from the top down by command and control, not by sharing and love. Decisions are made on a strictly objective basis and passed down as orders through layers of organization in which tasks are subdivided and specialized to the maximum degree. This yields highly efficient repetitive production. It also yields rigidity and alienation.

Reich tells us that the Era of Management ended when standardized mass production ceased to be a source of high and rising real incomes in the United States and other advanced countries. After 1970, capital, know-how, and education flowed around the world and permitted standardized mass production to be carried on efficiently in the low-wage, less-developed countries. For the advanced countries to remain advanced, their economies had to turn to something else—something the LDCs could not do. The correct response, according to Reich, has been production in the "flexible system." The source of high incomes will now be small-batch, specialized production constantly responding to changes in demand and to advances in technology. This requires a high degree of skill, constructive initiative from all parts of the labor force, and cooperative relations within the firm rather than fixed orders flowing from top to bottom.

Other industrial countries, notably Japan, have adapted to this new system. The United States has not. That failure, says, Reich, is the cause of our absolute and relative decline. He cites several reasons for the failure. We had a greater commitment, institutionally and culturally, to the mass-production system than did others. Our government policy was more protective and less adaptive. Our traditional outlook did not include a sense of justice within the firm and therefore prevented the emergence of a system of voluntary cooperation in production. American efforts to promote justice—which to Reich means equality—took the form of the welfare state rather than the welfare corporation.

This is an interesting hypothesis about the cause of the slowdown in American productivity growth. There may even be something to it. But there is no evidence in the book to show how much, if at all, this hypothesis explains the productivity lag. There are dozens of other factors that may have contributed to it. A great deal of hard research has been done in trying to quantify the contribution of each of these factors. I think of the work of Edward Denison, John Kendrick, John Norsworthy, Dale Jorgenson, and others. This work leaves a great deal unanswered; it does not rule out the possibility that Reich's hypothesis has some validity. But a hypothesis should be able to pass certain tests. It should be possible to move from the hypothesis to some effects, preferably measurable, on the size and age of the capital stock, the age-sex composition and educational attainment of the labor force, the interindustry distribution of resources, and other observable variables. Reich pays no attention to any of this work and in general makes no effort to test his hypothesis.

Suppose we agreed that the pattern of production in the United States is changing, for various reasons, and that it would be a good thing if business and labor adapted to this change more rapidly. Where would we go from there? We could preach to American business and labor, which is part of what Reich is doing, and I find no fault with that. We could point out that much government policy is obstructing adaptation and should be corrected. Reich does that too, in what I consider the best part of the book.

But he goes much further. He wants a radical transformation

of American enterprises under the leadership and sponsorship of the federal government. The business enterprise would become a cooperative venture in which worker and management discuss and agree upon long-run decisions about investment, location, product lines, and employment levels, as well as on daily work procedures. The enterprise would be the locus of justice—supplanting state and local government as the channel for providing medical care, training, unemployment benefits, and other aspects of what we have heretofore considered the welfare state. This development would be promoted by the federal government, which would provide protection, subsidies, tax benefits, and social-assistance payments to enterprises on the condition that they develop approved plans for adaptation and in general conform to the pattern of the cooperative company town. In passing, Reich throws in a system of wage-price guidelines worked out in "national bargaining arenas"—the kind of guidelines that in other countries "provide all segments of the population with highly visible opportunities to clarify goals, articulate demands, and negotiate precise trade-offs among inflation, unemployment, and structural adjustment."

In sum, the American economy would be reorganized on the model of the Israeli kibbutz or hippie commune, except that kibbutzim and communes would not arise spontaneously but would be generated and tended by a caring, farsighted, objective Big Brother in Washington. This surely is too heavy a policy load to be borne by Reich's weak description and diagnosis of our condition.

Some "Supply-Side" Propositions

The *Wall Street Journal,*
March 19, 1980

THERE is a rising tide of literature and talk about supply-side economics. For the benefit of noneconomists who may be wondering what this is all about, I will put down here my view of what are and are not "supply-side" propositions and what the current state of the evidence is.

The following are *not*, in my opinion, "supply-side" propositions. Although they all have to do with supply they were common currency long before the new school of thought emerged, about five years ago.

1. "Supply" is an important element in economic analysis. The first parrot who got a Ph.D. in economics for learning to say "supply and demand" knew that.

2. Increasing the supply of total output is important for individual welfare and national strength. That is what *The Wealth of Nations* (1776) is all about.

3. The supply of output depends on the supply of resources, or input. The early economist who first said "land, labor, and capital" knew that.

4. The supply of resources, and therefore total output, is affected by public policy. For example, economists 150 years ago argued against budget deficits on the ground that they diverted saving from productive investment. Moreover, the possibility of affecting output by policy remained an active element in public discussion. Thus, in the 1950s there was an intense public debate about economic growth with presidential candidates competing

to see who could offer the largest growth target. This was a debate about ways to increase total inputs.

5. The supply of resources will be influenced by the tax system. I remember learning about this in my high-school course in economics, which goes back almost fifty years.

6. A tax reduction will make the national income higher than it would otherwise have been, and the revenue loss from the tax reduction will therefore be less than if the national income had not been induced to rise. This was one of the pillars of Andrew Mellon economics.

7. A tax reduction will raise the national income by more than the amount of tax reduction. This was the essence of "trickle-down" theory as actively espoused by the Republican Congress in 1948 and 1954. If a tax cut did not increase the national income by more than the tax cut there would be nothing to trickle down from the immediate beneficiaries of the tax cut to the rest of the population. Whether this proposition was correct or not is unproved, but it is not a new idea.

8. A tax rate reduction will increase the total revenue. At this point we come to an idea that looks like the new supply-side economics and we must make a fine but important distinction. The idea that a tax rate reduction might increase the revenue has been a standard proposition in economics for many years— possibly forty—but it has heretofore been derived from "demand-side" or Keynesian reasoning. The argument has been that a cut of tax rates leaves more money in people's hands, as a result of which they spend more, and the total increase in spending exceeds the initial tax reduction, because the increased spending of one person raises the income of another person and induces him to spend more, and so on. Moreover, the increased demand thus created induces businesses to invest more. If these additional expenditures and investments are large enough they will raise the national income enough to yield an increased amount of revenue, even with reduced tax rates.

In a primitive form this was the "pump-priming" argument of the 1930s. In slightly more sophisticated form it became a key item in the New Economics of the 1960s.

A basic assumption of this line of argument is that there is a large quantity of unutilized resources available to be brought into production without any increase in real wage rates or in the return to capital. This makes it possible for the increase of demand to be translated into an increase of real output, and not simply to blow off in higher prices.

Valid or not, this proposition is old and surely not part of supply-side economics.

We may now turn from what, in my opinion, are not "supply-side" propositions to some that I believe fit that category.

9. A tax reduction, not accompanied by a reduction of government expenditures, will raise the total revenue, and will do so by operating on the supply side of the economy. We visualize a state of affairs in which the total output is limited to the supply of resources—that is, there are no unemployed resources—but there are more resources that would be supplied if the real rate of return to them was greater. A cut of tax rates will increase the after-tax return to productive resources, causing more of them to be supplied. That will increase the national income and the tax base. This increase in the tax base will yield more revenue at the reduced tax rate.

The basic point to note about this proposition is that it is not a proposition about ideology or even about economic theory but is a proposition about magnitudes. Theory does not even tell us whether a reduction of tax rates will increase or decrease the supply of labor or saving. But even if we bypass that argument, and stipulate that the effect is positive, the magnitude of the effect is all-important.

For example, suppose that we start with a tax system that takes 40 percent of the national income, leaving 60 percent as the after-tax return to the suppliers of productive resources. Then we cut the effective tax rate 10 percent from 40 percent to 36 percent. That increases the after-tax return from 60 percent to 64 percent, or by 6.67 percent. If the revenue is not to be reduced the national income must rise by 11.11 percent, so that the 36 percent tax rate will yield as much as the 40 percent formerly did. That means that a 6.67 percent increase in the return to resources must yield an increase of 11.11 percent in output, or one and two-thirds times as much.

Whether the quantitative relationships will be such that a cut of tax rates not accompanied by a cut of expenditures will increase the revenue is a question that we cannot answer with certainty. The answer surely depends on the kinds of taxes involved and on other circumstances. But one can be fairly confident that the relationships are not such that an across-the-board income tax rate cut will increase the revenues within any relevant period of time.

This form of the supply-side proposition is of critical importance for political reasons. That is, the tax-cutting prescription would be much less attractive if it were universally understood to be a recommendation for enlarged budget deficits or reduced government spending. Moreover, the proposition loses its claim to intellectual originality if it only says that taxes and spending should both be reduced or that a tax cut will reduce the revenue "less than some people think."

10. Less political and ambitious supply-siders might be willing to settle for the proposition that a tax rate cut, not accompanied by an expenditure cut, will nonetheless increase real output, even if it also reduces total revenue.

But even this more modest proposition is not axiomatically true and depends on magnitudes whose size we don't know very well. Again granting that a tax rate cut would increase incentives to work and save, we must also recognize the effect of the tax cut on the income left in people's hands. If their increased demand for consumption exceeds their increased output, and government spending is not reduced, there must be less investment.

This point was made by Michael Evans, whose econometric studies are frequently cited as support for supply-side propositions: "To the extent that the increase in private sector saving generated by tax cuts is offset by a decrease in public sector saving, additional funds will not be available for investment." And if the increase in private sector saving is less than the decrease in public sector saving (the increase in the budget deficit resulting from the tax cut) private investment will be crowded out and there is no reason for counting on an increase in the long-run growth.

The conditions required for a tax cut to lead to some increase of output are less demanding than those required to get an increase in output sufficient to raise the revenue. But the evidence for the existence of even these less onerous conditions is not strong.

11. An extreme, and currently very popular, version of supply-side economics is that the way to tackle the inflation problem is from the supply side, especially by cutting taxes. The argument is simply that inflation results from an excess of demand over supply, and there is no sense in correcting that by the painful method of restricting demand when it could be done by the pleas-

ant way of raising supply. The answer is of course equally simple. What we can do on the supply side is not big enough to solve the problem. We have demand growing by about 12 percent a year and supply growing by about 2 percent a year, which yields 10 percent inflation. To increase the rate of growth of supply by 50 percent from 2 percent a year to 3 percent a year, which is a difficult task, would still leave an enormous inflation, especially if the increase of supply is accomplished by means like cutting taxes which at the same time increase demand.

What I have said here is not an argument for or against cutting taxes, or for or against any other policy. It surely is not meant to deny that cutting taxes and expenditures, or restructuring the tax system, can be beneficial in many respects. I am only making a plea for modesty in recognizing the difference between what one knows and what one doesn't know.

Despite the tone of much of the current argument, the propositions of supply-side economics are not matters of ideology or principle. They are matters of arithmetic. So far one must say that the arithmetic of any of the "newer" propositions is highly doubtful. Supply-side economics may yet prove to be the irritant which, like the grain of sand in the oyster shell, produces a pearl of new economic wisdom. But up to this point the pearl has not appeared.

What Economists Do

The *AEI Economist,* January, 1984

*Recent public attention to the Washington experience of Martin
Feldstein, chairman of President Reagan's Council of
Economic Advisers, prompts these reminiscences and
observations by a former economic adviser to President Nixon.*

Joys and Travails of a President's Economist

On August 16, 1971, the morning after President Nixon startled
the world by announcing the imposition of wage and price controls, my son Ben called me and said, "Ideologically you should
fall on your sword, but existentially it's great."

I had spent much of my career arguing against wage and
price controls, even in World War II. And here I was, economic
adviser to the president who imposed the most comprehensive
and rigid controls in America's peacetime history. But also I was
an active participant in the most exciting event in the record of
economic policy. Both the frustration and the exhilaration were
present, and I cannot deny that the exhilaration was dominant.

Few days in the life of a president's economic adviser are
that exciting. Still, the life is well described by frustration at the
level of ideology and policy combined with high satisfaction at
the level of atmosphere and activity.

For me, the satisfaction came largely from the sense of being
on the stage—even if as an insignificant extra—where the greater
figures of history had performed. I worked in an office in an 1870
building where secretaries of State, War, and Navy had worked
for more than seventy years. When I went from my office in the
Executive Office Building to a meeting in the Treasury, my route

was through the ground floor of the White House, and I sometimes breasted crowds of wide-eyed tourists on a once-in-a-lifetime
trip. One would need a heart of stone not to be thrilled by the
feeling of "belonging" in the house where Lincoln lived.

But the White House economist's interpersonal relations are
not confined to those greats who are dead and therefore conveniently undemanding and uncompetitive. Most of his relations
are with living, breathing people, mainly people within the administration, and his relations with these people largely determine
the quality of the adviser's life. These relations in turn depend
mainly on the president, even though the adviser does not spend
much of his time with the president. The picture of the economic
adviser sitting constantly next to the president and whispering
in his ear is romance.

Economists and the Making of Economic Policy

Mostly the adviser does his advising in interagency committee
meetings. From the standpoint of good administration this interagency talk may be a waste. From the standpoint of the economic
adviser it is a blessing, because through these interagency meetings the adviser gets to say his piece and have some influence
over many matters that never rise to presidential notice.

The other participants in the interagency meetings—cabinet
secretaries and agency heads—feel no great need for the advice
of the president's economist. They pay attention to him only because of what they think is the respect the president accords him
and the willingness of the president to listen to him. It is in this
sense that the adviser's relation to the president dominates his
daily life.

I always thought that the quality of my own life in the administration was determined in a satisfying way early in Mr. Nixon's
term when we had the first meeting of the Cabinet Committee
on Economic Policy. Hendrik Houthakker and I, as members of
the Council of Economic Advisers (Paul McCracken was the chairman), were the lowest ranking people in the room. But President
Nixon turned to each of us and asked our opinion on the subjects
under discussion. That gesture naturally fortified my esteem for
Mr. Nixon, but it also helped establish my position in the administration.

My impression is that my experience was the usual one. People who become president are generally people who recognize and value those who are loyal and helpful to them. And if the president accepts his economic adviser as a member of this team, the other people at the White House will accept the adviser also. That acceptance is highly important to the adviser. He is going to take a lot of criticism from the outside world—deserved or undeserved. If he is to have enough self-confidence to continue doing his daily work, he must find when he goes into the White House mess for lunch not another group of critics but a group of friends who start with the assumption that he is right.

The notion that one, especially the economic adviser, should be a "team player" is the subject of much scorn these days. People who themselves go through their lives consciously or unconsciously toeing some conventional party line expect the economic adviser to be a Martin Luther nailing dissenting theses to the White House door. That would, of course, be impractical for both the president and the adviser. But everything depends on what the notion of team player covers, and that in turn depends on the president's attitude. The president can reasonably expect loyalty and helpfulness from his team. If he understands loyalty and helpfulness to mean prostitution, the relation will be intolerable and unproductive; but that is rarely if ever the case.

To return to the price control episode, Mr. Nixon knew that I thought the controls were a mistake. But I also knew that he had listened carefully to the arguments against the controls, arguments with which he sympathized, and that he had also heard economic arguments for the controls from people whose opinions were entitled to some respect. These people included many economists, at least one of whom was a past president of the American Economic Association. I could not hold that Mr. Nixon's decision was devoid of plausible economic rationale, even though I strongly disagreed. The president could expect that I would try to help make the controls work while they were in effect and, if possible, bring them to an early and painless end. Although he never asked that of me, I believed he deserved as good a public explanation of the economic reasoning supporting his decision as I could provide. I believe such team playing was effective and honorable on both sides.

There were exceptions to this idyllic picture of happy relations with the great ghosts and the important presences. For example,

I was disappointed when the president decided that the last seat on Air Force One on the trip to Moscow should go to his dentist rather than to his economist. But I mention this incident only to illustrate how trivial are the existential frustrations.

Economic policy performance is another matter. Some people think that economists know the answers to the big problems and that these answers are not heeded because the president and other politicians are ignorant or venal. They perceive this presidential attitude, therefore, as the source of great frustration for the economic adviser; but that is not really the problem.

It is true that presidents do not know much economics; they differ mainly in the extent to which they recognize their ignorance. It is also true that presidents do not make decisions exclusively on the basis of economic argument. But presidents are capable of comprehending cogent economic argument and are generally willing to give such an argument heavy weight.

The problem is that economists have difficulty giving sufficiently reliable answers to the kinds of questions that presidents confront. The questions for which answers can be found in the back of the textbook can be handled in the bureaucracy. The questions that come to the president always involve the balancing of uncertainties in the presence of ignorance. The economic adviser can help somewhat. He can rule out some things that "ain't so," and he can narrow the range of ignorance a little. He can add ideas that a president would not get if he relied on politicians, businessmen, or all-purpose intelligentsia alone. But still what he can do is disappointingly little, and the adviser becomes increasingly aware of this as his experience in office lengthens.

Sometime in 1973, after a meeting of economic officials, I said to George Shultz that I had the feeling of being one of a group of Boy Scouts who are allowed to sit in the City Hall for a day and pretend to run the city. That we were running the country was not believable. I should have added, but did not, that there was a big difference between those Boy Scouts and us. For us no group of mature, capable adults would be there to take over after we had finished our day. There would be nobody but us. Elections and the passage of time would change the names and faces but would not change very much the ability to cope with problems.

Newspaper stories currently emphasize alleged struggles between the chairman of the Council of Economic Advisers and

other officials of government. Even if such struggles exist, they
are not the main travails of an economic adviser. The main travails
are in the attempt to squeeze reliable advice out of a small and
squishy body of economics.

One lesson of this experience is not to put more decision-
making burdens on government than it is capable of handling. I
am tempted to add a second lesson, which is Harry Truman's
"Don't shoot the piano player; he's doing the best he can." But
that admonition is not necessary. Despite the occasional shooting,
the piano player is having an awfully good time.

Economists and the Making of Economic Policy

There are two extreme views among economists about the role
of economists in the making of economic policy. Both are, from
the standpoint of the economist, rather gratifying, although in
somewhat different ways.

The first view is that economic policy is dominated by economic thought. The classic exposition of this idea is the saying
of John Maynard Keynes at the end of *The General Theory of Employment, Interest, and Money:*

> The ideas of economists and political philosophers, both when they
> are right and when they are wrong, are more powerful than is
> commonly understood. Indeed the world is ruled by little else.
> Practical men, who believe themselves to be exempt from any in-
> tellectual influences, are usually the slaves of some defunct
> economists.[1]

The second view, associated with the name of George Stigler,
holds that economics is totally irrelevant to the making of economic policy. In this view economics is what the Marxists call a
superstructure or, in a favorite word of mine, an epiphenomenon.
The theory is that everyone involved in making economic policy—
from the average citizen to the president—knows his own interest
and how best to advance it, or at least knows these things better
than anyone else. These policy makers will do what their interests
and understanding dictate. The analysis of economists will not

[1] John Maynard Keynes, *The General Theory of Employment, Interest, and Money*
(New York: Harcourt, Brace and Company, 1936), p. 383.

change the policy but will provide rationalization for the benefit of those who want that.

The first of these views is attractive to some economists because it gives them a feeling of great power. It is especially attractive to those economists who have a vision of themselves as the possessors of that power—as the not-defunct economist to whom the practical men are slaves. The second view, of the economists' irrelevance for policy, is attractive to economists who think of economic policy as being generally a mess as measured by any objective criteria and who are happy to disclaim responsibility for the mess. Regarding policy as immune to economists' advice, they are content to confine themselves to the pursuit of pure science.

There is a third view, less extreme and probably more common than either of these. Unlike the second view, this holds that economists do in fact know superior answers to real problems, but, unlike the first view, it holds that the practical men in power do not listen to the economists, either out of venality or out of ignorance. This attitude is also satisfying for economists. It implies that economists really do know the answers to serious problems but that the illnesses of the economy are due to the failure of policy makers to take their advice. At the same time this view gives economists credit for superior knowledge but relieves them of responsibility for actual outcomes.

Each of these theories of the role of the economist in policy making is inadequate. The Keynesian picture of the practical man enslaved by economists ignores the fact that there are many economists in the world, with widely varying views. The practical man chooses which of these economists to heed, and in so doing the practical man becomes his own economist. Moreover, it is simply not true that practical people get all of their ideas about economic policy from economists. Lots of purveyors of economic ideas other than economists exist, and many of these are more persuasive than economists. Also, few practical people read economists directly. Most of them, insofar as they get the ideas of economists at all, get them at second or third hand, through editorial writers, preachers, and other intermediaries. Moreover, there are many practical people in the world, and many politicians, competing for influence and listening to different economists. Which economist's ideas get translated into action depends on which practical person wins the struggle for power.

So the attractive notion of the economist whispering in the ear of the powerful ruler is simplistic. But the notion that economics not only is irrelevant to policy but also should be irrelevant is both simplistic and too cynical. The underlying assumption is that the peanut farmer's influence on policy will be determined by his interest as a peanut farmer and that the peanut farmer knows perfectly well what policy will serve that interest. Because the peanut farmer does not need the advice of an economist about his own interest, he does not listen to economists and should not. But, in fact, there is no reason to believe that the peanut farmer knows his own interest without advice from economists. We accept as natural that he should want and need the advice of agronomists, lawyers, and investment counselors. Similarly he may need the advice of economists in thinking about public policy that affects the peanut interest. Moreover, and more important, it is wrong to think that the peanut farmer's interests are solely dictated by his position as a peanut farmer. He is a member of this nation and this society and he has an interest in their functioning well. He has a concern with the effects of budget deficits, of monetary growth, or of price and wage controls on the society, even aside from their effects on him personally and directly. He needs advice about those effects and is influenced in thinking about them by the ideas circulating in the country, including the ideas of economists.

The third view, that economists know the right answers but politicians do not listen to them, is wrong on both counts. Economists have to admit to a great deal of uncertainty on most important questions and are often wrong. And politicians do listen to economists, even though not exclusively to them, and would listen to them more if they gave more reliable answers.

Economists' Influence on Public Policy

The situation is more complicated than any of these three views suggests. Economics and economists have an influence on policy that is important, even though it is indirect and certainly not exclusive. On the whole this influence has been beneficial, even though there have been mistakes. Fifty years ago I had an economics professor who went around asking doctors how many years they thought it would be before doctors cured more people than they killed. I suppose that medicine has passed that point now.

It may be professional pride, but I think that economics has also.

One may take for granted that policy makers are politicians. One does not become or remain an important policy maker without being a politician, even in as nonpolitical a position as the chairmanship of the Federal Reserve. Politicians have political motives and objectives, high among which, of course, is their election and reelection. That statement does not mean, as the simple story would have it, that politicians are therefore unconcerned with the national interest. They do care about that. But politicians—at least successful ones—have a great capacity for believing that what is in their interest is also in the national interest. That belief gives them the courage and determination to seek and hold high office.

In making economic policy that conforms to their political objectives, policy makers are constrained within two kinds of limits. First, policy makers want to operate within the range of policies that the public, or parts of the public important to the politician, accepts as legitimate—kosher, so to speak. Thus, at present, a deficit in excess of $250 billion, the abolition of unemployment compensation, or an unemployment rate in excess of 15 percent would not be within the acceptable range. These limits do not necessarily reflect a judgment that all sound policy lies within the range. They are simply an indication of what the public is used to, has come to expect, or will not regard as too shocking. The range, of course, changes from time to time. I must emphasize that this is a range of policies and not a single point, so that the politician is left with freedom to choose policies within the range.

The policy maker–politician also wants to operate within the range of policies that he thinks are likely to work, both because that is important for his personal future and because he is interested in the future of the country. These policies also constitute a range. The policy maker cannot pinpoint the only policy that will work or the one policy that will work best, but he believes that he can identify a range within which the workable policy probably lies.

So the policy maker has the option of choosing policies within the range that is both acceptable to the public and likely, in his opinion, to work. It is within this range that his own judgment, political interests, and personal preferences can dominate; but politics is unlikely to lead him outside that range.

Economists and economics are among the factors that deter-

mine the limits of these two ranges. The range of what is acceptable to the public changes over time. It changes largely as a result
of experience; but it also changes as the result of thinking and
discussion. In fact, although experience is important, the experience itself usually has to be interpreted by thinkers of some kind.
Among those whose thinking and writing influence the public's
notions of acceptable economic policy are economists. They are
not the only ones who have this influence; but the influence of
economists has, I believe, been rising, because their communication with the public has been increasing. Much of this communication is indirect, through the media.

This role of economists in affecting public opinion is played
mainly by economists outside the government. Probably three
economists who have had the most influence on public opinion
in our time are John Maynard Keynes, Milton Friedman, and John
Kenneth Galbraith. Keynes was British, Friedman has never held
an important government position, and Galbraith has not held
an important economic position in government in forty years.

Policy makers—presidents, for example—form their own
opinions about what policy the public will accept. But, for reaching
an opinion about how economic policy will work, they usually
rely on advice. Of the ten presidents whose behavior I have studied
or observed, only two seem to be content with their own judgments about the economics—as distinct from the politics—of economic policy. They are Hoover and Reagan. The others depended
heavily on advice. This advice has not always come from professional economists: Eisenhower, for example, listened a good deal
to businessmen and bankers, some of whom were in his cabinet.
But increasingly presidents have relied on advice from economists
inside the government. The president receives economic advice
not only from economists who are officially labeled the Council
of Economic Advisers but also from other officials, notably the
secretary of the Treasury and the director of the Office of Management and Budget. These officials are usually not themselves
economists, but their advice is substantially influenced by the
economists on their own staffs.

According to a hackneyed story, President Truman said that
he wished he had a one-armed economist so that he would not
say "on the one hand and on the other hand." This complaint
reflects an erroneous view of the economist's function. It is not
the economist's function to tell the president what to do. As an

old professor of mine used to say, the expert should be on tap, not on top. The economic expert should inform the president of his options and of the likely effects of pursuing any of these options and should be candid in telling the president about the uncertainties of the economists' knowledge. If he does this he will leave the president with a range of possible choices, none of which can be ruled out by the economist's hard, scientific evidence. Economists in this position will indicate what their own preferences are, but that function is secondary. The effectiveness or success of an adviser is not measured by the number of times in which the president or other policy maker agrees with his preference or by the number of times he wins some interagency dispute.

In summary, economists influence economic policy in two ways. They are part of the process determining the range of policies that the public finds acceptable. They also advise policy makers about the range within which effective, workable policies lie. Economists are not the exclusive factor in the determination of either of those ranges; and even when those two ranges are known, a good deal of room is left for the policy maker to exercise his judgment, which may be good or bad.

These general propositions can be illustrated by describing the role of economists in some important policy developments of the last two decades.

Price Controls and Tax Cuts

The imposition of wage and price controls in 1971 was a dramatic case. Public opinion polls always show a majority of the population in favor of price and wage controls when inflation is recognized as a problem, even a fairly mild one. But in 1971, when the inflation rate was only 4 or 5 percent, a comprehensive, mandatory price-control system would probably not have been acceptable without the prior influence of a number of economists. Even if the majority of the public had been mildly in favor, there would have been significant groups that were strongly opposed. Certainly there would not have been a public demand for controls that would force a reluctant president to implement them.

The influence of economists appeared in a number of ways. The economists of the Kennedy-Johnson period had supported and tried to carry out a voluntary incomes policy, urging business and labor to hold prices and wages down; but they did not consider themselves to be advocates of comprehensive, mandatory controls. The public, however, could not be expected to make a distinction between voluntary restraint and mandatory controls—a distinction that is in fact less sharp than it superficially seems. The argument of these economists stimulated the call from the liberal media for some kind of controls. Probably even more important, a certain number of well-known conservative economists, most notably Arthur Burns, came out in favor of restraints on prices and wages. This backing enabled all supporters of controls to reject the idea that controls were inconsistent with the workings of a private, free-enterprise economy. It went far to make not only acceptance of controls but even demand for them seem nearly unanimous.

Economists contributed to the acceptance of controls in another quite different way—by mistake. Mr. Nixon was reluctant to point out that the ending of the inflation would involve a period of rising unemployment. The economists of the Nixon administration, of whom I was one, did believe that some period of unusually high unemployment would be necessary. But we significantly underestimated how much unemployment would be required. Therefore we did not sufficiently warn the president of what might happen or try hard enough to get him to warn the public. The administration was left saying that unemployment would not get much over 4 percent. As a result, when unemployment rose to be 6 percent and stayed there for a while, the whole policy looked like a failure; and the demand for a radical change of policy, which meant controls, became great.

Even though controls had become more acceptable and widely demanded, the president had a great aversion to them and probably would not have imposed them if he did not have economic experts on his own team to tell him that the controls had a reasonable chance of working. It was of no influence on him that an economist like Galbraith said that controls were a good idea; the president considered Galbraith hostile and unreliable. Many of the Nixon economists believed that controls would restrain inflation only temporarily and at great cost. But some economists whom the president regarded as part of his team told him that temporary controls would get the inflation down and that inflation would stay down after the controls were removed. These people were important to his decision.

It would be easy to say that President Nixon imposed the controls to win the 1972 election and that, from that standpoint, they were successful. But it would be wrong to stop the story there and exonerate the economists. Public acceptance of and demand for controls would not have been so great if not for the influence of economists, and so the political attractiveness of controls would not have been so compelling. And the president would probably not have imposed the controls, despite their political attractiveness, if the economic experts he trusted had unanimously opposed them on economic grounds.

There is a more recent example of the part played by economists in a policy that was misguided. That was the big 1981 tax cut, justified by the claim that the tax reduction would stimulate the economy enough to raise the federal revenue. Politicians do not need the advice of economists to be in favor of tax cuts: An old rule of politics is that one should support every tax cut and every expenditure increase. And the congressional Republicans did not even need the help of economists to develop the idea that tax reduction would raise the revenue. The necessity of reconciling their desire to cut taxes with their professed desire to balance the budget led the congressional Republicans to discover the idea that tax reduction raised the revenue. They used that idea to justify the tax cuts they made in 1948 and 1954. They returned to it during the Carter administration mainly because they were tired of losing.

But a small group of economists who began talking about the tax cut idea around 1976 did contribute to the policy that was finally adopted. They gave the idea an aura of scientific respectability that won it more respectful attention in the media than it would otherwise have had. They extended the application of the idea on a scale that an ordinary Republican congressman might have been reluctant to reach—that is, they justified an extremely large and broad tax cut. And they provided an effective way of demonstrating their point, in the form of the Laffer curve. Thus they helped to get the Republican party and the Republican candidate, Ronald Reagan, committed to the big tax cut.

In the period between his nomination and his inauguration, Mr. Reagan had the advice of a number of leading economists who believed that a tax cut would not raise the revenue, or at least not for a long, long time. Why did they not warn Mr. Reagan? There were several reasons. Some thought that the most important thing was to win the election. Some thought that the most important thing was to get taxes down, even if that would increase the deficit. And others feared that if they dissented they would be expelled from the circle of advisers, a risk they would not take.

After the election we had an example of the axiom that a president who chooses his own economists in line with his own thinking is his own economist. Support of the desirability of the big tax cut became the loyalty test for appointment to the administration, so there was little chance of the president's hearing any substantial dissent. By 1982 the administration's devotion to the idea that tax cuts would raise the revenue had substantially if not totally disappeared. This change of mind was mainly the result of brute experience: Everyone could see that the tax cuts already made had not raised the revenue. But the arguments of economists outside the government may have played some part in the conversion.

These two examples are cases in which the influence of economists on policy was probably unfortunate. So you may wonder about the earlier statement that by now economists are saving more patients than they kill. Therefore, I will conclude with another, much more important case in which the influence of economists has been on the whole beneficial, although not without some deviations: the development of attitudes and policies toward unemployment in the past fifty years.

Unemployment and Inflation

After the disastrous experience of the 1930s it did not take an economist to show that long-continued mass unemployment was possible, although it did take some effort of economists to show that what was directly visible was also theoretically possible. The work of economists, most conspicuously of Keynes, was required to show (a) that unemployment could be substantially reduced by public policy and (b) that the public policy to reduce unemployment did not require a basic change in the structure of the American economy but only better performance of its traditional budgetary and monetary functions. This latter point is interesting and ironical. Conventional conservatives have regarded Keynes as a dark and evil influence bent on undermining the free economic system. In fact, however, he helped to save the free system at a time when much more radical changes in the system were being seriously advocated.

As a result of the experience of the 1930s and the work of some economists, we came out of World War II with a commitment to maintain high employment by fiscal and monetary policy. For this achievement economists are entitled to credit. But in time this commitment was carried too far for a reason that was mainly political. Once the government assumed responsibility for unemployment, the rate of unemployment became a major test of the performance of a politician—especially of a president. This view led to a competition in promising and delivering a low rate of unemployment that became visible in the Kennedy-Johnson years and affected the early Nixon years.

The prevailing economic thought did not counter this political tendency but indeed encouraged it. Economists came to believe that the government could select a target rate of unemployment and achieve it. They recognized that if that target was very ambitious some inflation would accompany it. But they believed that the inflation would be stable, that is, the rate would steady and would not accelerate. Moreover, they believed that with an unemployment rate of 4 percent the inflation would be small and could be made even smaller by direct restraint on prices and wages.

These beliefs provided support for politicians to try to get unemployment down to a very low level; but this level in the end caused not only inflation but also accelerating inflation. Politicians might have done this without the support of economists, but the outcome was made more probable by the mistakes of economists.

Economists, however, can claim credit for recognizing this mistake before experience made the error obvious. The turning point came with the presidential address that Milton Friedman delivered to the American Economic Association in December 1967. This address was the most influential piece of economic analysis of the postwar period. In this paper Friedman showed that there was a natural rate of unemployment that could be achieved without any inflation. The attempt to get an even lower rate of unemployment would require not only some inflation but an inflation rate that would get higher and higher.

After that address economists in their public discourse began to nibble away at the notion that 4 percent unemployment was a proper and unchanging target for economic policy. Economic advisers within the government began to warn against setting overly ambitious goals. At first the implication of this warning was that the target for unemployment should be raised, from 4 percent to 5 percent or 6 percent, because of various changes occurring in the labor force and in other aspects of the economy. This evolution of economists' thinking interacted with what was occurring in the country. First, it became obvious that we were having higher and higher unemployment rates. Second, the 1974–1975 recession, in which unemployment rose to 9 percent, showed that the country would tolerate, without strongly adverse political reactions, a much higher unemployment rate than anyone had previously thought was politically bearable.

So the combination of economic analysis with visible experience gradually weaned policy away from obsession with excessively ambitious unemployment targets that would inevitably cause accelerating inflation and would threaten the survival of the free society. That was a considerable achievement. More recently this development has proceeded even further. The idea is now gaining ground that there should be no numerical target for unemployment, but only a determination to keep stable monetary conditions that will allow the market to generate as low a level of unemployment as is sustainable. The acceptance of that idea would, in my opinion, be another step toward a stable, noninflationary, high-employment economy.

One could describe other positive developments of economic policy of the past twenty years to which economics has made a constructive contribution. That contribution would include the increased emphasis on monetary policy as the instrument of economic stabilization and the move toward reduction of government regulations. But there is not the time or space for further elaboration of the history of economic policy.

Any such history would certainly conclude that economists have not known as much as one would want to know or even as much as economists have claimed to know. Moreover, economists have not been as objective and responsible as one could like them to be. Their increasing involvement in policy making has brought greater partisanship along with greater influence. Still, if one must admit that economists do not know very much about economics, one can claim that they know more than most other people who pontificate on the subject. And they are certainly not less objective that other people who participate in making economic policy. Economists do not have to bear sole responsibility for the mistakes of economic policy and can claim some credit for its successes.

What Happened to the Supply Side?

The *AEI Economist,* September 1982

THE decisions of the president and Congress on September 2 to raise taxes has precipitated a number of questions about the state of supply-side economics. Is it dead or only sleeping? Has the president abandoned it? Most important, does the course of the economy since the beginning of 1981 show that supply-side policy does not work?

As is often the case, the answer depends on the definition of the question. Specifically, it depends on what supply-side economics and supply-side policy mean. By some definitions supply-side economics clearly has not delivered what was promised, and hardly anyone believes anymore that it can. By other definitions the predictions of supply-side economics diverged from conventional economics and have not been supported, although not rejected, by anything that has happened or by any evidence that has been supplied in the past year and a half. In the absence of evidence to support the unorthodox view, opinion is gravitating toward the orthodox view. Finally, by some definitions supply-side economics fits squarely in conventional economics. That does not, of course, prove that supply-side theory is correct, though it does provide some presumption. Conventional predictions have been neither confirmed nor refuted by the experience of 1981–1982, but they remain the most probable expectations.

Extreme Supply-Sidism

The period of our experience with supply-side economics has been short and has, moreover, been complicated by a recession piled upon a disinflationary process. Thus this period could not provide a reasonable test of supply-side economics unless the theory was interpreted in such an extreme and short-run way that its consequences would stand out quickly and strongly even in a very confused environment. Indeed, some supply-siders did give the doctrine that kind of extreme interpretation. They maintained that output and employment were determined exclusively by the real return on producing and working, not by the demand for the product or the labor. They would say, for example, that people were unemployed because net real wages, after tax, were too low to induce them to work (or the unemployment benefits were too high). Reduction of tax rates would increase the supply of labor and capital by increasing the after-tax return, and this would raise output and employment. Moreover, this response would come immediately once tax rates were cut. (In reply to skeptics who thought that the results would come slowly, Arthur Laffer used to ask how long it would take you to pick up a hundred dollar bill if you saw it on the sidewalk.) The benefits of the tax cut would begin, in fact, before the cut went into effect, as soon as the cut was expected. The extreme supply-siders held that the stock market crashed in 1929, setting off the Great Depression, on the day the Senate Finance Committee approved a tax increase (the Smoot-Hawley tariff), even though the tax increase still had to pass the Congress. On that analogy, a marked improvement of financial markets and of the economy could be expected to start as soon as it became probable that the tax cut would be enacted.

This scenario, which was never credible, was not played out in the past two years. One could say, of course, that the tax rates were not really reduced, or were not reduced until July 1, 1982, the nominal rate reduction being offset by bracket creep. But some rates—on capital gains, on corporate profits, on the investment income of upper-income taxpayers—were really and significantly reduced. Grounds had been provided for expecting more real tax rate cuts in the future, and in any case, the rise of real rates was ending or markedly slowing down. Even if this was not a combination of developments from which a devout supply-sider would predict a surging economy, he would not have predicted the slump and rising unemployment we have had since the tax-cutting legislation was signed. Neither would he have predicted the sad days in the stock and bond markets, which, ironically, persisted until Congress and the president agreed to raise taxes.

Improbable Supply-Sidism

It is fair to say that the headiest version of supply-side economics has been discredited—for the time being, until the experience of 1981–1982 has been forgotten. There is, however, a less exclusive and extreme version that still deserves attention. Supporters of this version did not maintain that all the effects of tax cuts would be instantaneous. Neither did they hold that these effects would be so powerful as to offset all other forces in the economy. They would not, for example, raise output and revenue if monetary policy or cyclical developments were depressing the economy. But in some "reasonable" period—a period relevant to budget planning, say four or five years—a cut of tax rates would make output higher than it would otherwise have been, high enough to make the revenue higher than it would otherwise have been.

Even this more moderate proposition was, from the outset, highly doubtful in the light of conventional economic analysis and evidence. There was little argument about the claim that a reduction of tax rates would or might *to some degree* increase the supply of labor and capital. But there was no evidence at all to suggest that the tax cut would have this effect to the degree required to keep the revenue from falling, if the tax cut applied to taxpayers in general and not to a narrow category of taxpayers or transactions. Put most crudely, the question was this: If the tax rates of a person in the 40 percent marginal tax bracket are cut 10 percent, his marginal return from earning income rises by 6.67 percent. In order to keep the revenue from declining, he must do enough additional work or make enough additional investments to raise his before-tax earnings by 11.1 percent. Will an increase of 6.67 percent in his marginal return induce him to earn 11.1 percent more income, or one and two-thirds times as much? The evidence considered by economists suggested that the response would be much smaller than that. Moreover, if that was the case, so that the tax cut reduced the revenue, the deficit would rise unless the tax cut was matched by an expenditure cut. The deficit would have some negative effects on output. Therefore, not only could one not expect the tax cut to raise output enough to keep the revenue constant; one could not even be sure that the tax cut would not *reduce* output if the tax cut was not matched by an expenditure cut.

Experience of the past year and a half tells us nothing we did not know before about this brand of supply-sidism. The beneficial effects predicted from the tax cut could not have been expected to show up so soon. Moreover, the claim of this variety of supply-siders was only that the tax cut would make output and revenue higher than they would otherwise have been. We do not know, however, what they would otherwise have been or what would have been a correct forecast of them in the future, so it will be very difficult to tell, even after longer experience, whether the tax cut did what its enthusiasts predicted for it.

The problem may be illustrated as follows: In March, 1981, in the flush of optimism about supply-sidism, the administration forecast that the GNP in fiscal 1985 would be $4400 billion and the revenue, after its proposed tax cuts, would be $850 billion. Today a generally accepted estimate is that the GNP in fiscal 1985 will be about $4000 billion and the revenue about $750 billion, after the 1981 tax cut and the 1982 tax increase. Thus we have "lost" about $400 billion of GNP and $100 billion of revenue. One might say that this demonstrates the error of the supply-side predictions and the failure, now recognized, of the tax cuts to deliver what they promised. But that would be an improper conclusion: One could also say that the error was due to factors entirely different from overestimating the effect of the tax cuts and that without the tax cuts both the GNP and the revenue would be lower than they are now forecast for 1985.

We cannot say, on the basis of anything that happened in 1981 and 1982, that the supply-side process is not working, or will not work, to make the revenue higher than it would have been without the tax cut. What we can say is that two years have passed in which there has been a great deal of attention to the supply-side claims. The incentives to find evidence in support of the hypothesis that cutting taxes raises the revenue have been strong. Supply-side "believers" have had access to the data and research capabilities of the U.S. government to buttress their case, but the argument still relies on isolated anecdotes, *post hoc, ergo propter hoc* history, and quotations from fourteenth-century Moslem philosophers. The failure to find other evidence tends to support, even if not conclusively prove, the more traditional view.

Safe and Sane Supply-Sidism

There is a sense in which the supply-side movement is part of a return of economics to its traditional interests and attitudes after a diversion of a generation. The basic element of supply-sidism in this sense is the recognition that the long-term rate of growth of the nation's capacity is important, that it cannot be taken for granted, and that promoting it is a legitimate object of national policy. This element of economics was never denied, but it was ignored, for obvious reasons, during and after the Great Depression. Attention was then concentrated on policy for ensuring adequate demand for the nation's capacity to produce. Beginning in the 1950s, however, there was increasing attention to our problem of maintaining or accelerating the growth rate of potential output. This was manifest in the research of economists, in popular and political discussion, and in policy. Federal action about taxes, education, and research reflected this interest.

In its more conventional sense, supply-side economics is simply an extension of this interest in economic growth, an extension provoked by the marked slowdowns of growth in the 1970s. In this conventional sense, however, the policy implications and predictions differ markedly from those of the two varieties mentioned above. No miracles are promised. That is, it is recognized that policy can affect long-term growth rates only slowly and that to have a big effect on growth rates big actions are needed.

Moreover, the policy options relevant to this conception of supply-side economics are numerous. There is not the exclusive concentrating on taxes in general—the taxophobia—that has characterized the more eccentric supply-siders. Different kinds of taxes are seen to differ greatly in their growth effects, so that the structure as well as the total level of taxes is important. The size of the deficit is recognized as a variable affecting growth through effects on private investment. Some government expenditures—on research, education, infrastructure—may make a positive contribution to growth. The extent and character of regulation affect growth. There is also an important interaction between demand policy and supply policy, so that stabilizing demand management promotes rapid long-term growth.

Conventional supply-sidism tells us that there are government policies that will contribute to stronger growth, although slowly and in a limited degree. Government efforts have turned increasingly in this direction in the past twenty years and have done so most vigorously and articulately in the Reagan administration. So far, the main lessons seem to be of difficulties. Almost every growth-promoting policy has costs in some terms, which means not only that there will be political, that is, biased, resistance but also that even the most objective observer might not consider the policy worthwhile. Moreover, we do not really know very much about the magnitude of the growth-stimulating effects of various policies. It is difficult, therefore, to put together an efficient package that will deliver the desired growth effects at the least cost to other objectives.

Nothing that has happened in the past ten years, or in the past two years, tells us that we know how to promote economic growth. But neither does the experience invalidate the belief that something can be achieved. Indeed, the experience has shown the need to devote increasing attention and effort to this goal. It is in the recognition of this need that we are all supply-siders now.

Dressing for Dinner on the Op-Ed Page

Fortune, March 22, 1982

Iread George Will regularly in my daily newspaper. I watch him twice a week on TV. I can fairly claim to be a George Will fan. But I now see that I didn't fully appreciate him when I ingested him quickly with my orange juice or watched him on the flickering tube. It was only when I read his columns in large drafts, more slowly, as they are collected in his book *The Pursuit of Virtue and Other Tory Notions,*[1] that I got an adequate measure of the man. He is a marvel of style, personality, character, learning, and intelligence.

That is the kind of praise commonly reserved for people with whom one totally agrees. I used to think that I liked Will because I agreed with him. Reading this book I discovered that I admired his work more but also disagreed with him more, or at least was more puzzled by him.

I shall come to the disagreements or puzzlements later, but first a few comments on style. Will seems to attach much importance to style. I think it is one of his Tory notions—like the Englishman dressing for dinner in the middle of the jungle. Writing his elegant piece on the op-ed page of the *Washington Post,* Will is dressing for dinner in the jungle.

His writing is neat, colorful, and witty. Every article contains a turn of phrase that sparkles. I cite only one, which is representative not only of the style but of the content: "The public's preoccupation with the evangelical's finances reflects a preference for

[1] George F. Will, *The Pursuit of Virtue and Other Tory Notions* (New York: Simon and Schuster, 1982).

diving into the shallow end of every pool." This suggests a certain superciliousness, and there is much of that in the book. But it is not a dominating impression. In his quiet way Will conveys a range of emotions from humor to compassion to indignation to horror. A special word must be said for humor. The only other book that has made me laugh aloud in the past twelve months is the U.S. Budget for 1983.

Quotations are an important feature of Will's writing. The list of persons quoted includes Burke, Newman, Disraeli, Chesterton, Auden, Barzun, Kingsley Amis, Robert Conquest, Aristotle, Wilde, Solzhenitsyn, Raymond Aron, Baudelaire, Santayana, Henry Adams, and T. S. Eliot, which gives you an idea of where his heart lies. My favorite quotation is from a country-music song: "I don't know whether to kill myself or go bowling." That sentence seems to capture some of Will's attitude toward life. Things are terrible. They have been getting continuously worse since 1914— since the end of the Edwardian Era. Still, we go on with some hope and courage. There are good lives out there which show that much is still possible.

The Pursuit of Virtue contains 128 articles written as current comment between the beginning of 1978 and the middle of 1981. We get a full catalogue of Will's likes and dislikes—many more of the latter than the former. The dislikes include abortion, laissez-faire, totalitarianism, progressive education, pursuit of pleasure, materialism, capitalism, excessive claims to freedom by the press, zealous enforcement of sexual equality, homosexual rights, legalized gambling, sex education, palimony, Communists, bilingual education, reverse discrimination, assertions of commitment to peace, and Jane Fonda. The likes include the opposites of these (does Jane Fonda have an opposite?) as well as manners, environmentalism, conservation, military academies, nuclear energy, duty, Solzhenitsyn, Lech Walesa, Pope John Paul II, John Wayne, and Hubert Humphrey.

Will refers to Adam Smith briefly and inadequately, and to Keynes in passing. He gives no evidence of having read any other economist. I attribute to this deficiency his slighting remarks about economics, economists, markets, laissez-faire, and capitalism, and hope that he will yet have the opportunity to learn more about such matters.

In the wide range of subjects covered, two major themes stand out. One is suggested by the title Will gives to a section of his book, "The War Against the Totalitarian, 1939– ." We are engaged in the same war we were fighting forty years ago against the same evil, powerful enemy. The power and the menace of the Communist enemy are described with great force, and so are the terrifying weakness, blunders, and self-delusion of the Western response. "The Second World War," he observes, "began because of the moral more than the material weaknesses of the democracies." And it is good to read someone saying: "Occasional obduracy is good for a nation's soul, and standing. This would be a safer, better world if more nations had more occasions for muttering to themselves, 'We just have to understand how strongly the United States feels about this.' "

According to the society pages, President Reagan dines occasionally with George Will. It would be good if he read the section on totalitarianism once a week. I would like it to be read by all those congressmen who think that cutting the defense program is a sensible way to balance the budget, avoid a tax increase, avoid cutting social programs, and strengthen America.

But the book's largest theme, the one that provides its title and my puzzlement, is the role of virtue in societies. Will uses words precisely, and when he calls his book *The Pursuit of Virtue*, he doesn't mean the pursuit of happiness, liberty, affluence, power, or efficiency. Rather, his basic idea is that a good society, or just a good life, requires virtuous people. This idea has a well-established place in political philosophy, and it seems valid to me. Problems arise when we ask what is virtue, who decides, and who, if anyone, enforces virtuous behavior.

In Will's book the problems become clearest in an essay entitled "John Paul II: A Pope with Authority." Will argues that "Any community must have a core of settled convictions, and any community determined to endure must charge some authority with the task of nurturing, defending, and transmitting those convictions." And again: "But surely there must be points at which private judgment by any member of a community is circumscribed by institutional judgment. And some person or body—a Pope, a Parliament, a Supreme Court—must decide where those points are." The formulation seems ironic in view of Will's open contempt for the Supreme Court.

In the next sentence, Will switches to reliance on "authority that is rooted in tradition" as the arbiter of virtue. This only pushes the issue back a notch into the question of who decides what the tradition is. On a recent TV show, when Will invoked tradition as authority, Carl Rowan reminded him that not so long ago tradition authorized black slavery. I thought it a good point.

Elsewhere Will relies upon "self-evident" truth as a guide to what is permissible behavior. It is self-evident that a society may prohibit behavior that is destructive of the society. So he concluded that the right to prohibit Nazis from parading in Skokie is self-evident, and I agree. But I once knew a man who thought it self-evident that federal insurance of bank deposits was destructive of the society. What can one say to that?

Will sometimes seems to be slipping into the view that government should define virtue and perhaps—what comes next is not quite clear—enforce it, induce it, lean toward it, teach it. He says, "American public philosophy asserts, untenably, that popular government presupposes especially virtuous citizens, yet cannot concern itself with the inner lives of its citizens." Speaking with approval of the Republican platform in 1980, he says "Republicans believe the nation's moral makeup is, today, soft wax on which national leadership can leave a long-lasting impress . . . they are alive to the grandeur, when it is properly understood, of the political vocation."

But Will is not entirely consistent here. A few months later, he is speaking with warmth of "what Robert Nisbet rightly identifies as the major theme of Western conservatism: the defense of society against the political state." My puzzlement is about the unexplained apparent contradiction between his desire to have the government concern itself with the inner lives of the citizens and his awareness of the threat the political state poses.

There may be a way out. The answer may reside in other institutions, more decentralized and less monopolistic than government, that may concern themselves with our inner lives with less danger to our freedom. The author of newspaper columns and participant on TV talk shows is himself such an institution.

Don't Throw It Away

Fortune, April 2, 1984

*The annual report of the Council of Economic Advisers remains
a superior guide to the U.S. economy.*

T HE 1984 *Annual Report of the Council of Economic Advisers* has
already been critically reviewed by high authority. Secretary of
the Treasury Donald T. Regan has said that it could all be thrown
away. I believe that the report deserves a second opinion.

Secretary Regan was carefully distinguishing between the *Economic Report of the President* and the *Annual Report of the Council.*
The two reports are bound together and often confused, and
the confusion is magnified by the cover title, which makes it appear
that the entire volume is given over to the president's report
(which actually takes up only a few pages). The secretary, of
course, wanted to preserve the president's report while disposing
of the council's. Yet on the subject that seems to bother the secretary most—the significance of budget deficits—the president's report and the council's are not really far apart. It is true that the
council is more specific than the president in spelling out the
threat represented by the deficits, and this may have annoyed
the secretary. But the council's additional details refer mainly
to the crowding out of private investment by the deficits, which
is only an economist's way of describing what the president's report refers to as the "burden to future generations." The two
presentations are really quite consistent with one another, which
is not surprising since the council plays a major role in drafting
the president's report.

The events surrounding the book's publication illustrate once
again the troubles to which economists are prone in their relations

with politicians and other lay people. An economist tends to think that when someone says "two plus two" he also plainly means to say "four," whereas politicians frequently want to have the "two plus two" while retaining an option on "three" or "five." But enough on this point: the soap opera in which the secretary agrees with the president and the chairman agrees with the president but the secretary and the chairman disagree with each other has already received too much attention and is not the most interesting aspect of the council's report.

In my opinion, if you choose to read only one economic publication a year, you should pick the *Annual Report of the Council of Economic Advisers*, and this 1984 report is no exception. It combines professional excellence, relevance, and understandability.

Its value begins with its facts, which are presented in two formats. First, its statistical appendix offers 123 pages of economic data covering the national income accounts, employment, wages, prices, production, money and finance, government budgets, international transactions, and comparisons with other countries. The appendix data are well selected and well presented. With these reams of statistics plus a hand calculator, a little imagination, and a little nerve, you could set yourself up as an economic consultant. The tables alone are worth the price of the bound volume, which the U.S. Government Printing Office sells for $8, or $1.95 less than you would pay for a paperback copy of *Jane Fonda's Workout Book*.

The council's report is also full of other valuable data—the simple, specific, pointed facts that keep turning up in the book's chapters on various special issues and have a way of illuminating them. Three examples:

• Most Americans instantly think of Japan when our mounting trade deficits are mentioned, but the facts do not support this instinct. Between 1980 and 1983 the total U.S. trade deficit increased by $38 billion while our deficit with the OPEC countries declined by $30 billion; in other words, our deficit with the rest of the world increased by $68 billion. Only $10 billion of that huge amount came from an increase in our deficit with Japan. Our surplus with Western Europe, some $20 billion in 1980, had disappeared by 1983, and we had another $20-billion swing in Latin America, where we went from a $6 billion surplus to a $14 billion deficit.

• For all the talk about a decline of manufacturing in the

United States, our manufacturing output is around one-third greater than the 1970 level and over two and one-half times the 1950 level. Although employment in manufacturing has been a declining share of total employment, manufacturing output has been a relatively constant share of total GNP.

• About seven-eighths of total farm receipts are generated by the largest 29 percent of farms. These farms have average assets of about $1 million and average equity of about $800,000. In 1982 they received 78 percent of all direct government payments under farm programs.

Ever since Walter Heller's chairmanship during the Kennedy Administration, the council's report has had a standard format. Three chapters appear every year: one on general economic policy, one on the review and outlook, and one on the international economy. Then there are two or three chapters on special topics that change from year to year. This year the three special topics are industrial policy, food and agriculture, and financial-market deregulation. A strong sense of value of the free market runs through these chapters. The one on industrial policy, for example, contains a moderate, factual, and convincing debunking of common romantic notions about the miracles that government interventions have allegedly performed in Japan and Western Europe.

Elsewhere in the report the council makes a powerful case that trade protectionism, controls over capital flows, and intervention in exchange markets are inappropriate solutions to our balance-of-trade "problem." One of the most refreshing passages in the report is its persuasive demonstration that our trade deficit is not entirely a problem. The excess of imports, which is undeniably hurting some industries, is also generating an inflow of capital that is keeping interest rates here lower than they would otherwise be, which means that it is also supporting capital investment in the United States and in the industries that produce capital goods.

You might assume that such free-market attitudes are only to be expected from this particular administration. In fact, the reports of the council during the past thirty years have always been marked by respect for the market, although not always to the same degree. Even in the bad old Democratic days of Chairman Walter Heller, Gardner Ackley, Arthur Okun, and Charles Schultze, the council was, by comparison with the rest of the government and with much lay opinion, the champion of free trade, of a market-oriented farm policy, and of deregulation.

We have come a long way from the conceptions of economics and economic policy that inspired the Employment Act of 1946 (which mandates the annual reports by the council). The change has been gradual, extending over at least fifteen years, but the nearly complete disappearance of these earlier ideas is clearer than ever in the 1984 report. That is progress. The ideas reflected in the Employment Act were primitive, naive, and potentially dangerous. And yet the latest report also suggests, implicitly, that the disappearance of those ideas has left us with a gap in our thinking.

The original idea behind the 1946 act was that we could have full employment by flexibly using fiscal policy to maintain adequate demand in the economy. The president, with the aid of his economists, would calculate how much demand (measured as nominal GNP) would be required in order to achieve full employment. In his annual economic report he would recommend to Congress a budget policy—including federal expenditures, taxes, and a deficit or surplus—that was calculated to generate the required path of aggregate demand.

By the time it came out of Congress, the Employment Act of 1946 had fuzzed over these Keynesian ideas. Although the ideas were dominant in the economics textbooks of the time, they were never reflected with purity in the reports of the council or the policy of the government. But remnants of the ideas did linger for many years. One was the belief that the council's forecast and the President's budget recommendations were moving us toward a target for aggregate demand consistent with the full-employment goals of the 1946 act. This view of the policy process seemed plausible even to council chairmen who were not Keynesians.

Today only faint traces of this view remain. The 1984 report contains scarcely any reference to fiscal policy as a possible explanation for the sharp rise in total demand in 1983. It contains no suggestion at all that the budget policy proposed for 1984 and 1985 was designed to move the economy along the path forecast for those years.

The whole focus of fiscal policy, in the council and in the profession, has shifted from the short-run management of demand to the long-run management of supply. Most economists today are what I described in 1976 as "supply-side fiscalists." The phrase does not refer to the extreme notion that marginal rates of taxation are a lever capable of moving the world. It refers, rather, to the older and more sensible notion that the level and composition of taxes and government expenditures, plus the size of the deficit or surplus, have a significant long-run effect on the supply of capital and labor and thereby on the growth rate of potential output. This is not to deny that fiscal actions may have short-run effects, only to insist that such effects are not sufficiently manageable or important to make them the main consideration in fiscal decisions.

And yet the management of demand remains a critical matter. Stabilizing total demand from year to year is an essential part of any effort to maintain high employment, and keeping the increase of total demand moderate in the longer run is essential for avoiding inflation. Who should manage demand? It seems to be the council's view that demand management is primarily the responsibility of the monetary authorities. This view, spelled out even more in last year's report than in the present volume, is one that I believe to be correct.

But consider where that leaves us. What was originally conceived of as the main subject of the economic report—the management of demand—is no longer in the council's domain. It is in the Federal Reserve's domain. And given current concern for the independence of the Fed, the council is understandably inhibited in discussion of the subject. This leaves a large gap in the report, and the gap is only partially filled by statements from the Federal Reserve. Perhaps some day the Fed will give us a lot more to chew on; meanwhile, the council's annual report clearly remains the No. 1 economic publication of the year.

PART 2

An Economist Looks at Washington

and yes I said yes
I will Yes

The *New York Times,*
February 13, 1981

W ATCHING the other night on the MacNeil-Lehrer show—
that interminable drip-drip-drip of talk on the barely conscious
consciousness that is the penance we pay for watching television
at all—Edwin Meese 3rd and James Baker 3rd, outwardly so different, the one so cherubic and the other so Gary Cooperish, but
nevertheless so nearly identical, so interchangeable in words and
thoughts, carried my mind back through many administrations,
and many freshman White House officials appearing on television
talk shows in their charming innocence and confidence that they
knew what they were doing and that all within their purview was
in order, like newly engaged coal stokers on a tramp steamer,
decked out in dress whites and assuring all that everything was
neat and clean below, which could perhaps be forgiven because
they have not yet been there, or if they have been there nonetheless feel that there is about to be a new beginning, like a schoolboy
starting a new term, with newly sharpened pencils and an un-
marked notebook, who imagines himself capable of everything
but knows in the back of his mind that before the term is over
he will again be a struggling "C," a thought that is still far back
in the minds of new White House counselors and chiefs of staff
as, securely lodged behind the White House fence—significantly,
they did not come out to the TV studio but stayed in the Roosevelt
Room, where the cameras came to them—like novices in the ab-
bey, who will never have to go out to lunch, or look for a parking
place, or shop for a new suit, so well-clothed are they in their

official status, they expect always to agree with each other on what is right to do, and cabinet secretaries expect always to acknowledge the propriety of being denied access to the president, and the press always to accept the truth and reasonableness of what they have to say, and who cannot now imagine becoming a Hamilton Jordan, or a Haldeman or Ehrlichman or, who is for my generation the father of them all, a Harry Hopkins, the archetype of the cynical White House operator, but who at least had never claimed to be, or had given the impression of being, something else, which was at least in part because he never had the need or temptation to appear on TV, since it didn't then exist, or even on the radio—at least I don't remember, although I saw him in newsreels, ever hearing his voice, which I think of as being high and reedy, probably because he was thin and smoked a great deal, although that impression could easily be wrong—which is not to say that he had a passion for anonymity that his patron wanted in White House staff members, a requirement that I didn't appreciate until recently, when I understood that cabinet members live for two things, the attention of the president and the attention of the public, and if the White House staff denies them the former and competes with them for the latter there will be a prompt end to that innocence so charmingly displayed by Messrs. Meese and Baker, the only two who through no desire for preeminence, happened to be the ones on TV from among that happy and harmonious team that had just entered Washington, the courtiers of the newly crowned old king, bringing memories of those other courtiers who came with the newly crowned young prince twenty years ago, the best and the brightest who came to save us from the myths of "practical men" and whose fate it was to leave the stage before the end of the drama, before their "gallantry" had mired us down in Vietnam, before their "new economics" had enmeshed us in inflation, and before their "glamour" had transformed the White House into a set for a police thriller, leaving the stage to a new "crew," whose great conceit was their lack of conceit and whose pride was that they were not arrogant but accepted the role of stage hands assigned to clean up the mess left by the departed ranters and ravers, a role that we—for I was one of them, on that team, but on a special team of that team, like the members of the kickoff team whose sole function is to run down the field as fast as possible, four or five times in an afternoon, and keep the opposition from gaining ground, so we

were by no means the most conspicuous members of the team—
thought we understood, but that we could not play out consistently
to the end, but were in the end ourselves subverted by the foot-
lights and the audience and most of all by the stage sets, by the
White House mess with the ritual of the Mexican lunch every
Thursday, established by the departed king from Texas and continued by the new king from California, by the black car with
the reading light over the back seat, but much more by the trip
through the White House as the quickest way from the Executive
Office Building to the Treasury—up the steps of the West Wing,
past the press briefing room, along the colonnade next to the
Rose Garden (why are there no hawthorns in this dream? there
should be hawthorns) and along the ground floor of the White
House to the East Wing and out, breasting a flood of tourists
asking themselves, one thought, who this cool intimate of power
might be—the thought of using the White House as a short cut
itself dizzying, but not so dizzying, not so keenly evocative of *la
cour* as running up the narrow side steps in the West Wing to
attend a *levée* in the Oval Office or the Cabinet Room or the
Roosevelt Room, the *levée* itself not being so extraordinary as
was the feeling that it was ordinary, subverting our initial conceit
that we were capable of doing what could reasonably be expected
of us, because we knew how little could be reasonably expected
of any economists or any government, into the conceit that we
were capable of doing what had to be done because we were
especially chosen, intelligent, and powerful, although this infec-
tion struck different ones of us with different degrees of virulence,
some, among whom I count myself, having always been somewhat
ambiguous about it, as when I suddenly recognized during a meeting in the Roosevelt Room that we were a group of high school
seniors playing at being city-council-for-a-day, while others acquired so high an estimation of their own value that they could
make jokes about their own arrogance, secure in the knowledge
that the jokes could only be taken as jokes, since no overestimation
of the underlying value was possible and the jokes could only
be proof of the single virtue not fully evident, which is to say,
modesty, but even the more ambiguous of us finding ourselves
fine-tuning with vim and price-controlling with vigor, like our
predecessors, and claiming that the audience, bored by our performance as stage hands cleaning up the mess, insisted that we show
off as Don Quixote or some such thing, until at the end, all bal-

loons punctured by statistics, we returned, too late, to the modesty with which we started, not now a proud conceit but an inescapable necessity, felt with an intensity that life experience can give but that the history of others cannot, even for those few who read history, so that the innocence and confidence of Messrs. Meese and Baker on the MacNeil-Lehrer show, while refreshing, was also a little sad.

The Triumph of Illusion

Fortune, May 26, 1986

REVIEWING David Stockman's book objectively is difficult. His advance of more than $2 million consumes the reviewer with envy and, therefore, hostility. Also, he is a major character in his own book. There is a great temptation to review Stockman the brilliant budget director or Stockman the lousy team player rather than Stockman's book. Moreover, the book is a shot in a battle in which almost every eligible reviewer is a partisan.

Trying to be as objective as I can, I offer this assessment: Stockman has written a fascinating book that can make an important contribution to public discourse if it is taken seriously—which I fear it will not be. His warning that national policy is governed by dangerous illusions is already being drowned out by irrelevant clamor about his character.

The book's story is this:

By 1980 David Stockman had come to believe that the United States needed an economic revolution that would drastically reduce the role of the government as taxer, spender, borrower, and regulator. He joined the Reagan team with enthusiasm, having reasonable grounds for thinking that they shared his view. Well before the 1980 election he knew that the Reagan game plan was not going to work. The proposed tax cuts and defense increases were inconsistent with the balanced budget promised for 1983 unless cuts in the nondefense budget went far beyond the elimination of "fraud, waste and abuse" that was part of the campaign rhetoric. But he believed that once in office they could find cuts to bring the plan and the budget into balance.

After Inauguration Day in 1981 it was down hill all the way. The election of 1980 had not been the Reagan Revolution. It had only been the invitation to the Revolution. But hardly anyone other than Stockman came to the Revolution. His supply-side colleagues, led by Congressman Kemp, had never had any interest in cutting expenditures or any concern about the deficit. The president's Cabinet secretaries were as determined as any previous secretaries to expand their own budgets. The president's handlers in the White House wanted only to keep their Champ out of any fight in which he might get hurt. The Champ himself entered the fray only spasmodically, like Zeus above the shores of Troy.

By 1982 the country was facing endless deficits of around $200 billion a year. Stockman saw no hope of adequately reducing the deficits by expenditure cuts alone. So he turned to proposing fiscal packages that included, along with expenditure cuts, some tax increases—which infuriated his former team-mates. In his 1984 campaign the president made commitments—no tax increase and no cut in Social Security—which demonstrated to Stockman that the gap between reality and pretense would never be closed. So he left in 1985, convinced that the country was headed for an economic disaster because of the deficits.

This story has been told before. I told what an outsider could see of it in my book, *Presidential Economics*. Mr. Stockman told some of it in his interviews published in the December 1981 *Atlantic Monthly*. But he tells the story now with a wealth of intimate detail that makes it more exciting and compelling than it has been heretofore.

The blow-by-blow accounts of decision-making sessions in the White House are powerful. Sitting around the table are intelligent, honorable men who have had successful careers in the real world and will have such careers again when they return to it. But they are reduced to incoherence and deviousness by the need to operate in an unreal world—where tax cuts raise the revenue, where expenditure increases are savings, and where mounting deficits are the road to a balanced budget. Their economics is reduced to the rejection of economics. Their history is reduced to the recollection of personal anecdotes. Their vision of the future is that since everything is unpredictable everything will be all right. The stories are hilariously funny—the Marx Brothers in the White House—unless you think that it matters.

Denials of the Stockman version of the Reagan Revolution began to appear as soon as excerpts from the book were published in *Newsweek*. But some things are undeniable, such as the $200 billion deficit three years after the budget was supposed to be brought into balance. Samuel Johnson kicked a stone to prove that matter is real. You can kick the deficit and the debt. They are real.

A major issue, of course, is who did it. The Reaganauts blame Congress for not cutting expenditures as the president proposed. Mr. Stockman is naturally critical of the Congress. But he is particularly critical of the administration. After all, most of the Congress had not run on a promise to balance the budget. They were not part of the team that Stockman thought he had joined. During the five-and-a half years that Stockman was in office the president had never proposed enough expenditure cuts to bring the budget into balance, even by 1990.

The story of the budget negotiations of 1982 is told by the administration over and over again as proof that the deficit can not to reduced by raising taxes. The story is that the president reluctantly agreed to a tax increase in 1982 as part of a bargain in which Congress would cut expenditures by three dollars for every dollar of revenue increase. According to the administration story the taxes were raised but Congress never came through with the expenditure cuts. Stockman's version is different. "Of the spending cuts Congress allegedly owed, $100 billion consisted of savings in debt service that Congress couldn't do anything about; $40 billion was management savings that we had promised to come up with but hadn't; another $30 billion had actually been delivered in Medicare reimbursement reforms and other measures" (p.368). Most of the remainder was a $50 billion three-year defense cut that Weinberger refused to make.

The radical supply-siders have their own culprit—Paul Volcker. If only the Federal Reserve had made the money supply behave differently, they say, the supply-side plan would have worked, revenue would have increased, and there would have been no deficit. Mr. Stockman rejects this argument, more clearly in the appendix to his book than in its text. He explains that the administration's fiscal policy was inconsistent with realities of the American economy that monetary policy could not change. Monetary policy could not make the Laffer Curve work; it could only have concealed its failure by causing enough inflation, and enough bracket creep, to prevent the tax cut from being real.

Is Stockman going too far in identifying his frustrations as a failure of the Reagan Revolution? After all, haven't "we" gotten the economy moving again, tamed inflation, rebuilt the national defense, slowed the growth of nondefense expenditures, and stopped the upward creep of taxes? Stockman deals with this argument, but less thoroughly than he might have done. The country has enjoyed an expansion of about average size in output and employment during the Reagan years. The build-up of defense begun in the Carter Administration accelerated at first but then ran into the limits of revenue imposed by the administration's tax policy and is now about on the Carter path. The growth of nondefense, noninterest expenditures has been slowed down and replaced by a rapid growth of interest expenditures. The rise of the tax burden has also been slowed down for the present, but the debt created during this administration portends higher taxes in the future. There is now a chance that the budget may be brought into balance, at the expense of the defense program, by 1991, eight years and over a trillion dollars of debt beyond the promise of the 1980 camapign. The lasting positive economic achievement of the Reagan administration will probably turn out to be supporting Mr. Carter's chairman of the Federal Reserve as he got inflation down.

One may, if he wishes, call this a successful revolution. But Mr. Stockman is at least equally entitled to call it a failure—not by comparison with the achievements of other administrations but by comparison with the extraordinary claims this one made for its own unique virtues.

The figure who dominates this book, aside from David Stockman, is President Reagan. The president comes through as a mystery. We get more evidence of what we already knew, that by the standards of an accountant, economist, or budget director the president does not rank very high. But those are not the standards by which to appreciate presidents. A budget director knows many things, a president knows one great thing. But we do not discover in this book what is the one great thing that the president knows.

Mr. Stockman's book leaves some perplexing questions. Does anyone really care that there was no Reagan Revolution? Does it really matter? At the end of the book Stockman concludes that no one cares. The public wants its taxes cut, but also wants to keep its benefits and subsidies, and that means, arithmetically, that it wants the deficits. This conclusion comes as an anti-climax. Why has Mr. Stockman berated the politicians for 350 pages if they have only been doing what the public wants? Shouldn't the book have been called *The Triumph of Democracy* rather than *The Triumph of Politics*? Mr. Stockman is not very clear about whether it matters that there was no Reagan Revolution. He obviously thinks that the deficit matters, but his argument for that is rather perfunctory. Stockman strongly challenges the notion that there has been a Glorious Revolution. He is less strong in demonstrating what the adverse consequences of the failed revolution have been or will be. This is a comment on the book, not an exoneration of the fiscal policy of the past five years.

I have used the words "reality," "real," and "really" many times in this review. That is what the book is about—a political process that is losing its grip on reality. Politics is sliding into a world in which Jane Fonda is a pitiful farm wife testifying before a congressional committee, J. R. Ewing is an oil magnate, and Lee Iacocca is an actor in a television commercial. Politics is becoming a process of creating images to sell and then to live by as long as they sell. It is becoming a branch of show business. That did not start with Ronald Reagan and has nothing to do with his former profession. We all—peanut farmers, lawyers, investment bankers, divinity students, even economists—become actors when the little red light on the TV camera goes on. The difficulty is that the public can't just turn off the set and go back to the real world when the show gets boring. There are problems in the real world—the debt, the Russians, the alienated underclass—that those fellows up there on the TV tube are supposed to deal with. A hard look at Stockman's book may do a little to drag the politicians back into the real world.

Blind Confusion[1]

THE recent TV docudrama, "Blind Ambition," tells the story of Watergate as seen by a lawyer. Naturally, it is inaccurate at several points, especially in ignoring totally the role of economics in the drama, which was, of course, unknown to John Dean. I believe the time has come to tell the truth, however much that may hurt, to put an end to all this fantasizing.

When President-elect Nixon's head-hunter called me in December 1968 to ask whether I would be willing to serve as a member of the Council of Economic Advisers, I did not hesitate. Patriotism and principle dictated that I should make the sacrifice. I was prepared to give up my seven-by-twelve cubicle at Brookings for a forty-by-forty-foot study in the Executive Office Building. I was ready to give up my one-third interest in one preoccupied secretary for two efficient and beautiful ones. I was prepared to give up my daily bus rides to and from work for a chauffeured limousine. And I was willing to trade my peanut butter and jelly sandwich for the hot fudge sundae in the White House Mess.

I was willing to make these sacrifices because I considered it my duty to arrest the slide of the nation along the Road to Serfdom and to establish the country firmly on the course of economic freedom.

For two and a half years things went well. By the summer of 1971 I had acquired a third beautiful secretary. I had two color television sets in my office, on which the White House communications people could play back any football games I might have missed. I spent every week end resting at Camp David and every Wednesday evening in the president's box at the Kennedy Center.

This blissful period was interrupted one day in June 1971 when my red-white-and-blue telephone rang. One thing I loved about my EOB office was the telephones. There was a black one

---

[1] Not previously published; written in 1979.

for talking to my wife and staff, a yellow one for leaking to the *Washington Post,* a white one for the president and a red-white-and-blue one for H. R. (Bob) Haldeman. I knew that the *Post* was tapping my white phone and Haldeman was tapping my yellow one.

At the ring of the red-white-and-blue phone I stood to attention and pressed the receiver smartly against my ear.

"Stein here," I snapped.

"Achtung, Herr Profeszor! Higby here. Herr Haldeman will speak to you."

After a buzz, Haldeman came on the line.

"Listen, you curly-haired intellectual," he began, "we've had enough."

"What do you mean?" I stammered.

"For two and a half years you've kept us from doing anything in the economics field."

"But I thought that was what the president wanted," I protested. "I thought he wanted to leave the free market alone."

"Well, he doesn't want it any more. He wants to stop the inflation."

"But I've done my best on that," I replied in bewilderment.

"And what have you got to show for doing your best? A recession, that's what. The president doesn't want a recession either."

"So, what does he want?" I asked.

"He wants price and wage controls."

I was staggered, and almost sat down.

"But . . . but— My friends at the University of Chicago will be furious if we go into price and wage controls."

"F—— your friends at the University of Chicago," he argued in rebuttal. "You know what's going to happen if we don't stop the inflation?"

"What?"

"The president won't get reelected. And then the Democrats will take over. And after them the Commies. I suppose you know what the Commies will do to you and your friends."

"Sir," I replied firmly, "this is a matter of principle with me. I cannot sacrifice my principle to save my skin."

"Look," he said even more firmly, "the president wants this. If you don't go along we'll take away your privileges in the White House Mess."

I knew when I was licked.

"O.K. What do you want me to do? Do you want me to run a controls program?"

"No." He had it all figured out before the conversation began, as usual. "John Connally will be out in front. Then if it doesn't work we can blame it on Lyndon Johnson."

"And what should I do?"

"Just keep quiet. We don't want you outside the tent p——ing in."

"Yes, sir."

But I wasn't happy. The spell of being there, and of feeling that I was helping to save the world, was broken. I took to spending more and more time away from my office. I became a kind of international economics bum, flying from the OECD to the IMF to the IBRD to GATT to the ADB and back to the OECD. And when I was in the country I stayed as much as possible at Camp David, eating hot fudge sundaes. I really loved those hot fudge sundaes, I gave them the nickname "Mo," because when I ate one I wanted mo'.

It was there, one balmy June day in 1972, that Haldeman caught up with me again. There were red-white-and-blue telephones all over Camp David.

He wasted no time.

"Stein," he barked, "it isn't working."

"What isn't working?"

"The wage and price control system. We had a few good months, but the inflation rate is creeping up again."

"But," I explained, "I always told you it wouldn't work."

"Look, if I wanted a sermon I would have called Billy Graham. What do we do next?"

"Can't you just say that it isn't working and abolish it? You could blame Connally."

"That's out. Connally has become a Republican and the president's best friend."

I thought for a while before I came up with the solution.

"O.K., Bob." I was so sure that he would like this that I felt I could call him Bob. "We have to get to the heart of the problem, which is the Bureau of Labor Statistics. Nobody would know that the inflation rate was rising if the BLS didn't tell them so every month in the Consumer Price Index. What we have to do is get rid of the commissioner of labor statistics and put in someone who will give out better figures, at least until after the election."

"By George, Herb," he cried with excitement, "I think you're really getting on to this job. I'm going to ask the president to make you his special counsel."

"He can't do that, Bob. I'm not a lawyer. I wouldn't know what is legal and what isn't. Anyway, my suggestion is that you should kidnap the commissioner of labor statistics and keep him under wraps for about five months. Then the president can name someone reliable as acting commissioner—someone like Donald Segretti."

"Brilliant! Now where do we find this commissioner."

"Easy. His name is Geoffrey Moore and he lives in Watergate West, 2700 Virginia Avenue, Northwest, in Apartment 604. It won't be hard to get in there. People are always being robbed in the Watergate Apartments. You could hire a squad of Cubans to sneak in and snatch the commissioner."

"Wonderful, Herb. I won't forget this."

So I was ready for congratulations on the morning of June 18 when my beeper beeped. I called the White House operator and asked if she had a call for me. She said she sure did.

It was Haldeman.

"Stein, you traitor! You double-crossed us!"

"What are you talking about?"

"Our Cubans went into the Watergate and didn't find the commissioner's apartment. They wound up in an office building, and in the offices of the Democratic National Committee, of all places. They hardly realized where they were before the cops came in and nabbed them."

"But, Bob, they must have been in the office building at 2600 Virginia Avenue. I told you Watergate West, at 2700."

"Don't call me Bob!" he snarled. "You won't get away with this. I have plenty of friends in the TV industry. You'll never get your memoirs on the tube!"

And I guess I won't.

Metamorphosis II

The *Wall Street Journal*,
October 26, 1983

DAVID Stockman was the first one to see the enormous insect in the White House. It was about seven feet long and three feet wide. Its feelers waved continuously, but not in a menacing way. At first Mr. Stockman thought he would say nothing about it except to William Greider. But then he decided that his duty was to tell the President.

Mr. Reagan did not believe the story initially. He was used to the idea that Mr. Stockman tended to exaggerate the bad news. But a few nights later he woke with a start and a feeling that he was being observed. And there he saw the creature, standing on its hind legs, leaning against the door jamb and smiling. The smile was friendly, but the president thought he should reach for the button to summon the Secret Service just the same. As he did so the insect dropped to its eight feet and scurried away.

The incident puzzled the President and worried him greatly. He called in the chairman of his Council of Entomological Advisers (CEA) and described what he had seen. The chairman's response was in one sense reassuring, but in a more fundamental sense deeply troublesome. What the president had seen was one of the species *Blatta deficita*—the deficit cockroach. Such cockroaches had been common in the White House for fifty years. But what the president had seen was several times larger than the largest deficit cockroach previously seen.

The story was terribly embarrassing to the president. He had run for office on a promise to clean out the White House. And now he had this weird thing running around. For several weeks the president and his chief aides tried to ignore the creature, hoping that it would go away or, at least, not be noticed by outsiders. But the insect became increasingly bold in its excursions around the White House. It was even observed fleetingly in the Press Room. Evans and Novak ran a story that James Baker had smuggled a seven-foot moderate mole into the Reagan White House, and the *Washington Post* assigned investigative reporters to the Waterbug story. This led the president, on the advice of his communications director, to make a speech to the Republican Women's Club of Peoria ridiculing the media for suggesting that there was an insect in the White House.

Everything came out into the open, however, when the president held a televised news conference in the East Room. Just as Helen Thomas rose to ask her usual question about when was the President going to stop the Israelis from terrorizing the PLO the large, brown creature could be seen standing next to the president's podium. Correspondents shrieked and three fainted. A Secret Serviceman threw himself between the insect and the president, but the roach darted away.

In the analysis session on ABC afterward, George Will quoted archy the cockroach, who said:

> there is bound to be a certain amount
>   of
> trouble running any country
> if you are president the trouble happens
>   to you
> but if you are a tyrant you can arrange
>   things so
> that most of the trouble happens to other
>   people

More literal and less literate, David Broder thought it was all a dirty trick of the Democratic National Committee and Sam Donaldson was sure that the president was feeling out public reaction to a possible appointment to the Civil Rights Commission.

The next morning all the wake-up shows had professors of entomology as guests. They all agreed that what had been seen at the news conference had been a member of *Blatta deficita*, but of an extraordinary size.

The country, sensitized by a generation of horror movies featuring supernatural insects, was in a panic. The president had to deal with the situation, and called a meeting of his top officials

to review the possibilities. The chairman of the Council of Entomological Advisers argued strongly for spraying with a large dose
of taxation. But the president made it clear that he would not
consider such a course. He did not explain his reason, then or
later. But the fact was that the president was the only person
who knew what had happened. He had suspected it that first night
when he had seen the smile on the face of the insect leaning
against the door jamb of his bedroom, and he had confirmed it
by later close observation. The cockroach was a valued member
of his own team. Gregor K. had worked hard for Ronald Reagan
during the 1980 campaign. He had been the most vigorous advo-
cate and expositor of the idea that a big tax cut would raise the
revenue and balance the budget. After the inauguration, he had
become special assistant to the president. Constant exposure to
the budget numbers had depressed him and he had talked
about leaving. In fact, his colleagues thought he had decamped
a few weeks earlier. But Mr. Reagan knew what had become of
Gregor K.

So the president ruled out insecticide. The only other suggestion came from the secretary of the Treasury, who proposed that
the White House should announce that it had a new house pet—
an eight-legged one. The secretary of Commerce offered to put
a saddle on it and ride it around the South Lawn, but the weakness
of the insect's legs made that seem impractical. The president
bought the house-pet idea with one addition. He wanted to propose a constitutional amendment barring the use of insects as
White House pets after 1988.

The next day the press secretary held a news conference
on White House pets. He distributed pictures of Fala, King Tima-
hoe, Taft's horse, Caroline Kennedy's pony, and others—an equal
number of Republicans and Democrats. He also passed out somewhat blurred photographs of the insect, which he said was called
Fido and had been brought from Santa Barbara.

The public excitement faded after it became clear that the
creature had not come from outer space. The Sunday talk shows
gave up their effort to obtain a guest appearance by the insect.
Wall Street was occasionally upset by public disagreements between the secretary of the Treasury and the chairman of the CEA
over whether cockroaches caused high interest rates. But on the
whole, the country was calm.

The president was not calm, however. Whenever he sat down

to work he saw the cockroach, in reality or in his mind's eye. Trying to think about the size of the defense budget, or about an appropriation for the International Monetary Fund, or about a coming conference with the chairman of the Federal Reserve, the image of the cockroach came between him and his problem. He felt constantly rebuked and guilty—because there was a cockroach in the White House, because it was so large and, most of all, because it was his friend.

His mind was made up by Margaret Thatcher's visit to the White House. At two in the morning she awoke in the Lincoln Bedroom to see the creature staring at her. Being the Iron Lady, she did not scream but only shooed it away. The next morning, however, she lectured the president. She told him how unseemly it was for the head of Britain's greatest colony to have a cockroach in his house, and how she had cleaned out No. 10 Downing Street.

Two days later, the president called in his senior staff and informed them of his decision. He did not want to see the cockroach again. He and Nancy were going to move out of the White House into Blair House across the street. The staff would move out of the East and West Wings into the Old Executive Office Building. The White House would be left to the cockroach.

At first some members of the staff protested. But the president would not hear any objections. Staff attention then turned to the question of whose offices would be closest to the president's in the Old Executive Office Building, and this subject occupied the inside-Washington columnists for about two weeks. The move was consummated and things went on.

In the general opinion, the event demonstrated that cockroaches, even exceedingly large ones, did not really matter. Blair House was certainly big enough for the Reagans, or for most presidents, who usually do not have children living at home. The work of the government went on as efficiently or inefficiently from the Old Executive Office Building as it had from the wings of the White House.

But there were some who thought it was a sad and portentous day when the president of the United States was driven out of the White House by a cockroach.

The foregoing article in the *Wall Street Journal* evoked the following letters to the editor:

November 7, 1983

The Cockroach in Herbert Stein's "Metamorphosis II" (editorial page, Oct. 26) was indeed a double mutant, whether or not the mutation was caused by exposure to nuclear radiation. Not only was it unusually large, but it had eight legs rather than the six legs that have to suffice for all other insects. Of course economists, especially those who have had the ear of presidents, must get rusty in dealing with mere single-digit numbers.

Douglas B. Rose

Cleveland

* * *

For years I have attempted to tuckpoint the dreadful gaps in my education but with only limited success. What a comfort it is, therefore, to discover that the holder of so intellectually august a position as the A. Willis Robertson chair in economics at the University of Virginia has somehow escaped the knowledge that insects have six legs. My heart goes out to him.

E. F. Porter, Jr.

St. Louis

* * *

I suppose getting the numbers wrong is what economics is all about.

Dennis P. Waters

Binghamton, N.Y.

* * *

The White House's eight-legged creature must have been a spider, perhaps Lycosa tarantula, a large wolf spider whose bite is believed to induce an uncontrollable urge to send in the Marines.

Peggy Jacobi

Paicines, Calif.

November 16, 1983

My thanks to the readers who called attention to the error in my article (Metamorphosis II, Oct. 26) in which I described the deficit cockroach as having eight legs, whereas the correct number is six.

I can only offer the explanation that Samuel Johnson gave to the lady who asked him why he had defined "pastern" as the "knee" of a horse in his dictionary. He replied, "Ignorance, madame, pure ignorance."

Herbert Stein

Washington

You Read It in the
Times *First*

The *New York Times*, March 10, 1982

WASHINGTON—"To govern is to choose," said a senior White House official, who declined to be named, after the decision was made. The story of the process by which the decision was reached can now be told.

Until martial law was declared in Poland, no one in the Executive Office had any doubt that Nancy Reagan would wear a red dress for the ball celebrating the first anniversary of President Reagan's inauguration. Nancy Reagan always wore red. The president liked red. He liked it instinctively. He associated it with "Red, White, and Blue," "Red-blooded Americans," and "Red River Valley."

Mr. Reagan was once asked, in an interview, whether it wasn't inconsistent for him to like red so much when Franklin D. Roosevelt was his hero and Eleanor never wore red dresses. He explained that the public had a wrong impression because it saw Eleanor only in black-and-white newsreels and didn't know what color dress she was wearing. Also, polling data was produced that showed that of the 50.8 percent of the popular vote Mr. Reagan won in 1980, 2 percentage points were due to the constant sight of Nancy beside him in her red dress.

The White House staff did include, however, a few people who were not true-red Reaganauts and who regarded the attachment to red as "voodoo" couture. Some would have preferred a preppier image. Others, loyal to the memory of the Republican Roosevelt, would have liked to see the return of the Alice-blue gown. But as long as the First Couple were riding high, the deviationists kept quiet.

156

The imposition of martial law in Poland initiated a scramble in the government to find ways to show our disapproval of what was going on in the Communist, or "Red," world. The first indication that this might have some implications for Nancy's dress came not from the soft conservatives in the White House but from hawks in the Pentagon. Secretary of Defense Caspar W. Weinberger sent the National Security Council a memo outlining three options: A. Invasion of Poland. B. Declaration that Nancy would not wear a red dress. C. Blockade of Cuba. (The ordering of the options clearly indicated the preference.)

The Weinberger "Red Alert" memo, as it came to be called in the West Wing, was sent to the speech-writing staff, where the president's Christmas message was being prepared. There was an intense discussion of including in the message an embargo on red dresses, as a warning to Moscow. This idea was abandoned when the speechwriter came up with the line: "It is better to light a candle than to dress in darkness." That was too good to leave out of the speech, so candle lighting became the shot the administration fired across the Soviet bow.

By Christmas Eve, the "red vs. blue" issue had surfaced in loose cocktail-party talk. One senior adviser, just back from Europe, said there would be no way to get Helmut Schmidt to give up the Soviet gas pipeline if the United States did not give a signal by banning the red dress. On the other side, a blow-dried congressman urged the president to follow a policy of "Steady as you go!" He said: "You weren't elected to put a blue dress on Nancy's back."

The chairman of the Council of Economic Advisers sent the president a memo saying that the unemployment rate would probably be 9 percent by the time of the ball and suggesting that it might be inappropriate for the First Lady to be dressed so lavishly in the midst of such misery. He proposed a little black Republican dress. The memo came back with the comment: "What did Ginger Rogers and Fred Astaire wear in *Top Hat* during the Depression? R.R."

By this time, it was the day before the ball and the Blues were getting desperate. They arranged for the president to meet with a delegation of leaders of the United States Chamber of Blue Dress Manufacturers. They explained to him that they hadn't been able to sell a single blue dress since he took office. But they hadn't come to plead for their own selfish interests. They just wanted to remind him of the blue in Red, White, and Blue, of Navy Blue and Gold, of the Wild Blue Yonder, of "My Blue Heaven," and of "Blues in the Night."

The president was moved. After they left, he lifted the phone. "Nancy," he said, "I've made a decision. It's going to be the blue dress."

"But Ronnie," she replied, "you know I don't have a blue dress." And so she wore the red dress.

The next morning, everyone in the White House wore a red tie, and some had red hunting jackets as well. David A. Stockman said: "I was never for the blue dress. I only wanted the president to have all his options." The chairman of the Council of Economic Advisers said, "I'll never put my computer up against the man's instincts again." Evans and Novak said: "There's one Reaganaut in the White House, thank God. That's Nancy."

Some Washington Bedtime Stories

The *Wall Street Journal*,
June 24, 1980

Let My People Go

And the Israelites abided in the land of Egypt and toiled in the brickyards there. They labored diligently and produced many bricks per Israelite-hour, which pleased the Pharaoh, who rewarded them well.

Then it came to pass that the Pharaoh died and was succeeded by his son. The young Pharaoh had studied at the Karnak School of Economics, but had not graduated, having been expelled for driving his chariot too fast.

After several weeks the young Pharaoh summoned Moses, the leader of the Israelites, and spoke to him thus: "It has come to my attention that the environment in the neighborhood of the brickyards is polluted with straw. Therefore I have issued a regulation which requires that hereafter bricks shall be made without straw."

Moses carried this regulation to the Israelites, who grumbled but obeyed. To make bricks without straw was hard work indeed, and output per Israelite-hour declined.

Then the young Pharaoh summoned Moses a second time and spoke to him thus: "An Israelite brickyard worker has been found dead."

"Yes, Pharaoh," said Moses, "he was kicked in the head by one of your royal camels."

"That is as may be," replied Pharaoh. "But my royal surgeons have performed an autopsy and have found brick dust in his lungs. I am issuing an occupational safety regulation which requires that next to every worker in the brickyard there shall stand another Israelite to fan the brick dust away."

Then the Israelites did as the Pharaoh ordered. That greatly raised the cost of the bricks made by the Israelites and the people of Egypt began to buy bricks imported from Eastern countries, which were cheaper, and as a result many Israelite brickworkers could not be employed.

Whereupon the Pharaoh summoned Moses a third time and spoke to him thus: "It has come to my attention that many Israelites are unemployed and have no income with which to sustain their families."

"Yes, Pharaoh," said Moses. "It is true, and we are sorely vexed."

"Then I shall establish a fund, to be called the Pharaoh's Import Adjustment Assistance Fund, from which every unemployed brickworker will be paid weekly compensation equal to two-thirds of his weekly wage."

"Yes Pharaoh," replied Moses. "My people will be grateful. But . . ."

"But what?" asked Pharaoh.

"But where will the money come from?"

"Ah, yes. That is the other side of the coin. I am levying a tax on the production of bricks at the rate of one silver shekel per thousand bricks."

Then the cost of Israelite bricks soared and imports increased and unemployment rose more and more.

So the Pharaoh summoned Moses once again and spoke to him thus: "Moses, I am greatly disappointed in the Israelites. In the time of my father your people were productive and contributed much to the Gross Egyptian Product. But things have changed. Perhaps you have become too assimilated. Your productivity is down and costs are up. Imports are flooding the country, our balance of payments suffers and there is much unemployment."

"Yes Pharaoh."

"I do not accept this situation," continued the Pharaoh. "I will correct it. I am going to establish a corporation to be called the Brick Reindustrialization Corporation, and that will help you regain your productivity."

"But Pharaoh, my people have been making bricks since the time of Joseph and they are greatly experienced. Who will counsel them about the production of bricks?"

"The board of directors of the corporation will consist of the best and the brightest among my astrologers, courtiers, and professors from KSE. Moreover, they will have a fund of a hundred million shekels of silver which they can use to assist the brickyards that are having the most trouble. I will raise the money for this fund by a new tax on brickyards."

Then Moses could be patient no more and he exclaimed:

"You have regulated us and regulated us! You have taxed and taxed! The result has been the lowered productivity and increased costs and all the other evils to which you point. And now you propose to solve the problem by more of the same poison that has caused it—more regulation and more taxes. You will set bureaucrats and ignoramuses to tell us how to make bricks. And you will tax the efficient to subsidize the inefficient. That way lies ruin.

"There is only one solution to our problems. Get off our backs! Let my people go!"

Science at the Pentagon

President Carter announced today a major scientific breakthrough at the Department of Defense. A team of psychologists and systems analysts has discovered that military spending is inversely related to military strength rather than positively related, as had been previously thought. In layman's language that means that the more we spend for defense the less we get.

The President made his announcement at a hastily called news conference this afternoon. He said that he had wanted to keep the breakthrough secret but had been forced to reveal it when a Congressional move to increase the defense budget threatened to weaken the national security seriously.

In an effort to avert a dangerous disarmament race the president said that he will invite the Soviets to talks on the lowest allowable military expenditures, to be called the LAME talks.

Dr. Joseph Nudnick, leader of the team that made the discovery, was introduced by the president at the news conference. When asked for the origins of the idea he explained: "When I was a small boy the Russians launched a space satellite as big as a Buick. Then we launched one as big as a basketball and everyone said ours was better because it was smaller. That idea stuck with me and I wondered whether it was also true of defense. So we kept working on it until we proved it."

Judge Rosenman Rides Again

The president is meeting in the Oval Office with his troika—secretary of the Treasury, director of the Office of Management and Budget, and chairman of the Council of Economic Advisers.

> PRES: Well, you fellows have really gotten me in a fix. You persuaded me in March to promise a balanced budget and here we are, only three months later, and it obviously isn't going to be balanced.
>
> TREAS: But, Mr. President, you started that all by yourself back in 1976 when you promised to balance the budget during your first term.
>
> PRES: That was a promise to balance the budget four years in the future. That's always good politics. But you got me to promise it for a year that was only six months away. That was stupid.
>
> CEA: I meant we should promise to balance the budget at full employment.
>
> PRES: What does that mean?
>
> CEA: It means that tax rates should be high enough and spending programs low enough so that the budget would be balanced if we were at full employment.
>
> PRES: Well, that seems safe enough. At least, it doesn't sound as if they would ever catch you. But didn't I sign a bill saying that full employment is 4 percent unemployment? So why were we promising to balance the budget when you were forecasting over 7 percent unemployment?
>
> CEA: Four percent is only ultimate full employment. We've postponed that until 1985, after your second term. *Deo volente.*
>
> PRES: Then what is full employment now?
>
> CEA: We think the basic underlying unemployment rate now is 5.1 percent unemployment, but the nonaccelerating inflation rate of unemployment is 7.2 percent.
>
> TREAS: That's all too hypothetical. It doesn't give the financial community any confidence that the budget will ever be balanced. I think we should say that our policy is to balance the budget

over the business cycle. That would explain deficits in recession, like now, but show that they would be balanced by surpluses in prosperity.

PRES: And when did the recession start?

TREAS: It started in January.

PRES: Then why did you get me to promise a balanced budget in March if the recession had already started?

TREAS: But, Mr. President, we didn't know it had started.

PRES: Well, if the recession started in January 1980 then we weren't in recession in 1977 and 1978 and 1979. Why didn't we balance the budget then?

TREAS: We weren't following the policy of balancing over the cycle then.

PRES: So our policy now is to run deficits in recession, starting with this one and run surpluses in prosperity, in the future, right?

CEA: Unless we decide to go back to the old policy when the recession is over.

PRES: (Turning to the Director of OMB) What do you think, Jim?

OMB: I don't think it will fly. I think you should go back to the straightforward solution that Franklin Roosevelt found right here in this room forty-four years ago.

PRES: And what was that?

OMB: Well, in the 1932 campaign against Hoover, FDR had made a speech in Forbes Field in Pittsburgh promising to balance the budget. Then during the 1936 campaign he was planning another speech in the same place, also about the budget, and he was puzzled about how to explain his failure to live up to his promise of balancing the budget. So he called in his advisers and they came up with all kinds of complicated ideas, like today, until the President's Counsel, Samuel Rosenman, produced the solution. "Deny you ever said it," he told the President. That went over just fine.

PRES: (After musing for a moment) Why don't I have smart advisers like that. (Picks up phone and presses button) Ham, come in here. I want to give you some notes for a TV speech. And get me a long cigaret holder and a pack of cigarets. . . . No, no, just plain tobacco.

My Burn

Newsweek, July 29, 1974

HERB Stein threw the copy of *Newspeak* to the floor so hard the picture of Richard Nixon on the cover winced.

"What's the matter, dear?" asked his wife, looking up from her knitting. She was knitting an afghan with a pattern of the Consumer Price Index on it, and was halfway through the 1.1 percent increase of May.

"The thing that burns me up about these newsmagazines is their cult of personalization."

"Whatever that is, I'm sure it isn't the only thing that burns you up about them," she commented, reasonably.

Well, that's true. Practically everything about these magazines annoys me. But what I'm talking about is their practice of always telling the news in terms of a few identified people, presumably real. Look at this story called 'The Inflation Pinch.' "

"What's that about, life on the Via Veneto?"

"Very funny. No, it's about the way the American people are being hurt by inflation. They don't have any statistics in the article. It's all made up of anecdotes about particular people—a black autoworker, and a Jewish medical intern, and an Italian dry cleaner and a WASP family that can't afford to go away and has to spend its vacation around their backyard swimming pool. Why don't they give the facts?"

"But that's only their way. You know that people don't like statistics. They're much more interested in people."

"What's so interesting about this family with the swimming pool, unless they represent some large class of the American people? They aren't even movie stars. Nobody cares about them for themselves. The article is supposed to be about the American people, not about a family named Edwards in Keokuk. In the first place, how many people have swimming pools?''

"Oh, quite a few, I imagine. The Rockefellers up the street have one."

"And how many of them can't go on a vacation because of high prices?"

"I don't know, I'm sure."

"Well, do you think that *Newspeak* knows?"

"I don't know. I guess they interviewed one."

"Suppose I were to tell you that in June 22,611 families with swimming pools who usually go away on vacation had to stay home because of the high prices, but 27,859 families with swimming pools who usually stay at home made so much money from selling things at high prices that they went away on vacation."

"Herb, that's fantastic. You sure learn a lot on your job."

"Well, I made it up. No one knows things like that. *Newspeak* doesn't know them either. And unless you know something like that the story is meaningless."

"Tell me about the Jewish intern. Maybe you could arrange for him to meet Madeline."

"He's married. Anyway, his problem is he has to sell blood to buy gas for his Mercedes."

"How terrible."

"Don't worry, it isn't his own blood. You know how these doctors are. But the point is, the whole thing's a phony. These vignettes really aren't significant unless the people represent some general category. And we can only tell that from the statistics, however unreliable they may be."

"So what should we do, Pa?"

"Well, if they insist on personalization, they might at least use some representative situation. It might go like this:

" 'Joe Doakes gazed indolently at Archie Bunker on his twenty-seven-inch color screen. He felt a certain malaise. The show was a repeat and he had seen it before. Aside from that he was contented. His paycheck that week had been $154.72.' "

"Where did you get that odd number of dollars?"

"It just happens to be the average weekly earning of nonfarm workers in June 1974. 'Also, his wife had brought home $108.30.' Don't ask me where I got that. The average family has 1.7 wage earners so I just gave his wife seven-tenths of an average week's wage."

" 'Joe Doakes's family income was up 7 percent only a year earlier. He knew that his cost of living was up by 10 percent, so his real income was down 3 percent since last year. Actually he and his wife were short about $7.65 a week from what they would have needed to keep even with the cost of living in the past year. But still, he was pleased with himself and his situation. He knew enough not to take his economic temperature every week or month or even every year. Although he couldn't put numbers on it, he was aware that his real income was much higher than it had been ten years earlier and enormously higher than his father's had been at the end of World War II. So he didn't feel poor or depressed as he sat there watching Archie Bunker, although he wished they would do a new show.' "

"But, Herb, he still isn't as well off as he was a year ago."

"I know, but that's not my point. I'm not trying to prove that people are better off. But if you stick to the measured facts you find only a small difference between this year and last year, and only a minor ripple on the rising tide of economic welfare. That wouldn't be so dramatic, but we suffer from entirely too much drama already. The whole psychological underpinning of the society is being burned up to make dramatic spectacles for TV and newsmagazines."

"Now, Herb, you're being overdramatic yourself."

"Why do you say that?"

"Well, statistics show that lots of people don't read newsmagazines or even watch the TV news."

Throw Away the
National Debt

The *Wall Street Journal*,
March 30, 1984

I N 1946, after the end of World War II, the federal debt was $242 billion. Since then, Washington has run a total budget deficit of nearly $800 billion. But the federal debt today, in 1946 prices, is $232 billion. The real value of the debt is smaller today, despite the cumulative deficit.

This magic has been performed by inflation. We have gradually but effectively repudiated all of the postwar debt by inflation. How effective this repudiation has been can be seen from the following example: Suppose a person had bought a twenty-year Treasury bond in 1944 for $1,000. In 1964 he reinvests the $1,000 at maturity in another Treasury bond. This year he finally collects his $1,000. It is now worth $200. During this period the investor received interest, first at the rate of 2.5 percent and then, after 1964, at the rate of 4.2 percent. If we adjust the interest also for inflation, we find that his real rate of return on the initial investment was minus 1.2 percent per annum.

This repudiation-by-inflation has been mainly responsible for the decline in the ratio of the federal debt to GNP since 1946. In 1946 the debt was 115 percent of GNP; at present it is about 35 percent. Real growth of the economy also contributed to this decline, but less than inflation did.

In recent years, however, this repudiation-by-inflation has not been running with sufficient speed. It is not keeping up with the deficits. Since 1974 the real debt has increased, and so has the ratio of debt to GNP. Moreover, there's every expectation that the real debt and the ratio of debt to GNP will rise rapidly in the years ahead.

Unless something is done, we soon will be up to our keisters in real debt. But hardly anyone, I suppose, wants to speed up the inflation in order to keep the real debt from growing. We need a noninflationary way to repudiate debt.

Pursuing this line of thought led me to the conclusion that we should do in a straightforward, aboveboard way what we have been doing surreptitiously all these years. I was reminded of what the secretary of the Treasury, Salmon Portland Chase said, more than a hundred years ago about the way to resume gold convertibility, which had been suspended during the Civil War. "The way to resumption," he said, "is to resume." So, I say, the way to repudiation is to repudiate.

The government should announce that, from this moment, it will not pay interest or principal on the debt now outstanding. At one stroke we would be rid of the existing debt and the interest hereafter payable on it. Elimination of that interest would reduce the deficit by $125 billion in 1985, or by about 65 percent.

Some might think that such an action, wiping out almost a trillion dollars of assets, would have a depressing effect on the economy. But such an idea only shows an ignorance of modern economics. Although some people own this trillion dollars of assets, present and future taxpayers also have a trillion dollars of obligations, which accrue interest, represented by the debt. So repudiation of the debt is only a wash.

When I used to argue that taxes should be raised to reduce the debt, modern economists explained to me that there was really no difference between taking money from people by taxing and taking it by borrowing. That meant that there was no difference between owning a Treasury bond and owning a canceled check that had been used to pay taxes. If it would make the present holders of the debt feel better if we repudiate it, the Treasury could give them all canceled checks.

One might ask why we should go to the trouble of repudiating the debt if it really makes no difference—since there is really no net debt but only a gross debt matched by future tax obligations. In fact, repudiation should be stimulating to the economy. As long as the debt is out there, running up interest, there is a possibility that some misguided government will decide to raise taxes, at least to pay the interest. The fear of that future tax increase deters people from saving and investing now, because the income from that saving and investment might be subject to higher taxes. Alternatively, there is a possibility that a future government may be tempted to try again to repudiate debt by inflation. That prospect also is a source of current uncertainty and depresses the economy.

It may be said that repudiation is just another tax—a tax of 100 percent on holders of Treasury debt—and we already have too many taxes. As we have learned from the supply-siders, what is so bad about taxes is not that they take income from the private sector but that they take income at the margin from the additional earnings that people derive from additional work, savings, or investments. But that, of course, refers only to taxes on future work, savings, or investments, because that is all that can be discouraged. Repudiation is a tax on the income from past savings. Bygones are forever bygones. Repudiation is the ideal supply-side tax.

There is one economic problem in this proposal. About $180 billion of federal debt is owned by commercial banks. That far exceeds the amount of commercial bank capital. To wipe out that debt might tend to reduce the money supply, which would be depressing. (Bank examiners do not count as a liability the obligation of banks to pay taxes in the future because of the debt.)

To handle this problem the federal government should give the banks, in exchange for their current Treasury securities, nonmarketable, nontransferable consols whose face value would increase by 10 percent per annum and that the bank examiners would always appraise at their face value. That is similar to the way in which Latin American debt is now handled on the accounts of commercial banks.

One word of caution needs to be said in conclusion. Once a government has repudiated its debt it is likely to experience great difficulty in borrowing again. Even if the repudiation is covert, through inflation, investors get on to it, come to fear it in the future and demand high interest rates as insurance. The resistance to future borrowing by the federal government would be greater after an overt repudiation, unless assurance is provided that it will not be done again. Therefore, I suggest the constitutional amendment requiring a balanced budget should be amended to include a provision prohibiting future repudiation.

Feeding Baby the Budget Deficit

The *Wall Street Journal,*
December 3, 1984

DADDY, why are the newspapers so full of stories about the budget these days?"

"That's because there is a big deficit and the people in the government have to figure out what to do about it."

"But wasn't there a big deficit before the election?"

"Of course there was. Now, hurry up and eat your applesauce, darling."

"Didn't Mr. Reagan tell us before the election that he knew what to do about the deficit?"

"Yes, he did."

"Well, since he won such a big election victory, why doesn't he go ahead and do it?"

"The problem is that the deficit has turned out to be much bigger than the President thought during the campaign."

"Why is that?"

"It's mainly because the gross national product turned out to be lower in the third quarter than the president had expected during the campaign."

"Oh, really? What did the gross national product turn out to be?"

"In 1972 dollars it was $1.6465 trillion."

"And what did the president think it was, during the campaign?"

"According to the estimate that came out in October it was $1.6496 trillion."

"Well, using the handy calculator you attached to my crib, I see that's a difference of less than two-tenths of one percent. Is that what has Washington all upset?"

"It's not just the third quarter. It's what happens when you project out from the third quarter of 1984 to the year 1989, when the Reagan administration planned to have the deficit under control."

"Oh, really? So what happens, Daddy?"

"You see, the administration was counting on real GNP reaching $2005 billion in 1989. With the previous estimate of third-quarter 1984 GNP, that could be reached with an annual growth rate of 4.083 percent. Now that the third-quarter figure has been reduced, the required growth rate is 4.123 percent, and they don't think they can make it."

"Who is telling the president all that?"

"His economists."

"I thought the president didn't believe in economists. During the debate he said that the reason he couldn't keep his 1980 promise to balance the budget in 1983 was that the economists had given him bad forecasts."

"That was during a debate. Now he's back to work and in the hands of his economists again."

"So why doesn't he get the economists he had in 1980?"

"Oh Snookums, even at your age you should know that you can't sell the Brooklyn Bridge twice to the same customer. Now take some more applesauce."

"So, what's the big problem? During the campaign the president said he had this book with 4004 easy ways to cut the budget to $400 billion."

"I'm afraid that's out. One night Ed Meese couldn't sleep and he fell into reading one volume of the Grace Commission report."

"That's good, isn't it? Now the administration knows what to cut."

"No, that's bad. Mr. Meese discovered that the report calls for cutting benefits to veterans, farmers, retired military personnel, old people generally, sick people, and lots of people who voted Republican this time and are hoped will vote Republican in the future."

"Gee, that's tough. And I suppose a tax increase is out of the question after what the president said during the campaign."

"Well, the White House did have one good idea for getting around that, but it didn't quite work."

"What was that?"

"The president would appoint Fritz Mondale secretary of the Treasury. Mr. Mondale had said that he would raise taxes in 1985. If he were secretary of the Treasury he could recommend a tax increase to Congress while the president was out of town."

"Sounds brilliant. So what went wrong?"

"Mr. Mondale wouldn't take the job unless he could have a car and driver, and David Stockman wouldn't let him."

"It looks as if they're really up against it."

"Oh, they still have one option."

"What's that, Daddy?"

"They're going to give up the idea of balancing the budget."

"But how can they do that? Isn't the president still for the balanced budget amendment?"

"That's quite a different thing. The president can be for the balanced budget amendment without being for the balanced budget. After all, he's for equal rights without being for the equal rights amendment."

"O.K. You've sold me. But how is he going to sell that to the American people?"

"He's going to offer them something better than a balanced budget. He's going to offer them an equilibrium deficit."

"Sounds pretty impressive. But isn't the equilibrium deficit zero?"

"Oh, no. Think a minute. What's par on a golf course?"

"Usually seventy-two, but sometimes seventy-one or seventy."

"And what's normal body temperature?"

"Ninety-eight point six. I'm beginning to see where you're coming from."

"Right. And what's the freezing point of water?"

"At least that's zero."

"That's Celsius. Here we go by Farenheit. Anyway, you see what I'm driving at. Equilibrium isn't necessarily zero."

"Then what is the equilibrium deficit?"

"They haven't decided that yet. They have to decide on the revenues and expenditures first."

"Sounds backward to me."

"Oh, shut up and finish your applesauce."

Just the Fair Trade Facts, Ma'am

The *Wall Street Journal,*
October 21, 1985

I T looked like another dull day at the station. Business had fallen off a lot in the month since the president set us up as the Fair Trade Vice Squad. I'm lolling back in my chair, looking with half-closed eyes at the pinups on the wall—John Wayne, Mary Lou Retton, Ronnie—when the phone rang.

"Another one of those crazies," I think. "Probably just saw a Toyota."

But I pick up the phone anyway.

"Fair Trade Vice Squad, Sergeant Smoot," I snap, putting on my All-American, all business manner.

The voice at the other end was indistinct. Either using a South Korean telephone or covering the mouthpiece with a handkerchief. But I get the message.

"Tip for you. Clown Books. Twenty-second and Jay streets. Third shelf in the northeast corner." There was a click, and then silence.

My sidekick, Hawley, was snoozing in her chair. I wake her up and we roll down west to Twenty-second street and south to Jay. Yuppie area. They're the worst. Copped out of Vietnam, and now they buy French wines, Italian shoes, and Japanese cars.

Clown Books is all lit up, but quiet and empty except for a dowdy-looking dame behind the counter. I pay her no attention but go right to the northeast corner of the store, while Hawley leans on a post near the door, covering me.

On the third shelf I see what I'm looking for. Copies of *Com-*

plete Works of William Shakespeare. Big fat book. Hard cover. Price— $9.95. Too much for the money. Obviously dumped. New York publisher's name inside must be a fraud.

I saunter up to the counter with a copy of the book, not wanting to alert her. "Excuse me, Miss, how much is this book?"

She looks at me innocently through her thick cheaters. "Nine ninety-five. Just as it says on that little orange sticker."

Then I flick out my Fair Trade Vice Squad ID and flash it at her. "I want to see your cost accounting on this book."

"That'll take a little while," she says coyly.

"That's all right. I've got a little while."

But it only took a few seconds. She punches a few words on her keyboard, and green lights start showing up on the display. I edge behind the counter to read. It seems to be all there. Paper, printing, binding, markup. It makes $9.95 all right.

Then I see something missing. "How about the author's royalty?" I ask.

"But it's by Shakespeare."

"So what? Doesn't he get a royalty?"

"He's dead," she explains.

"Oh yeah? When did he die?"

"A long time ago. Three hundred and fifty years."

"Oh. Well, I missed it. So his children should get the royalties."

"As far as we know, he had no children." She was looking kind of smart-alecky. "Anyway, after fifty-six years the author doesn't get any royalty. That's the British law."

"Sure, that's the way the British sucker us."

"No," she comes back. "That's also the international law."

"Don't tell me about that Commie international law," I says, getting impatient. "Look, sister. If that book was by an American author—say, Louis L'Amour—he'd get two bucks a copy royalty, minimum. That book would have to go for eleven ninety-five. You know, there are perfectly good American authors, graduates of the University of Iowa, starving in garrets, driving taxis, or writing editorials for the *Washington Post,* because they can't get their books published. And you're bringing in this foreign stuff and dumping it."

Then I relax a little. "This seems to be your first time, so I'm not going to run you in. But I'm giving you a warning. Either you take the books off the shelf or you raise the price to eleven ninety-five."

Just as I'm saying that I notice the sound of music from the back room. Sounds familiar. "What's that?" I bark.

"Oh, that's the 'Beautiful Blue Danube,'" she comes back coolly.

Then I really get hot. "That's in Austria, isn't it? What's the matter with 'Swanee River,' or the 'Missouri Waltz'? You're running an import den here. I'm taking you in and throwing the book at you!"

With that, she snaps off her glasses and I see who she is. She's Mata Maru, the import queen. And she's gorgeous. She's also got a shiny Beretta in her right hand, one of those little Italian guns.

"Stand back, sap," she says, insultingly. "You'll never get me. We're going to flood this country with English books, Italian operas, French Impressionist paintings, Japanese woodcuts, and those cute African tribal masks. We're going to smother this country in foreign culture."

At the word "culture," Hawley reaches for her revolver. But it's a heavy Colt, and before she lifts her arm Maru lets her have it right between the eyes.

"Level playing field!" I holler. But Mata Maru is gone—out the back door.

I toss the Shakespeare in the wastebasket and Hawley into the back seat of the squad car. Mata Maru is somewhere out there, doing her dirty work. But we'll get her yet.

My Foreign Debt

The *Wall Street Journal*,
May 10, 1985

T HE latest thing I am supposed to worry about is that "we" are becoming net debtors to the rest of the world. I look around and say, "Who, me?" I try to visualize my balance sheet with the rest of the world. All I can think of is that a magazine has owed me 600,000 lire for about two years. But I have written that off in my mind long ago, so I conclude that my foreign assets and liabilities are both zero.

That is, however, a narrow way of looking at the situation. What about my indirect foreign assets and liabilities? Well, I have, like most people, a bank account, and I am indirectly a part owner of the bank's assets. Through the kindly ministrations of my bank, every year until recently I was acquiring more assets in Brazil, Argentina, Mexico, and so on. That was part of becoming a net creditor. In recent years, however, I have been acquiring few of such assets, which is one reason why "we" are becoming a net debtor to the rest of the world. I am, however, unable to find that a source of anxiety.

Directly or indirectly I own stock in a number of U.S. companies. Many of these companies have assets abroad. In recent years some of them have been borrowing abroad, usually to finance investment in the United States. In some cases this may have gone so far that their debts to the rest of the world exceed their assets in the rest of the world. So the company is a net debtor to the rest of the world, and as a stockholder so am I. But should that worry me? If their total debt exceeded their total assets I would be worried, but should I be worried if their debt in one part of the world exceeds their assets in that part of the world?

Presumably the company borrowed abroad because it was

cheaper to borrow there, and it invested here because this looks like a more profitable place in which to invest. That should be a reason for congratulating the management, not for worrying.

But, wise people say to me, that debt will have to be paid back, or, at least, interest will have to be paid on it. That, alas, is true of all debt, domestic as well as foreign. The companies that borrowed the money, whether they borrowed it at home or abroad, must have calculated that they could invest the money in a way that would yield a return adequate to service the debt.

The fact that the interest has to be paid to foreigners makes no difference to the company or to me as its stockholder. Whether the interest has to be paid in dollars or in some other currency would make a difference. Most of the debt of American companies to foreigners is an obligation to pay dollars, and it makes no difference to the company whether the dollars have to be paid to a creditor in Milwaukee or to a creditor in Milan. If the debt were in lire it wouldn't make any difference to the company if the lire were owed to a creditor in Milwaukee or to a creditor in Milan. A company that earns income in one currency and has debts in another one has an exchange risk, but the risk doesn't depend on where the debt is held.

Now, suppose that the company in which I am a tiny stockholder and a lot of other companies are paying more and more interest in dollars to people who live abroad. At some point these foreigners may not want to hold all those dollars but would prefer to convert more of them into some other currency—not necessarily their own. Then the dollar will decline. Isn't that something to worry about?

There are two things to say about that. First, the problem, if it is a problem, is not confined to dollars being acquired by foreign creditors. The basic fact is that the supply of dollar-assets in the world is rising rapidly. Most of these dollar-assets are owned by Americans. There are plenty of Americans who are just as alert as anyone in Frankfurt or Tokyo to the relative values of holding dollars, deutsche marks, yen, etc.—and just as quick to shift out of dollars as anyone else. The possibility of a decline in the value of the dollar as a result of an excess supply of dollar-assets does not depend on the dollar-assets being owned by foreigners.

Second, it is not at all clear that if the dollar does decline my hypothetical company that is now a net foreign debtor—that

is, has bigger debts to the rest of the world than its assets in
the rest of the world—will be a loser. It is probably not a net
debtor in foreign currencies, because most of its debt to the rest
of the world is in dollars whereas a large part of its assets in
the rest of the world may be valued in foreign currency or earn
income in foreign currency. Probably the net value of the company
in dollars would rise if the dollar declined.

Continuing an evaluation of my net foreign balance sheet,
I recognize that as an American taxpayer I owe part of the federal
debt, and part of that is owned by foreigners. Should I care
whether my piece is owned by someone in Omaha or by someone
in Osaka? I don't think so. It's all dollars either way. It might
look as if there is a difference because if the person in Omaha
buys a Treasury note for $10,000 he receives annual interest of
$1000 on which he pays tax, relieving me to some extent of having
to pay tax, whereas the income earned by the person in Osaka
is not subject to U.S. tax. That, however, is an illusion. If the
person in Omaha does not buy the Treasury note he has $10,000
to invest in something else that will yield an income on which
he will pay U.S. tax. I am concerned, when not otherwise occupied,
by the fact that my share of the federal debt is rising. I am not
concerned by how much of it I owe abroad and how much of it
I owe at home.

Perhaps this is an excessively worm's-eye view of a problem
that should properly be observed from a greater height. I do
not think so, however. The fact is that the American people, taken
all together, have a low propensity to save when the dissaving
practices of our government are taken into account. The United
States has turned out to be an exceptionally attractive place in
which to invest—attractive to foreigners as well as to Americans—
and so we export less capital than we used to and import more.
As compared with a situation in which the United States is a closed
economy, with no possibility of capital inflow, there is more investment going on here as a result of the capital inflow. Interest
will have to be paid on this capital, but it is financing investment
that the investors believe will yield a return sufficient to pay the
interest—and who is to say that they are wrong? As compared
with the closed economy situation, American workers are better
off because they have more capital to work with, higher productivity, and higher wages. American savers—suppliers of capital—are
worse off than if there had been no capital inflow, because the

capital inflow keeps interest rates in the United States lower than they would otherwise have been. Whether "we" are better off depends on who we are. Certainly the size of the total foreign debts of all Americans compared with their total foreign assets is irrelevant to judge the sustainability of the situation. Ability to service foreign debt does not depend on the amount of foreign assets; it depends on the amount of total assets and total capacity to earn income.

People say that the capital inflow, and the increase of "our" foreign debt relative to "our" foreign assets cannot go on forever. What economists know seems to consist entirely of a list of things that cannot go on forever, and this may be one of them. But if it can't go on forever it will stop. And if we never do anything that we can't go on doing forever we will never do very much.

Best-Selling Fiction: 3 Million Lost Jobs

The *Wall Street Journal*,
July 29, 1985

O NE of the most durable and widespread myths about the economy these days is that the United States has "lost" many jobs as a result of the trade deficit. In fact, there seems to be general agreement about how many jobs have been lost—three million. This number can be reached in any number of ways— all specious. The simplest is to observe that the U.S. deficit in foreign trade in goods and services is about $100 billion a year, or about 3 percent of gross national product, and that about 3 percent of total employment is three million. Grown men, including congressmen, say such things with straight faces, arguing for protectionist measures.

The whole thing is so silly that one feels like apologizing for discussing it, but the notion's prevalence raises an interesting question that, I confess, I cannot answer.

In 1980, when we had a surplus in trade in goods and services of about $9 billion, total U.S. employment was 100.9 million. Today, when we have a deficit of around $100 billion, total employment is 108.1 million. In 1980 total employment was 59.6 percent of the total population over age sixteen; today it is 60.1 percent. Where are the lost jobs?

One might just as reasonably say that we have a trade deficit because we have gained jobs as that we have lost jobs because we have a trade deficit. We have about seven million more people at work today than in 1980. They are out buying Hondas, Ferragamo shoes, and dinners at Taillevent. But I won't press that point.

Between 1980 (monthly average) and June 1985, private non-agricultural employment rose to 82.1 million from 74.2 million, or by 7.9 million. If we divide the private nonagricultural economy into thirty major industries, we find that between 1980 and 1985 employment declined in twelve of them; they had 1980 employment of 12.3 million, or one-sixth of the 1980 total, and their combined employment decline was 1.5 million. Eighteen industries with five-sixths of the 1980 total employment had a combined employment rise of 9.4 million.

The usual moaning about the loss of jobs implies that there is some connection between the loss of jobs and either an increase of unemployment or a decrease of employment. But that is wrong. In an ordinary year when unemployment is constant and employment is rising, probably about 10 percent of the work force will lose jobs and go through a spell of unemployment. Nobody thinks that is any problem. In the same year an equal number of people who had lost jobs and become unemployed will also find jobs. Probably since 1980 there have been about 50 million losses of jobs, but employment increased and unemployment rose only slightly, to 7.2 from 7 percent.

Even in manufacturing, to which so much attention is paid, there has been little deterioration of employment conditions. This May (1985) the unemployment rate for people whose last job was in manufacturing was 7.8 percent compared with 7.9 percent in May 1981 and 9.7 percent in May 1980.

So the fact that three million jobs were lost due to the trade deficit, if it is a fact, is of no special significance. Losing and gaining jobs goes on all the time, for all kinds of reasons. What is important is that if three million jobs have been lost, ten million have been found, because there has been an increase of seven million jobs.

Now, someone is sure to say that if we had found the ten million jobs and not lost the three million, there would now be three million more jobs than there are. But that would be the wrong conclusion. The causes of the loss of jobs are inseparable from the causes of the gain of jobs. When the United States imports $100 billion more of goods and services than it exports, the rest of the world earns $100 billion that, in one way or another, it invests in the United States. This investment creates jobs in the United States. It finances home building and business investment and defense expenditures and consumption that could not go on without it.

The basic fact is that the level of the trade deficit, or the rate of increase of the trade deficit if the increase is steady, has nothing to do with the total amount of employment or unemployment. Large short-run variations in the size of the trade deficit can affect employment temporarily, just as large variations in residential construction or automobile sales can. But such variations are not what is being complained of and are certainly not what proposed protectionist measures are supposed to remedy.

Over any extended period we can have few jobs with a trade surplus and we can have lots of jobs, as now, with a trade deficit. What counts is the number of people who want to work at a wage that does not exceed the value of their productivity. A clear example of this is the stagnation of employment in Western Europe, during years when their trade deficit was declining nearly to zero, in contrast to the rise of employment in the United States during years when our trade deficit was mushrooming. The difference between United States and European experience was in the labor markets, not in foreign trade.

The interesting question, which I cannot answer, is why these groundless allegations about the jobs lost from the trade deficit continue to circulate with little or no challenge. There is no surprise in these claims being made by representatives of industries that expect to benefit from restrictions on imports. After all, a congressman can hardly go on "The MacNeil-Lehrer Newshour" and say: "Some of my constituents don't think they are making enough money, so we would like the Congress to enact legislation to exploit the rest of the country for our benefit." He is expected to appeal to some general interest, like maintaining a high level of national employment.

The puzzle is why such fallacies persist for so long. Economists have a standard answer for this question. They say that the people with an interest in protectionism, even though they are a small minority, each have a strong interest, so it is worthwhile for them to push hard and propagate all the plausible arguments. For each of the large number of people who would lose by protectionism, the loss is small, so they have little incentive to organize and resist the pressures and propaganda of the protectionists.

There probably is something in this explanation, but less, I think, than there used to be. The costs of organizing and propagandizing seem to have declined relative to the incomes of the American people, so that even lightly felt causes can get represented. One or two zealots with a plausible cause, a mimeograph machine, and an idle millionaire looking for publicity can mount a national campaign, with full-page ads and Washington lobbyists. So the friends of the snail darter and the whale can withstand the business and government establishment.

But no one mounts a campaign for telling the truth about protectionism. Even though there are numerous and powerful industries that have an interest in resisting protectionism, they do not make themselves heard. Maybe the problem is that everybody wants something from the federal government—if not protection then tax relief or regulatory revisions or something else. Everyone recognizes that if he starts telling the truth about the other fellow's claim on the federal government, the other fellow will start telling the truth about him. So we have tacit collusion in not telling the truth, because although in some sense "everyone" might be better off if we all told the truth, no one could be sure that he would be better off.

Perhaps I am naive to ask the question. A wise man, Frank Knight, may have answered it over fifty years ago when he said: "Utterance which stands a chance of reaching any large public is either plain buffoonery, or solemn asininity, or worst of all, the mutual self-intoxication of popular oratory." Maybe that's all there is to it.

Remembering the Fifteenth of August

The *Wall Street Journal,*
August 14, 1981

O<small>N</small> August 15, 1971, President Nixon came down from Camp David and proclaimed to the nation a New Economic Policy. There had been other new economic policies before that and there have been others since. Undoubtedly there are more to come. But the Nixon policy was, with the possible exception of Roosevelt's closing the banks in 1933, the most dramatic, startling, and drastic in its effects of any so far.

This tenth anniversary is not an occasion for celebration. Mr. Nixon has said that much of what was decided then was mistaken. Few will disagree. But it was an important event from which we should try to draw lessons.

One element of the NEP, now commonly forgotten, was a tax cut matched by expenditure reduction of equal size. That was supposed to provide a noninflationary stimulus to output and employment. Many prominent economists sneered at this notion. They looked at the section of their elementary textbooks entitled "Balanced Budget Multiplier" and assured the nation that an equal reduction of taxes and expenditures would be depressing.

We (I was a member of the President's Council of Economic Advisers) tried to raise the discussion to the level of the intermediate textbook on public finance and argued that all taxes were not equal, all expenditures were not equal, and that the net effect of the package could not be deduced from the equality of the totals on the revenue and expenditure sides.

If we had thought of it we might have called our fiscal proposal a "supply-side" tax cut. That might have spared some economists the necessity of discovering America ten years later.

The only lesson from this venture in fiscal policy is the old one about the best-laid plans. The nicely balanced fiscal package that had been devised at Camp David was soon overwhelmed by other decisions and by unforseen events, so that the outcome for fiscal 1972 was quite different than had been planned. We never had a test of what the fiscal ingredient of the NEP would have accomplished.

The big news in the NEP was the comprehensive mandatory freeze on prices and wages. That is what people, including Mr. Nixon, have in mind when they speak of the mistakes of the program. There is no need to expatiate on what was and is wrong with price and wage controls. "Everybody" knows that mandatory wage and price controls are not a good idea in peacetime—everybody, that is, except Kenneth Galbraith and about 51 percent of the people.

The instructive point about the 1971 controls is that they were put in place by a president whose ideological opposition to them was fortified by a revulsion acquired during youthful experience on the staff of the wartime price control agency and who was advised by the free market "theologues," in Galbraith's term. The lesson is that being opposed to controls is not a sufficient safeguard against imposing them. What is required is a policy that will stop the acceleration of inflation without controls and without accompanying unemployment on a scale that the public considers unacceptable.

The great mistake which led to controls was that the administration, the Democratic opposition, and much of the intellectual leadership gave the public the impression that there was a way out of the inflation without unemployment. (In 1971, 6 percent unemployment was considered "much.") When this turned out not to be achievable, avoiding the move to controls was exceedingly difficult.

It is even less likely that Mr. Reagan will impose controls than it was that Mr. Nixon would do so, if for no other reason than that 1981–1984 comes after 1969–1972. But still, the probability even with Mr. Reagan is not zero, and it is worth taking the precaution of not promising economic results that may not be deliverable, in an effort to reduce the risk that public disappointment will force the government into policies it would not prefer.

From today's perspective the most interesting element of the policy of August 15, 1971 was the closing of the gold window, as it was then described. There is more attention now than in a long time to the idea of restoring the gold standard, and the decision of 1971 may shed some light on that idea.

Presumably, what is meant by restoring the gold standard is that the government would commit itself to keeping the free market price of gold constant in dollars, by buying or selling gold at the fixed price. Support for this idea is said to be provided by two propositions.

The first is that a commitment to a fixed price of gold would, if adhered to, yield a more stable general price level than any other conceivable rule of monetary policy. The rationale for this is the belief that the price of gold tends to be fairly stable relative to the prices of "things in general," so that if the price of gold in dollars is kept stable the price of "things in general" will be stable.

The second proposition is that the commitment to fixing the price of gold is more likely to be adhered to than any other rule, because abandoning the gold rule would be a dramatic, conspicuous act which would violate a deeply held public belief in the value, or even sanctity, of gold—even though, or perhaps just because, the belief is "irrational."

Thus, in a gold-standard system the government is confronted with a choice between following a noninflationary policy, politically inconvenient as that might be in the short run, and abandoning the gold standard, presumably an even more repugnant act politically. Faced with this choice, the government would opt for price stability.

What does the experience of August 1971 tell us about this argument?

Of course, when President Nixon "closed the gold window," saying that the United States would no longer be committed to paying gold to foreign treasuries and central banks at a fixed price on demand, the link between gold and U.S. economic policy had already become very weak. That link had been weakened by a series of actions of the previous sixty years—the establishment of the Federal Reserve System in 1913, the prohibition on ownership of gold by American citizens in 1933, the establishment of the International Monetary Fund in 1944, the elimination of gold reserve requirements against Federal Reserve liabilities to banks in 1965, and the 1968 agreement that the major central banks would no longer exchange gold with the private market, among other actions.

In fact, the gold window was already closed before Mr. Nixon declared it closed in 1971. That is, the major central banks of the world knew with a high probability that if they asked us for gold they would not get it, simply because we didn't have enough. When the British came in that August and asked for $3 billion of gold they were only checking whether that generally held belief was correct. The question at Camp David was whether to acknowledge the existing state of affairs or to try to postpone that acknowledgment in the hope that the condition would change.

Even though acknowledging that the window was closed does not, in this perspective, seem such a historic step, the people at Camp David that weekend did consider that they were cutting the dollar's last link to gold, with the possibly serious effects economically and politically. The issue did not appear in the conventional terms of sticking to the gold standard and fighting inflation versus abandoning the gold standard and tolerating inflation.

Insofar as there was a connection, closing the gold window did not permit less anti-inflationary action but required more anti-inflationary action. There were people, at home and abroad, who regarded our link to gold as an anchor against runaway inflation in the United States. If we were to cut loose from that anchor we would have to offer them some assurance, which was one reason for packaging the closing of the gold window with the price-wage freeze.

For some of the participants in the August 1971 meeting the choice was not gold versus inflation but was gold versus free markets. One must remember that in the summer of 1971 the country was going through one of its spasms of hysteria about the balance of payments, the balance of trade, and, particularly, competition from Japan Inc. This anxiety was stimulating demands for quotas or higher tariffs on imports and for retaining the controls on capital flows that President Nixon had promised to remove. Cutting loose from gold was a way of defusing these demands for restraints on trade and capital movements by increasing the possibility for achieving international adjustment through changes in the dollar exchange rate.

When President Nixon decided to declare that the gold window was closed he knew that there might be serious political repercussions. But these repercussions did not appear. For a great many people closing the gold window was welcomed as a declaration of national economic independence. A much larger number didn't care. There was no more sign of a deep-seated loyalty to gold in 1971 than there had been on any of the other occasions when the government took steps to dilute the role of gold.

This says nothing about whether the action on gold in 1971 was correct. I believe it was wise, but that is another story. The experience of 1971 does suggest that it is unrealistic to think that the gold standard will present governments with an unequivocal choice between inflation and adherence to gold which governments will be forced to make in favor of gold because the public has a strong emotional attachment to it.

The Chief Executive as Chief Economist

Reprinted from *Essays in Contemporary Economic Problems: Demand, Productivity, and Population* [1]

Summary

Presidents have been playing an increasingly active role in the management and exposition of economic policy, especially policy relating to inflation. Power and responsibility has moved to the president from the subordinate executive agencies, from the Congress, and possibly also from the Federal Reserve.

Presidents typically come into office little prepared for this function—less prepared than for the performance of their other functions. Such experience as they may have had with economic problems has usually not extended to macroeconomic problems but has been confined to the concerns of single states or to a few sectoral interests. Moreover, people who become presidents tend not to be the kind of people who have much interest in economics as a "scientific" subject, being more happy and more able at less abstract, more personal matters. The process of running for the presidency and of taking stands on economic issues does not serve to educate the candidate. It is more likely to enmesh him in commitments that have not been carefully thought out and that turn out to be embarrassing if he is elected.

A president will, therefore, be highly dependent on advice in the field of economics, more dependent than he is in the other

[1] American Enterprise Institute for Public Policy Research, Washington, D.C., and London, 1981, pp. 53–78.

major fields of his concern. How he organizes to get that advice is important.

In earlier times presidents seem to have relied on outside advice—advice from people outside the government in whose knowledge and judgment they had confidence. Some presidents have set up formal bodies of outsiders—such as labor leaders and businessmen—to advise them. And there are many self-designated study groups prepared to advise the president. The contribution of outside advisers has, however, been small. The outsiders usually do not learn enough about the current issues, or do not learn soon enough, to get into the decision-making flow in government. The outsiders can make a contribution insofar as they influence the general pattern of opinion in the country about the general and durable questions, and so affect the climate within which the president operates. But that always makes them irrelevant with respect to the decisions immediately before the president. Moreover, those close to the president often doubt the outsiders' loyalty to the president and therefore the trustworthiness of their advice.

The Reagan administration has established a body of economic advisers who could be called outside insiders. These people are not in the government but have been supporters of Ronald Reagan and, for the most part, have worked in previous Republican administrations. Whether this board will be valuable remains to be seen, but in the best of cases its influence is likely to be small relative to that of the people continuously on the scene.

New presidents always say that they intend to rely on the cabinet for advice. But experience with the cabinet or cabinet-size committees in several administrations shows that procedure not to be workable or durable. It involves too many people talking too much about subjects of which they know too little.

At the other extreme from the cabinet system of advice would be a one-to-one relation between the president and a chief economic adviser on whom he counts for information, discussion, and advice. This system has not existed in the case of economics as it did, for example, in the Kissinger-Nixon relation in foreign policy. The one-on-one system would be dangerous in the field of economics, where so much is in dispute and where it is essential that the president be aware of a range of views. Especially where the president is innocent of economics it can result in the adviser playing the role that should be played by the president.

The organization that seems always to emerge and that meets the needs of the situation is a small central committee of high-level economic officials who advise the president on what issues require his attention and on his options. The core of this committee is the secretary of the Treasury, the director of the Office of Management and Budget, and the chairman of the Council of Economic Advisers. In certain economic conditions other officials may be added more or less permanently to the group if their continuous participation is essential, as was the case when general economic policy was heavily affected by the price controls of the Nixon administration or by energy policy a little later. Other officials may be added on a case-by-case basis.

The effectiveness of this central committee will depend heavily on the way in which its members appreciate their relation to each other and to the president. The secretary of the Treasury is the senior economic official of the government and the natural chairman of the committee. He must not use his position to dominate the group or to exclude it from the decision-making process. The members of the group must be able to distinguish between the critical issues on which their differences need to be brought to the president's attention and those issues on which they should reach a consensus before approaching him. Each must be willing to work through the committee process and not to seek an end-run into the Oval Office. They must accept this process as part of their duty to the president and not try to manipulate him. This implies that they should be willing to give him a fair representation of all his eligible options, and not only the ones they prefer.

Since this committee process is very important, a major qualification for appointment to the positions that make up the committee, and especially for its chairman, presumably the secretary of the Treasury, is that they should be temperamentally suited for operating as members of such a consultative, advisory team.

The president will inevitably, and properly, be influenced in his economic decisions by considerations of political feasibility and attractiveness. The president's economic advisers cannot be expected to ignore such considerations. They should, however, try to make clear how much their judgments are based on economic factors and how much on political ones. The president will presumably look to others for advice on the political aspects of economic policy. He should seek political advisers who have a talent for giving political advice—a talent not necessarily demonstrated by long tenure in Washington or on the campaign trail. Also, an effort should be made to educate the political advisers on the main issues of economic policy before they give their advice to the president.

No relationship is of more potential value to the president in his conduct of economic policy than his relation with the Federal Reserve. There are abundant channels for the conduct of this relationship. On the whole, however, this relationship has been too distant, mistrustful, and even hostile. There should be much more recognition by both sides of their interdependence. The Federal Reserve needs the political support of the White House if it is not to be excessively vulnerable to public misunderstanding and congressional demagoguery. The administration needs the support of the Fed if it is to have a successful economic policy, and the administration cannot count on the Fed to provide a consistent policy, especially a consistently anti-inflationary policy, if the Fed cannot count on the political support of the administration. Developing a more candid and intimate relation between the president and the Federal Reserve is the most critical requirement for improving the process of economic policy making. The Federal Reserve and the administration should be able to agree on the objectives of macroeconomic policy for the next several years and on the way in which monetary policy would contribute to the achievement of these objectives. The agreement should also include recognition by the administration of the risks in the policy and of its obligation to stand by the Fed when it is attacked.

Forcing Presidents into Economics

Dissatisfaction with the performance of the economy, notably with inflation, has increasingly focused attention on the performance of the president as the nation's chief economist. We are used to the idea that when there is a major national problem, and inflation surely is one, the federal government has a responsibility for solving it. Moreover, inflation is an especially "presidential" problem. Its consequences are widespread, and the measures required to deal with it so comprehensive, that decisions cannot be delegated to cabinet secretaries, shared with Congress, or left to an independent agency, the Federal Reserve. Also, decision making about inflation and other macroeconomic problems is interwoven in a peculiar way with economics as a "science," if that is not too presumptuous a word. The usual qualities of a good president—foresight, persistence, judgment, persuasiveness, firmness, and so forth—are all important in dealing with inflation. Yet they are not sufficient. There must be an input from economics as a science. At the same time, the science is uncertain and divided. If the president cannot rely simply on intuition and native wit, neither can he look in the back of a textbook for reliable answers to his questions. He must use economics and not be used by it. Finally, since it is now generally recognized that the problem of inflation and its cure lie largely in the realm of public psychology, the president's unique role as communicator to the public has become a major aspect of anti-inflation policy.

All of these points are illustrated by the Reagan administration. Mr. Reagan has accepted, and asserted, responsibility for bringing down inflation. He has proposed a program whose success depends on the accuracy of forecasts of many economic magnitudes that most economists would regard as highly uncertain. He has chosen a rather eccentric school of economics and economists and has eschewed the opportunity for reducing his responsibility for error by staying close to the mainstream. In relations with Congress he has been unusually insistent that only the precise program he has proposed will solve the nation's economic problems. He has been unusually explicit in public advice and direction to the Federal Reserve. And he has vigorously played the role of public spokesman and salesman for the economic program.

Thus we see the president as the dominant decision maker in economic policy, as the judge of economics and economists, and as the major figure attempting to set the psychological tone of the economy. In those senses he is the nation's chief economist. But, of course, he is not an economist in the sense that 15,000 members of the American Economic Association are economists. That is, he is not a professional in this field. To be a professional economist is not a requirement for being a good president, although it is probably not a disqualification, either.

Few presidents have, when they enter office, even the level of understanding of economics one might find in an interested amateur or a fairly good third-year college student. Herbert Hoover was probably the most recent exception, the president in this century who was most abreast of the economics of his time. John Kennedy is said by his advisers to have been interested in economics and to have read some economics after his Harvard College days, but the evidence is weak and the authorities are suspect. Richard Nixon had a course in economics at Whittier College that he later described as having negligible intellectual content. Ronald Reagan is said to have read both Milton Friedman and Ludwig von Mises, but a reasonable guess is that it was the political and ideological writings of these authors rather than their scientific economics.

Even if future presidents have little book learning in economics, they have almost all been public officials and have had some experience in that capacity with economic problems and policies. A senator or congressman with twenty years of service will have acquired an amazing amount of knowledge of economic programs of government. Yet experience in Congress, or in a state governor's office, usually does not produce much knowledge of macroeconomic problems like inflation. Probably only two recent candidates had a useful background in this field. They were Richard Nixon and Hubert Humphrey, both of whom had been vicepresidents. Moreover, the value of this empirical background has been limited during a period increasingly dominated by a condition new to the United States, serious inflation, and less dominated by reverberations of the depression. In fact, one of the advantages of joining theory and history with personal observation is that it prepares one for the emergence of conditions outside one's personal experience. It must be confessed that economists trained in theory and history were not as quick as they should have been to adapt to the shifting state of the economy, but they were not the last to recognize the change.

People who run for the presidency usually have an idea of their general stance with respect to economic policy—a stance that may reflect their own convictions or their ideas of what the public likes to hear or, probably, a convenient marriage of the two. Thus, Kennedy thought of himself as a "liberal," Nixon regarded himself as a "modern conservative," and Reagan views himself as a "classical conservative." This kind of self-identification is not entirely meaningless. It does provide a president with some guidance in the choice of macroeconomic policies after he gets into office. Nevertheless, it still leaves a wide range of options open. Ronald Reagan's views of economic policy were probably more precisely defined than those of any other recent candidate who was not an incumbent. He wanted to free the private economy and revive the growth of total output and productivity, deemphasizing the reliance on public services and income redistribution as sources of the people's welfare and reversing the trends of the recent past. His various articulations of this theme before he became president, however, left open a great many possible strategies of macroeconomic policy. It was a tent big enough to cover supply-siders, monetarists, old-time-religionists, and probably many chastened veterans of Kennedy's New Economics. It signified nothing about whether the candidate was for or against "the gold standard" or "balancing the budget," or, if it may be taken as gospel that all politicians are "for" balancing the budget, when and under what conditions. It left open innumerable questions about the size of the budget and about monetary policy. The conspicuous exception, the point on which the Reagan philosophy had a concrete and specific embodiment, was a commitment to a 30 percent across-the-board tax cut to be put into place in three equal annual installments. Still, for those to whom that specific tax cut was not the totality of economic policy, that specific proposal raised many questions about the other measures that would have to be accommodated to it.

One might think that in an era when economic concerns such as inflation seem to dominate politics, a presidential campaign would provide the occasion and necessity for the candidate to formulate an economic policy, an exercise that would educate him and the public. But, of course, that is not the case. Candidates run on the economy, not on an economic policy. The candidates who are out of office run on the terrible state of the economy but do not get very specific about how they would make it better. The incumbent maintains that things are not so bad now and were worse when he came in or are getting better.

Thus, the campaign is unlikely to be an educational experience for a future president. In fact, it is more likely to be a diseducational experience. For the purpose of getting votes, the candidate finds himself saying things that he comes to believe and that will interfere with sound policy if he does become president. With respect to inflation, specifically, he may be led into thinking that the problem is due to some obvious and peculiar deficiency of his predecessor that will be easily overcome by his own arrival in the Oval Office. This is, of course, a mistake that may for some time keep the new president from appreciating the gravity of his task.

Although the campaign will not be an educational experience for the president, at least not where economics is concerned, it may yet be a period of preparation for the job that lies ahead. It has become standard practice for a candidate who is not an incumbent to appoint a number of task forces of experts to work during the campaign preparing issue papers that will be available to the candidate and his top officials after the election if he should win it. The contribution of these papers to policy seems to have been small. They are generally not read by the new president or given much weight by his economic officials, if, indeed, they read them either. On many matters the issue papers reflect much less information than will quickly become available to the new administration after it is in office or even during the transition, when it has access to the bureaucracy. If in the confusion of the transition they get into the hands of anyone in the new administration, it is likely to be either someone who already knows enough not to need the advice or someone who does not yet know enough to know that he needs it.

There is probably a more fundamental reason for the failure of these campaign-year issue papers to have more influence. The papers are the product of outsiders. During the campaign the candidate will have a group of economists traveling with him and advising him on the positions he should take in order to get elected. These are the insiders. They are the people who know what the candidate thinks and in whom he has confidence because they have demonstrated their usefulness and, above all, loyalty. The writers of issue papers are at some distance from these insiders. That is partly because the insiders are too busy and partly because some of the experts on the task forces do not want to become intimately involved in the political process. Usually the task forces are established without any clear idea of how their product will get into the decision-making flow if the election is won. The task forces serve the purpose during the campaign of demonstrating that the candidate wants to draw upon the assistance of "thinkers" and that a certain number of "thinkers" are willing to help him. When the campaign is over, that purpose has been served. Then the issue paper commands no more attention from the people who are inside than would similar papers volunteered by, say, the American Enterprise Institute or the Brookings Institution or an editorial in the *New York Times* or *Wall Street Journal.* The issue paper does not command more attention because it is not regarded as coming from "us," from members of the team.

Conceivably the national committees of political parties, especially the party that is out of office, could play a role in educating and preparing future candidates and presidents. They have concentrated on the problem of getting elected and have ignored the problem of governing once elected. The party out of office commonly does establish a committee or council to think and write about issues. During the Carter administration the Republican National Committee established a large network of such committees, including one on economics with several subcommittees. Still, the work of these committees is not taken very seriously, because everyone knows that the program of the party will be the program of the next candidate, whoever he may be, and that he is unlikely to be much influenced by the work of the party and may be embarrassed by it. There may still be a role for the party committee to play if it will try to promote discussion of basic philosophies and policies rather than to formulate specific programs. This might at least alert the potential candidates to the options and uncertainties before they get themselves too much committed, and the potential candidates may be more receptive to such guidance if it comes from their own party than if it comes from some other source. To undertake such an effort would, of course, require the party to recognize that good policy will not automatically spring full-blown from the brow of the next president if only he is one of theirs. So far this condition does not exist.

We may take it for granted that a new president will arrive on the scene, on the day after the election, with little preparation in economics or in economic policy. (The day of transformation has, of course, become the day after the election, not the day after the inauguration, because that is when he stops running and starts governing.) The new president may have a fairly specific and comprehensive program—that is, a list of things he wants to do. Recollections of Roosevelt's Hundred Days have put a premium on "hitting the ground running." Still, having a program is not the same as having a policy. A policy is what tells you what to do when you cannot get your program, or when conditions change, or when the program does not work—all of which are things that are quite likely to happen. In that sense presidents do not come into office with an economic policy.

Of course, despite what may be suggested by higher criticism from the media and academia, a person does not become president without being intelligent and a quick learner. A president will certainly learn a good deal about economics and about economic policy on the job. How much and what he learns, however, will depend in part on how he organizes to do his work, which is the subject of this essay.

An example of the possibilities and problems of learning from experience is provided by a conversation I had with President Nixon in the spring of 1973. He was considering restoring a freeze on prices and wages such as that which he had imposed in August 1971. I said, quoting Heraclitus, that you cannot step into the same river twice. He replied that you could if it was frozen. My lesson from experience was that the success, economic and political, of the 1971 freeze depended on conditions that would not recur, partly because we had had that freeze. His lesson was that the 1971 freeze had been a great success. The decision went his way—a freeze was restored—and the outcome went my way— the new freeze was an instant flop. That experience tells something about advising, also.

The obvious consequence of a president's inevitable limitations in the field of economics is that he will delegate many decisions and depend heavily on advice. This is true in all fields, of course, but it is much more true with respect to economics than with respect to foreign policy, usually the other main area of presidential attention. There are several reasons why.

Presidents tend to be skillful in interpersonal relations and to enjoy them. Foreign policy seems to them to be an area in which much can be achieved by dealings with other individuals— "Brezhnev and I"—across the table. Economic policy deals with abstractions or statistics or masses. The president cannot confront the GNP eyeball to eyeball, or even "the consumer." Some presidents think they can deal with economic problems on a person-to-person basis, the opposite number usually being the president of the AFL-CIO, but that is a mistake and leads to disappointment.

Presidents like to associate themselves personally with dramatic events, for reasons of vanity as well as of politics. There is hardly anything in economic action that can compete with the televised picture of the president alighting from Air Force One on the Peking airfield. The only similarly dramatic event in the field of economics in the past forty-five years was President Nixon's announcement of the price-wage freeze and the closing of the gold window on August 15, 1971. Still, even on that occasion President Nixon doubted that the public would be interested in a speech about economics and was reluctant to speak on a Sunday evening for fear of annoying millions of citizens whose favorite TV program, "Bonanza," would have to be preempted. A later attempt to dramatize and to personalize economic policy, President Ford's Inflation Summit, was a great bore, and its accompanying WIN buttons became a subject of ridicule.

There are two other reasons why presidents have not wanted to become involved personally in economics. Economics has been the scene of more defeats than triumphs lately, and presidents do not like to be closely associated with failure if they can help it. There is comfort in having an inflation czar who can be removed or forgotten if things go wrong. Also, the gap between amateurism and expertise may be greater with respect to economics than with respect to foreign policy and most other fields with which a president has to deal, and therefore he may be more inclined to rely on economic "experts." Perhaps that is a parochial opinion of mine, but presidents seem to share it. Richard Nixon, for example, regarded economics as almost a "hard" science, unlike the other so-called social sciences.

President Reagan seems to be an exception to these generalizations in some respects. He has identified himself personally with his economic program to a greater extent than his predecessors have done and has taken the role of the chief spokesman and salesman for it to the Congress and to the public. He has made the economic program his "moral equivalent of war." Whether he is really an exception remains to be tested. As this is written the Reagan program is mainly promises. Whether he will retain close identification with it in 1982 if these promises are not being met will be the test. In any case, the Reagan administration is not an exception to the proposition that presidents rely heavily on advisers for guidance on economics.

Outsiders as Advisers

There are many ways in which presidents can organize to get the advice they require about economic issues, including which decisions are sufficiently important to receive presidential attention and which can be largely delegated to others. In the past, presidents may have obtained significant amounts of advice from outsiders—people outside the executive branch. One has the picture, perhaps apocryphal, of President Eisenhower consulting with friendly CEOs on the golf course or around the bridge table. If that ever did happen, it happens no longer. Perhaps it is more difficult to exchange ideas while jogging or riding horseback than while playing golf or bridge.

Later presidents have attempted more formal ways of getting outside advice. These are usually "commissions" of business, labor, and possibly "public" representatives (typically professors) with whom the president has met from time to time. Presidents Nixon and Ford occasionally met with small groups of private economists. Mr. Nixon once said that he wanted to run the whole gamut, from Friedman to Rinfret. Still, these exchanges were too infrequent, too brief, and too superficial to have much effect on decisions.

The president delegates the function of receiving advice from the outside to his insiders, which of course increases his dependence on them. On some occasions this outside advice can be extremely useful—I think particularly of the advice we received when we were planning Phase II of the price-wage control system in the fall of 1971. On the whole, however, this outside advice has not been very helpful. There are undoubtedly many reasons, but two seem especially interesting and important.

One reason has to do with the character of the advice. From the standpoint of the president and his team, the outsiders almost always engage in special pleading—that is, they attempt to advance some special interest, as distinguished from the national interest. That is even true of economists, whose personal reputations are often tied up with certain doctrines, which they therefore feel compelled to advance in all circumstances. Only a rare person fails to take advantage of an opportunity to promote his own interest if he has an occasion to advise the White House.

It may be naive to suggest that outside advisers represent special interests, in distinction to the national interest represented by the president. Perhaps it would be fairer to say that the outside advisers represent special interests that are different from the special interest that the president represents. Yet this formulation does not change the situation from the standpoint of the president and his people, which is that the outside opinion has to be discounted.

I do not know whether it was ever thus. I have the impression of an earlier time, in the first fifteen years after World War II, when some private citizens accepted a responsibility to give objective advice on national policy. That may be only a romantic recollection of my younger days, however, when I participated in an organized effort to provide such counsel.

The other reason for the limited usefulness of outside advice lies in the character of the decisions the government makes. Where lasting strategy—questions of principle—are concerned, outside advice can be timely and informed. Such decisions are made infrequently, they are usually changed slowly, and they rely on general attitudes and experience about the way the world is, not on inside information. Outside advice can influence such choices, but they are obviously not the bread and butter of government. Typically an issue arises, an ad hoc group is assembled to work on it, a body of information is hastily pulled together, the whole decision-making apparatus is seized with the question for a few weeks, a conclusion is reached, and then the process is repeated for the next issue. The wave rises, peaks, and subsides before the outside world can mobilize to offer opinions.

Outside Insiders

The Reagan administration has established an economic advisory unit that has some of the characteristics of an inside group and some of an outside group. That is the President's Economic Policy Advisory Board. The members—thirteen as of April 1981—are insiders in the sense that they are all Republicans and were all supporters of the Reagan candidacy. All but three of them held office in the Nixon or Ford administrations. Yet they are outsiders in that none of them holds office in the Reagan administration. Their inside quality may give them a credibility with the administration that a more diverse group might not have, although that is bought at the expense of limiting the range of views represented. Their outside quality may still expose the administration and the president himself to a variety and independence of advice that might not surface from inside sources alone.

No one knows how this will work, and although the conception seems excellent, the implementation could be delicate. Much will depend on the willingness of the economic officials of the administration to expose to outside criticism ideas on which they have not yet committed themselves and on which various ones of them may have taken different positions with the president. Effectiveness will also depend on the candor of the advisory board members in expressing disagreement with the president or with some of his officials. If the board is merely a council of elders called in to bless the president's decisions, it will not be very useful.

The basic problem here, as in other aspects of the advisory relationship, is that the president has little basis for judging the quality of economic advice. Even if he could tell who are the best economists, he could not be certain that they would be the best advisers. He therefore tends to give very great weight to loyalty as a test. Still, the value of the advice will depend on its independence. There is danger of confusing loyalty with dependence and independence with disloyalty. The outside advisory board, consisting of independent people, will succeed if it can exercise its independence without suggesting a lack of loyalty that will make opinions suspect.

One value of the board is that it will bring a body of experience that the new team will not have. That will be a transitory advantage, however, or it will seem so. The new group will acquire its own experience, which the board members will not have, and that may seem to make the older experience obsolete.

The Cabinet System

Despite these questions, the board of outside insiders may prove to be a highly valuable device. Nevertheless, we may expect the president to continue to rely primarily on insiders. If he follows precedent he will think, when first elected and confronting the problem, that he will rely on the cabinet for advice. Nothing seems more reasonable. The cabinet officer charged with a particular subject—the secretary of the Treasury, in the case of most economic questions—will explain the problem to the group of wise, objective, broad-gauged men and women gathered around the cabinet table; and out of their discussion the president will get what he needs for making a decision.

The trouble is that the cabinet is not like that. The cabinet usually consists of capable men and women, but being wise, objective, and broad-gauged is the lesser part of the qualities for which they have been chosen. They have been selected for knowledge of a particular subject, ability to manage a large enterprise, political influence, and fulfillment of the requirement that women, blacks, Hispanics, and so forth be represented in the top levels of the government. There is nothing wrong with these criteria, given the usual functions of a cabinet member, but these are not the people the president would most want to rely on for advice about fields not their own. Moreover, they tend to be ambitious and to see pleasing the president as one way to advance their aspirations. Some of them, through a lifetime spent on the stump, have become intolerably long-winded and are boring talkers in a small group. As a result, even a president who tries is likely to find soon that the cabinet is not a useful consultative body.

An effort to bring something like the cabinet into an advisory role on economic matters was made by President Nixon in 1969, when he set up the Cabinet Committee on Economic Policy (CCEP). This committee was not set up because anyone thought it would be the best way to make economic policy. It was created in part to comfort certain cabinet members who thought they were entitled to participate in the decision-making process.

The CCEP consisted of the president and vice-president, all the cabinet members whose main responsibility was economic, a representative of the State Department, the director of the Bureau of the Budget—later the Office of Management and Budget (OMB)—the chairman of the Council of Economic Advisers (CEA), and the president's two counselors—twelve people in all. The two other members of the CEA participated regularly, as did some other people occasionally. The president carried through gamely, meeting with this crowd about once a month for a year. It served at least one purpose for him: It enabled him to watch in action some of his cabinet members whom he had not known before and to acquire some impression of their qualities. Still, it was not an efficient way to make decisions. Too many people spent too much time talking about subjects about which they knew too little. Moreover, the president was not going to share his thoughts with so many people who had no need to know them. At the end of 1969 the president turned the chairmanship of the group over to the vice-president. That was for all practical purposes the end of CCEP, because the cabinet members had no interest in attending meetings chaired by the vice-president.

Mr. Reagan's experiment with the use of the cabinet as a

committee to discuss economic policy was even briefer. After about one month of his term he decided to use instead of the cabinet, an economics group which, however, as initially established was almost as large as the cabinet. Nevertheless, it immediately appeared that this group was not the scene of the action either.

At the other extreme from using the cabinet as a source of advice on economic policy is the one-on-one system. The president meets regularly with one chosen adviser who serves as his source of information, ideas, and recommendations and with whom he discusses his thinking during the process of reaching a decision. This is the kind of relation that both Presidents Nixon and Ford apparently had with Henry Kissinger. No president has had quite that relation with anyone in the field of economics, although the relation between Richard Nixon and John Connally approached it for a time.

The one-on-one system can be dangerous. The president is likely to be, or at least to feel, quite inadequate in his understanding of economic questions, compared with his adviser. The result can be that the adviser becomes the policy maker, which is a mistake. Even if the two parties are in the proper relation to each other, the two-handed decision-making process may be too unstable. That is, it may not take much of a change of mood or perception by the two people to produce a lurch of policy, which might have been avoided if a larger number of people, with different temperaments and viewpoints, had been consulted.

President Carter came into office with the idea that he was going to operate by what was called the "spokes-of-the-wheel" system. He would meet separately with each of his economic officials and advisers, obtain the views of each on the current economic policy issue, and make his own decision on the basis of what he had heard. This is a clearly unworkable process. It is wasteful of the president's time. More important, it deprives him of the advantage of seeing the interaction among his advisers. He does not get the assistance he should get from each of his experts in evaluating the arguments of the others.

The Central Committee

In recent years, although some administrations have made starts in other directions, the organization for giving advice on economic policy to the president has always boiled down to a small committee, of three to six people, which could be supplemented as necessary by others who had special knowledge or responsibility in a particular field. This committee set the economic agenda for the president and the executive office, made some decisions on its own, recommended decisions on other matters to the president, and on the most important matters, presented to him an analysis indicating the more eligible options and the arguments for and against them.

During the 1960s the central committee was called the Troika, consisting of the secretary of the Treasury, the director of the Bureau of the Budget, and the chairman of the Council of Economic Advisers. To some extent this composition of the group reflected the view that federal economic policy was fiscal policy. As Arthur Okun, chairman of the CEA in the later days of the Johnson administration, explained the rationale for the Troika: Treasury had the revenue, Budget had the expenditures, and the CEA had the deficit. There were, however, strong reasons for these three to remain the core of the central committee even when presidential economics expanded far beyond fiscal policy. The secretary of the Treasury is the senior economic official of the government. The director of the OMB, with the assistance of an expert and mainly permanent staff, is the best-informed person in the administration on all the programs of government, by virtue of his agency's responsibility for monitoring the expenditures of all the agencies. Of all the economic officials in government, the chairman of the CEA is institutionally the most objective in the sense that he has no parochial departmental or agency interests. Of all the professional economists in government, the CEA chairman is the most presidential, and of all the presidential advisers he is the most professional.

As presidential economics expanded beyond fiscal policy, the Troika was also expanded, in two quite different ways. A new organization, the Quadriad, was established to join the chairman of the Federal Reserve with the Troika. The relations of the president with the Federal Reserve have a special nature, which will be discussed below.

The other expansion of the Troika was the addition of other executive office people on a more or less equal basis with the original three, as the rise of particular problems dictated. In January 1971 a new White House agency, the Council on International

Economic Policy (CIEP), was established in an effort to coordinate
the often contradictory behavior of the State, Treasury, and Commerce departments and other agencies in matters of foreign economic policy. The director of CIEP then began regularly to attend
meetings of the Troika. When price and wage controls were insti-
tuted in August 1971 and became a major expression of presidential economic policy, the director of the Cost of Living Council
was added to the group. In 1973 when economic policy seemed
dominated by energy policy, the official mainly responsible for
energy was added.

This lineup has changed from time to time as economic conditions suggested a change of emphasis. Also, other agencies, such
as Agriculture or Labor, might be added for the consideration
of particular issues in which they had responsibility or competence. In general, as the situation has emerged, the Troika forms
a continuous core. It retains exclusive jurisdiction with respect
to budget policy and with respect to forecasting and analyzing
the macroeconomic condition. There may be two or three other
agencies that function as members of the central group on all
other questions, and the identity of these agencies changes from
time to time. Other agencies are brought into the circle on an
ad hoc basis for the consideration of particular issues. The Ford
and Carter administrations followed a similar pattern.

The secretary of the Treasury is the natural chairman of the
central committee, since he is the senior official, and in ordinary
circumstances the only "regular" cabinet member on the committee. There was a period when another official, designated as assistant to the president, served as chairman. That is not likely to
be a workable relation unless the designated person has quite
unusual personal stature, relationship to the president, and skill
in mobilizing a small group of near-equals. If he does not have
these qualities, the secretary of the Treasury, at least, will not
accept the committee as the normal channel through which his
advice goes to the president. He will seek his own approach, known
as the "end-run" in Washington, others will follow his example,
and the committee system will break down. That can happen even
if the Treasury secretary is the chairman; if he is not strong or
respected by the others, they will try to function outside the system
to the extent that the president permits.

A strong leader of the committee may operate either in an
exclusive way or in an inclusive way. On the one hand, he may

try to minimize the role of the other members and essentially use the committee as a facade for promoting his own ideas and influence. He will control the committee's agenda and be its most regular channel to the president. Thus, he can keep out of the committee's purview those subjects on which he wants the president to hear his views only, or first, and he can give the president his interpretation of the committee's advice.

Obviously, this exclusive approach forfeits the advantages of the committee system, however, and gets back to the difficulties of the one-on-one arrangement discussed above. The committee system works well only when the leader adopts an inclusive strategy, giving all members an opportunity to be heard in discussion of all major issues and to be represented in the advice that is communicated to the president.

In the Ford administration, the executive committee of the Economic Policy Board, which was what I call here the "central committee," operated with divided, or shared, leadership. The secretary of the Treasury served as chairman and chief public spokesman. A presidential assistant provided the secretariat, managing the agenda, assuring that all relevant agencies had an opportunity to be heard, and supervising the drafting of position papers for the president. This arrangement seems to have worked well. Among other results, it keeps the secretary of the Treasury as the leader of the group but it reduces the danger of his dominating it. The need for this arrangement, or its utility, was associated with rather special conditions in 1974. There was a secretary of the Treasury who had not been appointed by the new president and whose relation with the new president was uncertain—to the secretary, to the president, and to all the other people in the administration who need to know. At the same time there was a presidential assistant with long and close ties to the new president and with some background in the field of economics. The joint arrangement solved a number of problems. It is not, however, the ideal arrangement if there is a secretary who is close to the president and has his confidence and who is trusted by all the other participants to deal openly with them. In this case, as generally, the pattern of organization must be adapted to the persons on the stage.

The foregoing remarks have implications for the qualifications to be sought in a secretary of the Treasury. Secretaries of the Treasury are commonly chosen from the ranks of executives of large, successful financial or business firms. The qualities that attainment of such a position demonstrates are useful for the Treasury secretary. Still, it is not his only or even his principal function to run a large organization and exercise skill in dealing in the financial markets. At least as important is his role of leading but not dominating a group of diverse thinkers about economic policy, organizing and synthesizing but not settling issues, presenting issues fairly to the president, and representing his views persuasively to the Congress and the public. The qualities needed to perform this role may be found in Wall Street, but Wall Street success is not necessarily evidence of them.

The Options Paper

The key function of the central committee is to advise the president on what his critical decisions are, what the most eligible options are, and what the arguments for and against each of the options are. This advice can be presented in writing, orally, or in some combination, and the actual combination has depended on the preference of the president. President Nixon relied heavily on written presentations, reserving oral discussion for the most critical and difficult matters. President Ford preferred a larger element of face-to-face discussion with his advisers. Still, however much oral discussion there may be, a written basis seems essential. Writing down the options forces the committee members to concentrate on the main points and to specify the alternatives and arguments as precisely as they can. It also increases the opportunity for each member to see that his position is fairly stated. There is a danger that if the decision-making process relies too heavily on oral discussion, it may be too much influenced by persuasiveness and force of personality rather than by evidence and logic.

The options paper is the noblest work of the president's advisers—the most difficult and the most responsible. Its function is to help the president make a decision but not to make the decision for him. There are two dangers in writing an options paper. One is to tell too much, to include all information that is not demonstrably false or irrelevant and all options that might conceivably be chosen. That does not give the president the help he is entitled to have from his advisers. He is left foundering in a sea of facts and opinions that his advisers would have been more capable of dealing with than he is. It is the responsibility of the advisers to narrow the information and argument down to what is most probably true and relevant and the policy options that are most likely to be worth considering. Thus the preparation of an options paper requires the exercise of judgment about questions that cannot be conclusively answered by the facts. It is not only a prelude to decision making but also itself a decision-making process.

The other danger, which is more serious and more likely to occur, is that the options paper excessively limits the president's freedom of choice. One option can be described so much more attractively than the others that no reasonable person could fail to choose it. (The technique is suggested by Kissinger's Law of Options Papers, that the author should make his preferred policy "option B," because that is the one the president usually chooses.) This is likely to happen even if the authors of the paper do not consciously intend it. They will naturally attach more weight to the arguments for the option they prefer and present them more persuasively. One reason for relying on a committee rather than on a single person to advise the president is that differences among the members provide some protection against excessive restriction of the president's choices. More than that is required, however. The authors of the options paper must make a deliberate effort to give a fair presentation to the options worthy of consideration and not stack the deck in favor of their preferred option.

This points to some qualifications that a senior economic adviser should have. He should understand and share the president's general philosophy sufficiently that he does not exclude from consideration any options the president would want to consider if he knew about them. He should also be sufficiently loyal and responsible to the president, and sufficiently modest, not to try to force his own views upon the president by illegitimate means.

There is an anecdote that masters of ceremony who know little about economics love to use when introducing an economist as an after-dinner speaker: Harry Truman said that he wished he had a one-armed economic adviser, who would not say "on the one hand this and on the other hand that." But this longing for certainty reflects a mistaken conception of economics and economic advisers. On most of the issues that come to presidents, at least two possibilities should be considered, and often more. It is the responsibility of his economic advisers to inform the president of these possibilities.

Economics and Politics

Of course, the president's decision is not absolutely confined to the options presented in the options paper. If the president feels strongly enough he can certainly get his preferred option included in the paper and can even be sure that it is recommended by at least one of his advisers. If necessary he can broaden the circle of his advisers until he finds one who will recommend what he wants. Thus, it probably never happens that the president makes a decision that is not supported by some adviser.

Still, for the president to make a decision outside the range of options spontaneously suggested by his economic officials and to force his own preference into the range of eligible options is rare. There is a view, especially congenial to academic economists, that the president's economic advisers make suggestions to him that are sound economics and that the trouble begins when he departs from these suggestions for "political" reasons. This is a naive view of what happens. As I have already suggested, his advisers give the president a range of options from which to choose, which means that they are options that cannot be ruled out on economic grounds. The president must bring something other than economics into the decision-making process. He can exercise some judgment about the relative probability of the various possibilities and about the extent to which they conform to his own vision of the way the world works or should work. He will probably also consider the political implications of the various options.

If the decision turns out to be wrong, it is unfair to attribute the error to the perversion of sound economics by politics or to attribute it only to that. The fault is usually with the economics in the first place. If the economics had been better, the erroneous policy would not have been included in the list of options from which the president chose. This is clearly illustrated by two seriously mistaken policy decisions that I had the opportunity to observe. One was the decision to impose price and wage controls in August 1971, and the other was the decision to push an expansionist fiscal policy at the beginning of 1972. Each of these decisions was politically useful to the president. Still, each of them was recommended by some of the president's economic officials, including economists, and was supported by a large number of economists outside the government. Probably neither of these decisions would have been taken if they did not have endorsement by some economists, especially by some the president regarded as part of his "team."

The presence of political considerations in presidential decisions about economics is certainly not surprising and is not necessarily to be decried. There are, however, three cautionary comments to be made about this.

1. The president should know when the advice that he gets is based on economic analysis and when it is based on political judgments. When President Truman's chairman of the Council of Economic Advisers, Leon Keyserling, told the president that a certain course of action should be taken because it was good politics, the president is said to have responded: "Don't try to teach your grandmother to suck eggs." It is probably unrealistic to expect that in their advice to the president, his economic officials will avoid considerations of political feasibility or political effectiveness. They live in an atmosphere where such considerations are always present. Still, they are not the people on whom the president would rely most for political advice, and they should try to make it clear to him what they believe as professional economists and what they believe as political amateurs.

2. It should go without saying that when the president relies on political "experts" for advice about that aspect of economic decisions, he should seek the best qualified individuals he can find. The credentials of the people who can pass as political experts in the White House are quite uneven. Although some are people of experience and outstanding judgment, others have arrived at their position by serving as advance men in a victorious presidential campaign or by working as administrative assistants to defeated congressmen. The problem is not that there is too much politics in the decisions but that the politics is often too shallow. Also, the president's political advisers cannot well appraise the political implications of proposed economic policies if they do not understand their economic implications. This calls for a serious effort to explain these matters to the president's aides whom he is likely to call upon for political advice.

Efforts to bring the political advisers into the discussion of economic policy at an early stage are not likely to be successful. The economic officials will not want their recommendations to be influenced by the political judgment of a political adviser, whom they will certainly consider ignorant of economics, before those recommendations have gone to the president. They recognize that the president will make a political judgment and that he will be influenced by his political advisers, but they do not want the president's judgment to have been foreclosed by their prior agreement with a political adviser. At the same time the political adviser will not want his judgment merged with that of a group of economists before he has had a chance to present his views to the president. Responsible advising of the president will depend upon the effort of the economic advisers and the political advisers to understand the position of the others and to respect the difference in their functions.

3. Although the president must operate within the political constraints that exist and cannot adopt policies that the public will not tolerate, he can also to some extent change those constraints by using his unequaled opportunities to talk to the American people. The president is not confined to choosing the option that he considers most acceptable politically. He also has a responsibility to try to make the economically desirable policy politically acceptable. Presidents commonly take too defeatist a view of the possibility of moving public opinion and too readily accept the constraints imposed by the existing state of opinion. One reason is that they are too short-sighted and place more value on conforming to today's opinion than on trying to change tomorrow's. What is commonly called communication with the public is usually an effort not to change public opinion but to mobilize existing opinion in support of the president's program.

Speeches as Policy

One of the main instruments by which the president can try to influence public opinion or economic policy is his speeches. The importance of speeches and speechwriters in the formation and implementation of economic policy is usually underestimated. A speech is not only a way of influencing public opinion so as to make policy acceptable. It can also be itself a policy action in the sense that it can directly influence confidence and expectations and so influence economic behavior in the private sector. Moreover, the preparation of a speech can precipitate precise decisions on policy issues on which there would otherwise have been vagueness and differences of interpretation within the administration, and after the speech is delivered it serves as a guide throughout the government to the president's thinking.

Some presidents may make a large and specific contribution to their own speeches. This is unusual, however. A president will not get good speeches unless he wants them and recognizes one when he sees it, and he will usually rely heavily on a speechwriter. The success of the president's economic policy will depend greatly on the qualities and position of this person. He not only should be a good writer but also should have a good relation with the president, so that the president will communicate his wishes freely to him and be receptive to the writer's ideas. He should be able to work closely with the economic officials, be able and willing to receive instruction about economics from them, and have sufficient status to negotiate points of disagreement among the persons who participate in deciding on the form and content of a major presidential speech.

Relations with the Federal Reserve

No relationship is of more potential value to the president in his conduct of economic policy than his relation with the Federal Reserve and especially with its chairman. In principal this relation can run in both directions. That is, advice and influence can flow from the chairman of the Fed to the president and from the president to the chairman.

The advice that flows from the chairman to the president can be extremely helpful for several reasons. It will often be true that the chairman has much more experience with national economic policy than the president or any of his inside advisers. The chairman will have the services of a larger economic research staff than the Treasury, the OMB, and the CEA together contain. Through his contact with the twelve Federal Reserve Banks he will be informed about what is going on in the regions of the country, and through his contacts with foreign central banks he will be informed about economic conditions in the rest of the world. Also, the chairman has a degree of independence of the president, even if he has been appointed by the president then in office, which may make him more likely than other advisers to tell the president the bad news or to question the policies the president has adopted or is considering.

The flow in the other direction, the opportunity to influence monetary policy, can be even more valuable to the president. Nothing that happens in Washington is likely to be more critical for the achievement of the president's economic goals than the conduct of monetary policy. It is important that the president's goals and the Federal Reserve's policies should be in harmony with each other. The Federal Reserve's policy for monetary expansion should contribute to achieving the president's goals for the expansion of the economy. That does not necessarily mean that the Fed's policies should be attuned to the president's goals, but it does mean that there should be mutual adaptation. That is to be sought in the relation between the two parties.

Fairly elaborate procedures have grown up for the exercise of this relationship. The chairman of the Federal Reserve meets weekly with the secretary of the Treasury. The three members of the Council of Economic Advisers meet every two weeks with the seven members of the Board of Governors of the Federal Reserve. The Quadriad, consisting of the chairman of the Fed, the secretary of the Treasury, the director of OMB, and the chairman of the CEA, meets with the president on no fixed schedule but on the average eight or nine times a year. Other involvements have developed from time to time. When the administration's economic policy became focused on the Cost of Living Council during the Nixon price-wage control period, for example, the chairman of the Fed met with the council, although he did not become a member of it.

These procedures seem adequate to their purpose. Still, the relationship between the president and the chairman has not developed to its full potential value, the degree of the shortcoming varying with the personalities of the parties. On the side of the advice from the chairman about the administration's economic policy, the main problem seems to be one of trust. The same independence that makes the chairman's advice peculiarly valuable means that he is not a member of the president's team. His objectives will not be thought to be identical with the president's, and that will be correct. Moreover, the president's inside advisers may feel threatened if the chairman gains too much influence, and they may resent public statements by the chairman that are not supportive of the administration's policy. For these reasons there may be a tendency not to take the chairman's advice on the administration's economic policy at face value. These are not, however, very serious difficulties and can be largely overcome by persons who appreciate the importance of doing so.

The difficulties on the other side, the obstacles to achieving any specific and operational agreement between the administration and the Fed on monetary policy, or even to having any constructive discussion of monetary policy, seem more serious (although I must acknowledge that this view may be biased by my having been on the administration side of this relation rather than on the Federal Reserve side). The problems here are organizational and intellectual rather than mainly personal. Discussion with the chairman of the Fed is inhibited by the fact that he cannot speak for the board as a whole. Discussion with the board is inhibited by the unwillingness of the members to reveal to outsiders the differences among them. The Federal Reserve's tradition of secrecy is also an obstacle to discussion. An even more important difficulty is the Federal Reserve's posture, only now changing a little, that all decisions are open for review at least as often as every four weeks, when the Open Market Committee (the board's chief policy-making body) meets.

The main problem, however, is the usual interpretation of the Federal Reserve's independence. This has led to the extreme delicacy on the part of the administration in pushing any precise policy upon the Federal Reserve and extreme reluctance on the part of the Federal Reserve to enter into any specific discussion of monetary policy.

All of this is understandable, but its inadequacy is becoming clearer and clearer. The country urgently needs a moderate-term disinflationary economic policy in whose durability there can be confidence. President Reagan has promised such a policy. This policy will have to be a joint policy, agreed to by the administration and the Federal Reserve. If it is the president's policy alone, without commitment by the Federal Reserve, there will be real doubts that he can carry it out. If it is the Federal Reserve's policy alone, there will be real doubts that the agency will have the political strength to carry it out.

The Reagan administration, at least in its early months, seemed to have embarked on a new tack in the relations between the presidency and the Federal Reserve. Instead of the previous hesitancy about openly and admittedly giving advice or directions to the Federal Reserve, the new administration made strong public statements about what it thought the Federal Reserve should do, in highly specific terms, that not only were highly critical of the Federal Reserve's practice of the immediate past but also seemed at variance with the Fed's current conception of its proper policy. Specifically, the administration put much more emphasis on the stability of the rate of growth of the money supply in the short run than the Federal Reserve did. At the same time, the administration asserted its regard for the independence of the Fed and showed no wish to take over its responsibilities in a formal way.

It is doubtful that this confrontational approach will be more successful in getting the president and the country what they need than the previous more delicate approach was. There is a rationale for the independence of the Federal Reserve. That independence was given, or justified, by the need for the Fed to do politically unpopular things. Such need, in this time of dangerous inflation, is greater than ever. Ways to get around that need are conceivable—the gold standard or a constitutional amendment controlling the rate of growth of the money supply. But if these are solutions at all, they are not for the next few years. For now it is necessary to strengthen the resolve of the Federal Reserve to fight inflation, and that requires strengthening the ability of the Federal Reserve to resist the attacks that will be made upon it in the course of the fight against inflation.

The main reason for the failure of the Federal Reserve to restrain inflation is its fear of the popular dissatisfaction and congressional attacks that will ensue if the anti-inflationary process results, as is likely, in higher unemployment and higher interest rates for a time. Public criticism of the Fed by the administration weakens public regard for the independence of the agency—contributes to undermining the idea that this institution should be treated with special respect—and increases the vulnerability of the Federal Reserve. The administration cannot expect to have a monopoly on criticism of the Fed. The danger that the Fed will be attacked when the less pleasant consequences of its disinflationary efforts appear, or that the Fed will be excessively timid for fear of such attacks, is increased if the administration has publicly discredited the monetary authority. That danger is especially great if the administration has given the public the impression that the disinflationary process need not involve any unpleasant side effects.

The Federal Reserve needs the political support of the White House just as the White House needs the economic leverage of the Federal Reserve if a national macroeconomic policy is to succeed. Developing a more candid and intimate relation between the president and the Federal Reserve is the most critical requirement for improving the process of economic policy making. Through such a relation the administration and the Federal Reserve should be able to agree on the objectives of macroeconomic policy for the next several years and on the way in which monetary policy would contribute to the achievement of these objectives. That need not include agreement on operating procedures or on day to day policy, although there is no reason why such matters should not be discussed between the parties. The agreement should also include a recognition by the administration of the risks in the policy and of its obligation to stand by the Fed if and when it is attacked. Such an agreement could do much to supply the confidence now lacking in the continuity and determination of anti-inflationary policy.

PART 3

The Old Conservatism

A Grumpie Talks to Yumpies

The *Wall Street Journal*,
August 13, 1984

LIKE the Yippie radicals and the Yumpies (Young Upwardly Mobile Professionals), we Grumpies (Grown-up Mature People) experienced the civil-rights struggle, Vietnam, and Watergate. We were impressed with those experiences and learned from them. But we have experienced more history than that. We experienced the Great Depression, the rise of Hitler, Munich, World War II, the revelation of the concentration camps, the subjugation of Eastern Europe by the USSR, the Berlin Wall, and forty years of unparalleled prosperity in the United States, Western Europe, and Eastern Asia. There are about 38 million of us who were fifteen years of age or older in 1939, and so remember something of the Depression and the origins of World War II.

This experience does not leave us with much nostalgia for a bygone golden age. We believe that in this time and in this country, we are as close to a golden age as we have ever been. We live in a society that is more free, more just, not to say richer, than any ever known before, or known now elsewhere in the world. One thing that distinguishes us from the Yippies and the Yumpies is that we consider ourselves extremely fortunate to be here. This is especially true for those of us, and there are many, who knew a parent or grandparent who came to this country, mostly from Europe. We bless them for not leaving us to be born somewhere else.

We also know that this happy state we are in did not come naturally and was not given to us free. It had to be paid for,

221

fought for, and died for. Much of this paying, fighting, and dying was done by preceding generations. But we also did our share, and we take pride in that. We do not think that our generation was a failure that left the world and the country in a mess that the Yippies and the Yumpies now have to clean up or flee.

Some 400,000 Americans of our generation died in World War II. We do not think it was a mistake to fight the war. The world would be a truly horrible place today if the Allies had not fought World War II. But there was a lesson there. If the United States and its Allies had been more farsighted, if they had had a more realistic conception of the danger that existed in the world, if they had rearmed earlier and stopped aggression sooner, most of those lives could have been saved. The lesson is not to be afraid to be strong.

It was not only by military means that our generation defended the Free World (a phrase that we consider full of meaning). We paid for the Marshall Plan, which Winston Churchill described as the most magnanimous act in the history of statecraft. (Quoting Churchill is a sign of being a Grumpie.) This was a vital step in the reconstruction of the European and world economies. Moreover, we paid for tens of billions of dollars in economic aid to the less-developed world. The Yippies and Yumpies did not invent the nonmilitary element in foreign policy.

Most of us were too young to participate in the policy-making process of the Great Depression, even as voters. But we saw enough to realize that the economic travails of the 1930s were incomparably more severe than anything experienced since. And we also see that it was mainly due to policies initiated in the previous generation and followed by ours that the Yippies and Yumpies have been spared a repetition of the 1930s.

We are impressed by the fact that we came through the 1930s—a time of real crisis and wild ideas—with the free system basically intact in America. This is a tribute to the fortitude of the American people and to the loyalty to the American system that is in their bones. The Depression showed that change was required. There was a great deal of policy experimentation. What survived was, on the whole, consistent with the free system and in some respects enhanced freedom.

Our generation witnessed a great increase in the economic security and economic opportunity afforded the American people—across the board. If these gains did not come equally to all, probably being realized more by the middle class than by either the very top or the very bottom, they were pretty widely shared. The gains were partly the result of public policies building on the start made during the Depression. The sharing of the gains was partly the result of the demands of the disadvantaged, which resulted in corrections through changes both in private attitudes and in public policy. As the ruling class of the period, white males may feel some guilt at having resisted claims of blacks and women for equal treatment. But we may also say that our resistance was not very strong or prolonged, and that many white males helped the claimants from an early stage.

Most of the gains so widely shared during the last generation resulted from the big increase in national output and productivity that began after World War II. Our generation produced that mainly by our private behavior in saving, investing, and educating ourselves and our children. We also contributed through public policy, including public expenditures for education and research. Because of national security requirements, plus interest on debt accumulated during the Depression and World War II, combined with new programs for the elderly and disadvantaged, our federal budgets were much larger, relative to GNP, than they had ever before been in peacetime. Although we were less religiously devoted to balanced budgets than previous generations, by and large we paid for these expenditures through taxes. From 1946 to 1980, the total federal deficit was only 1.1 percent of the total GNP. Federal deficits did not divert much of the national output from private investment.

There are Yippies and Yumpies of the extreme right who believe that the development of the Keynesian welfare state in our generation was a great mistake. They feel that they have been called to rescue the nation from our softheadedness. We reject that, just as we reject the claim of the Yippies and Yumpies of the left that they have a call to rescue the nation from our hardheartedness. No one who remembers the depressed 1930s, or even knows anything about the prosperous 1920s, can deny that the concern and compassion of our generation have made society better. We feel confirmed in that opinion by the Reagan experience. This administration, less sympathetic to the developments of the past fifty years than any other, still found little to undo when it came to responsibility.

We know that there is work still to be done. Much is required to defend the Free World, to broaden opportunity further and to assure continued economic growth. We do not think that the nation can rest on our achievements or simply repeat the policies of our generation. But we think it is wrong to disregard or belittle our experience.

We are especially irritated by the cult of "new ideas." Most of the things bearing this label are not ideas at all, but only platitudinous longings. And of those that might reasonably be called ideas, very few are new. What is meant by a new idea is one that is not now being implemented. But usually there are good reasons why these ideas are not being implemented. Either experience or analysis has rejected them. What is needed in policy is not the capacity to generate or revive "catchy" ideas, preferably reducible to bumper stickers. What is needed is good judgment in selecting among the ideas that are out there and in executing the ones that are selected.

Our great worry is the way in which our national security problem is being viewed by the Yippies and Yumpies (of all ages). The problem is being looked at excessively through the experience of Vietnam. One can understand that if this experience is considered in isolation—as a war in itself—it might yield the lesson that military action does not pay. But Vietnam was a campaign in a larger war, what George Will calls "The War Against the Totalitarian 1939– ." (George Will is too young to be a real Grumpie, but I would nominate him for honorary membership.) Vietnam was not a successful campaign, but the war continues. The United States cannot afford to withdraw from it. The cost of failure and the possibilities of success are both too great for that. We realize that the war has economic and moral dimensions as well as a military one. But it is only in the military dimension that the United States is in danger.

Our worries about the future of America—about the national security and about the growth of the economy—are not worries for ourselves. We have reached an age where we are not very likely to be much affected by what might happen in either area. But the Yippies and Yumpies are our children and the parents of our grandchildren. We are concerned for them. We would feel more confident of their future if they showed more capacity to learn from our experience.

Conservatively Speaking

Public Opinion, February/March 1981

THE temptation for conservatives to stretch the limits of responsible discussion of economic questions has been strong in the past twenty or thirty years for several reasons. The background noise of liberal talk was loud, and the popular media were not receptive to conservative discourse. To penetrate the media curtain and be heard against the background of liberal talk, it seemed necessary to express conservative views in extreme, black-and-white letters.

Also, when conservatives were few, they had to huddle together for protection and could not allow differences among them to be exploited by the opposition. I have had some recent experiences with this problem. About a year and a half ago, belief in the wisdom of a constitutional amendment requiring a balanced budget was considered a test of loyalty to conservative doctrine. How long ago that seems! I wrote an article questioning the idea, and as a reward I have been frequently quoted by Arthur Schlesinger, Jr., as a witness against the balanced budget. He quotes me not because he has a high regard for my opinion, for he never quotes me on any other subject. He just finds it convenient to be able to say that even the conservative Herbert Stein is against the balanced budget. Similarly, a few months ago I wrote an article raising questions about some of the arithmetic used by Governor Reagan during the campaign. This was soon quoted at great length by Tom Wicker, who also had never quoted me on any subject, but who exploited the opportunity to cite a conservative against the conservatives. This kind of reaction naturally causes reluctance to say what you really think about specific items in the conservative creed, if you agree with the creed in general.

Finally, when they were a small minority, conservatives had the luxury of making policy proposals for the sake of their didactic and attention-getting effect, without having to worry that the proposals might actually be put into operation. The constitutional amendment calling for a balanced budget is an example. I believe that this has been true for some, although not all, supporters of the Kemp-Roth bill. As a minority, the Republicans could use the 30 percent tax cut proposal to put the Democrats in the unpopular position of refusing the tax relief the citizens wanted. Now that the tax cut means a huge *Republican* deficit, they have to think harder about it.

This situation, in which one could explain and understand a certain looseness in conservative talk on the ground that the conservatives were a minority far from power, has been changing gradually over the past few years, and changed dramatically with the election of 1980. What conservatives say now will be more adequately reported and more seriously considered than it was in the past. The possibility that conservative proposals will become national policy is greater than it once was. We are all conservatives now, even though we may not all know, or all be in agreement, about what that means.

This change imposes a new responsibility upon conservatives. It is a responsibility to try to tell the whole truth, not just the aspect of the truth that has been ignored in prevailing liberal discourse. It is a responsibility to put forth proposals we might really want to see enacted instead of slogans to rally our own troops. There is an old saying that a platform is something to get in on, not something to stand on. Much conservative talk in the past—big tax cuts, balanced budgets, indiscriminate references to getting government off our backs—has been a platform to get in on. Now the conservatives have to discover what they want to stand on.

I will give some examples of what I mean with reference to one of today's big economic problems—productivity.

Conservatives have made a major contribution to current American thinking by emphasizing the importance of increasing productivity. For too long, prevailing American thought took a high rate of productivity growth for granted, as a never-ending source of additional national income which we could use for whatever purposes we preferred at the moment. This attitude badly distorted national policy.

Conservatives can take credit for helping to restore the growth of productivity to a place in the top rank of national objectives and, just as important, for stressing that the objective had to be promoted by deliberate policy. I do think that some proponents of these ideas have been too much impressed with their own uniqueness and originality. Enthusiasm for economic growth, and optimism about ability to promote it, was shared by all candidates in the 1960 election, for instance. Also, the acceptability of these ideas was much enhanced after the slowdown of the growth of productivity became undeniable in the statistics. Still, the national awareness of the productivity problem owes much to the conservatives' effort over the past ten years to call attention to it.

Yet it must also be said that those who have been properly emphasizing the importance of rapid growth of productivity and output have been improperly belittling the worth of other objectives, or denying the possibility of conflict between growth and other objectives. The country has undoubtedly gone too far in subordinating economic growth to the pursuit of environmental purity and occupational safety. Getting the last one percent of impurity out of the water is surely not worthwhile. But it would also be wrong to act as if these other objectives did not exist, and did not sometimes justify measures which will retard growth as we usually measure it. Economic growth, unless defined tautologically to include all good things, is not all that life is about.

There has also been a tendency to claim unrealistically that economic growth would by itself achieve other objectives, or to imply that other objectives could not be advanced by measures which would in any degree interfere with growth. A leading illustration is the problem of reducing the amount of poverty in our country. It is sometimes implied that this problem can be satisfactorily handled by speeding up economic growth, and that any measure intended to alleviate poverty which has as a consequence the slowing down of growth must be counterproductive. This attitude is justified by a quotation from John F. Kennedy—ironically the apostle of many new conservatives—that "a rising tide lifts all the boats." Unfortunately, that is not true. A rising tide does not lift the boats that are under water. One can readily see many kinds of poverty that will not be significantly relieved by faster growth of productivity. If we recognize the reduction of poverty as an independent objective of national policy, there must certainly be cases where it is worthwhile to sacrifice some growth of productivity to achieve it.

A more critical tradeoff now exists between economic growth and national defense. Here, too, there is some tendency to deny that the tradeoff exists. It is said that we cannot build a strong national defense on a weak economy. This is true, in a sense, but misleading if intended to refer to our present situation. In any sense that is relevant to our national security, the American economy is enormously strong, and will continue to be so for many years even if productivity grows slowly. Our military establishment is, in the relevant sense, not strong. Our national security will be greater if we have a GNP of $5 trillion in 1985 rather than of $4.5 trillion. But if the choice is between a GNP of $5 trillion with a four-hundred-ship navy and a GNP of $4.5 trillion with a six-hundred-ship navy, there is little doubt that we would be more secure with the smaller GNP and the bigger navy.

Those who have done so much to establish, or reestablish, economic growth in the scale of national values, have a responsibility now to face the difficult task of striking a better balance between growth and other objectives. This cannot be done by denying the other objectives or the conflicts among them.

It will be necessary, if we are to offer responsible prescriptions for speeding up the growth of productivity, to be more realistic about the causes of the recent slowdown, or at least more modest about our knowledge of the causes. Popular explanations of the slowdown of productivity growth emanating from conservative sources have focused almost entirely on the lag in the rate of business investment in plant and equipment. I have no doubt that this lag of investment is part of the explanation. But scientific investigation of the matter leaves grave doubt as to the predominance of this explanation. The fact is that we cannot with any great confidence assign quantitative values to the large number of factors which have probably contributed to the slowdown. To mention only a few factors involved: the rate of improvement of the educational attainment of the labor force has probably slowed down; there may have been a decline of the "work ethic"; inflation is distorting economic decisions to an unmeasured extent; and economists are far apart in their estimates of the effects of the energy problem.

From an oversimple explanation of causes comes an oversimple conclusion about the necessary remedy. The remedy for productivity growth slowdown, of course, is tax rate reduction. Again, the preaching on this subject—coupled with the taxpayers' own resentments at their burdens—has contributed to a desirable change of national attitudes. But it is also true that the preaching about taxes has given support to a nondiscriminating taxophobia, which considers all taxes to be equally the enemies of growth. While it may be true that all taxes are the enemies of growth, it is almost certainly not true that all taxes are *equally* the enemies of growth. This taxophobia can lead to tax rate reductions which have little beneficial effect—or even a negative effect—on growth per dollar of revenue loss.

The whole tenor of the recent discussion of productivity has generated the expectation that rather simple and pleasant measures will yield large and prompt results in the form of more rapid growth. This is dangerous in many ways. One of the most serious ways is that it supports the belief that the inflation problem can be solved simply by speeding up the growth of productivity, without having to take any of the bitter medicine of spending cuts, tight money, high interest rates, and unemployment. This belief is almost certainly in error, and basing policy upon it will lead to more inflation and to slower rather than more rapid growth.

This reliance on the easy solution is connected with another common element in conservative talk. That is the belief that the economy can be "psyched" into good behavior. If the right words are said on the right occasion—preferably an inaugural address or a prime-time TV speech—if the right signals are sent or the right symbols offered, the private sector will respond in the right way. It is not suggested that this symbolism should be without objective policy content. That is to be included. But the expected reaction derived from the psychological effect is much larger and quicker than would be expected from the policy measures alone.

Many examples come to mind. Herbert Hoover in 1932 recommended a tax increase in the thought that it would help restore "confidence" and so get the economy moving again, and this idea was supported for its psychological effect even by people who saw that its objective effect was probably negative. Franklin Roosevelt's "nothing to fear but fear itself" was a psychological weapon in the war against the Depression. Later, in 1937, faced with his own recession, Roosevelt authorized his secretary of the treasury to talk about balancing the budget again, in the hope of reviving "confidence." Skipping thirty-five years to the age of inflation, we find Richard Nixon imposing wage and price controls, not because he thought they would "really" cure inflation but because he thought that a period of months in which prices did not rise would lead the public to expect price stability, and that would result in actual price stability. And a little later Gerald Ford showered the country with WIN buttons as symbols that would mobilize the country to anti-inflationary behavior.

Reliance on symbolism is not confined to conservatives, although all of the preceding examples have a conservative context, even including FDR in a conservative mood. But the method of argument seems to have a special appeal to conservatives. There may be two reasons for this. Conservatives tend to regard investment as the key to economic performance, and this is not only because many conservatives are businessmen or investors. Confidence and expectations are probably more important for investment decisions, which look far into the future and involve much uncertainty, than for other aspects of economic behavior. Also, conservatives are typically leery of government action, and so they like to believe in homeopathic solutions for the problems they see—solutions which give big results for little action.

The relation of economics to psychology is not news. The study of the economic behavior of Robinson Crusoe on his island is not a study of geology or meteorology or zoology; it is a study of Crusoe's psychology. And economics has always recognized that the economic behavior of men and women in a society is heavily influenced by the culture or opinion of the society. The supply of labor is influenced by the strength of the work ethic in the society. The propensity to invest, as Keynes emphasized, is dependent on the animal spirits of investors, which are also culturally determined. Theories of the business cycle which depend on alternating waves of optimism and pessimism are very old. And the emphasis on what may be called macropsychology in economics is greater than ever today, as is evidenced by the central role of the words "expectations" and "credibility" in all current economic discussion.

So the reliance on symbolism as an instrument of economic policy is not without "scientific" basis. But the historical examples I have just given, from Hoover to Ford, provide a warning. All of those cases were failures. Hoover's tax increase did not restore confidence, or at least not enough to stop the slide of the economy.

Roosevelt's "nothing to fear" speech—a speech we now think of as a triumph—was part of a package which helped produce a recovery in 1933 that soon subsided and left the country to suffer many more years of depression. His later attempt to generate recovery in 1937, by saying the words he thought the business community wanted to hear, yielded no results. Nixon's effort to create the expectation of price stability, through controls to keep prices stable, only created the expectation that when the controls were lifted, inflation would take off again. And Ford's WIN buttons only created the expectation of more jokes about WIN buttons.

There are two problems in manipulating the economy with symbols. First, although a change of psychology may alter economic behavior for a time, it is unlikely to alter it durably if the psychology gets out of touch with reality. There is a certain reality in the economy. Although psychology is important, it is not everything, and it is not likely to float for long detached from reality. Roosevelt's inaugural address, for example, was part of a bootstrap program which attempted to lift the economy without correcting the deficiency of money and income from which it was suffering. The balloon rose briefly but then settled to earth again. Similarly, symbolic gestures may reduce inflationary expectations and slow down inflation for a while, but if the growth of the money supply is undiminished, money balances will build up and revive the inflation.

The new buzz word in economics is "rational expectations." This is a rejection of the notion that the economy can run for long periods on illusion, as some earlier theories implied. The key is the "rational" part of rational expectations. As I described the idea earlier, it means that the girl in the box cannot be fooled by the illusionist who pretends to saw her in half. Participants in the economy cannot be permanently fooled into believing something that their own experience shows to be untrue.

This does not deny that for a period, the duration of which is uncertain, people can be fooled. On the other side of the coin, policies that are objectively effective can fail to work as well as they might, if they are not explained and understood. Symbolism and communication are *something;* they are just not *everything.* There is, however, another problem in the attempt to psych the economy into good behavior. In many cases no one knows what is the right symbol to make the economy behave. We don't know what bell makes the economy salivate. For example, in 1937, Treasury Secretary Morgenthau persuaded President Roosevelt that a promise to balance the budget would revive business confidence and promote recovery. But that didn't work. Balancing the budget was not what the business community was seeking, and the promise did not inspire them. This incident illustrates another point. There is a strong tendency for people to believe that what gives them confidence will give the rest of the country confidence, as Morgenthau believed about balancing the budget. And some people who may not believe that nevertheless find the confidence argument a convenient one to make in favor of whatever policy they prefer, since it is hard to deny that any particular measure might have the desired psychological effect.

The concern with psyching the economy has been much in evidence in the discussion of steps President Reagan might take at the beginning of his term to deal with economic problems. Emphasis has been placed on the need for quick, visible, and dramatic announcements of actions, in the belief that if announced in this way, the actions will have a much prompter and stronger effect than could be forecast from their objective workings alone. Thus, measures which, abstracting from the change of psychology, might reduce the inflation rate slowly over the course of five years, are counted on to change private expectations so radically that the inflation rate will come down quickly. Further measures that might objectively promote a slow increase in the rate of productivity growth are counted on to change the "atmosphere" to one in which everyone works, saves, and invests more energetically, producing a flood of output. But the fact is that the magnitude of these psychological effects is uncertain and easily exaggerated. We don't even know, in some cases, the direction of the effect. Will a big tax cut be anti-inflationary because of its expected effect on productivity, or will it be inflationary because of its effect on the deficit and the connotations that traditionally it has for inflation? No one can be sure.

Conservatives have come into a position of greater influence and responsibility than they once had because they advanced certain general principles that were valid, that conformed to the obvious condition of the time, and that were in tune with the public mood. They have made important points about economic policy. But they have not formulated or enunciated a comprehensive economic policy. They have been telling half the story—a half that had been ignored and needed to be told, but a half that is not sufficient to govern or live by.

It is now necessary for conservatives to learn and tell the whole truth. One might say that I am applying a double standard. The liberals, after all, remained in power for almost fifty years while believing and selling illusions. Should not the conservatives have a chance to do the same? I think there are two answers to that. In the first place, and speaking pragmatically, I am not sure that conservatives can retain influence if they do not tell the truth and deliver results. In a contest of demagoguery, the liberals will probably win. In the second place, conservatives, being more devoted to the free society, do have more of an obligation to practice the civic virtues of the free society, including the virtue of honesty and responsibility in discussion.

8 Questions for Conservatives

Fortune, January 11, 1982

T HE spirit of the conservative economics on which I was brought up is clearly indicated by the title of a pamphlet published in 1934 by my teacher Henry Simons, *A Positive Program for Laissez-Faire.* The spirit of today's conservative economics, as it seems to animate the Reagan administration, is indicated by the slogan "Don't just stand there, undo something!"

Given the huge increase in government intervention since 1934, a lot of undoing was necessary, and the Reagan administration deserves credit for the undoing thus far. So much harmful or wasteful policy was in effect that a slashing negative attack was almost bound to be constructive, and may have been the only way to go. But a negative approach will not continue to be sufficient. If conservative economics is going to be a satisfactory and durable strategy for our times, it is going to have to develop a positive program.

There seem to me to be several sizable problems about the administration's economic policy today.

First, it has specified a desired path of money growth that seems inconsistent with the desired path of the GNP. By conventional standards, and by the reckoning of most economists, the administration's desired rate of monetary growth is not sufficient to yield the growth rate of nominal GNP that the administration counts on.

Meanwhile, the administration's specified growth rate for real, inflation-adjusted GNP—4 percent a year for several years—seems inconsistent with the desired reduction in the inflation rate. Our experience does not suggest that such rapid growth can be continued over four or five years while the inflation rate is coming down.

There is a certain ambivalence about relations with the Federal Reserve Board. The administration has declared its devotion to the independence of the Fed, yet it has been unusually specific in its public guidance to the Fed.

There has been ambiguity about budget balancing. The administration specified an arbitrary schedule for achieving a balanced budget by 1984, but it did not make clear its rationale for this schedule or even its rationale for *wanting* to balance the budget. President Reagan has said that balancing the budget is "only a goal," has recently added that the goal is important, but has left open the question whether the administration is willing to sacrifice anything to achieve it by some specific date.

Many administration statements still reflect the notion that taxes are not only an evil but an unnecessary evil. This is a vestigial remnant of the theory, prominent during the campaign, that a reduction of tax rates would increase tax revenues, in addition to having a number of other good effects. Although hardly anyone believes this anymore, the taxophobia rationalized by this idea remains an element of administration thinking.

Finally, the administration's statements often suggest that a sufficient rule about nondefense expenditures of the federal government is "Less!" That rule probably was sufficient when the first $30 billion or $40 billion was being cut out of the budget. But the rule becomes less reasonable and less salable the further the cuts go.

These ambiguities and inconsistencies have resulted in some large uncertainties about future policy. It is uncertain whether the administration will lower its GNP goals, or try to pump up the rate of monetary growth, if it becomes clear that the path of money is not adequate for the desired path of GNP. Similarly, it is uncertain whether the administration will moderate its ambitions with respect to output or will try to pump up the economy, even at the expense of speeding up the inflation, if the desired growth of real output cannot be achieved with the projected reduction of the inflation rate. It is unclear whether the administration will respect the independence of the Federal Reserve, or will instead apply increasing pressure on the Fed, if the Fed is not following the course preferred by the administration. And now that the budget clearly cannot be balanced at any foreseeable date with present policies, it is unclear what policy will be followed with respect to the size of future deficits. If the administration decides that balancing the budget is not a high priority, if it has a religious aversion to taxes, and if it cannot agree with Congress on which expenditures to cut—against this background, it is hard to specify a limit to the deficits that will emerge.

Uncertainty about these matters is one of the things troubling the capital markets. The problem is not only that the private sector has different and less optimistic forecasts than the government, which it has. People in the private sector are unusually uncertain about even their own most probable forecasts, because they are unusually uncertain about which way the government will go. They don't know what to expect from the administration when it accepts that its forecasts and plans won't be realized. This is a very ironic situation because it is a basic principle of conservative economics that the private sector is essentially stable and has a strong tendency to regain equilibrium after temporary disturbances. According to this view, however, the government's own policies must be stable and well known to the private sector. But we now have a situation in which uncertainty about the behavior of a conservative administration is unusually high. The administration, and conservatives in general, have not yet developed any agreed-upon and specific theory for the operation of government or the management of fiscal and monetary policy. It seemed true in previous administrations, including previous Republican administrations, that we knew, more or less, what kind of textbook the answers were being drawn from. The economic officials of the government were operating with a textbook that was basically neo-Keynesian, though it had an increasingly monetarist tinge. The new conservative economists have not yet produced their textbook; at least, they have not yet produced one they agree upon.

It would be nice to believe that the recent decline of interest rates shows that the uncertainties have been removed and the financial markets now have confidence in a known course of policy and in the probable future reduction of inflation, interest rates, and deficits. In fact, the recent decline of long-term interest rates has been mainly due to the recession. There is a widespread feeling that rates will rise again, as a result of which many corporations are rushing in to borrow long term now, even though rates remain around 15 percent. Long-term corporate rates peaked at around 17 percent in October, compared with about 9.5 percent two years earlier. Uncertainty about future inflation may keep rates from falling enough to permit a healthy recovery of the economy.

How might conservatives go about removing the uncertainties that now beset the financial markets and corporate planners? In my judgment, they must supply operational and credible answers to eight questions:

1. Does the government want a managed monetary system or does it think it can escape from the necessity of a managed system, or improve upon it, by some form of gold standard?

2. In general, how can the credibility and stability of policy be protected against narrow and shortsighted political considerations? Concern about this question has led many conservatives to espouse constitutional amendments limiting economic policy. A few years ago, many Republican congressmen had endorsed constitutional amendments requiring that the federal budget be balanced or spending limited. Others have supported amendments to control expansion of the money supply. Now that they have responsibility, conservatives must decide whether they are still serious about such constitutional limits.

3. What should be the guide to monetary policy? Should it be specified in terms of some measure of the quantity of money or should it be specified in terms of some measure of economic performance, like GNP or employment?

4. How should responsibility be divided between the Federal Reserve and the administration?

5. Should budget balancing be accepted as a categorical imperative or should it be regarded as a goal to be evaluated pragmatically in relation to its effects? The administration has opted de facto for the pragmatic approach, but there are still many certified conservatives, including some in Congress, who consider balancing the budget akin to a moral law.

6. Assuming that decisions about the size of the surplus or deficit are made pragmatically, what considerations are to be used in determining the proper policy? Is the decision to be made each year, from scratch, in the light of current conditions, or are some more durable rules possible and desirable? In either case, should we be concerned mainly with the effects of a deficit or a surplus on the stability of the price level, on the rate of private investment, on the level of government expenditures, or perhaps on all of these—and if on all, then how are they to be accommodated to one another?

7. Having generally rejected the more extreme supply-side

claims about the incentive effects of tax reduction, while remaining convinced that taxation is a drag on economic growth and efficiency, how do conservatives reach some realistic view of the magnitude of these adverse effects, thus enabling them to make informed judgments about choices among higher taxes, lower expenditures, and bigger deficits? Also, how do they decide about the relative merits of different kinds of taxes?

8. What is the conservative view of the functions of government, and the proper level of expenditures, especially in providing assistance for those who are poor or disadvantaged?

Conservatives need to bear down on such questions and try to agree on some workable answers. These are intellectually and politically difficult questions, but they must be answered if a conservative administration is to know where it is going, and if the rest of the country is to know. Let me suggest the *kinds* of answers that seem appropriate.

1. *We should stop flirting with the gold standard.* This flirtation only creates uncertainty about the determination of the government to stick by a responsible, restrained, anti-inflationary policy. It gives the country the idea that the government thinks, unrealistically, there is some magic potion that will solve all our problems painlessly. The case for the gold standard is exceedingly weak. The historical record does not suggest that it has been any guarantor of long-run price stability, or of long-run economic stability in general, and it is very unlikely that we can recreate the conditions under which the gold standard served to discipline governments. That toothpaste can no longer be put back in the tube.

2. *We should stop flirting with constitutional amendments as a solution to macroeconomic policy questions.* We may have some notion of what would be desirable policy for the next five years. We certainly do not know what policy should be in the year 2081 and shouldn't be presuming to prescribe rules that will be binding fifty or a hundred years from now.

3. *An effective monetary policy requires that the administration and the Federal Reserve first agree on the objective for a period of five years or so, and this objective should be stated in terms of nominal GNP.* Objectives stated in terms of real GNP or employment or unemployment almost inescapably invite inflation. There is an irresistible temptation to set the real goals too high and then to try to pump up the economy to achieve them. If we can achieve stability in nominal GNP growth, or in the price level, then the forces of the market

will in time get real growth to a sustainable rate, and that is the best we can do. Nominal GNP has been rising at an annual rate of about 11 percent. There is no way the inflation rate can be significantly reduced if that continues. Monetary policy might aim to reduce that steadily to about 5 percent by, say, 1985. That rate would accommodate 2.5 percent real growth and a 2.5 percent inflation rate, which seems a satisfactory and possible combination.

4. *The Federal Reserve should retain its independence in pursuing the agreed-upon goals.* If we are ever going to get the inflation rate down in this country, we must go through a transitional period that will involve pain in the form of high unemployment and high interest rates, and the Fed must be supported against political attack when it carries out such a policy. It is the responsibility of the administration to give the Fed that support.

5. *Running a deficit should be regarded as a legitimate way of financing government, like collecting taxes.* Much conservative rhetoric to the contrary, running a deficit is not a cardinal sin. Everybody knows that, really, yet everybody goes around pretending he doesn't know it because he thinks that other people don't know it. The choice between borrowing and taxing should be recognized as no more than a choice between the adverse consequences of crowding out private investment (a result of deficits) and the adverse consequences of less economic efficiency (a result of high taxes).

6. *The decision about the size of the deficit or surplus should be regarded as a decision to be made for the medium term—not every year, but also not forever.* Making the decision every year opens up too many dangers. If the decision is made in the context of each year's legislative tussle over spending and taxing, the size of the deficit or surplus is likely to be a residual of that tussle and the political pressures will almost certainly yield excessively large deficits. On the other hand, we do not know what will be the desirable size of the deficit or surplus twenty or thirty years from now. What we can say now is that, after about eight years in which productivity has grown minimally, it is probably desirable to give somewhat higher priority to growth than we might have done earlier or than we may give at some future time.

The implication of this posture for the budget is that we should be seeking to achieve a balanced budget, or at least smaller deficits than we have been running, in order to leave more of private saving available to finance productive private investment. We should be aiming to reduce the size of the deficit relative to GNP as the economy moves along the path that monetary policy is trying to achieve. All of which implies that the desirable size of the deficit (or surplus) depends on the state of the economy. It is meaningless to state a goal for budget policy—for example, that the budget should be balanced—without stating the economic conditions under which the goal is to be achieved. And it is misleading to state a goal for the budget that is to be achieved, or could only be achieved, under economic conditions that are not feasible and desirable. Failure to see this was one of the causes of the undoing of the Reagan budget projections. They promised achievement of a balanced budget in 1984, but they predicated the balance on economic conditions that cannot be achieved, or that should not be achieved because they would be excessively inflationary.

7. *Some tax increases may be desirable.* The Reagan tax bill of 1981 incorporated some changes that probably will significantly stimulate economic growth and efficiency. This was notably true of the reduced top rates for the individual income tax and of the speedup in allowable depreciation charges. But the bill also included other cuts, causing tens of billions of dollars of annual revenue losses, which probably will have little "supply-side" effect. This is certainly the case for the rate reductions applicable to the lower- and middle-income brackets. These cuts were desirable to the extent that the government had no compelling need for the money and in the sense that it is always desirable for the income earner to retain his income if the government's need is not compelling.

But one cannot credibly maintain that those rate cuts were essential for the health of the U.S. economy (except insofar as they were a "Trojan horse" making essential tax changes in the top rates politically possible). Much additional revenue could now be raised without seriously adverse economic consequences if there is a compelling reason to do so—to finance needed defense expenditures, to avoid excessive deficits, even to finance nondefense expenditures. This is not an invitation to hefty increases of tax rates. The danger of that is slight. The government has not brought itself to raise tax rates, other than Social Security taxes, in peacetime since 1935, so one can assume the political resistance to be adequate. Recouping some revenues now might involve the use of excise taxes, say, rather than a politically difficult (and embarrassing) effort to cancel some of those rate cuts. But we should not be prevented from doing anything important by the fear that raising revenue must have seriously adverse economic effects.

Conservatives need to recognize that tax reform is a two-way street, and includes the closing of loopholes favoring some taxpayers. There are opportunities to improve equity in the treatment of different taxpayers without injury to economic efficiency and without loss of revenue and sometimes with an increase of revenue. For example, we might consider some sort of cap on the deductibility of mortgage interest. Such tax reform would also permit conservatives to demonstrate that their concern with strengthening the supply side of the economy is not a cover for policy tilted toward the rich.

8. *Conservatives need to give much more attention to appraisal of the proper functions of government and of efficient ways to perform these functions.* The government cannot continuously be run on the assumption that "the government is the problem" and that any expenditure cut is a good thing. Such shibboleths are untrue and will not last. The administration needs to accept that it is here to govern, that it has certain positive responsibilities, and it needs to figure out how to discharge those responsibilities and not how to deny them. This also means that the public must be educated to a more sophisticated attitude, because once you recognize that there are legitimate functions of government and legitimate expenditures of government, you are then obliged to decide what are the proper limits, and such decisions are much more complex and difficult than simply casting government as our enemy or as our savior.

Probably the main function of government about which conservatives need to develop a philosophy and a policy is the relief of poverty. It is not sufficient to say that a rising tide lifts all boats. It is not true. Neither is it accurate to deny that there is a widespread feeling in the country of obligation to assist the poor and that the government needs to recognize that obligation and discharge it to some degree. It is necessary to recognize that some sacrifice of economic efficiency and growth may be desirable for the sake of helping the poor, while also recognizing that the help should entail a minimum sacrifice of efficiency and growth. The initial attitude of this administration was a proper one. It was going to maintain a safety net to protect the truly needy while cutting expenditures that had been improperly justified as useful for the needy but that mainly benefited the middle class. The safety-net concept has proved much more difficult to implement in practice than it was to describe in general terms; nevertheless, it is a commendable first step toward achieving what needs to be done. In the next round of expenditure cuts, it will be harder to avoid hurting the poor.

These decisions facing conservatives are difficult ones, both intellectually and politically. But conservatives cannot avoid facing these questions and doing their best to answer them. Conservatives should not think that they came into office with a mandate to do some list of specific things that were well known to the country. They came into office not with a mandate, but with an opportunity—with a chance to try to do better in solving our nation's economic problems than their predecessors had done. And conservatives must prepare themselves for meeting in 1984 the question that Ronald Reagan raised so powerfully in 1980: Can you truly say that you are better off now than you were four years ago?

Conservatives should not delude themselves into thinking they are now riding some irresistible wave of opinion and support for right-wing policies. This might have seemed the case a year and a half ago, but we have seen lately that the tide of world political opinion is shifting wildly. The only constant seems to be that whoever is in gets turned out. In France, in Greece, to a lesser degree in Canada, and elsewhere, relatively conservative governments have been ousted and more liberal or radical governments have been put in place. This should be a reminder to the American conservatives that theirs will not be a winning team unless they play a game that deserves to win.

How to Pay for Survival

Commentary Magazine, August 1980

A reluctance to face the full magnitude of our task and
overcome it is a coward's part. Yet the nation is not in this
mood and only asks to be told what is necessary.
—J. M. Keynes
"How to Pay for the War," February 1940

A RECENT *Washington Post* story bore the headline "5-Year Military Build-Up to Cost U.S. $1 Trillion." The headline and the text were clearly meant to suggest that a trillion dollars is a lot of money, although the reporter was fair enough to say that the expenditure "will not make the United States the undisputed No. 1 in global military might." But in the period under consideration in the article (1981 through 1985) the trillion dollars would only be a little over 6 percent of the total value of U.S. output.

The basic fact is that we start from a low level of expenditures for defense—relative to the size of the U.S. economy. Even a fairly rapid increase in this low level of spending will still leave the total small—again, relative to the size of the U.S. economy. In 1979 we devoted about 5 percent of the U.S. national output to defense. That was, to provide some standard of comparison, about 25 percent more than consumers spent for furniture and household equipment in that year. If the 1979 level of defense spending were to increase by 10 percent per annum in real terms for four years, and total output rose by 2.5 percent per annum— not an unreasonable rate of output growth—defense spending in 1983 would be still only about 6.6 percent of GNP.

Perhaps it is as unconvincing to rely on the intuitive notion that 5 percent or 6.6 percent of GNP are small numbers as it is to rely on the notion that one trillion dollars is a large number. A better idea of what is implied by such numbers may be obtained by considering the output that would be available for nondefense purposes—for personal consumption, for private investment, and for the nondefense programs of government—with defense programs of various sizes. I will compare possible programs. One is the Carter budget of March 1980, which calls for an annual average increase of 3.4 percent in real defense outlays from 1979 to 1983. A second, which I call "medium," would involve average annual increases of about 10 percent. This is, by my rough calculations, the rate of increase implied in the defense program suggested in May by the Committee on the Present Danger, and the rate of increase that (according to newspaper reports) Governor Reagan's defense advisers are considering. A third program, which would raise real defense outlays by 15 percent per annum, I call "high," although it would certainly be far from exhausting the economic capabilities of this country. This third program would raise defense outlays as a percent of GNP to about 8 percent in 1983, which would be midway between our recent ratio of 5 percent and the 10 to 11 percent ratio of the Eisenhower years. We did not consider ourselves "poor" in the Eisenhower period. Indeed, some social critics of the time thought we were suffering from excessive affluence. In retrospect it seems a time in which the economy performed well. In comparison with our recent performance, the inflation was negligible and growth was vigorous.

The table below compares the state of the economy in 1983 under each of my three hypothetical defense programs with the condition in 1979 and in 1958. I assume for 1983 the GNP level projected in the president's March 1980 budget revisions.

Gross National Product and Its Uses
(1972 Dollars)
(Figures for GNP, Defense, and Nondefense
Are Expressed in Billions of Dollars)

FISCAL YEAR	GNP	DEFENSE	NONDEFENSE	NON-DEFENSE PER CAPITA
1958	$ 673	$ 74	$ 599	$3454
1979	1428	69	1359	6174
1983				
Carter defense	1570	79	1491	6548
Medium defense	1570	101	1469	6452
High defense	1570	121	1449	6364

Clearly, with any of the defense programs considered here, output available for nondefense purposes per capita will be enormously greater in 1983 than it was twenty-five years earlier—90 percent higher with the Carter defense program and 84 percent higher with the "high" defense program. In this perspective, the difference between the effects of the two programs on the nondefense economy is trivial. The difference of per-capita nondefense output in 1983 between the "high" and the "low" defense program would be about 3 percent. That is, a 53 percent larger defense program would cost a 3 percent reduction in per-capita nondefense output. This is less than the loss of per-capita output which has been caused by environmental, health, and safety regulations in the last seven years. With any of the defense programs, per-capita nondefense output will be higher in 1983 than it was in 1979. In general, even with the largest of these defense programs we would be economically better off in 1983 than in 1979, twice as well off as in the Eisenhower years, and three times as well off as in 1944 when we were defending the country against Hitler.

What then is the problem? Why should there have been a great struggle this spring in the Congress, and between the president and the Congress, about a proposal to spend a few additional billions of dollars, one- or-two-tenths of one percent of GNP, for defense? Part of the opposition came from people who believed that increased defense spending would endanger our national security by provoking the Russians. Some, like the president, thought that more money would weaken the national defenses, presumably because the Pentagon did not have enough wit to spend more money in a useful way. But the main problem was that people who believed that more defense spending would be useful could not agree on who should pay for it, or how. Some were for more defense but not if it was to be financed "on the backs of the poor," as they would say, meaning not if it was to be financed by cutting "social" programs of government. Some were for more defense but not if it was to be financed by an increase of taxes. And, at least in the political and economic circumstances of the spring of 1980, no one wanted to finance more defense spending with a budget deficit. Given these disagreements on how to pay for an increase of defense spending, only a tiny increase was possible.

Those who held these positions did not believe, or would not have said, that they were subordinating national security to some other objective. They would have said, and probably believed, that the other objective was also essential to the national security. That is, the national security could not be defended if the disadvantaged part of the population were alienated by the inadequacy of social programs. Or the national security could not be defended if the nation's economic base were undermined by high taxation. Or the national security could not be defended if the country were racked by inflation as a result of budget deficits.

This all means that we have an allocation problem which is politically acute and may be serious in its economic implications also. In the aggregate, even the largest of the defense programs considered here does not require any great sacrifice from the American people. But there will be *some* sacrifice, in the sense that there will be less output available for nondefense purposes than if the defense program had been smaller. The problem is to find the best way to allocate that sacrifice. Or, if there is no "best" way, as there probably is not, we must find a way to allocate the sacrifice that we can agree upon as preferable to not defending ourselves adequately.

Operationally, these allocation issues come into focus in the federal budget. Thinking about the budget problem has to start with the fact that the total Carter expenditure estimates—defense plus nondefense—for 1983 would take a larger share of the estimated GNP for that year than we are now paying in taxes. In other words, if we continue to pay the same share of the GNP in taxes, we will not be paying for his defense programs, let alone for any higher ones.

There are four ways to finance such defense programs: cutting nondefense spending below the Carter projections, raising the tax ratio above the present level, running a budget deficit, and raising the real gross national product above the level assumed in the Carter budget projections. Each is possible. None is easy, or free of problems. I shall consider each in turn.

Cutting Nondefense Expenditures

We are so used to the idea of extravagance and excess in the nondefense budget that it may come as a surprise to be told that the Carter estimates of nondefense spending for 1983 are low. But that is the usual condition. Estimates for a year three years into the future usually show little increase, but when that year is reached the actual expenditures far exceed the estimate made three years earlier. I start here, however, with the official estimate of expenditures for 1983, not with a realistic estimate of what expenditures will be if we pursue politics as usual for the next three years. To hold actual expenditures to the official estimates will require a great effort. I am concerned here with the possibility of cutting *below* the official estimate.

From 1958 to 1979 real nondefense expenditures increased at an average rate of 5.5 percent a year. The projection for 1983 implies an average annual increase of 1.8 percent. There are two ways to look at that. On the one hand, after twenty-one years of such rapid increases we ought to be able to afford a few years of little or no growth in this area. On the other hand, there is a strong trend of rapid increase which will be difficult to arrest. There is something to both these points. During the easy years, when inflation was raising the revenue rapidly, when defense spending was declining, and when we were still impressed with the ability of the government to cure poverty, injustice, pollution, and all other ills by spending money, programs were added which had little or no payoff. But also during this period things were going on, like the aging of the population and the increase of the public debt, which made some increases of expenditures inevitable and irreversible.

A large part of the increase in government expenditures in recent years has been the increase in transfer payments to individuals—payments for which no service in return is expected. Such payments (by all governments, federal, state, and local) rose from 8.5 percent of GNP in 1972 to 10.2 percent in 1979. This has led to suggestions that returning the ratio to its former level would provide funds to finance most or all of the needed increase in defense spending. However, such a shift is much more difficult than it seems. In 1979, 83 percent of those transfer payments were for social-insurance benefits (for which the beneficiaries had made prior payments), for military retirement pensions, and for veterans' benefits. The remainder, mainly direct relief and food stamps, was only 1.1 percent of GNP in 1979, down from 1.2 percent in 1972.

Still, it would be a mistake to say that the nondefense expenditures cannot be cut below the level projected in the Carter budget, or that cuts would have to come out of the hides of the poor.

Several categories of expenditures are most eligible for reduction:

1. The part of programs nominally addressed to the poor but which is spent on middle-income people including parts of the food-stamp, education-assistance, school-lunch, and housing programs.
2. Programs nominally addressed to the poor that don't work, like employment and training programs.
3. Industrial interventions that have no rationale as anti-poverty programs, such as agriculture assistance and regulation and "promotion" of the energy industry.
4. Grants to state and local governments for purposes that could be better financed at the state or local level.

The larger the cuts sought the more difficult they will be to achieve, not only because the political resistance will be greater but also because the real costs per billion dollars of cut are getting larger. These costs have to be compared, in a judgmental way, with the costs of raising taxes or running deficits. But I would suggest that a cut of nondefense expenditures by 1 percent of GNP below the Carter projections for 1983 is feasible in the sense that it is not ruled out by existing legal or moral commitments. That would be a cut of about 6 percent from the level projected by the Carter administration, and of about 16 percent from the more "cuttable" part of that projection, which is the part left after excluding social insurance, veteran's benefits, and interest. The feasibility of this much of a cut is indicated by the estimates made in President Ford's last budget, issued in 1977, and by a study done earlier this year by the Congressional Budget Office, which canvassed the possibilities of reducing expenditures without radical changes of policy.

Increasing Taxes

Cutting nondefense expenditures by 1 percent of GNP would permit balancing the budget without any increase in the overall tax burden above its present level if we stick to the Carter defense program. But present taxes would not be sufficient to pay for the medium defense program, let alone the high one.

The idea that we should raise taxes to pay for the defense program will strike some people as politically impossible. We haven't had a general revenue-raising tax bill in peacetime in about forty-five years. But, of course, we are raising taxes all the time, every day. We do it by inflation which, without any law being passed, raises the ratio of revenues to incomes by pushing people into higher tax brackets.

In fact, if we do nothing, leaving the tax laws just as they are, the ratio of federal revenues to GNP will rise from 20.7 percent this year to 22.8 percent in 1983. That will result partly from the new windfall profits tax and the social security tax increases already enacted. But it will result also in large part from the 28 percent increase in the price level which Carter's budget assumes will occur between 1980 and 1983.

This built-in tax increase would finance the medium defense budget plus Carter's projected nondefense expenditures for 1983. It would come close to financing the high defense budget with a cut of nondefense spending equal to 1 percent of GNP.

So it is not difficult to raise enough taxes to finance an enlarged defense program. The problem is that the tax system which would result from keeping the rates we have while the inflationary process runs would be an unsatisfactory one. In fact, the inflation of the past ten years has already substantially distorted the federal tax system. It has subjected a large number of middle-income people to much higher marginal rates of income tax than they have been used to paying. It has especially increased the tax burden on income from business investment, primarily because businesses cannot charge off the true cost of replacing capital used in production when they calculate income subject to tax.

For years many people have been looking forward to the opportunity to reduce the overall tax burden—the ratio of taxes to GNP—as a way of correcting these distortions accumulated during the inflation. To continue the present tax rates while the inflation runs would not only preserve the existing evils but also add new ones. And then there is the possibility that the inflation may be reduced below the rate projected by the administration, in which case all the projected revenue would not be available.

There are, however, ways to revise the tax structure that would preserve the revenue yield while correcting features of the system that are the subject of most complaint. This would involve reducing the present highest rates of individual income tax and relieving the burden on business investment in any one of a number of ways. The corporate-profits tax rate could be reduced, dividends could be relieved, in whole or part, from taxation at the corporation or individual level, or more ample provision could be made for depreciation. The revenue loss from these reductions could be recouped by increasing taxes on consumption. One way to do this which is attractive at the present time because of its beneficial effects in reducing oil imports would be a high tax on gasoline, or on oil products in general. This could be properly described as a "defense tax" because of its contribution to reducing our vulnerability to disruption of oil supplies. Other possibilities are a value-added tax or a progressive tax on consumption administered through the income tax. In any of these cases provision could be made for relieving the very poor from the added tax burden.

Of course, the tax revision suggested here will not be attractive politically. It will be easily described as transferring burdens from the rich to the poor, even though its long-term effect may be beneficial to the poor. Not the defense burden alone but that burden combined with political power and prejudice may keep us from having a tax system that is favorable to economic growth.

It may be realistic to suppose that such a revision of the tax system is not possible, and that a tax program to finance higher defense expenditures will have to be pretty much like the present one but further distorted by inflation. This would not mean that financing the higher defense program is impossible, or not worthwhile. Its chief economic significance would be that during the period of the defense buildup the rate of business investment would be smaller than would be optimum, and the future level of total output would also be smaller. The magnitudes involved in a short period are not frightening, however. At an improbable extreme one might assume that the budget was so financed that the entire difference between the low defense program and the high defense program came out of private investment. How much difference that would make for the total level of output in 1983 would be a subject of considerable disagreement among economists. But the difference is unlikely to be more than 2 percent of GNP and more likely to be around 1 percent. In a longer period this difference would become larger. The need to reform the tax structure would be greater if the defense program were to continue rising relative to GNP for a long time. But our need may be for a spurt in defense spending for a period of four or five years, while we make good certain deficiencies in our forces, after which spending would decline as a fraction of GNP. In that case, reform of the tax structure, while desirable, would not be imperative because we could look forward to tax reduction later. Anyway, even for a longer period, tax reform would not be the necessary condition for our security.

This is an appropriate point at which to comment on the proposition that a strong economy is essential to national security. The proposition is true if we are not too fussy about what "strong" means, and it is relevant in some circumstances. But it is not relevant as implying any limits to U.S. defense policy or U.S. economic policy today. The total output of the U.S. economy is about twice that of the USSR. The output of the industrial democracies is four or five times that of the USSR. It is not because the West is economically weak that it is militarily vulnerable today. A difference of 1 or 2 percent in U.S. GNP in 1983, or even 5 or 10 percent in 1990, will not significantly affect our national security. What will be important, and what has been lacking, is will and wisdom in using the resources that our economy makes available.

Running a Deficit

The foregoing discussion has assumed that increased defense spending has to be financed within a balanced budget. This may seem a bizarre assumption. The federal budget has been balanced in only one year of the past twenty. Why should we suddenly become so finicky about balancing the budget when our defense expenditures may be rising rapidly?

The conventional answer is that deficits cause inflation, which has many adverse consequences, including bad effects on total output, without any offsetting benefits. But the connection between deficits and inflation is loose and probably not necessary. Even a deficit equal to several percent of GNP will not be inflationary unless it is financed in an inflationary way, by excessive increase in the supply of money. Whether in fact deficits in the past have caused excessive monetary expansion is in dispute among students of the subject, but there is little doubt that a determined monetary authority could avoid an inflationary monetary increase. It is probably prudent not to put too much strain on the determination of our monetary authority, the Federal Reserve, by running a very large deficit, but a deficit of 2 or 3 percent of GNP is unlikely to exceed our ability to avoid inflation.

The consequence of a deficit which is more serious because it cannot be avoided is the absorption of savings into financing it. The larger the deficit the smaller will be the fraction of savings available to finance private investment and the slower the rate of economic growth will be. This general proposition will not hold in recessions, when demand is temporarily inadequate, but we cannot count on carrying on a defense program only in recessions.

Thus, the objection to financing the defense program with a deficit is much like the objection to financing it by taxes of a kind which bear heavily on investment and therefore on future growth. Whether a deficit will have more or less growth-inhibiting effect than taxes of equal amount will depend on the nature of the taxes, and also on the nature of the future taxes that taxpayers expect to confront as a result of the present deficit. If the tax program which is the alternative to the deficit is of the conventional type, like a combination of our present individual and corporate income taxes, the growth-inhibiting effect of the deficit is probably larger than that of the taxes, although one cannot be sure of that. In any case, the adverse effect of the deficit is more an argument in favor of taxes than an argument against enlarging the defense program.

We have typically financed wars by deficits as well as by tax increases. The classical tolerance of deficits in wartime, in violation of the standard rules of peacetime finance, rests on two propositions. One is that war expenditures serve a more imperative national need than most other government expenditures and are therefore more worth making even if they have to be financed in a way that retards growth. The second is that the costs of the war are concentrated in a short period while its benefits are more lasting and it is desirable to spread out the final allocation of the costs over a longer period. These arguments may also justify deficit financing of the defense buildup.

Increasing the Size of the Pie

Undoubtedly the most attractive way to provide the resources for an enlarged defense program would be to raise the total national output so that it is not necessary to divert output from nondefense uses by cutting nondefense expenditures of government or raising taxes or increasing the deficit. Unfortunately, we do not know with any reliability how to raise the national output on a scale which would relieve us of these painful necessities.

The arithmetic is essential and simple. In round numbers, in 1979, before the recession, taxes were 20 percent of GNP and with output growing by 2.5 percent per annum we would need taxes equal to 22 percent of GNP in four years to pay for the projected expenditures including the medium defense program. Then to avoid the need for the tax increase we would have to make the GNP higher in four years than it would otherwise have been, and not only higher but higher by at least a certain amount. Specifically, it would have to be 10 percent higher. To get there, the GNP would have to rise by 5 percent per annum for four years, instead of by 2.5 percent. We have never achieved that for four years in a row except in recovery from a recession, and we don't know how to do it.

It is probably true that if the ratio of taxes to GNP were held at 20 percent instead of raised to 22 percent, the GNP would grow more rapidly. But there is no evidence to suggest that it would grow *sufficiently* more rapidly to supply the needed revenue.

One may say that even if tax restraint or tax reduction will not solve the whole problem of financing the defense program, it will solve part of the problem by making the GNP grow more rapidly. But if the lower taxes do not solve the whole problem they may not solve even part of it. That is, if the lower taxes mean a higher deficit, the deficit may make the GNP lower rather than higher by crowding out private investment.

It is not absolutely impossible that lower taxes would raise the national income enough to yield higher revenue, but the available evidence indicates that the possibility is very low. The risk in a policy that seeks to finance an enlarged defense program by lower tax rates is that it will result in larger deficits. As I have indicated above, that is not in itself necessarily fatal. The great danger is that a combination of lower revenue and insistence on balancing the budget or minimizing deficits will squeeze the defense program down to an inadequate size. Advocates of the low-tax route who are also devoted to a large defense program must recognize that defense may suffer if the bet on the revenue-raising power of low taxes does not pay off.

Enlarging the American defense program will not be free.

The case for it is that failure to enlarge the program will be infinitely more costly. The fact is that even a substantial increase of the defense program, relative to its present size, will require only marginal sacrifice from the American people. This sacrifice can be borne in ways that do not weigh upon the very poor, do not need to cause inflation, and do not seriously slow the growth of the American economy. There are various combinations of policies with respect to taxes, nondefense expenditures, and government borrowing that can bring about the desired result. Different combinations will have different effects, and people will have different preferences among them. But for people who take the defense problem seriously, insistence on the preferred method of financing an enlarged defense program cannot be allowed to stand in the way of achieving the defense program we need.

Why Disarm Unilaterally?

The *Wall Street Journal*,
February 11, 1983

I CANNOT understand the mad rush for unilateral disarmament
on the part of usually sensible, cautious and responsible people.
I refer, if you didn't immediately recognize the description, to a
large number of members of the Congress—probably a majority.

Two years ago the president, on the advice of the secretary
of defense and the Joint Chiefs, recommended an increase of
defense expenditures for the succeeding five years. Congress approved this. According to polls it had overwhelming support in
the country. The authorized defense expansion was a response
to a common observation that a decade of very low defense expenditures in the United States and very high outlays in the USSR
had left the United States in a seriously weakened relative position.
Moreover, Soviet behavior, notably in Afghanistan, and the behavior of Soviet accomplices in many parts of the world, left little
doubt that Soviet military power was intended to be used whenever it would be effective. The increase in U.S. defense spending
was an answer to the threat posed by the relative strength and
the intentions of the Soviet Union.

Now there seems to be wide demand for a substantial cut
in this program. Polls show that a majority of the public thinks
the defense program is too large. Businessmen, editorialists, and
other leaders call for cuts. And there is hardly any congressman
or senator too conscious of his own ignorance to assert that the
program should be cut.

What is going on here? I suppose that there is very wide

support for agreed reductions or limitations of arms on both sides. But that isn't what we are talking about. We are talking about unilateral disarmament by us. We are talking about actions which would make the United States defense forces in 1986 or 1987 or in any other year weaker than they would otherwise be, and we are talking about doing that without asking or expecting any reciprocal reductions from the Soviets. Why are we in effect telling Mr. Andropov that the reason he doesn't have to negotiate mutual arms reduction in Geneva is that Congress will reduce United States arms for him?

Congressmen and others who assert the need for cutting the defense program hardly make any argument about the Soviet threat. The assertion is almost always based on one or more of the four following propositions, which must surely constitute as flimsy a basis as has ever been offered for a major national decision.

1. *There is waste in the defense program.* By some ideal standard that is certainly true, but it is also irrelevant. The relevant question is whether, if the defense program is cut, the cut will come entirely or almost entirely out of the waste. The cuts will be made by the same people whose decisions led to the waste. It is pitiful to hear congressmen plead with defense officials to tell them where the waste is.

There is and always will be waste in the Defense Department, just as there is in General Motors and in my household and yours. If we cut the defense program there will be some cut in waste and some cut in muscle. The notion of the defense spending cut that doesn't impair security is simply another illustration of the free-lunch fallacy.

The waste argument often casts doubt on specific weapons. MX in dense pack is the leading example. I do not myself find the dense-pack idea reassuring. But the conclusion that dense pack doesn't work wouldn't mean that the defense budget could be cut. We would still need a survivable land-based missile, and the superior alternative might be more expensive. There isn't any reason to think that correcting the mistakes of the Pentagon will save money.

2. *Increasing defense expenditures while nondefense expenditures are being cut is "unfair."* This is the typical reaction of a congressman who regards the whole function of government as the passing out of goodies among special interest groups in accordance with

the principle of greasing the wheel that squeaks loudest. They think of the defense program as a handout to a special class—like handouts to peanut farmers. But defense is a program for the benefit of the nation and for everyone now in it and yet to be born into it. To cut defense isn't "fair" to anyone.

There is a fairness issue about defense. That is the issue of how to pay for it. That is certainly debatable, but it isn't an issue about the size of the program.

3. *The survival of the free democratic system depends not only on military defense against foreign aggressors but also on internal support for the system.* That is probably true but surely irrelevant to our present situation. It implies that we are on the verge of great general disaffection with the system because of government's failure to provide some social benefits. The picture conjured up is of mobs rioting in the streets of Moscow on the eve of the Russian Revolution because there wasn't enough to eat. The whole idea is absurd. To suggest that the danger to our system comes not from Soviet missiles but from internal disaffection—in a country which in its last four presidential elections chose Richard Nixon twice, Jimmy Carter, and Ronald Reagan, where the whole active political spectrum runs from Alan Cranston to Jesse Helms, where poverty even by generous American standards afflicts less than 10 percent of the population, where real per capita consumption is at an all-time high—is sheer fantasy. We may need to spend more on school lunches, food stamps, or fixing potholes. But they are not alternatives to defense.

4. *The increase in the defense program will weaken the economy upon which our security ultimately depends.* This is the favorite argument of "hardheaded" people—businessmen, budget-conscious congressmen, and such. It sounds like an argument which should be expressible in numbers. How much will the increase of defense spending reduce real output, investment, consumption, or whatever else is supposed to be the content of the weakening of the economy? I have never heard any critic of the defense program attempt an answer to such questions. All we get is adjectives—"disastrous," "horrendous," "frightening," etc.

I would like to make a stab at quantifying the economic consequences of cutting or not cutting the defense program. The program included in the president's budget would raise defense spending from about 6.2 percent of GNP in fiscal 1982 to about 7.9 percent in fiscal 1988. What would be the effect on real GNP if the defense program were cut by 1 percent of GNP—meaning a cut of about $30 billion this year rising to about $50 billion in 1988? The answer depends on how much of the cut in defense goes into increased investment, and how much goes into increased consumption. I will assume that all of the cut in defense goes into increased investment, because that is the assumption which makes the effect on real GNP greatest.

So the question is how much difference it would make if investment were 1 percent higher as a fraction of GNP than it would otherwise have been. This is a question on which economists are divided, but from the standpoint of the defense issue the division isn't very great. One of our leading students of the sources of economic growth is Edward F. Denison. The conclusion of his work, as I simplify it, is that if net investment were increased permanently by 1 percent of GNP, the annual rate of increase of real output would be raised by one-tenth of one percentage point. That is, if the growth rate would otherwise have been 4 percent, it would be raised to 4.1 percent. Many economists think that is too low an estimate. But at the other extreme, if all economic growth that doesn't result from an increase of hours of work is attributed to capital investment—which means that none is attributed to research, education, increases of scale, and the like—increasing net investment by 1 percent of GNP might raise the growth rate from 4 percent to 4.33 percent.

The Council of Economic Advisers estimates that real output will rise by 4 percent a year from 1983 to 1988, reaching a total of $1.819 trillion in 1972 dollars in 1988. By my estimates in the preceding paragraph, cutting the defense program by 1 percent of GNP and devoting the savings to private investment, starting right now, would raise 1988 real GNP by between 0.5 percent and 2 percent. That is, it would give us between $9 billion and $36 billion of real output in 1972 dollars in 1988. I can hardly believe that is what people mean when they say that cutting the defense program is needed to keep the economy strong.

I do not claim any great precision for these estimates, though I would be extremely surprised if the truth were different enough to alter the conclusion that spending 1 or 2 or 3 percent more or less of GNP on defense would have little effect on the economy. But the main point is that those who see disastrous effects have an obligation to spell out the size and nature of these effects. The size of the defense program is too important to be decided by frightening but fuzzy adjectives.

The Undelivered
Basic Speech

The *Wall Street Journal*, May 28, 1980

Fellow Americans:

It is my duty to tell you that the country is in grave peril. Our fortunes, our lives, our security, and our freedom are in greater danger today than at any time since 1942 when the Battle of Midway made ultimate victory of the Allies in World War II certain.

For ten years or more the American defense forces have been starved and stagnating. At the same time the Soviet Union has been devoting massive resources out of its weak economy to building up its military might. They have now achieved superiority in many respects and if present trends continue they will achieve military superiority in every respect.

No one can any longer have doubts about the aggressive intentions that motivate this Soviet buildup. For those to whom Communist doctrine and the experience of Hungary, Czechoslovakia, Cuba, Angola, and Ethiopia were not sufficiently clear the invasion of Afghanistan was the final proof.

The United States now has a choice between two options. We can rapidly rebuild our military forces so that they will soon be strong enough to assure our survival. Or we can prepare to live under the conditions the masters of the Soviet Union will dictate to us.

It will be my first priority, if elected, to restore the military strength of the United States to a position where it cannot be challenged.

That will be expensive. We must do everything we can to eliminate waste in our armed forces and make them more efficient.

As I shall make the strengthening of our military forces the highest national priority, I shall hope to attract into the defense forces the highest intelligence, ingenuity, and imagination our people can provide. But I would be deluding you if I promised to restore our defenses cheaply.

I propose to increase our expenditures for defense in real terms (that is, above the cost of inflation) by 15 percent a year for the next four years. This would make our total defense expenditures for the four-year period one-third higher than planned with the present program. In 1980 dollars defense expenditures for the four-year period would be about $190 billion higher than with the present program. This surge of spending is necessary to make up for the deficiencies accumulated in the past decade.

This big increase in defense expenditures is well within the capacity of the American economy and the American people. After four years of this increase annual defense expenditures would be about 8 percent of our total production. In the Eisenhower administration we spent 10 percent of our total production for defense. In those years the economy grew vigorously and there was little inflation. We did not feel oppressed by the burden of defense.

The big increase of defense expenditures I propose would still permit the total of public and private nondefense expenditures to rise in the next four years. If total output rises at the same rate as in the past twenty years, real total nondefense expenditures will still be rising by about 2 percent a year. We will still be a nation of great affluence.

But, nevertheless, this proposed increase of defense expenditure will require sacrifice from the American people. The output available for nondefense purposes—for private consumption, for nondefense programs of government and for private investment—will not rise as fast as it has in the past ten years or as fast as the American people have come to expect. Because we will be devoting a larger share of our production to defense we will have a somewhat smaller share for other purposes.

The main implication of this will be for taxation. The American people are heavily taxed and this taxation is slowing down the growth of the economy. For many years I, like others, have believed that the growth of federal expenditures should be held down, so that federal spending as a share of our total production would decline. That would permit a reduction of the share of our incomes that we had to pay in taxes. There would be a cumulative benefit. The reduction of government expenditures relative to the national income would leave more real resources available for private investment, which would in time raise the national income and permit further reduction of taxes.

During the period of the rapid defense buildup the restriction of government's nondefense spending will be more important than ever. We will be less able than ever to afford waste in government and programs, of which there are many, that do not deliver what they promise to deliver. I will do my best to cut this spending. But it would be unrealistic to expect to cut it enough to outweigh the rise of defense spending during the next few years.

Reducing tax rates while total government expenditures as a share of national income are rising will not promote economic growth but will retard it. The rise in the government share means that the private share, consisting of consumption plus investment, must fall. Any comprehensive large cut of tax rates will to some degree raise consumption, which will reduce investment and slow economic growth. A country, like a family, can have more income later if it invests more now, but to invest more now it must consume less now.

If the country tries to spend more for government functions (defense plus nondefense) and at the same time stimulates consumption by cutting taxes, it will have less income later.

We shall have to pay for our rapid defense build-up by restraining the nondefense expenditures of government and by deferring tax reduction. Indeed, during the period of most rapid defense build-up we may have to pay more taxes. We are now paying about 21 percent of the GNP in federal taxes. That may have to rise temporarily to 22 or 23 percent, depending on how much we are able to cut nondefense spending.

Unfortunately, shortsighted policies of the past have brought us to the position where a temporary tax increase of 1 or 2 percent, or even a deferral of tax reduction, is extremely difficult. The easiest course would be to keep the tax rates we have. Then if inflation continues at its recent speed the inflation will raise the tax revenue enough to pay for our defense. In fact, that would even permit what would look like tax reduction but would be only a return to taxpayers of part of the revenue surreptitiously taken from them by inflation. But that is an unacceptable choice.

We must check the inflation, and if we do that we will not have the revenue that inflation yields. In fact, the past inflation has already distorted the tax structure in ways that need to be corrected. Heavy real taxation is being imposed on unreal incomes—on incomes that after recognition of inflation are much smaller than they seem, or are even losses.

We are surely able to find better and more honest ways to pay for the national defense than by the surreptitious route of inflation. We need to make explicit, responsible decisions about raising revenue. Two objectives are most important. First, the very poor should be sheltered from the burden of additional defense. Second, we should seek to reduce the particular tax burdens that bear most heavily on savings, investment, and economic growth.

This points to the need for shifting taxation to the consumption of people with incomes above the poverty level as the way to pay the costs of defense while protecting the very poor and promoting economic growth. There are various ways in which this can be accomplished. It could be done by imposing a heavy tax on gasoline, by introducing a general sales tax in the federal tax system or by reducing the income tax on income that is saved and raising it on income that is consumed. Any of these methods could be accompanied by safeguards for poor people.

I want to emphasize that the first priority is to increase defense expenditures rapidly. I have certain beliefs about what is the best way to pay for that. But I recognize that decisions about that— about how much nondefense spending should be cut and where, and about how the tax system should be restructured—will have to be made by the president and the Congress cooperatively and with due regard to public opinion. None of us should allow insistence on a preferred way of paying for defense to stand in the way of getting the defense program the country needs.

It is many years, almost fifty, since the federal government has made an explicit decision to raise any taxes, other than Social Security taxes, in peacetime. Conventional political wisdom warns against proposing that. But we have the economic problem of war, not of peace. We face the need, as in war, to divert a larger share of our national product to defense, and to do that quickly. That calls for high taxes. I am confident that the American people are willing to pay for their survival and the survival of the country.

I do not make this statement to be frightening. If we are

awake to the danger we can meet it. But the president cannot rearm the country, and meet the costs of doing that, if he does not have the full support of the American people. I want my intentions to be perfectly clear, so that my election will be understood, at home and abroad, as an affirmation of the American people's support for rebuilding our strength and of their willingness to bear the sacrifices needed for that purpose.

How World War III
Was Lost

The *Wall Street Journal*,
December 3, 1982

T HERE were people who never accepted the term World War III. George Will, a respected columnist of the Carter-Reagan period, called it "The War Against the Totalitarian, 1939–   ." The implication, of course, was that it was all one war, first against the Nazis and then against the Communists. Today, if he were still writing, Mr. Will would be able to complete the dates, making it 1939–1987. For, whatever the war was called, by 1987 the democracies had lost it.

Not a shot had been fired, and no article of surrender had been signed. But the defeat was clear to all when the United States agreed to a United Nations resolution establishing a committee to monitor the world press, television, and radio to prevent the dissemination of anti-peace–anti-people statements, the committee to be composed of delegates from Bulgaria, Cuba, Nicaragua, Angola, and Cambodia. The *Wall Street Journal* and *Commentary* magazine were closed.

There had been other signs of course. In 1983 the Organization for Economic Cooperation and Development had agreed to an economic agreement with the Soviet bloc under which the West would extend credit to the bloc at a fixed interest rate of 5 percent. In 1984 the convention of the Democratic Party had ruled the candidacy of Senator Sam Nunn for the presidential nomination out of order after the Stockholm International Peace Research Institute denounced him as a militarist.

In the same year the Republicans refused to renominate Ronald Reagan, choosing instead Senator Chamberlain, who had just returned from Moscow with a letter from Comrade Andropov offering to buy one million American automobiles a year on long-term, low interest credit. The leaders of an effort to establish a Freedom Party disappeared.

But the beginnings of this defeat came earlier, when the United States decided that it wouldn't pay the cost of defending the Free World or itself. For a time it had looked as if the United States had made the contrary decision and would turn to rearming itself adequately after a decade of somnolence. America's humiliation in Iran and the invasion of Afghanistan had awakened even President Carter to the need for strengthening the armed forces.

Ronald Reagan ran for the presidency, and was overwhelmingly elected, on a platform of rebuilding military strength. He proposed a substantial increase in the defense budget. This would have raised real defense expenditures by 9 percent per annum, raising them as a share of GNP from about 5.5 to 7 percent, which was still less than the 10 percent spent in the Eisenhower-Kennedy years. There were some experts, such as the Committee on the Present Danger, who thought the Reagan defense budget was inadequate. Still, the Reagan program was a significant movement toward a stronger military posture. And it was adopted without much dissent by the Congress, Democrats as well as Republicans.

But in the winter of 1981–82 and the spring of 1982 things began to change. The president had to agree to some cuts in his defense budget. On June 10, 1982, the Republicans and conservative Democrats in the House adopted a budget which cut the president's proposed 9 percent annual increase in defense spending to 7 percent—a cut of more than 20 percent. That was regarded as a triumph. Even people devoted to defense agreed that it was the best the president could get. But it was clear then that the rebuilding of America's military strength was bogged down in a morass of special interests and that the United States would not pay the costs.

This became even clearer after the 1982 election, when Congress returned with a determination to cut the defense budget. This attitude was a reaction to the high rate of unemployment, though no one had shown that cutting defense was a way to increase jobs. So in a special session of Congress in December 1982 the defense budget was cut a further 10 percent.

In a cliché expression of those days, this action "sent a signal." As the Committee on the Present Danger had said: "Any budgetary revision by the Congress cutting the projected levels of defense funding or deferring or stretching out the proposed five-year program, against the will of the president, would give a dangerous signal to the Soviet Union and our Allies."

The Soviets got the signal that they did not have to worry about America's rearmament. The U.S. strategy of confronting the Soviet Union with a choice between arms limitation and an arms race was defeated because the threat of an arms race was seen not to be credible.

The Western Europeans also got the signal. They saw that they could no longer count on defense by the United States and therefore felt it necessary to cozy up to the Soviet Union. That accounted for the European drive, to which the United States acceded, for larger economic relations with the Soviet Union, even if on concessionary terms from the West.

And that gave the United States a signal back. With the Soviet Union increasingly adamant and Western Europe decreasingly cooperative with us, the value of what remained of the U.S. military buildup was increasingly in doubt. More and more it appeared that the choices for the United States were conciliation or suicide. And this led to a whittling down of the military program to a point at which the Soviets could simply instruct the United States not to seek military parity or survivability.

Those months between October 1981 when the Reagan defense program seemed invincible and December 1982 when it was clearly impossible are crucial for the history of the loss of World War III. What happened then?

Of course, there had always been people who opposed the program either because they thought the Soviets were weak, or because they thought they were peace-loving or because they didn't mind adapting to the Soviet way of life. These people were quiet during the year following Mr. Reagan's election, which was the period of his maximum popularity and power. The country was all conservatives, nationalists and hawks then, and the few doves had no desire to expose themselves to ridicule.

But as the year wore on Mr. Reagan began to suffer the fate of other presidents. Overexposure, trivial mistakes, and inevitably controversial policies cut him down to a size that made attack at least feasible. When that happened the anti-defense "pro-peace" chorus in the country rose. This was undoubtedly rein-forced by the world-wide "peace" movement which was, in part, a Soviet reaction to the fear of Western rearmament after the invasion of Afghanistan.[1]

But the rising resistance of the peacenicks wouldn't by itself have been sufficient to turn the tide. What ended the Reagan rearmament effort was the disaffection or weakening of people who considered themselves, and were, supporters of a strong de-fense program. They had registered their support in 1980 by electing Mr. Reagan and again in 1981 by backing his defense budget. But they had done that when they thought that the defense program was free—that they wouldn't have to give anything up for it. The magic wand of economic growth would provide for everything.

As 1982 progressed it became clear to many of those people that defense was not free. And when that happened they discov-ered that while defense was important it wasn't the most important thing.

For some, a defense expansion of the Reagan magnitude was less important than maintaining the growth of nondefense pro-grams, mainly social programs. For others defense expansion was less important than preventing the budget deficit from exceeding a certain magnitude, which for some unclear reason turned out to be $150 billion. For others, defense expansion was less impor-tant than holding down taxes.

None of these people thought or said that they were prepared to sacrifice national security for some other objective. They all maintained that their combination of less defense and more of something else was the best strategy for national security. Those who preferred larger social programs held they were essential for the social solidarity which was a prior requirement for national security. Those who preferred to hold the deficit down said that was necessary to prevent an economic crisis which would make a continued defense buildup insupportable. Those who put lower taxes first said they were indispensable for the economic growth that was essential to national survival.

It happened that many in each group that placed the military buildup second to some other objective had a special interest in

[1] See Vladimir Bukovsky, "The Peace Movement and the Soviet Union," *Commentary,* May 1982.

the other objective. Those who were most protective of the nondefense social programs in the budget tended to have constituencies which thought themselves the direct beneficiaries of those programs. Those who put restraining the deficit first tended to have an interest in financial markets that was not equally shared by the rest of the country. Many of those who put low taxes first were large taxpayers.

This didn't mean that they were insincere. They all honestly saw matters from their own perspective. Of course, they were all wrong. As the country learned later—too late—the danger to the free world was not the inadequacy of American social programs, or the size of American budget deficits, or the height of American taxes. It was the inadequacy of the actual and prospective American military establishment.

In any case, the upshot was that, even though a large majority of the people thought that defense was important, they couldn't agree on how to pay for it. They couldn't agree on what to give up in order to have a larger defense program and could, therefore, agree only on a smaller one.

The tragic irony is that in the end, after World War III, the American people paid more than it would have cost to defend the country. They paid more even in the common coinage of taxes and deficits, because they had to raise the fund assessed by the United Nations upon America as its contribution to WEEP—the World Economic Equalization Plan. But far beyond that, they paid more in the rare coinage of freedom and the lives of those who would fight for it.

National Security and the Economy

The *AEI Economist*, January 1980

In the golden age, thirty years ago, we were all certain that the U.S. economy made a decisive contribution to our national security. This contribution came in several ways:

- The unequaled productive capacity of the United States would enable us to support a defense force that no one else could match. We could afford the defense we required and still satisfy the nondefense needs of our population on a scale never before imagined.

- We could provide economic assistance to build up the capabilities of those countries that shared our national security interests, which meant, essentially, Western Europe.

- We could limit the economic development of our enemies—the Communists—by denying them access to goods and technology that we controlled.

- We were invulnerable to external economic pressure because we had within our borders almost all the resources needed for our economic growth.

- We could provide economic assistance to the less developed, and nonaligned, countries which would help to create stability within and among them and to make them friendly toward us or, at least, desirous of maintaining our friendship toward them.

- The obvious success of our political-economic system in meeting the needs of our population would make other countries want to emulate us, which would be a force for peace and friendship with us. In the end, the attractiveness of our economic performance might even induce in the Soviet Union changes of internal and external policy which would reduce its threat to us.

This confidence in our economy as the bulwark of our national security began to erode in the 1960s, and the process of erosion speeded up in the 1970s. Although defense expenditures as a share of the gross national product (GNP) or of the budget declined, argument over whether we could afford those expenditures became more acute. Our foreign policy became increasingly dominated by fear of an interruption of oil supplies from abroad. The greatly increased economic strength of Western Europe and Japan, which we had fostered, made them more independent of us politically and raised new sources of friction. In an effort to obtain trade advantages, we felt obliged to relax trade restrictions against the Communist countries, which we had thought were of national security advantage to us. We came to expect popular movements around the world to be anti-Western and anti-capitalist.

The low point in this decline of confidence was probably reached around the first half of 1979. The economy had come to be regarded not as a source of strength but as a source of weakness and vulnerability. The loss of confidence in the economy, over the course of thirty years, coincided with the change in the national mood from "We can!" to "We can't!"

Undoubtedly, there was much that was naive and shortsighted in our view of the economics of national security thirty years ago. We were looking at a balance of world economic power which resulted in part from the war devastation of Europe and Asia and which could not be expected to last. Our own independence of imported supplies was an unusual situation for a major power and would diminish, especially as our own growth increased our demand for raw materials and our own policy promoted open exchange. Our notions of the connections between economic aid and economic development, and between development and political solidarity, were too simple.

But, still, the reaction to a feeling of economic weakness went too far. What we should have learned is not that our economy is weak or that economic strength doesn't matter but that economic strength is not the same as military and political power and does not necessarily yield such power. But economic strength can be a mighty source of military and political power if it is used with will and intelligence. The deficiencies in our world position today are not due to weakness of the economy but to inadequate and shortsighted use of the economy's capabilities. This is true even if we look at the area of our greatest, and apparently most hopeless, vulnerability—our dependence on oil from the Middle East. If, when the danger was already clear six years ago, we had begun applying our economic capacity to accumulating stockpiles, to strengthening our military posture in the Middle East, and to increasing our domestic sources of energy, our vulnerability today would be radically less than it is.

This feeling of being up against the economic limits is now being questioned. The evidence of our military weakness which came out during the SALT debate has made it almost inevitable that we will increase at least a little the share of the GNP going to defense. Events in Iran have prodded us into trying to demonstrate that we can live without Iranian oil. The Soviet invasion of Afghanistan has led us to test the possible usefulness of trade embargoes as an instrument of force short of war. But these are altogether small and tentative moves; Gulliver is stirring beneath his bonds but has not yet broken them. Therefore, it is worthwhile to consider some of the main facts about the relationship between the economy and our national security.

Can We Afford Defense?

Mr. Carter has proposed to increase defense expenditures by 4.5 percent a year for five years in real terms—that is, beyond the added costs resulting from inflation. That was before events in Afghanistan taught him something about the intentions of the Soviet Union. Possibly his new lesson may induce him to support an even bigger increase in defense spending.

The prospect of increased defense spending will certainly raise questions about the ability of our economy, beset as it is by many ills, to support a heavier defense burden. The fact is that, by any reasonable standard, our defense burden is very light and our ability to bear a heavier burden very great. This fact is commonly denied, and the opposite is often taken for granted. It is necessary, therefore, to review the basic evidence.

Defense expenditures in the United States, in real terms, have been lower in recent years than at any time since before the Korean War—that is, since before 1951. In the three years of the Carter administration we spent $107 billion a year for defense, in 1979 dollars. In dollars of the same value we spent $128 billion a year in the seven Eisenhower years after the end of the Korean War.

We spent at about the same rate, $129 billion a year, in the five Kennedy-Johnson years before the Vietnam buildup. After the Vietnam War we never regained the previous rate of spending. In the four Nixon-Ford years after Vietnam, 1973 to 1976, the rate was only $110 billion, and it fell under Carter.

In view of our recent low level of defense spending and the well-documented increase in Soviet spending, the deterioration of our military position should be no surprise. These figures do not, however, tell the full story of the decline of our defense *burden.* For that we should look at the ratio of our defense spending to our total output because the GNP is the best measure of our ability to bear the defense burden. (See table.) We see the startling fact that the ratio of our defense spending to our GNP in 1979 was lower than in any year since before World War II—that is, since the days when we thought, mistakenly, that we were protected by the British Navy and the French Army.

In the seven Eisenhower years after the Korean War we devoted over 11 percent of the GNP to defense. In the five Kennedy-Johnson years before the major involvement in Vietnam we spent a little over 9 percent for defense. In the Nixon years the ratio was 5.4 percent, and in the Carter years it fell to 4.6 percent.

It is worth remembering that in the years when we were devoting about 10 percent of the GNP to defense we enjoyed strong economic growth and admirable price stability. This does not mean that a defense burden of 10 percent is good for the economy, but it does indicate that such a burden, for a country as rich as ours, is not a necessary source of economic difficulty.

The proposed increase of defense expenditures at the annual

THE BURDEN OF DEFENSE
(Billions of 1979 Dollars)

	AVERAGE ANNUAL GROSS NATIONAL PRODUCT	AVERAGE ANNUAL DEFENSE EXPENDITURE	DEFENSE SPENDING AS A PERCENTAGE OF GNP
1954–1960	1124	128	11.4
1961–1965	1385	129	9.3
1973–1976	2039	110	5.4
1977–1979	2301	107	4.6

rate of 4.25 percent for five years would still leave the defense burden much lower than it was from 1954 to 1965, when we bore it lightly. If GNP did not rise at all, the proposed rate of increase of defense would bring the ratio of defense to GNP up to only 5.7 percent. If real GNP was rising by 2 percent a year, a small increase by historical standards, the ratio of defense to GNP would rise to only 5.2 percent of GNP, or about half the figure we lived with between the Korean and Vietnam wars. The amount of output available for nondefense purposes would still rise by almost 10 percent over the five-year period.

For the ratio of defense spending to GNP to reach the 10 percent figure of 1954–1965, an increase would be required in defense spending of 17 percent a year for five years—even on the extreme assumption that total GNP does not rise at all. That would be almost four times the rate of increase proposed by Mr. Carter. In short, we are a long way from any economic limit to the ability to increase defense spending.

Some will ask why we can afford more government spending on defense, but not on health, education, welfare, and housing programs. The answer is clear: the survival of the country is not threatened by the inadequacy of our provision for these social programs. It is threatened by the inadequacy of our provision for defense.

Of course, during the earlier period when we were devoting 10 percent of the GNP to national defense, we were not also devoting 15 percent of the GNP to nondefense federal expenditures, as we are now doing. This means, as a matter of arithmetic, that if we are to restore the ratio of defense spending to the GNP to 10 percent, we will require a reduction in the nondefense-spending ratio, a higher tax burden than we previously bore, or a very large budget deficit. The conclusion is obvious that defense spending will not return to the previous ratio unless there is a strong feeling in the country, supported and advanced by responsible leadership, that priorities have radically changed and the nation is in danger. The budgetary constraints do not, however, change the basic fact that, in view of the large growth in the economy since the Eisenhower-Kennedy days, we can regain the previous ratio of defense expenditures while still enjoying much higher per capita nondefense output, public and private, than we experienced in the past.

Oil Paralysis

The rationale of our recent policy in the Middle East is a mystery. Still, it has been difficult to escape the idea that we were heavily influenced by the fear that the Arabs would use the oil weapon against us. In a world where everything influences everything else, everything must be taken into account. It is inevitable and rational that a major change in the world's oil situation should influence United States policy. But the policy should be influenced by a realistic appraisal of the situation and not by an exaggeration. There is every reason to believe that our policy has been unnecessarily inhibited, and our independence unduly limited, by excessive fears of our vulnerability and magnified ideas of the costs to us of reducing our vulnerability.

There have, in my opinion, been several kinds of error in the national assessment of the oil situation and the implications for United States policy. We have exaggerated the ability of the Arab oil producers to injure us without cost to themselves, as if their production were higher and their prices lower than necessary to maximize their own long-run revenues, or as if they didn't care about income. We have exaggerated the adverse consequences for us of an increase in the balance-of-payments deficit of the oil-importing countries. We have underestimated the amount of alternative kinds of energy, especially natural gas, that would be forthcoming with higher prices. We have underestimated the possibility of conversion from oil to other kinds of energy, especially coal, that would be induced by a higher price of oil. Our political leaders have overestimated popular resistance to higher prices of energy and have encouraged that resistance by exploiting the idea that the main significance of higher oil prices is that they enrich the oil companies. As a result of these misconceptions we have tolerated a greater degree of dependence than was economically necessary and have lived under an exaggerated fear of the degree of dependence that we actually have.

The problem of energy vulnerability is essentially a question of time. If we do nothing, and if we do survive, our vulnerability will come to an end. By and by the supply of oil in the Middle East will be exhausted, and we will find ourselves living without it. Presumably we will be living mainly on energy from domestic sources and possibly in an economy that uses much less energy in relation to its total output than we now do. Even before the oil runs out the real price of energy will have risen to a point that induces more domestic production of energy and less consumption.

We can, by our policies, either bring this date of reasonable independence closer or push it further off. On the whole, our actions of the past six years have tended to prolong our dependence by holding down energy prices here, thus discouraging incentives for more domestic production and encouraging continuation of a high-energy way of life. There is now some evidence of a change in this policy. The price of natural gas has been allowed to rise, and we are now permitting the price of crude oil to rise gradually to the world level. The effect of the decontrol of oil prices is, unfortunately, blunted by the misnamed "windfall profits tax," but some beneficial effect still will be felt. Probably the most powerful force moving us toward independence is the increase in world oil prices.

Unless there are technological breakthroughs which no one now foresees, the cost of obtaining energy is going to rise and that will slow down the growth of real output to some extent. That would happen even if we were not importers of oil, or if all our imports come from secure and friendly sources. How severe the negative effect on us would be of the world energy "shortage," or of the rising real cost of energy, is a matter of dispute. I have previously estimated that it might reduce the normal rate of growth of the United States real GNP from 3 percent per annum to 2.8 percent per annum over the next twenty-five years.[1] Whatever the cost may be, it is not a source of vulnerability.

Our vulnerability arises from dependence on insecure imports. We can reduce the period of our dangerous dependence, at a cost. For example, we could impose a heavy duty on oil imports; this would discourage some domestic consumption and encourage some domestic production that would only be profitable at a price above the world price.

The cost of shortening the period of dependency will depend on how much we want to shorten it. To achieve security by the

[1] See Herbert Stein, "Energy—The Wrong Summit," *AEI Economist,* July 1979, pp. 1–8.

year 2000 will cost less than to achieve it by 1990 because the
longer period would require less premature replacement of the
existing capital stock and allow more experimentation with new
processes. To achieve energy security within a very short period
by this "economic" route of developing domestic production and
changing patterns of use may be too expensive and not worthwhile. This doesn't mean that the achievement of security is impossible, or that it shouldn't be sought, but only that it shouldn't
be sought by those means. How do we protect ourselves this
year against the possibility that the Soviets might threaten to sink
all tankers carrying oil to the United States unless we agreed,
for example, to get out of Western Europe? We don't protect
ourselves by preparing to get along for a year or two, beginning
right now, without imported oil. We protect ourselves by maintaining a political and military posture which makes it unwise for
the Soviets to threaten us in that way, including naval forces to
prevent the tankers from being sunk and strategic forces to
threaten dire retaliation if they are sunk. And that is the only
efficient way, and maybe the only possible way, to protect our
ability to refuse a demand put to us in the near future by a coalition
of major oil-producing countries.

In the short run our security against the use of the oil weapon
depends not on our energy position but on our general military-
economic-political strength. We have been reluctant to recognize
this fact, or at least to talk about it, for several reasons:

• Since Vietnam an important part of the American establishment has found it unthinkable that the United States should ever
use power to protect any national interest.

• We have found it difficult to imagine that the oil weapon
would be used to threaten any interest vital to the United States,
except insofar as we have underwritten the security of Israel.
Therefore, it must have seemed to many that we could always
avert the use of the oil weapon against us by putting a little more
pressure on Israel.

• The big oil producers seemed immune to our power because
their huge monetary reserves made them economically unassaila-
ble and because direct military assault would result in the destruction of the oil fields.

Recent developments, especially in Iran, are disabusing us
of the first two notions. We are finding that, despite our own
abstention, others are quite prepared to use force in ways that

are injurious to us. We are beginning to face the fact that power is loose in the world, and unless we are willing to allow our lives to be dominated by the power of others we must be prepared to use ours. It is obviously absurd for us to be spending $120 billion a year on military power if there are no vital interests for which we would use it. Moreover, we have seen that our only potential conflict of interest with the oil-producing countries does not relate to Israel. Iran has been willing to cut off oil shipments to us, as well as to imprison our nationals, in an effort to force us to return the Shah. We can imagine other unacceptable demands being placed upon us as a result of nationalistic, religious, or ideological conflicts in the Middle East, and these demands being backed up by the threat of cutting off oil supplies.

The Iranian situation has forced us to begin a reconsideration, in a realistic way, of the proposition that the oil-producing countries are immune to our power. We began with the freezing of Iranian assets. Other moves to apply economic sanctions followed. The support of the European allies and Japan was sought, and the United Nations was asked to impose limitations on economic dealings with Iran. Also, certain tentative and limited military moves were made. An aircraft carrier with escorting naval vessels was dispatched to the neighborhood of the Persian Gulf. The administration announced plans to establish forces in the Indian Ocean and began negotiations with countries of that area for the acquisition of bases.

Whether or not these measures help to release the hostages in Iran, they are important as reflecting a greater willingness, in and out of the government, to explore the use of American power in the Middle East. If this exploration is continued, it will reveal that America is not powerless in the area. Middle Eastern oil is a tremendous asset for those who control it. Because it is such an asset there are many contenders for control, and outside parties, like the United States, have an opportunity to influence who controls by the disposition of their economic and military assistance. Moreover, whoever controls the oil can enjoy the benefits of it only in exchange for the goods and assets of the rest of the world, and this can be interdicted by outside powers such as the United States.

The United States, if it is willing to use its economic power, or the military power its economic power can support, can strongly influence the behavior of those who control OPEC oil. Our ability to do this is complicated, but not eliminated, by the possibility that our use of force might result in the "destruction" of the oil fields. This means that production of some part of the world's oil might be suspended for a period. Willingness to use force can shorten the period during which we might be deprived of imported oil and that would be a major contribution to our security. We would still require measures to enable us to survive that period. The most important measure would be the accumulation of reserve stocks of oil in the United States. Unfortunately, our own policy on reserve stocks has been terribly delinquent. The prospect of price controls and allocations has weakened the incentive for private accumulation of stocks. At the same time, the government has fallen far behind its targets for the accumulation of federally owned stocks.

The geographical distribution of the world's oil makes the achievement of our security more expensive than it would have been if all the oil were within our own borders and more expensive than it seemed to be thirty years ago when our energy requirements were smaller. But this additional expense is certainly not unbearable and probably not even very large relative to the capacity of our economy. Our situation at the end of World War II, in which we were self-sufficient in essential materials, was most unusual. The usual strategy by which great powers ensured their supply of essential materials was to use their general economic capability to support a military force adequate to assure access to foreign resources. That was one of the main functions of navies. Our economic strength provides us with the capacity to do the same thing.

Economics as Irritant

After World War II, the United States national security interest in helping to rebuild the economic strength of Western Europe seemed obvious. Such rebuilding was useful, and perhaps essential, to keep the devastated countries of Western Europe from falling into the Communist orbit. A reconstructed Europe could contribute to the common defense against the Soviet Union. And an economically viable Japan would be a key base for American forces in the Pacific.

American efforts to assist the restoration of the Western European and Japanese economies were dramatically successful, and the basic national security benefits sought from those efforts were achieved. No one can doubt that this has been a net gain for the United States. Some problems have arisen, however, as the European and Japanese economies became stronger.

Economic issues have become the subject of conflict between the government of the United States and the governments of our chief industrial allies. Competition in trade has been the main source of this contention. Since the other countries were gaining in competitiveness as they recovered from the effects of the war, it was usually the United States that was the complainant. We alleged that the others were dumping their products on our markets and that they were excluding our products by devious means. At various times we have claimed that the policies of other countries were forcing us into balance-of-payments deficits. We have tried to persuade or pressure our allies to restrain their sales to us and to change regulations that we thought discriminated against our exports. We have asked them to adapt their fiscal and monetary policies to assist us in reducing our balance-of-payments deficits.

Complaints have run in the other direction also. For many years other countries believed that we were exporting inflation to them by our own expansionary policies, which forced them to acquire dollars and which increased their money supplies more than they liked. Recently there has been criticism of our failure to restrain our oil imports, which put upward pressure on the world oil prices that they, as well as we, pay. The economic action that angered our allies most was probably our embargo on the export of soybeans in 1973.

These economic issues set off bilateral or multilateral negotiations which almost never end with general satisfaction. The result is often irritation and suspicion, which weaken the psychological basis needed for political and military solidarity.

How serious such conflicts over economic issues may be in the conduct of foreign affairs is seen in the observations of Henry Kissinger, stimulated by his experience in the negotiation of an agreement under which Japan would limit its exports of textiles to the United States.

> But the real problem, of course, was deeper, and it is of fundamental importance to the future of all the industrial democracies. While

Japan, the United States, Canada, and the nations of Western Europe are political and military allies, we are also inevitable economic competitors. As democracies, indeed, our systems disperse economic power as well as the political authority by which decisions are made on economic questions. No government has solved the problem of how autonomous national economic policies can be pursued without growing strains with political allies who are also trade rivals; even less have we solved the challenge of coordinating economic goals to reinforce the cohesion of free peoples. We proclaim interdependence but we have been reluctant to accept that this involves a measure of dependence.

Thus trade disputes among the industrial democracies are still with us; the competitive and protectionist pressures surged again after the 1973–1974 energy crisis threw the industrial world into a protracted recession. The textiles fiasco was one major lapse in Japan's otherwise impressive record of economic decision-making. Yet the vulnerability of American policy to protectionist pressures, which forced us to stake so much on the effort to get such an agreement from the Japanese (if only to head off more brutal legislative impositions), remains a serious weakness of the American system. Protectionism is the resort of the economically weak; a wiser national policy would seek to enhance the mobility of labor and resources so that we can shift out of declining industries and expand our more productive sectors. And protectionism is above all an untenable posture for a nation that seeks to be the leader of the alliance of industrial democracies. This has thrown us into conflict when the necessity of statesmanship is to reemphasize in the economic field the fundamental community of interest that would surely operate in the face of obvious external threats to our security. The danger, conversely, is that economic clashes of mounting bitterness could undermine that very unity of interest and aspiration that is the bulwark of our freedom. We have yet to rise to this challenge.[2]

The ironic, but also fortunate, aspect of the situation which troubles Kissinger is that most of the conflicts he was looking at were not conflicts of interest between the United States and other countries. They were at most conflicts of interest between some sectors of the American economy and some sectors of the economies of other countries. Thus, in the case to which Kissinger referred, there was a conflict between the United States textile industry and the Japanese textile industry. But there was no conflict between the Japanese textile industry and the United States

[2] Henry Kissinger, *White House Years* (Boston: Little, Brown, 1979), p. 340.

as a whole or the American people as a whole. Indeed, for most of the American people, the unlimited importation of cheap textiles from Japan would have been a benefit, and most objective observers would say that the American people as a whole would have benefited. Similarly, the Japanese people as a whole had no economic interest in imposing artificial barriers to imports from the United States.

Much the same can be said about the controversy that has surfaced repeatedly in the past twenty years over the balance-of-payments deficit of the United States. We have tended to regard that deficit as a great evil for which we have blamed our economic partners. But in fact a balance-of-payments deficit is, in many circumstances, not an evil. In the ordinary course of events some countries will have deficits and some surpluses, which means that the surplus countries are supplying resources to the deficit countries, and this may be a beneficial condition for both parties, just as private borrowers and lenders typically benefit from the economic relations between them. In any case, if a particular country is dissatisfied with its deficit or surplus position this creates no obligation for its economic partners to correct it.

The basic fact is that our economic relations with the other countries of the non-Communist world have been almost entirely to the benefit of all parties. The conflicts among us over economic issues have not usually resulted from real conflicts of national interests. They have resulted, rather, from ignorance or from the subservience of national policy to special interests. These are, of course, conditions that exist. But they should not be allowed to overshadow the national interest in open economic relations and in harmony with our major allies.

Economic Relations with the Communist World

There has been a marked change in the economic relations between the United States and the Communist countries since the early postwar years. In those days we severely limited our trade with those countries. This policy was mainly based on the theory that denial of American supplies would significantly limit the military potential of the Communist countries and also, by depressing their standards of living, cause internal unrest. We have now had a substantial liberalization of trade and of credit to the Communist world, especially to the Eastern European satellites, but also to the Soviet Union and most recently to the People's Republic of China.

A number of beliefs, some political and some economic, have led to this change of policy:

- that the Soviet, or Communist, economy has become so strong and self-sufficient that its effectiveness as a military base or its internal stability cannot be affected by the with-holding of economic relations with the Free World
- that "regularization" of economic relations would help to make the Communists, the Soviets particularly, less aggres-sive—in part because they would fear loss of an economic relationship on which they depended
- that strengthening economic relations with the Eastern European satellites would make them more independent of the Soviet Union
- that strengthening the People's Republic of China would make it a more reliable counterweight against the Soviet Union in the world's balance of power
- that the availability of supplies and credit from other sources greatly diminished the leverage that the United States could exercise over the Communist countries offering or withhold-ing economic relations
- that the United States would gain significant economic bene-fits from increasing trade relations with the Communist bloc

The judgment that closer economic relations with the Soviets would lead to less hostile political relations was not supported by the history of trading partners, on, for example, the European continent. Neither is there evidence that the behavior of the Sovi-ets since we liberalized trade and credit with them has been "paci-fied" by that move. Possibly the case on political grounds for expanding economic relations with the Eastern European satellites and with the People's Republic of China is greater.

The point here, however, is not to evaluate the political, or national security, gains or losses from the decision to increase economic relations with the Communists. Our concern in this essay is with the economics of the matter. Have the Communist economies become so strong that goods and capital from the United States are of little significance to them? Can't they be expected to make any political concessions in exchange for economic relations? Wouldn't they be weakened by the absence of such relations? Have the economic benefits to us from those relations become so great that we must seek to achieve them even if the political results are problematical or negative?

The Communist countries are undoubtedly much more productive than they were thirty years ago. But the demands upon their economies have also increased greatly. We can see, for example, that the Soviet Union is intermittently dependent on grain imports to maintain the standard of food consumption that the government considers it important to maintain. Moreover, the Soviets have also apparently found a cutback of their plans for investment to be necessitated by their rapid increase in military expenditures. Thus, one should not conclude that the economic benefits of its external relations are unimportant to the Soviet Union. Clearly, the Soviets will not be deterred from any action for which they would risk nuclear war by the threat that we would also cut off trade with them. But there may be some actions short of nuclear war but nevertheless hostile to us which could be deterred by the economic weapon, if we felt free to use it.

The main point is that we have been inhibited in the use of our trade as a bargaining chip for political advantage by the thought that we have a significant gain to be realized from such trade. That is a mistake. Our trade with Communist nations varies from year to year with their harvests, but it is typically not more than about 2 percent of our total exports or two tenths of one percent of our GNP. But the *gain* from the trade is even less than these figures might suggest. If we sell the Communist countries $2 billion worth of product the gain to the United States economy is not $2 billion. The gain is the excess of that $2 billion over the value that the same resources would have produced if they had been devoted to some other use, either for export or for domestic consumption. That gain would ordinarily be much less than $2 billion.

The utility of trade as a lever in dealing with the Soviets would, of course, be greatly enhanced if the industrial democracies acted in unison. Some of the other countries, such as West Germany, have relatively much more trade with the Communists than the United States does, and therefore would have more to lose from a decision to withhold trade. But even for those countries the potential losses are not great, and that is surely true for the industrial democracies considered as a group. Again, that is not to say that cutting off trade with the Communists would enhance our security. It only means that having the option to do so would be useful in some circumstances, and we should not feel inhibited in the use of that option by the fear that we would suffer serious economic consequences if we did.

The Free Economy as Model

We were not wrong thirty years ago to believe that the free economy, on the United States style, had enormous benefits to offer the people of the world. The expansion of opportunities and improvement of living standards enjoyed in the United States, Western Europe, and Japan since 1945 are evidence that we were correct. And the experience of Taiwan, South Korea, Hong Kong, Singapore and Israel shows that the possibilities are not confined to the old industrial countries.

But we were, apparently, wrong in thinking that the superiority of this model would attract much of the world to emulate it and that such emulation, or convergence of systems, would be a force for peace and security. Probably the basic thing to say is that much of the world has not been free to choose. But it also seems true that even where the possibility of struggle for freedom exists, the establishment of a Western-style, capitalist, free system is not always one of the eligible options.

Some of the weakness of the U.S. model as an attraction for others is undoubtedly due to our own attitudes. We have lost much of the confidence and pride in our system that we had thirty years ago, and consequently we project a much less clear image of a society that is to be admired and emulated by others. Perhaps because the blessings and achievements of our own society have been taken for granted, discussion has focused on the deficiencies. An outside observer of American talk and writing about ourselves would conclude that we are an oppressed society, but he would not be sure whether the white males of the corporate establishment are oppressing the black, female, and poor, or the bureaucrats of government are oppressing the industrious yeomen and workers. He would conclude that we produce an overwhelming amount of valueless material but also that our productivity is withering. He would find that we are polluting the earth's atmosphere and consuming its resources, and giving nothing back in return. He would see that we are either the aggressive, militaristic arm of multinational corporations, or a helpless, pitiful giant, terrorized by a handful of Iranian students. He would find us ditheringly incapable of managing inflation, the dollar, and the balance of payments.

Most of this would be without foundation, and would, moreover, omit the most fundamental aspects of our society. But it is the picture an observer would get from us—not a picture calculated to inspire resistance to the forces of collectivism.

In the world of ideas, as in others, we have squandered the opportunities our economic system provided us. We have squandered the opportunity to maintain an adequate defense posture. We have squandered the opportunity to attain reasonable energy independence. We have squandered the opportunity to use access to our markets as an instrument of our national security. And we have squandered the opportunity to present to the world the true picture of a free society offering unparalleled benefits to the mass of its citizens. But it is probably not too late. At least, it will never be earlier.

PART 4

Recurring Issues

The Decline of the Budget-Balancing Doctrine,

or

How the Good Guys Finally Lost

From *Fiscal Responsibility
in Constitutional Democracy*,
Martinus Nijhoff Social Sciences
Division, Leiden/Boston, 1978

I HOPE it is understood that the title of this paper, part of which was assigned to me and part of which I chose, is not to be taken seriously. The title implies that there was a budget-balancing doctrine in 1929, when my story begins, that this doctrine subsequently declined, and that this decline was a defeat for the good guys. I am not sure that any of these propositions is true. However, I want to discuss them and also the question of how the change of attitude towards budget balancing, to use the more neutral term rather than decline, happened.

Initially one should distinguish between at least two possible meanings of the budget-balancing doctrine. One is the idea that the budget should be continuously balanced, or at least balanced in every fiscal year. The other is the idea that the budget should be balanced over a longer, unspecified, period, with the deficits of some years being balanced by the surpluses of other years.

Later we shall have occasion to refer to somewhat more complicated meanings of budget balancing, such as balancing at full employment.

We should also distinguish, where we can, among four different meanings of the idea that the doctrine exists:

1. That the doctrine is followed in practice
2. That public officials believe in the doctrine
3. That economists believe in the doctrine
4. That the public believes in the doctrine

Surely, annual budget balancing was not the practice of the federal government, even before 1929. In the 140 years of the nation's history from 1789 to 1929 there were forty-seven years of budget deficit, about one-third of the total. There were always deficits in war years, including the years of minor wars—the Mexican War and the Spanish-American War (although we managed to fight the Battle of Little Big Horn without a budget deficit). We also generally ran deficits in years of depression, or right after. The depression of 1873 was an exception, but the budget did go from a surplus of almost $100 million in 1872 to a surplus of only $2 million in 1874.

Whether our pre-1929 practice should be considered one of balancing the budget in the long run depends on how literally one interprets balance. The federal government, which started with a Revolutionary War debt and incurred some more in the War of 1812 repaid it all, except for about $37,000 by 1834. However, this result was at least in part accidental. We had that lovely protective tariff, which was not imposed for revenue but which yielded a large amount of revenue nonetheless. Since the federal government had no budget bureau it didn't know what to do with all that money and so used it to repay the debt.

After the Civil War there was a run of twenty-eight years of consecutive budget surpluses—surely as much as one can reasonably expect—and the debt was reduced from about $2.75 billion to about $1 billion. This was a big cut, but it still left the debt about ten times as large as it had been before the war.

In eleven consecutive years of surplus after World War I the debt was reduced from about $25.5 billion to about $16 billion, which was still fourteen times as large as the prewar debt. Whether this experience reflects a fierce determination to eliminate the debt is hard to say. From today's standpoint the achievement of the budget surplus in the 1920s seems easy. We were having our first important peace-time experience with that marvelously elastic revenue producer, the income tax, individual and corporate. Expenditure programs had not yet adapted to the fact that in a period of prosperity and economic growth this tax would yield strongly increasing revenues. That is, they did not build in expenditure increases to absorb the growing revenues. So surpluses came easily. Some of these surpluses were given away in tax reductions. However, the revenues frequently exceeded the estimates so that unplanned surpluses emerged. Secretary of the Treasury Mellon claimed that the increased revenues were the result of the tax reductions. However, he was cautious about testing this theory further by making bigger tax cuts.

All of these numbers about the size of the debt up to 1929 look small to us today, and there is a temptation to say that for all practical purposes the debts were eliminated after the Civil War and World War I. But that would not be quite accurate. In 1894, when the Civil War debt reached its low point it was still three times a year's federal revenues and the interest was about 10 percent of the total revenues. In 1929 the federal debt was about four times a year's revenues, and the interest on the debt was about 17 percent of the revenue. By these standards it seems an exaggeration to say that the pre-1929 practice was to eliminate the wartime deficits in peacetime.

Perhaps a more relevant standard is the relation of the federal debt to the GNP. Of course, measurements of the GNP for earlier periods are pretty rough, but the federal debt in 1894 was probably about 7.5 percent of the GNP. In 1929 the ratio was about 16 percent. These are not insignificant fractions.

In summary, budget balancing in the years before 1929 meant in operation that there would be deficits in wars and depressions, which would be followed by surpluses that reduced the debt absolutely and relative to the GNP, but that did not reduce it to zero. The long-run trend of the debt was up, absolutely and relative to GNP. Whether one should say that the United States practiced budget balancing is a matter of taste.

The opinions of responsible federal officials about budget balancing in the pre-1929 period are unclear. During World War I the secretary of the Treasury and other officials were quite concerned with the inflationary consequences of excessive reliance on debt financing, and their discussion of the question in general terms seems fairly modern. What was most lacking was any notion of the relevant quantities. The administration therefore made the predictable decision to finance the war half by borrowing and half by taxation. In actuality the part financed by borrowing was more than half.

After the war, during the 1920s, officials made frequent reference to the desirability of balancing the budget, but without ever revealing what they meant by it or why they thought the budget should be balanced. As far as I can see, they were not then concerned with possible inflationary consequences of deficits. About the most that can be inferred from the statements of Presidents Harding and Coolidge is that the debt should be reduced in order to reduce the interest payable, by reducing the principal amount of the debt and by getting the interest rate down as a result of reducing the government's demand for credit. This reduction of the interest burden was desired as a necessary condition for getting taxes down. But why this year's taxpayers should forego tax reduction in order to run a surplus which would allow future taxpayers to enjoy tax reduction was never discussed.

As the unbroken string of surpluses continued through the 1920s, devotion to the idea of balancing the budget each year became more religious, and the reason for that devotion more obscure. In 1922 President Harding faced the prospect of a budget deficit with equanimity, in view of the probability of a surplus in the next year. (Actually the prospective deficit did not materialize.) By 1929 the director of the Bureau of the Budget was giving the federal officials an inspirational talk about saving money to keep the string of surpluses going like a Big Ten coach who needed one more win to get to go to the Rose Bowl.

However, the practice of budget balancing in the 1920s was child's play, as I have already explained. The real test of meaning and will was to be faced by Herbert Hoover, when revenues fell off in the recession and demands for expenditures to provide employment and relief mounted.

At first President Hoover accepted his deficits as the natural and necessary consequences of the depression. Although he resisted what he regarded as extreme spending proposals, he initiated some expenditure increases himself and certainly made no great effort to balance the budget. In his budget message of December, 1930 he said that he did not view with great concern the deficit for the current fiscal year, noting that we could confidently look forward to the restoration of surpluses with the general recovery of the economic situation.

In September 1931 President Hoover turned very actively towards budget balancing and recommended a large tax increase to achieve it. In my opinion this did not result from any dogmatic devotion of Hoover to a doctrine that the budget should be balanced at all times. He concluded that he was hemmed in by a particular set of circumstances which made a desperate attempt to balance the budget, or at least reduce the deficit, imperative. The British went off gold and there was fear that the United States would be next. Interest rates were rising sharply. Banks were dropping like flies. The president felt the need to demonstrate to the world, especially to the financial community at home and abroad, that the dollar was sound and that our credit markets would not continue to be depressed by enormous additions to the federal debt.

However, it must be said for Hoover that the hard facts of the situation were pretty bad. For one thing, he had to deal with an especially uncooperative Federal Reserve. I treasure as an example the following note of George L. Harrison from a meeting of the Federal Reserve Bank of New York on January 7, 1932: "If we are to deviate from straight and narrow central bank theory because of the terrible economic situation, the government must do all it can to improve the situation—we require an authoritative pronouncement of its intentions with respect to borrowing between now and July 1 and a commitment to operate on a balanced budget beginning July 1, 1932."

As I shall mention below, economists generally considered to be more sophisticated and modern than Hoover saw reasons why the conventional acceptance of depression deficits might not be appropriate in 1932.

The general pre-New Deal view of government officials about budget balancing was that deficits were acceptable in wars and depressions, that the wartime deficits should be limited because of their inflationary consequences, and that the debts accumulated in wars and depressions should be subsequently repaid. The reason for the repayment was apparently the desire to reduce future tax burdens. This gave no clue to the desirable pace of debt reduction, and it did not imply a need to run a surplus or even balance the budget every year, or in every year of peace and prosperity.

I will now turn to the doctrine of budget balancing as held

by economists before 1929 or 1932. Two things immediately strike a modern reader surveying economic literature of the 1920s on budget balancing. One is that the literature is so slight and the other is that there is such a wide gulf between general economics and the discussion of business cycles, unemployment, and so on, where the question of budget balancing comes up in its modern context. Either the economists of the 1920s were much less infatuated with budget balancing than we later came to believe they had been or they took its virtue so much for granted that they did not feel the need to argue about it.

I take as an example the economics textbook that I used in high school. It was a good little book, prepared under the editorial supervision of Allyn A. Young, Professor of Economics at Harvard. The subject of public deficits or debts comes up only once, in a listing of the various sources of revenues, and is completely covered by the following paragraph:

"Sale of bonds and treasury notes. This is a temporary method of raising revenue; such loans must be repaid."[1]

Another sample of 1920s thinking is a college text, *Public Finance,* by Jens P. Jensen. This book identifies three occasions for public borrowing. One is occasional random errors in estimating or planning the relation of revenues to expenditures. A second is the financing of capital improvements. A third is emergencies, mainly war, but also including earthquakes, floods, and epidemics. Depressions are not mentioned. The repeated lesson of the book is to borrow as little as possible and repay as soon as possible. The apparent reason for this is to preserve the government's credit.

Jensen's text of 1924 should not be dismissed as of antiquarian interest only. It did say: "The enormous debt of New York City, for example, is eloquent testimony to the danger from too much borrowing."[2]

I do not find in the American writing of the 1920s the classic argument that deficits are to be avoided because they absorb private savings and so cut the rate of economic growth. During the debate of 1917 on war finance Senator Stone made this point, and quoted John Stuart Mill in support of it. Perhaps this argument

[1] Eugene B. Riley, *Economics for Secondary Schools* (Boston: Houghton Mifflin, 1924), p. 259.
[2] Jens P. Jensen, *Problems of Public Finance* (New York: Thomas Y. Crowell, 1924), p. 471.

was assumed by American economists. If so, it is worth noting that the argument does not say anything about whether there should be deficits at any particular time. It is logically only an argument against a deficit in a current accounts budget, from which capital investments have been excluded. And it is a valid argument only to the extent that priority is to be given to economic growth.

Neither do I find in the American discussion of this period any reference to the related argument which was then known in England as the Treasury view. This was the view that government spending financed from borrowing could not stimulate output and employment because the government borrowing would crowd out an equal amount of private spending. It took our Treasury fifty years to acquire the British Treasury view.

In fact it is unclear who did hold the British Treasury view. Keynes in 1929 attributed that view to Winston Churchill, who was chancellor of the exchequer. However, he misquoted Churchill, who did not say that it was his view. At the same time Keynes insisted that no leading economist of the United Kingdom would endorse that view. Presumably it was the property of Treasury bureaucrats.

Probably this argument did not go on here in the 1920s as it did in Britain because we did not then have a depression as Britain did. But there was in the United States a group of people concerned with planning to deal with a future unemployment problem—having been stimulated by the 1919 depression. They believed that increased public works expenditures financed by borrowing would be helpful, particularly if the borrowing "was assumed by America."

As soon as the issue became an immediate one, with the coming of the Depression, there were large numbers of economists who believed that deficit finance was both inevitable and desirable. Without having taken any poll, I would say that was the standard view among economists.

However, even among economists who took this position there were some who in 1932 were hesitant about the feasibility of expansionary deficit finance, given the international and domestic monetary situation and the state of confidence. I think of Jacob Viner and J. M. Clark in this connection. Viner did suggest that Hoover had created his own problem by insisting that a balanced budget was essential to the national credit until a psychology was created in which it was true. That was probably a little unfair to the president.

In sum, the state of thinking of American economists about budget balancing at the beginning of the Depression can probably be best described as undeveloped. It was for budget balancing but it also recognized a number of real, important conditions in which deficits would be appropriate. It did not rule out deficits in depressions and was ready, when confronted with the problem, to assert the desirability of deficits in such circumstances. Its argument for budget balancing was an argument for balancing the budget in the long run. But even this argument was not very forceful. It was less a demonstration that a balanced budget is optimum than an expression of fear of the lengths to which the government and the people would go if relieved of the belief that a balanced budget is the normal, natural state of affairs.

I will not try to describe public opinion, as distinguished from the opinion of government officials and economists, about budget balancing in this period. There are no polls and I have no other data. Politicians clearly thought then, as they do now, that there was a considerable body of public opinion out there in favor of the balanced budget.

My principal observation from this is that the commitment to the balanced budget before, say, 1932 was not very great, whether in practice or in thought.

How have things changed since? In some respects, or at a certain level of generality, not much.

As far as practice is concerned, we have continued to have a variable budget position, with bigger deficits in some years and smaller ones or surpluses in other years. The biggest deficits come in big wars and smaller deficits come in smaller wars or in recessions. After the big wars, World War II for our generation, the debt has been sharply reduced relative to the national income.

But in other respects there have been changes. The variations in the size of the deficit or surplus associated with fluctuations in economic conditions have been greater, whether measured in relation to the size of the budget or in relation to the size of the GNP. Although these variations continue to be mainly the result of the automatic response of revenues and expenditures to the change in economic conditions, the automatic responses have been increasingly supplemented by discretionary changes. Also, these discretionary changes have increasingly come on the revenue side of the budget, rather than on the expenditure side.

The main change in performance of the past generation, as compared with the earlier periods, is that the average level around which surpluses and deficits revolved has been a deficit, rather than a surplus. This means simply that after the Civil War for about thirty years the debt was reduced and after World War I for about ten years the debt was reduced, but after World War II the debt was increased greatly and almost continuously.

Despite this difference in the behavior of the absolute size of the debt, the reduction of the debt relative to the GNP has been comparable to that in earlier periods. The federal (i.e., Union) debt after the Civil War was probably about 50 percent of the GNP. At its low in 1894 it was about 7.5 percent. At the end of World War I the federal debt was about 30 percent of the GNP. By 1929 it had been reduced to 16 percent. At the end of World War II the federal debt was over 100 percent of the GNP. It is now about 30 percent.

While the debt is now larger relative to the GNP than it was on the earlier occasions, it is much smaller relative to the federal revenues. Even after the deficit forecast for fiscal 1977 the debt would be about 1.6 times the year's revenues, as compared with three times in 1894 and four times in 1929. Interest on the federal debt would be about 10 percent of the revenues, the same as in 1894 and less than in 1929.

Now it is true that a large part of the reduction of the ratio of the debt to GNP has been due to inflation. If there had been no inflation after 1946, and the debt had followed its actual course, the ratio of debt to GNP would have fallen from 100 percent to 75 percent, rather than to 30 percent. Whether the fact that the debt was rising in absolute size, even though less rapidly than real output, caused or contributed to the inflation is an interesting question which I assume to be beyond my present assignment.

The inflation may not have reduced the interest burden on the debt, because the inflation tended to raise interest rates.

This difference of performance, the increase of the debt after World War II contrasted with the decrease in its absolute size after the Civil War, does not necessarily reflect doctrinal differences. The circumstances since 1946 were in some respects more difficult than in the earlier period. We did have two wars after 1946, whereas the periods 1865 to 1894 and 1918 to 1929, when the debt was being reduced, were years of peace. Even when we were not at war we had a heavier military burden than in earlier periods. Also, we have had more serious recessions than during the 1920s, although not worse than in the 1870s.

So, even if there had been the same determination to reduce the debt absolutely as in the earlier periods less might have been accomplished because the obstacles were greater. However, the fact is that there was less determination. One evidence of this is that there was no provision after World War II, as there was after World War I, to set up a sinking fund and make annual reduction of the debt a regular charge against the budget.

The cumulative deficits of the post-World War II period through 1975 have been around 1 percent of GNP. To have kept the absolute size of the debt from rising would have required that on the average surpluses should be larger and deficits smaller by 1 percent of GNP. The swings from surplus to deficit between peace and war or between prosperity and recession could have been of the same magnitude as they were. But everything would have gone on at a higher level of surplus or smaller level of deficit. This would not, I think, have made stabilization policy any more difficult, or the management of war finance any more inconvenient. It would not have been impossible. But it would have required a willingness to pay more taxes relative to the expenditures, and this would in turn have required a belief that over the long run avoidance of absolute increase in the debt was highly valuable. This belief has not been present.

The change in the view of the budget problem held by public officials in the past forty or fifty years is pretty obvious, despite their periodic regression to the language of more innocent days. Whereas they had always, or almost always, accepted the fact that they would have deficits in depressions, they now came to accept much larger deficits, relative to the GNP or to the budget. Moreover, they came to accept the notion that they should take active steps which would increase the deficit in recessions and that the proper size of these steps was the size needed to get the economy back to where it should be in the short run. It was a short-run economic problem.

That is, they became true believers or camp followers of functional finance, of the view that the proper deficit or surplus is the one that gets the economy onto its optimum feasible path. Presidents have been uneasy with this position, which leaves the debt at the mercy of the economy and the economists, and they have sought some more reliable or familiar anchor. Thus Roosevelt toyed with the idea of balancing the budget over the cycle, or with balancing a current-accounts budget. When Truman proposed a deficit during the 1949 recession he consoled himself and the country by explaining that the budget would return to balance at full employment. Eisenhower, Kennedy, and Nixon each at times described his policy in terms of balancing the budget at full employment. But this was mainly salve for their own consciences or for what they believed to be the public conscience. It did not much deter them from doing what they thought was in the short-run economic interest and within the limits of political feasibility.

A policy of functional finance does not necessarily mean that the deficit cumulates over long periods. It only says that we should have the size of deficit or surplus at any time that will get us on the optimum feasible path. Whether this policy leads to deficits or surpluses in the long run will depend on how the optimum feasible path is defined, how the economy behaves spontaneously in relation to the path, and how other policies which might affect the behavior of the economy, such as monetary policy, are managed. The fact that functional finance has yielded a long-run deficit during the postwar period does not mean that Alvin Hansen was finally right and that we have entered the age of secular stagnation. It may mean that we have defined the optimum state of the economy too exclusively in terms of the unemployment rate, and of too ambitious an unemployment rate, so that inflation accelerates and the needed deficit increases. This is probably part of the explanation for the tendency of functional finance to lead to long-run deficits in the postwar period.

Another aspect of functional finance needs to be mentioned in this connection. To conduct a policy of functional finance requires estimates of the size of the surplus or deficit needed to get on the optimum path. But the president's economists cannot tell him within a wide margin what that proper size is. Within that range he has to make that choice himself, and he is not neutral about where he makes it. If his economists cannot tell him that a $10 billion deficit is better than a $20 billion, he is likely to choose the $20 billion, because the voters like tax cuts and expenditure increases. This bias is increased when the Congress enters the picture.

From time to time the classic argument against deficits on

the ground that they absorb saving and slow down economic growth has surfaced in official thinking. President Eisenhower used this point in recommending a budget surplus in 1960. We have been hearing it again recently from Washington, especially from the secretary of the Treasury. However, I believe that Eisenhower's push to balance the budget was primarily motivated by shorter-run considerations—fear of inflation and worry about our balance of payments.

The meaning of the current interest in "crowding out" is unclear. It could mean that beyond some size a deficit is undesirable because it makes the economy rise too fast and is inflationary. Alternatively it could mean that beyond some size a deficit is excessive because it undesirably restrains private investment, even though it does not cause an excessive rise of aggregate demand. Or it could mean that beyond some size a deficit is contractionary, because its restrictive effect on private investment outweighs whatever stimulative effects it may have.

I find the third view, that a larger deficit is contractionary, hard to credit, although it sometimes seems that it is what is being said and it is always possible to get any results one wants if one is free to choose assumptions about confidence and psychology. The second interpretation seems to be a more logical possibility, but it would involve the government in saying that it wants to slow aggregate expansion below its optimum rate in order to get private investment up to its optimum. I don't think the government is saying this. I think that for the present it is only saying that too big a deficit would be too inflationary. They may be trying to stake out some claim for a budget surplus in the future to speed up growth, but that is to happen only when it is possible, presumably meaning when the ordinary canons of functional finance would call for a surplus anyway. There is no explanation of how that condition is to be brought about in the future if it so rarely occurred in the past thirty years.

In sum, official attitudes toward budget balancing now ignore the size of the debt, the burden of the interest charges, and the long-run size of the deficit. We are all functional financers now, concerned to find the best size of this year's deficit for this year's economic conditions. President Ford may feel more of a twinge of pain at an $80 billion deficit than, say, Senator Humphrey does, but that is not the reason for a difference in their policies. The reason is that President Ford thinks that in the particular economic circumstances of 1976 a deficit of that size is more inflationary than Senator Humphrey thinks it is, and that President Ford thinks inflation is more damaging than Senator Humphrey does.

There is probably little reason to discuss the doctrines of economists about budget balancing separately from the views of public officials. There is little difference between the views of the officials and the predominant views of the economists. Many of the politicians are economists and even more of the economists are politicians.

However, I will attempt some classification of the opinions of economists. This shows considerable difference of opinion. However, it shows little support for the idea that there is a presumption in favor of balancing the budget, over either long or short periods. It seems to me that the following schools can be distinguished.

1. *The pure, old-fashioned Keynesian functional financers.* They believe there is a direct, unique connection between the deficit or surplus and the state of the economy, so that if you know the desirable state of the economy you know the desirable size of the deficit or surplus, aside from difficulties of estimation. That is the size of the deficit or surplus you should have. The cumulative deficit or surplus will be the sum of these short-period deficits and surpluses, and should be; there is no other test of the desirable long-run behavior of the deficit or surplus.

2. *The fiscal-monetarists.* They deny that fiscal policy has any direct effect on aggregate demand, which is governed by monetary policy. However, they believe that monetary policy is governed by fiscal policy, in such a way that if there is a big deficit there will be rapid monetary expansion. Therefore, there is always one and only one size of deficit or surplus which will yield the right rate of monetary expansion to yield the right rate of rise of aggregate demand. They wind up in the same place as the old-fashioned functional financers.

3. *The monetarist-Parkinsonians.* They believe that the behavior of aggregate demand is determined by monetary policy and unaffected by fiscal policy. Also there is a political law which says that the government will spend all its tax

revenues, over a reasonably short period, and will not spend more, so there is no realistic question about deficits or surpluses. The object of policy is to hold the size of government down, which can best be accomplished by holding down taxes.

4. *The monetarist neutrals.* They also believe that the behavior of aggregate demand is determined by monetary policy. The size of the deficit or surplus in the long run affects the rate of economic growth, through the effect on the supply of saving available for private investment. However, what is the desirable rate of growth is not a question that economists can answer for the society, given that growth is not free. The size of the surplus or deficit has to be decided in the political process, and there is no presumption that the answer will be or should be a surplus.

5. *The supply-side fiscalists.* They also believe that aggregate demand is determined by money. However, aggregate supply is determined by taxation, including negative taxation, or transfer payments. Both inflation and unemployment can be reduced by reducing taxes and transfer payments, and that should be the objective of policy. It may be implied that surpluses are better than deficits, but probably only because they are the route to tax reduction.

6. *Conventional eclectics.* They believe that both fiscal policy and monetary policy affect aggregate demand. Therefore, the optimum behavior of aggregate demand can be achieved by any one of many combinations of fiscal and monetary policy. However, since they have not yet figured out how to put these combinations into their models, they continue to operate as old-fashioned, one-dimensional, functional financers.

7. *Growth-oriented eclectics.* These believe in the possibility of different fiscal-monetary mixes to achieve specified behavior of aggregate demand. They also believe that more rapid economic growth is desirable. Therefore, they recommend a policy with long-run budget surpluses, and whatever complementary monetary policy is needed to get high employment. However, the time to get on this policy is later, not yet.

As far as I can see, none of these schools implies any presumption for budget-balancing, in the short run or in the long, except for the last, which has not yet been tested in the crucible of any specific decision.

I will turn now from the opinions of officials and economists to the opinions of the general public on the subject of budget balancing. For as long as we have had public opinion polls, that is, for a little more than forty years, about 70 percent of respondents to such polls have given answers that showed some belief in balancing the budget. We have no direct evidence from polls on how deeply they felt about that. However, we do know that they went on voting for presidents and congressmen who produced deficits, so I would conclude that they did not feel very deeply about it and did not rank devotion to budget balancing very high among the criteria by which they judged public officials.

Something more may be said about the views of one sector of the public, the business community, partly because its views are more often elaborated in print and partly because I have myself had more direct contact with it than with other sectors.

The businessman is traditionally the fiscal conservative and defender of the balanced budget. In the 1930s, in the early days of the New Deal, the utterances of business organizations and business leaders were thick with complaints about the administration's failure to balance the budget. However, my reading of that literature convinces me that they really didn't care much about that, and only emphasized it to put themselves in line with a feeling which they thought was widespread in the country and against the Roosevelt administration. What they really cared about was keeping down taxes, especially on business, and fending off government regulation.

One rather sad evidence of this came after the recession of 1937. Treasury Secretary Morgenthau tried to convince Roosevelt that the way to get recovery would be to restore the confidence of the business community by promising it a balanced budget, and Roosevelt was briefly tempted by the idea. Morgenthau then went to talk to a group of businessmen and made a speech about balancing the budget which he thought would evoke warm support. Instead he got a cold reception, he was discouraged, and Roosevelt turned in the other direction.

I had my own experience on this subject in 1947 when I worked for the Committee for Economic Development (CED) and we were writing the policy statement that recommended the policy of balancing the budget at high employment. This statement was intended to be about tax reform and we got into the question of budget policy only as a way of determining how much revenue we had to raise. We made some estimate of the minimum necessary expenditures and quickly decided that the revenues should be sufficient to yield a surplus of X at high employment. We then faced the question of how high X should be. It was recognized that although there might be some level of X that would be inconsistent with the achievement of high employment, nevertheless there was a range within which we could choose. The higher X was, the larger the surplus would be, or the smaller the deficit, in the long run. Also, the higher X was, the higher the level of taxation would have to be. The committee's decision was dominated by the desire to keep taxes, including business taxes, low. Therefore they chose as small an X as they thought would look respectable.

I think it is also of some interest that in the recent furor about the capital shortage, it is not the businesspeople who are plumping for budget surpluses as a solution. That is the route chosen by economists, and "liberal" economists at that. The preferred route of the business community is tax reduction, especially reduction of taxes on capital. This difference is perfectly natural because the issue is not only, or mainly, how much capital formation there should be but who should own it and what the return on it should be.

My conclusion is that there is nobody out there who cares very much about balancing the budget. There wasn't a strong belief in this as a primary objective of national policy in the 1920s, and there is less now. How did this change occur?

The change in practice and doctrine is the result of a long list of developments in the real world and in theory since 1929, which I will put down here in no particular order:

1. Hoover was inhibited about continuing to run deficits by the uncooperativeness of the Federal Reserve about financing enough of the deficits to keep interest rates from rising. The Federal Reserve has since been more cooperative.

2. Hoover was also inhibited by fear of the response of foreign holders of dollars to the sight of our budget deficits. For a great variety of reasons we have become much less worried about what foreigners think of the dollar.

3. We had willy-nilly, by the sequence of Great Depression and Great War, a long string of large deficits and woke up to discover that none of the bad consequences which were predicted had come about, or at least that they could not confidently be pinned on the deficit. This was extremely damaging to the popular prejudice against deficits. There was even a belief that the deficits of the 1930s had contributed greatly to the recovery from the depression, which was at least debatable but became part of the mythology nonetheless.

4. There was the Keynesian Revolution, which converted a generation of economists and other intellectuals to the belief in the efficacy and harmlessness of deficit finance.

5. The big increase in the size of the federal budget relative to the GNP automatically increased the size of the fluctuations in the surplus or deficit relative to the GNP. It accustomed us to bigger deficit figures.

6. The change in the composition of the federal revenues and expenditures made them more elastic with relation to the GNP and so increased the variability of the deficits and surpluses and made the task of keeping the budget in balance much more difficult.

7. The huge absolute size of the debt at the end of World War II, instead of making the need to reduce it seem great, made the possibility of any significant absolute reduction seem remote.

8. At the same time, at the end of World War II, we were becoming acquainted with the figures about the rate of national growth, and impressed with the prospect of being floated off the real burden of the debt by rising GNP. It seems to me that belief in the high probability of rapid growth is important in explaining willingness to assume and maintain large debts. Essentially the classical argument works in reverse. Why should I pay taxes to reduce the debt so that private investment can exceed private spending, accelerating economic growth and making my grandchildren richer than I am, when it is likely that they

are going to be richer than I am anyway? At the end of 1974 the federal debt was twenty-one times as high as at the end of 1929. At the end of 1974 private consumers' credit was twenty-seven times as high as at the end of 1929. The same attitude that we are going to be richer later may help to explain both phenomena.

9. Perhaps this is saying the same thing, but the claimants on government programs also became used to the growth of the economy and of the revenues, and programs were shaped to absorb the revenues. There was no growth dividend to which a vigorous claim had not been asserted and which could be painlessly applied to reduction of the debt.

10. The business community, which might have been the claimant for debt reduction, was staggered by the tax burden it faced and was not inclined to put debt reduction ahead of tax reduction.

11. Our whole generation was saddened and frightened by the experience with unemployment in the Great Depression and so became extremely sensitive to the need for supportive, and deficit-creating, action by the federal government when faced with a rise of unemployment.

12. Whatever mystique there was once about the budget-balancing rule, and there was some, it could not be transferred to a new, more realistic rule devised by human heads and not handed down from Mount Sinai. We discovered that in the CED with respect to the rule of balancing the budget with a moderate surplus at high employment. Even the committee that wrote the rule was not prepared to be disciplined by it, perhaps because they knew that its origins were not divine. The rule involves a number of arbitrary decisions. How much is high employment? How much is a moderate surplus? Which of the possible definitions of the budget is to be used? If provision is made for exceptions, how are the exceptions to be identified? How are we to estimate what the revenues and expenditures would be under conditions we have never experienced, and how would we ever know if the estimates had been correct? Now it is possible to show that the same or similar arbitrariness is involved in the old-fashioned budget-balancing rule. But that only

serves further to demystify the old rule. It does not transfer any mystique to the new one.

I seem to have come out to the same point as I did in my book. The revolution was not really revolutionary. It was a change. The good old days before the change were not so terrible. We are feeling unhappy because we have discovered that we really don't know enough to manage the economy as well as we would like. But we never did. And we can't create new myths, at least not consciously by holding conferences for that purpose. The only way out of our present predicament is to try to go forward and learn more, not to try to go backward and unlearn what we have learned.

Reflections on
Economic Growth

The *AEI Economist*, September 1985

G ROWTH is now the great god before whom all participants in the discussion of economic policy bow their knee. Merely to allege that a policy will promote growth is sufficient to make a case for it. While almost everyone acknowledges the supremacy of growth, one particular cult claim to have special legitimacy as guardian of the sacred flame—the cult of neo-cons, supply-siders, and evangelists of the opportunity society, as distinguished not only from liberals but also from conventional conservatives. This cult claims to know the magic words that please the god "Growth," the magic words being "less government" and, even more, "lower taxes."

I do not propose to sustain this metaphor but will now under-take the more prosaic task of examining three questions: (1) Who is for growth? (2) What do we know about how to get growth? (3) Is growth the only thing? The answers to these three questions are, respectively, (1) Almost everyone, (2) Little, and (3) No.

First, to keep the discussion from being totally amorphous, I must say a few words about what is meant by economic growth. I cannot allow everyone to have a private definition of economic growth as the increase in the quantity of what he or she wants to increase, because then the argument that growth was the only goal would be almost tautological, and for two more people to discuss whether we had had economic growth or how we could get it would be quite impossible. Quite simply, I think of economic growth as the increase in total and per capita output—or an increase in the supply of goods and services as valued by the public in the market—over a period longer than a business cycle. I suppose that is what most of the people now talking about it mean.

Who Is for Growth?

The idea that economic growth is good has a long history. Robert Nisbet gives evidence back to Athens in the fifth century B.C., without implying that the idea began then.[1] Moreover, in the United States the idea that the federal government should have a prominent role in the promotion of economic growth is at least as old as the republic.[2] The tariff, the inland waterways, the subsidization of the railroads, the Homestead Act, the land grant colleges were major reflections of this idea. The role of government in economic development was not a partisan issue, although there were fights about particular policies and about the division of responsibility between the states and the federal government. Some people—such as Thoreau—were hostile to the idea of economic progress in general, but they were far from the mainstream. Indeed, intellectual complaint about American society focused on what was thought to be excessive concentration on economic growth.

The current controversy and alignments can be conveniently dated from the 1930s and are connected with the progressive income tax on the one hand and with Keynesian economics on the other. Even when the federal income tax was reintroduced in 1913 with rates from 1 to 6 percent,[3] there were warnings of the adverse economic consequences it would have. In the 1920s, Treasury Secretary Andrew Mellon pushed for, and got, reduction of the rates of individual income tax, which had been raised during World War I. His argument was that the reduction of the rates would raise the tax base and increase the revenue. Since the rates were reduced and the revenue did rise, Mellon has since been

[1] See Robert Nisbet, *History of the Idea of Progress* (New York: Basic Books, 1980).

[2] See Alexander Hamilton, *Federalist Paper No. 12:* "The prosperity of commerce is now perceived and acknowledged by all enlightened statesmen to be the most useful as well as the most productive source of national wealth, and has accordingly become a priority object of their political cares."

[3] A federal income tax had been imposed during the Civil War but an attempt to impose such a tax in peacetime was declared unconstitutional in 1895. The constitutionality of such a tax was established by the Sixteenth Amendment in 1913.

the patron saint of supply-siders, regardless of the fact that tax revenue almost always rises in the United States and the lack of evidence that the Mellon tax cuts had contributed to the rise of revenue in the 1920s.

The outrage of upper-income and corporate taxpayers boiled over during the New Deal when President Roosevelt proposed raising their taxes in 1935 and 1937. Their point was not simply that they did not like to pay higher taxes. They cast themselves as the instruments and custodians of economic growth, as distinguished from the "liberals" who would accidentally or deliberately kill the goose that laid the golden eggs.

But Roosevelt could and did maintain that it was he who was promoting the future growth of the country. He was engaging in massive public works projects that were investments in the economy, like the Tennessee Valley Authority. He could also point to a contribution that was less physical—his programs were providing the purchasing power without which the productive capacity of the economy would not be utilized and, if not utilized, would not continue to grow.[4]

Still, the conservative, Republican, taxpayer critics of the New

---

[4] Mr. Roosevelt was much impressed by a memorandum to him from Beardsley Ruml on April 1, 1938. This memo was summarized in Herbert Stein, *The Fiscal Revolution in America* (Chicago: University of Chicago Press, 1969), pp. 110–111, as follows:

> According to the memo, the whole course of American economic advancement had been accompanied and permitted by the alienation of the national domain to create purchasing power for the growing national product. First the gold under the ground had been turned into money—national domain into purchasing power in one step. Then the public lands had been alienated, given to railroads and homesteaders, who borrowed on the lands from the banks and in the process created money—national domain into purchasing power in two steps. Then franchises, public grants of right to engage in certain kinds of business, had been given to corporations, which established enterprises, which borrowed on the strength of their prospective earnings and thus generated money—national domain into purchasing power in the three steps.
>
> The gold, land, and franchises had never been in the federal government balance sheet. Their alienation had not appeared as a diminution of a federal asset or increase in a federal liability. Now it was necessary to continue the process one step more. It was necessary to use a small part of the government's tax claim upon the future national income as a basis for borrowing to create purchasing power which would stimulate the national economy.
>
> The government had two choices. It could try to push private production, hoping thereby to generate purchasing power, or it could push consumption, thereby generating production. The latter was the democratic method.
>
> This was a line of thought well calculated to impress the President. It made the whole thing seem very elemental, rather than a complicated financial or economic technicality. It put the President in the picture as an agent of a long historic process, and appealed to his pleasure in the role of prudent manager of the national domain— a role which he himself had said he enjoyed. Also, it was a democratic solution, not a surrender to business.

Deal had a point. The Roosevelt administration did not give a high priority to growth. It was naturally and properly concerned first with the immediate problem of getting the economy up to full employment and, after that, perhaps less properly, concerned with social security, justice, and, of course, cementing the new Democratic majority. After about 1935 the relative neglect of growth had intellectual underpinnings derived from Keynes. Keynes had said both that in the long run we are all dead and that in the long run we are all going to be so rich that there will be no economic problem and the capital stock will be so large that its marginal productivity and the rate of interest will be zero. Thus we had no need to be concerned about the long run because we will be either rich or dead. The Keynesian argument was popularized and carried further by Alvin Hansen with his theory of secular stagnation. He held that economic growth was propelled by exogenous forces—population growth and strategic technological advances, such as the steam engine or the internal combustion engine. Since none of these forces was in sight, the best that could be done was to prop up the economy by running a budget deficit that would absorb the savings that could not be absorbed in private investment. Surely there was no need to reduce taxes on the rich or on corporations, which would only increase the already-redundant savings.

After World War II the congressional Republicans, business establishment, and conventional conservatives continued as advocates of economic growth via tax reduction. When the Republicans controlled Congress, in 1947–1948 and 1953–1954, they put through major tax reductions against the opposition of a Democratic president in the earlier case and a Republican president in the later one. The cuts were supported as contributions to economic growth, through a combination of arguments about purchasing power, savings, and incentives. Leadership in these moves was taken by the Republican chairmen of the House Ways and Means Committee, Harold Knutson and Daniel Reed, about as old-fashioned Republicans as one can imagine. Later, leadership of the same cause was taken by a Republican president and a new breed of politicians and intellectuals.

Economic growth was not, however, left as the exclusive possession of the conservative–business community. As obsession with mass unemployment faded after World War II, the Keynesian economists discovered that they too had something to say about economic growth. Not surprisingly, what they had to say about growth was also what they had been saying about unemployment. Growth depended on the increase of the capital stock, which meant investment. Investment depended on the actual and expected increase of output; businessmen would invest when they had or expected a market. The way the government could generate the actual or expected increase of output was to ensure the adequacy of demand, notably by running a deficit when needed. One element in that story was what would now be called "crowding in." That is, a budget deficit would increase total output and so induce, crowd in, more private investment. This was a restatement of what Keynes had called the paradox of thrift—that an excess of thriftiness would depress the economy and so cause less, not more, investment than if thriftiness had been less. The government's role was to keep private thriftiness from retarding investment and growth. During the Truman administration when the reports of the Council of Economic Advisers turned from immediate cyclical concerns to the question of growth over somewhat longer periods—which was not very often—the approach was through the maintenance of adequate demand to induce a high level of investment.

During the Eisenhower administration concern with economic growth became more general and somewhat more intense, partly because some of the European countries and Japan were seen to be growing more rapidly than the United States for reasons that could no longer be described as recovery from the devastation of World War II. The apparent rapid growth of the Soviet Union was a cause for alarm, and even the growth of our friends seemed to be a challenge, indicating that the United States was not exploiting all possibilities for growth.

In the late 1950s, the promotion of economic growth rose to a higher position on the agenda of moderate or liberal conservatives, of which the Eisenhower administration was itself, of course, a leading representative. This school had a more eclectic view of what was needed to promote growth than either the early Keynesians or the more conventional conservatives. An important element in this view was the emphasis on investment in "human capital"—the education and training of the work force and research to increase the knowledge incorporated in the work force. The idea that most of what we call labor is really a form of capital, not originating in nature but created by human investment activity, had been clearly spelled out in the 1930s by an economist at the University of Chicago, Frank H. Knight. In the 1950s several economists, including Edward F. Denison and Theodore W. Schultz, began to measure the amount of this human capital or to estimate its productivity. They found in general that the productivity of investment in human capital was high—higher than for investment in physical capital—and that economic growth could be efficiently promoted by more investment in human capital. This line of thought was stimulated by the launching of the Soviet *Sputnik,* which raised doubts about the adequacy of American education and technology.

Attention to human capital changed the ideological aspects of the growth issue profoundly. Much, perhaps most, of the investment in human capital was done by government. Much of it was financed by taxes. So if increasing the human capital stock was an important part of a program for increasing economic growth, the program could not be simply anti-government and anti-taxes.

A good example of the eclectic, liberal-conservative attitude toward economic growth is found in a policy statement "Economic Growth in the United States: Its Past and Future," issued in February 1958 by the Research and Policy Committee of the Committee for Economic Development (CED). The CED had been founded in 1942 by a group of unorthodox businessmen—unorthodox by the standards of the Chamber of Commerce and the National Association of Manufacturers. By 1958 the center of public opinion had probably moved so much that the CED was right on it, but the CED was still regarded as liberal by the conventional conservatives.

The CED statement presented a long list of the factors that it believed had contributed to economic growth in the past, including

- the decentralized economic system
- the amount of capital goods
- the quality of business management
- the quality of the labor force
- the diffusion of education
- the high degree of mobility
- technological change and advancement
- the mass market and advertising
- consumers' credit, savings, and income
- the growth of the money supply

Some of the items appeared on this list because the subcommittee that prepared it included several people from retailing and publishing. Even with some allowance for that circumstance, however, the approach was notably catholic.

The committee's views on the future of economic growth and on what might hinder it were similarly inclusive. Warning was given about the adverse effects of excessive taxation, including rates in the federal personal income tax which then rose as high as 91 percent. Even more space was given to the need to provide adequate education, to avoid government regulations and private monopolies that might impede mobility, to maintain reasonable economic stability, and to keep an open world economy.[5]

President Eisenhower's economic reports gave increasing attention to the goal of economic growth as the years of his administration passed. His suggestions for the achievement of growth were broad and certainly without heavy anti-government or anti-tax bias. One recurrent theme was that the growing population would need an expanding infrastructure, provided in large part by the federal government in the form of highways, navigational aids, and research and development. The responsibilities of state and local governments for education were also emphasized. The 1960 budget message reflected the president's view that a federal government surplus that was used to retire debt would contribute to economic growth by making possible a higher rate of private investment.[6]

The 1960 presidential campaign clearly indicated how far the stimulation of economic growth had risen in the nation's priorities. In fact, the campaign turned out to be a competition in promises about growth, although the competitors were generally innocent of the difference between growth and short-run fluctuations. The Democratic platform, on which John F. Kennedy ran, said:

> We Democrats believe that our economy can and must grow at an average rate of 5 percent annually, almost twice as fast as our

[5] Edward F. Denison was on the staff of the CED and did the background research for this statement. His subsequent classic work on the sources of economic growth developed out of his efforts to quantify the generalities contained in that statement.

[6] See Stein, *The Fiscal Revolution in America*, pp. 350–351.

average annual rate since 1958. We pledge ourselves to policies that will achieve this goal without inflation.

As the first step in speeding economic growth, a Democratic president will put an end to the present high-interest, tight money policy.

Nelson Rockefeller, who was the "liberal" aspirant for the Republican nomination, committed himself to at least the 5 percent growth goal and held out the prospect of 6 percent, which he considered feasible. Richard Nixon, who was the Republican candidate, did not offer a numerical target. Perhaps that was because as vice-president he had served as chairman of the Advisory Board on Economic Growth and Stability and learned something of the limitations of the government's ability to forecast or manage growth. He did say, however, that "I would say that my goal, and I think the only proper goal, for those who do not buy the theory of government-manipulated growth, the only proper goal is a maximum growth rate. It might, in some instances, be 3 percent, in some instances 4, in some instances 5." Nixon said that he recognized the need for government investment but rejected the Kennedy policy of manipulating interest rates and government spending to achieve growth.

In 1959, President Eisenhower had established a Commission on National Goals, which was to report after the 1960 election and to be, in a way, his legacy to the nation. Formation of the commission seemed to reflect less an awareness of problems than a concern over the apparent lack of problems to focus national attention and civic spirit. The chairman was Henry Wriston, former president of Brown University, and the membership encompassed the Establishment from Crawford Greenewalt, president of du Pont, to George Meany, president of the AFL-CIO, with assorted college presidents and former government officials making up the middle.

The commission, in its report "Goals for Americans," concluded that economic growth was indeed a national goal. It said that "the economy should grow at the maximum rate consistent with primary dependence upon free enterprise and the avoidance of marked inflation." The commission gave three reasons for believing that such growth is essential: to provide jobs for an approximately 13.5 million increase in the work force during the next ten years, to improve the standard of living, and to "assure United

States competitive strength."[7] (The 13.5 million estimate was almost exactly correct.)

The list of ways to achieve the growth goal covered all the bases. The first mentioned was increased investment in the public sector, said to be "compatible" with the goal, which seems a rather defensive claim. The climate for new investment should be improved, particularly by an overhaul of the tax system, including depreciation allowances. Good words were said about maintaining full employment (with a target of unemployment below 4 percent), promoting research, and education. Mr. Greenewalt appended a footnote placing greater emphasis on the need for tax reduction.

The commission avoided taking a position on the competition in growth targets then under way. It referred to a background study that had been written for it by the present author and Edward Denison: "The chapter by Messrs. Stein and Denison presents carefully documented evidence indicating an annual increase in the gross national product of 3.4 percent without extraordinary stimulating measures. Other estimates made with equal care indicate higher growth rates up to 5 percent annually." In separate statements three members, Mr. Meany, and two university presidents, Clark Kerr and James Killian, indicated their preference for and confidence in a goal closer to 5 percent. (From 1960 to 1970, the ten years usually contemplated by the commission, the growth rate was 3.9 percent per annum; from 1960 to 1984 it was 3.4 percent per annum.)

Having been elected on a promise to achieve 5 percent per annum growth, the Kennedy administration seemed to take that promise fairly seriously. In 1961 the chairman of the Council of Economic Advisers took the lead in establishing a target for the member countries of the Organization for Economic Cooperation and Development (OECD) to grow by 5 percent a year for the next five years. Whether that goal was intended to apply to the OECD countries as a whole or to each country separately was uncertain at the time, but certainly the agreement was intended to legitimize Kennedy's goal for the United States. (As it turned out, the growth rate between 1960 and 1965 was 4.7 percent per annum.)

[7] Commission on National Goals, *Goals for Americans* (New York: Prentice-Hall, 1960), pp. 10–11.

The Kennedy administration, or at least the economists within it, had a more sophisticated plan for achieving rapid growth than the simple easy-money policy of the Democratic platform. Although these economists were Keynesians, economists had passed beyond first-generation Keynesianism to something called the neoclassical synthesis, which recognized the interaction between fiscal and monetary measures and the relevance of the supply-side as well as demand-side factors. This synthesis led to a prescription that included not only monetary expansion but also a budget surplus to increase savings available for private investment and keep real interest rates low. Also the government would initiate or expand programs for improving education and training and increasing the mobility of the labor force. Paying for that and running a budget surplus would preclude tax reduction. Thus what was envisaged was a high-tax, big-government, low-interest strategy—in direct contrast to the later supply-side strategy. It was a strategy for what Keynes had called the euthanasia of the rentier, not for his enrichment.

The Kennedy administration was unable to pursue this strategy, for several reasons. The United States was running a balance-of-payments deficit that, in the presence of a commitment to maintain the exchange rate of the dollar, was considered a serious problem. A low-interest-rate policy would have encouraged the outflow of capital from the United States and so would have worsened the balance-of-payments deficit. Congress was reluctant to approve Mr. Kennedy's plans for increasing federal aid to education and other investments in human capital. Mr. Kennedy's effort in 1962 to jawbone the steel industry into holding prices down had alarmed and irritated the business community, and this reaction seemed to be connected with a sharp dip in the stock market and signs of an incipient business recession. The administration felt the need for prompt measures to support the economy. Given the balance of payments problem, and perhaps given the predilections of the Kennedy economists, these measures had to be fiscal rather than monetary. Given the opposition of Congress to the administration's favorite spending plans—except for defense—and the felt need to mollify the business community, the natural step was tax reduction. Thus the administration arrived at the Kennedy tax cut plan, enacted after his death in the Johnson administration.

The tax cut plan was proposed initially at the end of 1962 as a way of achieving two objectives—preventing a recession in the short run and promoting growth in the long run. As the debate over the tax bill dragged on during 1963, the need for an anti-recession policy faded. The administration then put more emphasis on the long-run growth-promoting virtues of the plan.

Economic growth fell somewhat in the scale of national priorities after 1965. For one thing, the growth problems seemed to have been solved. The revival of the economy after enactment of the Kennedy-Johnson tax cut was commonly taken as evidence that the Keynesian economists had discovered the key to stable and rapid economic growth, as shown by a *Time* cover story in December 1965 featuring J. M. Keynes. Even rather cautious people then thought that an annual growth rate of 4 percent was to be the U.S. norm. Meanwhile attention was diverted from economic growth by the Vietnam war, the war on poverty, and alarms about the environment.

After about 1975 doubts about the optimistic growth projections increased. Productivity seemed to be rising slowly; but no one could be sure whether that slow growth was due to presumably transitory forces—the energy crisis, the inflation, and the recession of 1974–1975—or to some more durable problem. The immediate difficulties—the inflation and the energy crisis—dominated attention, and one could think that overcoming them was the most important contribution that could be made to economic growth.

Nevertheless, economic growth came increasingly to the fore as a national concern and goal in the latter part of the 1970s. Four schools of thought in favor of growth could be identified in this period.

PLANNERS

The great economic difficulties and uncertainties of the 1970s encouraged the emergence of an idea never far below the surface in American thinking—that more or better planning by the government could achieve national economic objectives, in this case economic growth. For example, at the urging of several members of Congress, the Ford administration set up the Advisory Committee on National Growth Policy Processes. The committee, of which

I was a member, produced a report of little content and less consequence. The planning notion survived, however, in popular discussion and was embodied in several pieces of legislation that were taken seriously at the time, such as the Humphrey-Javits Bill and the Humphrey-Hawkins Bill.[8] The Humphrey-Hawkins Bill was passed in 1978, after the death of Hubert Humphrey. Although formally an amendment to the Employment Act of 1946, this one was called "The Full Employment and Balanced Growth Act of 1978." The word *Full*, which had been fought over and finally excluded from the 1946 act, was now restored. The idea of growth, missing in 1946, was introduced; but the growth was to be "balanced"—meaning something other than the growth that comes out of the play of the market. Although the act had been the subject of much controversy and some foreboding, it has had no effect except to reduce from four to two the number of regular reports made by the Federal Reserve to Congress each year.

The planning approach to economic growth reappeared in 1980 under the name "industrial policy" and attracted attention for a few years. This line of thought was also of no practical consequence and is of interest here only as evidence that economic growth is espoused as a goal by the most liberal or anti-market school of thinking about the American economy.

CONVENTIONAL LIBERALS

The reports of the Council of Economic Advisers during the Carter administration are good representations of this point of view. Successive annual editions of these reports showed increasing concern about the slowdown of productivity growth and of potential output. The remedies proposed were like those of the Kennedy administration fifteen years earlier, except that there was less thought about increasing federal spending programs for education and training. Demand management policy should be sufficiently expansive to keep the economy near full employment. If that policy were followed, existing taxes and expenditure trends would lead to a large surplus of federal revenues over expenditures. If nothing were done, the surplus would be so large as to depress

[8] See Herbert Stein, *Economic Planning and the Improvement of Economic Policy* (Washington, D.C.: American Enterprise Institute, 1975).

the economy and so depress private investment. Still, it would be consistent with a high level of activity and helpful for growth to end the deficits we had been running during the 1960s and 1970s, which would leave all of private saving available to finance private investment. So there was room for tax reduction, and this reduction should concentrate on business taxation, both to increase the incentive to invest and to increase the savings of business. Personal tax reduction was to be avoided because that would not contribute to investment but would increase consumption and reduce the savings available to private investment. Some tax changes aimed at stimulating investment were enacted in 1978, and the Carter administration proposed others in 1980, but they were not enacted before his term ran out.

CONVENTIONAL CONSERVATIVES

Leaders of the business and financial community were the chief spokesmen for this group. In fact, their thinking was not different from what I have called the conventional liberals except in the single-mindedness and intensity of their focus on capital shortage and on reduction of business taxation as the key to remedying the shortage. Although the conventional conservatives did not look upon the elimination of the budget deficit itself as a positive contribution to savings and investment, as the liberals did, they were nonetheless limited in their tax-cutting recommendations by concern for the size of the budget deficit. As a result, their pro-growth tax program was also an exclusively pro-business tax program, at least in its direct effects, which, of course, interfered with its salability.

THE NEW CONSERVATIVES

The conventional conservatives were thus faced with a dilemma. A tax cut that concentrated on stimulating investment was politically unattractive, but a tax cut that also extended its bounty to the great mass of personal taxpayers would seriously increase the deficit. In the late 1970s a group of conservatives emerged (or reemerged) to resolve this dilemma by denying it. The heart of their argument was in the relation between tax reduction and economic growth. Tax reduction—across the board and not confined to investment incentives—would stimulate growth. Growth in turn would increase the revenue with the lower tax rates enough to eliminate the budget deficit or, at least, so that the remaining deficit could be financed by the increased savings resulting from the growth and the tax changes. This was a program of tax reduction for the sake of growth and of growth for the sake of tax reduction. At its inception this policy seemed to be the opposite of the 1961 Kennedy-style growth policy. That was a high-tax, budget-surplus, low-interest-rate program. This was a low-tax, budget-deficit, high-interest-rate program. In the end they had one feature in common, however; they both became growth-via-demand-expansion programs. Since the program of the 1980s depended on growth to validate the tax cuts, and the tax cuts did not themselves yield the required growth, some other route to growth had to be found. That route was monetary expansion.

So we can see that economic growth has been espoused as a high-priority goal by all sides of the American political and ideological spectrum—the choice of means for achieving the goal varying according to the interests or preconceptions of the several groups. In many, perhaps most, cases, it was the means rather than the goal that people wanted. Some groups, however, have dissented, or have seemed to dissent, from the very idea of the desirability of growth.

CLUB OF ROME TYPES

These people believe that rapid economic growth depletes the world's stock of exhaustible resources at an excessive rate. This belief is, I think, erroneous for several reasons. Even if it were correct, it should not be interpreted as opposition to growth. Instead its basic thesis is that excessively rapid growth today may make growth in the future very small or even negative. Thus, some restraint on present growth can be defended as necessary for a high rate of economic growth measured over a long period of time.

EXTREME INDIVIDUALISTS

Some people argue that economic growth is not the responsibility or function of government. That position is not against growth, but it does imply that the optimum rate of growth is the one that results from the decentralized decisions about saving or investing of all private individuals. This position is certainly defensible, but it runs into the practical difficulty that the government inevitably makes some decisions that affect the rate of growth, such as decisions about taxes, or the budget deficit. Defining what would be a neutral policy, one that would leave the growth rate as if government had no influence, is difficult.

DEFENDERS OF "HIGHER" VALUES

There have probably always been some people who believed that economic growth, in the sense used here, causes ugliness or other ills. Some who think this way are romantics or elitists, longing for an earlier, purer time, or simply contemptuous of the public's tastes. This position could, however, be reached by another route. One might accept the proposition that each individual is a good judge of what is good for him or her and that to have more of that is good, but still believe that getting more for each person has negative effects on others, via congestion and pollution, for example. In that case all may benefit from measures that slow down growth. That is the rationale for environmental restraints on the free market, even if they slow growth as commonly calculated. But probably only a few people would accept this rationale as justifying more than a marginal restraint on economic growth.

What Do We Know about How to Get Growth?

What has already been said suggests that we do not know much with confidence about how to get more economic growth. If we knew more, such diverse ideas about pro-growth policy would not persist for so long.

The sources of economic growth can be divided into two parts. One part is the increase in the quantity of productive resources, and the other is the improvement in the efficiency with which the resources are used. The productive resources include physical capital, both private and public, and human capital embodied in the population by education and training. Economists disagree radically about the size of the contribution to growth that would be made by an increase of a certain amount in the rate of increase in the stock of a particular kind of productive resource.

Our ignorance is great with respect to the efficiency-improvement contribution to growth. The amount of this contribution to past growth is conventionally measured as a residual—that is, it accounts for all the growth we cannot otherwise explain. We can give labels to some elements that improve efficiency: technological advance, improvement of management, improvement of the market, the vigor of entrepreneurship, and the cooperativeness of labor. But we do not know how to measure any of those factors or their contribution.

That is only the beginning of what we do not know, however. Even if we understood the contribution of the various factors to growth, we would still not know much about the policies that would increase the contributing factors. We might know, for example, that increasing business fixed investment by 1 percent of GNP would increase the annual growth rate by a certain percent— which might be large or small. We would not know how to increase business fixed investment by 1 percent of GNP. Presumably a cut in the tax rate on the return to investment would work in that direction, but we would not know how much of a cut would be required to achieve the 1 percent increase in investment. The problem is complicated because most policies for increasing growth require the rearrangement of the uses of a total of resources that is given at the outset.

These rearrangements often have negative as well as positive consequences for growth, and the direction of the net effect is hard to tell. A cut of tax rates may stimulate the desire to invest, for example. But if, as is likely, the tax cut increases the budget deficit, the larger deficit will reduce the supply of saving available for investment and reduce the amount of investment. Economists are still arguing about the net effect of this situation. Another current argument is about the net effect of a tax change that increases the average tax on the return to investment but reduces the diversity in the tax rates applied to different kinds of investment. The measure might reduce total investment but make the distribution of investment more efficient, and we do not know what the net effect would be. Similarly, shifting taxation from capital to labor might increase the supply of capital but reduce the supply of labor, with uncertain net effects on growth.

Decisions do have to be made, and these decisions often have to involve some judgment about their effects on economic growth. But three generalizations can be offered about such judgments.

First, great results should not be expected from small measures. Probably the most important of all lessons about growth is that the difference between 3 percent growth and 4 percent growth is not 1 percent but 33.3 percent. As a first approximation one should expect that raising the growth rate from 3 percent to 4 percent will require an increase of one-third in the resources devoted to growth. That means a very big increase in private and public investment, education, and research.

Second, since the results of growth-stimulating measures are highly uncertain, large commitments should not be based on the expectations of the results of such measures. For example, a long-term budget policy predicated on achieving a significant change from historic trends in the growth rate by new measures is risky. If the policy is adopted, some preparation should be made for adaptation of the budget plan as the results for growth become measurable.

Third, one-dimensional explanations of growth and approaches to the increase of growth are almost certainly wrong. The leading case today is the view that government spending and government taxing are the enemies of growth and that the sure and sufficient way to get more growth is to cut expenditures and revenues relative to GNP. Looking at American history is instructive at this point. In the thirty-seven years from 1948 to 1985, federal expenditures have averaged around 20 percent of GNP and federal revenues around 18.5 percent. In the thirty-seven years from 1892 to 1929, federal expenditures were around 4.5 percent of GNP and revenues around 3.5 percent. (Most of the difference was run up in World War I.) In the early, small-government period, real GNP rose at an annual rate of 3.4 percent. In the later, big-government period, real GNP also grew at an annual rate of 3.4 percent. In the small-government period, real GNP per capita rose by 1.5 percent per annum; in the big-government period, it rose by 2.1 percent per annum. In the small-government period output per worker-hour rose by 1.5 percent per annum; in the big-government period, it rose by 2.3 percent per annum. These figures are not meant to demonstrate that big government is good for growth; and, of course, one must consider the consequences of big government for values other than growth. These simple facts do suggest, however, that the truth is much more complicated than it is often claimed to be.

Is Economic Growth the Only Thing?

Simply to ask this question is to answer it. No sensible person thinks that economic growth is the only worthwhile goal. Neither in our private lives nor in public policy do we act as if economic growth were the only objective. Simply stated, almost everyone thinks that economic growth is good, and no one thinks that it is the only good. So rational discussion of public policy would seem to require some explicit consideration of the relative importance of economic growth and other values. But we do not get that at all. Economic growth has become the shibboleth that everyone must utter as a sign of belonging to respectable society. Questions of the value of growth in relation to other values are bypassed by asserting that no choice is necessary because growth yields all good things and all good things yield growth.

People say, for example, that cutting national defense expenditures in order to permit a tax reduction that will allegedly promote growth is not deciding to sacrifice national security because growth is essential to national security. On one hand, cutting social welfare expenditures to make growth-stimulating tax reductions is defended, not on the grounds that more growth is more important than assisting the poor but on the grounds that more growth is the best way to assist the poor, because "a rising tide lifts all the boats." On the other hand, social welfare programs are defended as essential to economic growth because they create the social solidarity without which an economy cannot function.

The current obsession with economic growth in public discussion does not mean that we are too much obsessed with it in policy. That is partly because, as already noted, we do not know much about how much growth we get out of any policy and partly because the discussion is unrelated to policy decisions and is only the cover under which real struggles go on. Still one would be gratified, at least aesthetically, to hear some candid discussion of the importance of accelerating economic growth in a society that is by most standards already very rich and has every expectation of becoming richer.

As a contribution to such a discussion I offer the following observations:

First, two points made by Frank H. Knight: What people want is not so much the satisfaction of their wants as the acquisition of new wants, and these wants relate less to absolute conditions of life than to position relative to and power over other people.

Second, a statement by the late Henry C. Simons of the University of Chicago:

> There is, first of all, a question as to whether society should make large sacrifices to further accumulation. To stress obligations to our children's children is often a means of diverting attention from patent obligations to our contemporaries. For the future there is a responsibility of maintaining a respectable proportion between population and resources—which surely admits of more than one method. Of course progress should be encouraged; but its costs should give us pause, in a society mature enough to exercise some deliberate control. Both progress and justice are costly luxuries—costly, above all, in terms of each other.[9]

Finally, the conclusion of the study that Edward Denison and I wrote for the President's Commission on National Goals in 1960:

> There is a limit to the number of goals that the American people or any people can pursue, the number of crusades they can engage in. There is a limit to our supply of leadership for "pointing the way" and to the supply of attention and followership. In this sense, any goal is proposed at the expense of others that are or might have been advanced, and the cost of elevating accelerated economic growth to the front rank of goals is that something else is deprived of that position. The number of goals calling for our attention is large—to help set the underdeveloped world on the path of economic progress, to reduce the barriers of nationalism and racialism, to strengthen our national security, to improve the lives we lead with our immense flow of goods and services, to set a floor of economic security and welfare for all. We need not feel guilty of negativism or passivity if we decide that accelerating growth is not one of our most critical needs.[10]

---

[9] Henry C. Simons, *Personal Income Taxation* (Chicago: University of Chicago Press, 1938), p. 24.

[10] *Goals for Americans*, p. 190.

The Deficit-Dollar-Trade Nexus

The *AEI Economist,* July 1985

F OR some time now concern about economic policy has focused on the intertwined factors of the U.S. budget deficit, the interest rates in the United States, the dollar exchange rate, the U.S. trade deficit, and the inflow of capital into the United States. Attention has focused on this complex in the rest of the world as well as in the United States. Even the recently arisen fear that the United States is about to enter another recession has not diverted attention from those conditions. Instead, the prospective recession is seen as a reflection of one or another aspect of that complex.

The purpose of this essay is to describe how the United States got into that combination of conditions, to evaluate the numerous complaints that are commonly raised about it, and to discuss what should and should not be done to deal with it.

Background

A convenient point at which to start the background of our present situation is the Reagan economic policy of 1981. The main ingredients of that policy were the big tax cut and the initiation of a rapid buildup of defense expenditures. These two measures were responses to real needs in the country—or, rather, to the need for a restoration of our military strength and to the strong desire for lower taxes. This combination of measures produced the large budget deficit. Although warnings were sounded at the time, the resulting deficits were commonly either denied or disregarded.

327

The belief that the measures of 1981 would not cause large budget deficits was based on three assumptions that turned out to be erroneous and should have been known to be erroneous at the time. First, policy makers assumed that an across-the-board cut of tax rates would raise, not reduce, the revenue—supply-sidism in its extreme from. Second, they assumed that making cuts in nondefense expenditures on a scale that would keep total spending from rising would be both desirable and politically feasible. Third, they assumed that the rate of inflation could be reduced without the economy's passing through a period of recession that would temporarily increase the deficit and leave behind a permanent increase in the federal debt and interest burden.

Some people at the time, including possibly some in the administration, would have preferred the course chosen even had they been fully aware of the implications for large deficits. They would have given priority to cutting taxes and raising defense spending over holding down the deficits. That was not the stated position of the administration, however, and it is doubtful that the American people generally thought they were choosing large deficits.

The 1981 tax package was especially powerful in reducing taxes on the return to investment by the introduction of accelerated allowances for depreciation. This move was justified at the time as a way of offsetting the effect of inflation that tended to increase the real tax burdens on investment. As the inflation rate declined, however, the effect of the 1981 tax changes turned out to be a very sharp cut in taxes on the return to investment—probably a sharper cut than would have been defended if the decline of the inflation rate had been foreseen.

The combination of the budget deficit and the reduction of the tax on capital raised interest rates and the after-tax return to investment in the United States and increased the attractiveness of investment here, to foreigners as well as to Americans. At the same time developments in the rest of the world reduced the attractiveness of investment outside the United States. The European economies were slow to adapt to the decline in the world's inflation rate, so that production stagnated, profits declined, and investment became more unattractive. European corporations found it more profitable to invest in United States assets, including even U.S. Treasury bills, than to invest in their own productive facilities.

The less-developed countries suffered even more as the world inflation declined. The loans that reckless governments had assumed with the encouragement of overoptimistic banks in the industrial world turned out to be bad. The flow of capital from the industrial world, including the United States, slowed to what little was necessary to preserve at least the appearance of soundness in the existing debt.

The Current Situation

These factors were the primary causes of the present situation. They have left us with present and prospective deficits that will run to 4 or 5 percent of the GNP for many years, by common estimates, unless something effective is done to reduce them. That estimate compares with deficits of about 2 percent of GNP during the "bad" years of the 1970s. The deficits would exceed 50 percent of net private saving in the United States. Moreover, there is a danger that the deficits will exceed the current estimates. For one thing, the common projections do not include the possible consequences of a recession, which would surely raise the deficit, the debt, and the continuing interest charges.

The deficit combined with the tax measures that made private investment, and borrowing to finance investment, more attractive has given us unusually high real interest rates. Although the nominal rates quoted in the financial markets are much lower than they were, say, four years ago, so is the actual inflation rate and probably also the expected inflation rate. So lenders are getting and borrowers are paying higher real interest rates than they did during most of our history. Borrowers have been helped to pay these interest rates by the benefits of the 1981 tax act.

The net capital inflow generated by the factors I have already mentioned has been enormous, way beyond anyone's expectations. I remember that three years ago when someone suggested that net capital inflow might offset a substantial part of the federal budget deficit I thought that was impossible, because we had never had a net inflow of more than $15 billion. But we have been running a net capital inflow of around $100 billion a year compared with essentially zero four years ago. The switch has been about equally composed of a decrease in U.S. capital outflow, mainly to the less-developed countries, and an increase in the capital inflow, mainly from Japan and the developed countries of Europe.

The capital inflow has enabled the United States to have a fairly high ratio of investment within the country to GNP. In that sense, the capital inflow has offset the effect of deficit. The ratio of investment *owned by Americans* to GNP has been rather low, however. In that sense the inflow of capital cannot offset the effects of the deficit. That is, the deficit absorbs some of the savings of Americans, even though foreigners may be investing more within our borders than they did before. The total amount of capital within our borders is rising fairly rapidly, but the net assets owned by Americans are rising fairly slowly.

The big inflow of capital has raised the exchange rate of the dollar quite dramatically. The rise of the dollar has depressed U.S. exports and increased U.S. imports. We have a net excess of imports of about $100 billion a year, also an enormous figure. The net imports are the only way in which the net capital inflow can be translated into real productive capacity.

Present Concerns—Valid or Invalid?

That combination of conditions—the budget deficit, the interest rates, the exchange rates, the capital inflow, and the net imports—has generated a flood of complaints and fears, at home and abroad. I will first list these complaints without much elaboration and then turn to evaluating their validity.

• It has been said rather regularly in the past three years that the budget deficit would prevent the United States from having an economic recovery or would make the recovery unusually weak and short. Recently, after GNP growth in the first quarter was estimated to have been at an annual rate of only 0.7 percent, claims were heard that reducing the budget deficit was necessary to prevent us from sliding into recession.

• The conventional view that budget deficits would cause inflation is not heard quite so much as it was a few years ago, but it has still not disappeared from popular thinking.

• A concern, much older even than the concern with inflation, is that the budget deficit will slow down economic growth by absorbing saving that would otherwise be invested in growth-promoting activity.

• Probably the most common complaint in the United States these days is that the high dollar and the accompanying excess of imports are depressing the U.S. economy, or will do so. This concern gathered intensity after the results of the economy for the first quarter of 1985 were announced.

• Some particular industries in the United States are being hurt by the excess of imports, and some people imply that this situation should be a matter of national concern even if the economy as a whole seems to be prospering.

• Some people look at current developments and say that the United States is in the process of becoming a service economy, a condition they view with horror.

• Similarly, people look at the prospect that the United States may become increasingly a debtor nation—with Americans' net debt to foreigners exceeding their net foreign assets—and regard that as improper and intolerable.

• In Europe the main complaint about our policy and situation is that the United States is inhibiting the recovery of European countries and keeping them in stagnation. The route by which this situation is supposed to be developing is that high U.S. interest rates keep European interest rates high and deter the investment that would be necessary for economic recovery and expansion.

• Finally the less-developed countries complain that U.S. policy is absorbing capital that would go to them and promote their development.

In my view, some of all this concern is true, but much of it is not. Enough is true to require some changes of policy, but failure to see which is true and which is not can lead to the wrong changes of policy. Moreover, complaints that turn out to be groundless weaken resolve to correct the real problems.

Clearly the deficits of the past four years did not prevent us from having an economic recovery and did not make the recovery weak. In fact, the recovery has been a little stronger than the average. Moreover, the idea that the deficits would depress the economy had no basis in economic thinking. The conventional argument was that the deficit would raise interest rates and crowd out investment, without which we could not have a "healthy" or "balanced" recovery. In fact, the deficits crowded out net exports, not domestic investment, and they crowded out net exports because of a strong demand, derived from the deficit, for domestic uses of capital and labor. The deficit shifted the composition of output away from net exports toward domestic uses, but did not reduce total output and should not have been expected to do so.

Some of the measures associated with the deficit—mainly, the pro-investment tax cuts of 1981—may have caused a temporary surge of demand for investment in the United States. If so, when that surge passes there will be a depressing effect on the U.S. economy. But if this scenario is probable, it would have developed even if the same tax cuts had been made within the confines of a balanced budget. That is, the source of the instability is in the particular kind of tax cut, not in the budget deficit. Moreover, the tax cuts that generated the surge of domestic investment also generated the surge of capital inflow. When the stimulus from those tax cuts wears off so will the stimulus for the capital inflow, the dollar will decline, and there will be a shift toward net exports, which will be at least in the direction of offsetting the decline of domestic investment.

Another recession will certainly occur sometime, but when it does come it will probably not be due to the present policy imbalances on which so much attention is focused.

We have now demonstrated—or, more accurately, the Federal Reserve has now demonstrated—that running large deficits for a considerable period without inflation is possible. I suppose that economists always knew that to be true as a matter of economics. They did not think that it was true as a matter of politics. They thought that big budget deficits would cause high interest rates and a politically irresistible pressure to expand the money supply in an effort to keep interest rates down. That pressure has been, so far, politically resistible, however. An inflationary danger does exist in continued high and escalating deficits in conditions to be discussed later.

Some industries are surely being hurt by the combination of policies and conditions that led to the capital inflow and the high dollar. Many of the industries hurt the worst were already suffering from relatively high wages and slow productivity growth that would have forced some adaptation even without the rise of the dollar. The high dollar made the injury greater, however, and spread it to other industries that would have gotten along well without the rise of the exchange rate.

That these injuries occurred in an economy in which total output and employment were rising satisfactorily shows that other industries were thriving. The same factors that were causing the high dollar were stimulating consumption, defense, and domestic investment and so helping industries concentrated in those activities. The basic fact is that we made, not entirely consciously, a shift of priorities in 1981 that entailed a shift in the location of economic activity—away from exporting and import-competing industries. If that shift of national priorities was good and necessary, the complaint that it distributed some gains and losses among various industries does not seem legitimate. (As it happens, I do not think we made a good shift of priorities; we would have been better off had we not stimulated consumption so much by a large tax cut; but that is another matter.)

Of course, instability and uncertainty are always to be avoided. If the shift out of the export industries is now to be reversed by a sudden decline of the dollar, one might complain that the whole process was wasteful and should have been, or still should be, moderated in some way (such as by raising taxes). People who worry about the dollar today do not seem quite sure whether they should be worrying because the dollar will not come down or because it will.

The strong recovery in the United States from 1982 to 1984 while our import surplus was rising showed that an import surplus is not in itself depressing. Appropriate monetary policy can generate enough demand to absorb all the goods and services produced domestically plus all the goods and services imported from abroad. It is not as if some fixed total of goods and services were demanded to be supplied either from domestic production or from imports. If net imports fluctuate unpredictably, they can cause fluctuations in total output, as the decline of net imports in the fourth quarter of 1984 and the rise in the first quarter of 1985 caused first a rise and then a decline in the rate of increase of total output. But fluctuations in housing, business investment, or automobile sales, for example, can similarly cause economic fluctuations. There is nothing special about imports in this respect.

As for the fear that the United States is becoming a service economy, two things should be said about that. In the first place, there is nothing particularly wrong with being a service economy. If the rest of the world will supply us with steel, oil, and other hard goods in exchange for reruns of "Dallas" and essays on economics, and if the terms are good, there is nothing wrong with that situation. In the second place, however, we are not becoming a service economy. In 1984 the output of goods was as large a proportion of total output as it had been in any year since 1957. The output of durable goods was a larger proportion of total output than it had been at any time since World War II.

The fear that the United States will become a debtor nation is similarly groundless. For individuals, companies, and countries, the relation of their assets to their liabilities is important; but the location of their assets and the nationality of their creditors is not. For the United States there is no disadvantage or danger in that people in the rest of the world find the United States a good place to invest, which is how we are becoming a net debtor. There is an exchange risk in having assets in one currency and liabilities in another, but the extent of this risk is not measured by a comparison of American assets in the rest of the world with American liabilities in the rest of the world. All of the liabilities of the U.S. government and most of the liabilities of U.S. companies to the rest of the world are in dollars, and these liabilities create no more risk than liabilities to Americans.

A more serious complaint, one that has dominated international economic conferences in recent years, is that the American deficits and the resulting high interest rates have caused the stagnation of European economies. This complaint is invalid, however. The attraction of capital to the United States did hold down investment in Europe, but low investment in Europe was due mainly to European policy that was adverse to investment. Moreover, the depressing effect of the capital outflow from Europe was balanced by the stimulating effect of the increase of Europe's exports. In fact, Europe has not suffered from a deficiency of demand. In the past four years demand for output increased by about 10 percent per annum, but output rose only by about 1.4 percent per annum. Europe's problem is a European condition, that too little of the demand gets translated into output and too much into inflation.

So we now come down to the real problems and dangers involved in the present combination of conditions. The basic fact is that the U.S. budget deficit absorbs a large part not only of U.S. saving but also of the world's saving and thereby keeps that saving from being invested to increase the world's productive capacity.

If the deficit is of more than a critical size, it will escalate.

The deficit increases the federal debt. If the deficit is big, it will make the debt increase faster than the GNP. That increase will make the interest on the debt rise faster than the GNP; and unless something is done to stop it, the deficit will rise more and more relative to the GNP. Unless checked, these deficits not only will crowd out all net investment but will make net investment negative, so that the capital stock actually diminishes. Sooner or later any government will feel the need to stop this escalation. Unfortunately, there will be a great temptation to stop the escalation the easy way, by inflation that reduces the real burden of the debt. That is the ultimate danger of inflation in the deficit.

But even if that extreme situation is avoided, a large U.S. deficit slows down the growth of total output by slowing down the growth of the stock of productive capital. Since capital flows freely around the world, this situation does not show up entirely as a slowdown in the growth of the U.S. economy. The growth of the world's capital stock is reduced; and some of that reduction, indeed most of it, may appear outside the United States. But the capital stock owned by Americans declines, and the growth of the future income of Americans is retarded.

Policy Implications

The foregoing appraisal of our present situation leads to some suggestions of policies that should or should not be followed.

First, protectionism is not a solution to our problem. Erecting barriers to imports will raise the value of the dollar and not reduce our trade deficit. These barriers may protect some industries, but others will suffer, both from the higher dollar and from retaliation by other countries.

Second, intervention in currency markets is not a solution to our problem. It will reduce the value of the dollar only if the Federal Reserve creates enough dollars to raise the U.S. price level, but then U.S. export business will not benefit and will lose as much from the higher U.S. prices as it gains from a lower dollar. More generally, proposals for reform of the international monetary system have little content. The monetary system is reflecting the underlying economic factors in the world and nothing more should be expected of it.

Third, we must avoid the temptation to try to lower interest rates by monetary expansion. The interest rates also reflect real factors that monetary expansion cannot change. The result of an effort to reduce interest rates by monetary expansion will only revive the inflation traumas of the 1970s. In fact, one of our great needs is for a firmer and more durable commitment of the Federal Reserve to concentrate on the prevention of inflation.

Fourth, the Europeans can do things that will revive their economies, reduce their unemployment, and help retain more European capital in Europe. Basically they need to reduce real labor costs by cutting back on excessive social benefits and impediments to labor mobility. This policy would be good for Europe, but there is no reason to expect any economic benefits to the United States from it.

Fifth, the Japanese could take steps to keep more of their savings at home, including increasing their budget deficits. Although many Americans urge these measures upon the Japanese, hoping to reduce the capital flow to the United States and get the dollar down, I see no general value to us from such a policy. Some U.S. industries would gain, but on the whole we benefit from the inflow of capital.

Sixth, that capital is now flowing out of the less-developed countries, rather than to them, is a real problem, for us as for them. We have both a political and a humanitarian interest in their economic growth. The solution to this problem is partly in the hands of the less-developed countries themselves. They have much to do to create conditions that will attract private investment again, but they probably cannot do enough to generate a substantial private inflow in the near future. The governments of the industrial countries, notably the United States, should reconsider their present rather negative attitudes to the provision of government economic aid.

Finally, we come to topic A, the U.S. budget deficit and the need to reduce it for the sake of long-run stability and growth. One must emphasize that we are dealing with long-run effects, not with something that is hurting us today or will hurt us tomorrow. That is the main reason that getting effective action is so difficult.

The minimum requirement is to get off the path on which the federal debt, the interest burden, and the deficit all escalate relative to the GNP. That path would at some point confront us with the terrible choice between continued erosion of our capital stock and debt repudiation via inflation. Probably this minimum objective would be met by getting the deficit down to around 2 percent of GNP in ordinary economic conditions, accepting the larger deficits that would occur in recessions.

The budget proposed by the president in February 1985 and the budget resolution being considered by Congress would both have met this minimum requirement. There are, however, several major worries about the present situation.

- The budget is only in its earliest stages of congressional action. As this is written, the House and the Senate have not agreed on a budget resolution. When they have, we will still need incorporation of the budget resolution into specific appropriation and authorization legislation.

- The most important parts of the deficit reduction provided by the resolution would come not next year but in the second and third years. We have a long record of failure to realize the deficit reductions that we have projected two or three years ahead, however. Constant vigilance and effort will be needed to keep on the path now outlined.

- The 1985 budget resolution now being considered, even if fully carried out, meets only the minimum requirement. It will keep the federal debt from exploding. We could probably go on forever with a deficit equal to 2 percent of GNP and a federal debt stable at about 40 percent of GNP. But the question will remain whether we should not go further and try to get the deficit down lower for the sake of faster economic growth.

- Most important, all ways of reducing the deficit are not equal, and some ways of reducing the deficit are worse than not reducing it at all. Specifically, we will not gain if we reduce the deficit by weakening the national defense and endangering or losing our security and independence. This consideration is not an academic or a formal one. The defense program proposed by the president has been significantly reduced to obtain congressional approval. No argument, however, has been presented to show that the defense forces we are planning are unnecessary. There has been a good deal of evidence of waste in the defense establishment, but that is a stronger argument for spending more than for spending less. It would be a tragic irony if those who seek to make the nation more secure by preventing a buildup of the federal debt should contribute to making it less secure by building down the national defenses.

Agenda for the Study of Macroeconomic Policy

A Study in Contemporary
Economic Problems, 1982[1]

As the 1970s came to an end, it appeared that the poor economic performance of the preceding fifteen years, accompanied by new economic analysis, had led to a revolution of thinking about macroeconomic policy and would lead to a revolution of practice. The revolution could be most simply described as anti-Keynesian and pro-monetarist; other adjectives had to be invoked to give its full flavor. Those adjectives included "supply-side," "anti-government," and "anti-intellectual," or at least "anti-intellectual-pretensions," meaning great skepticism of claims to ability to understand, predict, and manipulate the performance of the economy.

More specifically, the revolution rejected the notion that the proper central strategy of economic policy was the discretionary, "fine-tuning" management of the federal budget to keep aggregate demand at a level that would maintain full employment. Instead the revolution called for stabilization of the money supply to provide a stable and predictable overall economic environment in which private market forces would bring employment and output to their "natural" or "equilibrium" level, whatever that might be. The revolution rejected or at least deemphasized government measures to redistribute the national income in favor of low-income people or other preferred objects and emphasized government policies, mainly negative, to make the national income grow more rapidly.

[1] American Enterprise Institute for Public Policy Research, Washington, D.C., and London, 1983.

The impact on policy of this revolution in economic thinking was already evident in the Carter administration. In October 1979 the Federal Reserve announced a change of strategy that was generally understood to be a major step toward more emphasis on controlling the growth of the money supply to make it steadier and slower. The president and Congress took steps to reduce the taxes believed to bear most heavily on investment and productivity. The rise of government spending was slowed. When the deficits implied in President Carter's budget of January 1980 seemed to shock the financial markets, he proposed revisions designed to reduce them. The recession of 1980 was accepted without expansive fiscal action.

But it was natural to expect the revolution in economic policy to be carried on much more radically in the Reagan administration. (Reagan would be Lenin to Carter's Kerensky.) He had used the anti-Keynesian, monetarist, supply-side, anti-government language in extreme form during the campaign. After his inauguration the language continued and was translated into action to an unusual degree. A specific path of restrained monetary growth was made part of the administration's program in a way that had not been seen before. An unprecedented tax cut was enacted. It was accompanied by expenditure reductions that were large in relation to common expectations of political feasibility, though not in relation to the size of the tax cut. Devotion to a balanced budget was reaffirmed, and a long-run budget plan was laid out that would bring the budget into balance by 1984. The administration's determination to shun the past course of "stop and go," "fine-tuning" fiscal policy was emphatically, and disdainfully, restated.

But at what might have been the moment of great triumph for the new economics, questions flooded in again, and consensus began to dissolve. Uncertainties appeared in both monetary and fiscal policy. Although the major change in Federal Reserve policy had promised more stable growth in the quantity of money, in fact the money supply was more volatile after the campaign than before. Once this became apparent, more attention had to be paid to the question whether this volatility had serious consequences. Although strong claims were made about this, the answer was not clear, and the general propositions about monetary policy that constituted the revolution did not imply how much volatility over what periods was consistent with "stable" monetary policy.

Moreover, questions arose about whether, if a much higher degree of short-run stability was needed, failure to achieve it was due to inadequacy of the control instruments, or to something else, or was inevitable. The period of the new, stabilizing monetary policy was also a period of unusual change in the composition of the public's moneylike assets, which raised questions about the reliability of the relations between overall economic behavior and the quantity of some particular "money." These questions about conventional monetarism kept alive interest in an entirely different version of anti-Keynesian monetary policy—the gold standard. In the fall of 1982 the Federal Reserve announced a "temporary" relaxation of its previous devotion to announced targets for the money supply, a devotion that critics claimed had never been very great. The significance of this deviation was unclear except that it both reflected and raised questions about the adequacy of the monetary rules by which we had been guided.

So after about two years the meaning and validity of monetarism were much less clear than they had seemed when it was only an idea in opposition to prevailing practice. There was a similar development on the fiscal side. In fact, it turned out that merely rejecting Keynesian fine tuning did not constitute a prescription for fiscal policy. The natural alternative to the Keynesian policy was balancing the budget, and that was how the new fiscal policy was conventionally described. But once the revolution was installed, the difficulty of balancing the budget in practice became evident, and the question arose whether balancing the budget was imperative, or was sufficiently important to require the painful steps needed to achieve it, or, indeed, mattered at all. The reversal of roles on this question was illuminating. In the political realm, many of the people who had been the stoutest champions of balancing the budget previously, when they were out of office, began to find sophisticated arguments for not balancing; whereas those who had been defenders of deficits for almost fifty years discovered the virtues of the old-time religion of the balanced budget. This led some cynics to the view that there never had been anything to the balanced-budget idea but a stick with which the outs could beat the ins.

But if budget balancing was not a useful principle and Keynesian functional finance was out, what did we have for guidance on fiscal policy? And even if one did think there was something in budget balancing, there were unanswered questions about what it meant. People who had once rejected the idea of "balancing the budget at high employment" as a subterfuge, or as unworthy compromising with the Keynesians, had to recognize that balancing the budget could not mean balancing the budget all the time regardless of economic conditions. But what were the conditions, if any, in which it should be balanced? This became a glaring issue as it became obvious that seemingly minor changes in the economic assumptions on which budget projections were calculated could do more to change the apparent size of deficits than painful decisions about tax rates and expenditure programs. So the whole debate about the budget took on an unreal look, concerned with numbers based on assumptions that could not be checked even in retrospect.

Moreover, as attention turned to the question whether deficits mattered, a number of different reasons for being concerned about deficits emerged. But then it appeared that corresponding to every reason for being concerned about the deficit was a different definition of the deficit that was relevant. So the notion of balancing "the" budget became as complicated as the notion of stabilizing "the" money supply.

To add to the list of causes for uncertainty about the meaning and validity of the new macroeconomic policy, the common-sense view that one way to reduce a deficit was to increase taxes and raise the revenue was forcefully attacked. Two quite different objections were raised to the common-sense view. One was that raising tax rates reduces the revenue, by reducing the taxable national income. This interesting hypothesis led to puzzlement about why we had any taxes at all, since no one seemed to like them. The other objection was that raising tax rates would indeed raise the revenue but that the government would spend any additional revenue, so that raising the rates would not reduce the deficit. In this view, the deficit was not a policy variable, but was given by some political force. In the summer of 1982 the administration seemed to return to the old-fashioned idea that raising taxes was a way to reduce the deficit, but it did so apologetically, and many of its supporters did not agree.

Earlier thinking had been that the expenditure side of the budget was too encrusted with particular programmatic considerations to be used as an instrument of macroeconomic policy, a role that had to be left to the revenue side of the budget. Now it was held that the revenue side of the budget was useless for that purpose.

To add one more without exhausting the list of reasons for

uncertainty about the state of macroeconomics, the experience of 1981–1982 opened wide the question of the relation between restraint of the nominal side of the economy and the behavior of the real output and employment side. The hopeful view at the beginning of 1981 had been that a policy of monetary restraint, publicly accepted with sufficient credibility, could reduce the rate of growth of nominal GNP and the price level without any adverse effect on output and employment, or at least without any serious adverse effect. In 1981 we had an announced change of fiscal and monetary policy in a disinflationary direction, in what would have seemed the most favorable political conditions for achieving credibility. But the slowdown of nominal GNP growth and inflation then realized was accompanied by an unusually large decline of output and rise of unemployment. What did this imply about the steps needed to achieve credibility, or about the credibility theory itself?

This state of confusion and skepticism about the new macroeconomics is not surprising. Putting the new theory into operation would obviously require answering many specific questions that did not have to be answered when we were talking about big, general, largely negative ideas. The process of selling the new ideas inevitably involved making more extravagant claims for them than could ever be fulfilled. For this reason, all "new ideas" once installed will be disappointing. Economic discussion is political discussion, at least when the discussion reaches the public. Once the new ideas were applied, they became objects of political attack on a greater scale than previously. And once the new ideas became the slogans of the party in office, they acquired responsibility for all the ills the economy suffered, whether that responsibility was legitimate or not. The new ideas, moreover, were basically ideas about how to keep the economy in a state of equilibrium. They were stabilizing ideas. They did not have much to say about how to get to equilibrium from a condition of high inflation, with its accompanying expectations and constraints, and high unemployment.

The present uncertainty about the new macroeconomics does not mean that it is invalid. Still less does it mean that we should return to the naive Keynesian liberalism of the Kennedy-Johnson days. With the passage of time and with constructive discussion, some of the questions would be answered, some of the expectations would be moderated, and if the policy was only fairly successful, the transitional difficulties would be left behind.

Still, the current uncertainty about the meaning and validity of the new macroeconomic policy that became the nation's standard doctrine at the end of the 1970s presents dangers. First, there is obvious danger that seriously wrong decisions will be made. Even if this should be escaped, the economy suffers from lack of knowledge about what policy is coming next and from lack of confidence in whatever policy may eventuate. Some of the economic problems of 1982 are due to unusual uncertainty about what fiscal and monetary policy will be in the next several years and what the effects of that policy will be, rather than to current errors of policy or to a settled conviction that policy will be wrong in the future.

There is great need to resolve the uncertainties that now exist. That means more than that economists need to learn the answers to the unsettled questions about macroeconomics. Of course they need to do that. But the fact must be accepted that this learning is going to come slowly. Meanwhile, the country must learn what to do in the state of limited knowledge—which is our perpetual condition. More than that, we must seek a consensus on policy, because predictable stability of policy may be more important than the "best" policy, and predictable stability requires that there be some agreement. Otherwise, policy is a political football, which may change direction radically after any election or in anticipation of any election.

The present situation of uncertainty and disagreement about macroeconomic policy is reminiscent of the situation around the end of World War II. The country had been through a decade of disastrous economic failure. We were determined not to repeat that. But we also knew that the country had not found the formula for dealing with the depression, even after ten years. The war had only declared an intermission in that effort. There were people who thought they knew what needed to be done, but in fact what they knew was very general—an attitude rather than an operational program—and there was wide disagreement about the attitude.

By that time, the latter days of World War II, the predominant viewpoint in the economics profession was Keynesian. The Keynesians thought they had the key to our economic problem— use of fiscal policy (which meant government spending) to sustain adequate demand and so maintain full employment—but they were only beginning to recognize the economic, administrative, and political difficulties of carrying out such a program. There were a number of economists who, having originally been sympathetic, had fallen off the Keynesian bandwagon when they saw the extremes to which the Keynesian enthusiasts were going. These dissenters gave considerable weight to money—the term monetarist had not yet been invented—but they had no specific plan for the management of money. There were still fundamentalists around who believed that the depression had been caused by the New Deal and that the needed course was to get the government out of the economy—whatever that meant for fiscal and monetary policy. There were others who took from the wartime management of the economy the lesson that similar management would be needed in peacetime. And there were still others who knew only that something had to be done to keep the country from sliding back into depression.

When the United States entered the war, no one could tell what postwar economic policy would be like. But within a few years after the war ended, a substantial consensus had been achieved, a consensus on policy that worked fairly well and survived for about fifteen years. An unusual national discussion of economic policy contributed to this result. There was a widespread awareness of the existence of a major national economic problem and a general desire to participate in the search for a solution. The discussion was addressed to long-run issues rather than to immediate decisions, but the discussion of long-run issues had an unusually large practical and operational content. Moreover, the discussion rose above partisan and parochial interest to an unusual degree.

Some specific components of this discussion may be listed to indicate its character:

- the statements of the Committee for Economic Development, an organization of businessmen established specifically for the purpose of formulating economic policy for postwar America
- statements of the National Planning Association—representing business, labor, agriculture, and academic experts
- unusually thoughtful statements of their position by the Chamber of Commerce and the National Association of Manufacturers
- a contest, sponsored by the Pabst Brewing Company, for essays on how to maintain postwar employment, in which there were 46,000 entries and national publicity

- writing by several leading economists on macroeconomic strategies, notably Friedman's "Monetary and Fiscal Framework"[2] and a symposium, *Financing American Prosperity*, published by the Twentieth Century Fund[3]
- reports of two task forces established by the American Economic Association
- the hearings and discussion on the legislation that was finally called the Employment Act of 1946
- the hearings on economic policy held by a subcommittee of the Joint Economic Committee under the chairmanship of Senator Paul H. Douglas

The national discussion, of which these were only the most conspicuous parts, led to a national consensus. As I have written elsewhere, it domesticated Keynes and liberated monetary policy. It led to a normal rule of budget policy: balancing the budget at high employment. It established the revenue side of the budget as the main instrument for stabilization policy, defined the unified budget as the relevant measure, and identified 4 percent unemployment as the standard of high employment. Monetary policy was recognized as an equal partner and freed from the commitment to fixing interest rates. The Council of Economic Advisers and the Joint Economic Committee were created to advise the president and the Congress.

This consensus, we can see now, was not ideal. Still, it was great progress from where we stood in 1939 or 1945. And there was sufficient agreement to provide reasonable stability and predictability of policy for some time.

What we need now is not a return to the postwar policy consensus but a return to the postwar discussion process—and we are not getting it. The utterances of economists, with few exceptions, are either incomprehensible or incredible. Political discussion is myopic and intensely partisan. The statements of business organizations and of other special-interest groups are simply that—expressions of special interest. The validity of these observations can be checked by comparing any issue of the *American Economic Review* for 1982 with any issue for 1947, by comparing

[2] Milton Friedman, "A Monetary and Fiscal Framework for Economic Stability," *American Economic Review*, June 1948, *38:*248.

[3] Paul T. Homan and Fritz Machlup, (eds.), *Financing America's Prosperity: A Symposium of Economists* (New York: Twentieth Century Fund, 1945).

any current statement of any business organization today with those of the Committee for Economic Development thirty to forty years ago, or by comparing the discussion of the Employment Act of 1946 with the discussion of the Full Employment Act of 1978 (the Humphrey-Hawkins Act).

There are undoubtedly many reasons for the difference in the quality of the postwar discussion and the present discussion. Our present problem is intellectually and politically more difficult than the problem envisaged in 1945. Then we were overwhelmingly concerned with the simple problem of full employment. Today we know that we have a complex problem of inflation, growth, full employment, efficiency, welfare or justice, and freedom. Economists, having become more sophisticated, are more aware of the limits of their knowledge and in their scientific roles more reluctant to give advice, whatever may be true in their political, publicist roles.

But there is, in my opinion, one chief explanation for the difference between 1945, say, and 1982. In 1945 the country had been through the agony of the Great Depression and the great war. There was a generation of leaders who were acutely aware that the nation could be in mortal peril. They accepted the responsibility to make the intellectual effort and the moral effort—to rise above their ideological commitments and private interests—in order to save the nation. That feeling seems rare today. Perhaps our economic condition is not yet critical enough. But we should not have to experience disaster before turning seriously and objectively to dealing with economic policy issues.

The obvious contradictions of policy in 1982—the difference between our professions and our realizations in fiscal and monetary policy and the related worries about a depression or revived inflation—may provide some stimulus for the needed discussion. There are hopeful signs. The annual report of the Council of Economic Advisers issued in February 1982 wrestled with the meaning of budget balancing in a constructive way. The Gold Commission recommended a congressional study of rules of monetary policy, which could be the occasion for trying to synthesize present thinking about money. Even the proposal for a constitutional amendment requiring a balanced budget shows awareness of the current problem and, although it is not in my opinion a good idea, may precipitate serious discussion of the principles of budget policy we really mean to live with.

But the kind of discussion we need will depend basically on the private sector. Government agencies and congressional committees can provide a forum, but they cannot rise above the quality of thinking that goes on in the private sector. There is need for private research bodies, organizations of business, labor, and other sectors, and individual economists to try to make the leap to a more constructive, durable, objective formulation of policy, which might have general acceptability.

Questions for Consideration

In the remainder of this paper I discuss what seem to me the main questions about macroeconomic policy on which attention needs to be focused and answers need to be sought. I want to make clear that I am not primarily proposing an agenda for research, but an agenda for thinking, discussing, agreeing, and deciding. Of course, more research is needed and would be welcome in the process I am describing. But the fruits of research in this field will come slowly. Our urgent need is to try to bring the present state of knowledge to bear and to decide open-mindedly what to do in the limited state of our knowledge.

IS THERE MACROECONOMICS, AND WHAT IS IT?

The notion that there is a macroeconomic policy that differs from other aspects of economic policy implies that there are certain "overall" policy instruments, which have an effect on the "overall" behavior of the economy in ways that other instruments do not and which affect only the "overall" behavior of the economy. As an extreme example, one might say that the quantity of money determines the price level and only that, relative prices being unaffected, and that nothing else influences the price level. But we know that the world is not really like that. All the instruments that we conventionally consider macroinstruments have micro-effects; that is, they affect the allocation of output and the distribution of income. And at least a great many of the instruments that we do not conventionally consider macroinstruments do have effects on such overall aspects of the economy as total output, nominal GNP, or the price level.

The fuzziness of the distinction between macro- and micro-policy is clearest in fiscal policy. We usually think of total government expenditures, total tax revenues, and the difference between them—the deficit or surplus—as macroinstruments. But it is hard to think of a statement about the effects of these aggregates that might not also be true of some subaggregates. One might say, for example, that the choice between taxing and borrowing is a macroeconomic decision, which has an effect on the overall rate of economic growth. But to some degree a choice between consumption taxes and income taxes has such an effect, and choices among forms of income tax do also. Moreover, the choice between taxing and borrowing does not have only overall effects on the economy. The choice will, for example, affect Oregon and Michigan differently from California and Florida. Different kinds of taxes or expenditures or methods of managing the debt have different macroeffects, and different actions about the budget aggregates have different microeffects.

The same thing is true, though probably not to the same degree, of monetary policy. Change in the rate of growth of the money supply, usually regarded as the macroinstrument in the monetary field, does not affect only the price level or some other macrovariable. At least in the short run it will affect the distribution of income and output. We could also have, and sometimes have had, policy instruments to control separately the quantity of different kinds of financial assets, and the use of these instruments would have macroeffects as well as microeffects.

If economists knew all about everything, there would be no need for the distinction between macroeconomic policy and microeconomic policy. There would be one enormous model of the economy into which all possible policy actions could be plugged and from which all possible consequences could be read out and the combination of actions that maximized some social objective could be calculated. But, of course, economists do not know everything.

At this point there are two alternatives. One is to try to do our best as if we did know everything or at least would bring to bear on every decision everything we know, however little, about all its consequences. In deciding whether to build the B-1 bomber or refit the B-52s, we would consider the effects of the decision on the general price level. In deciding whether to raise the money supply by 5 percent or 6 percent, we would consider the effect of the decision on the relative prices of corn and lima beans in South Succotash.

The other alternative is, when trying to affect the overall objectives, to focus on those instruments that we believe *mainly* affect those objectives, even though we recognize that other instruments also have *some* overall effect. When trying to decide on the use of those instruments, we would focus on their overall effects, even though we recognize that they also have some specific effects. This would be a recognition that if we try to think of everything at the same time, we will not make good decisions. If we tried to stabilize the price level by thinking of all the things that affect the price level, we would be bogged down in decisions of great uncertainty and little relevance.

Probably most people would agree that the second alternative is the only workable one. Yet it is surprising how many people, when asked to think "fundamentally" about the causes of inflation and its cures, for example, come up with lists of scores of demographic, psychological, political, and technological factors. This is more likely to be true of "practical" people than of economists.

Adopting the second alternative means accepting the fact that macroeconomics and macroeconomic policy are abstractions made for pragmatic reasons, because we cannot think of everything at the same time. Thus it is no serious objection to a macroeconomic policy that it leaves out of account some instruments or some effects—unless those instruments or effects are so important that leaving them out of account worsens the decision-making process. Moreover, this way of looking at macroeconomic policy already implies a partial answer to the perennial question about rules versus discretion. That is, if "discretion" means that all possible information must be taken into account in making every decision, the idea that there is macroeconomics means the rejection of discretion because it calls for concentrating on a certain kind of information in making certain decisions.

In fact the notion of discretion in the sense just mentioned is unrealistic. No person or organization can make decisions by continuously taking in "all" information and processing it in all possible ways. Everyone operates by some decision-making rules, conscious or unconscious, that limit the information to be taken into account and its use. The argument about rules is an argument about which rules—how simple, explicit, and durable—and from whom they come.

It is significant that the 1936 essay by Henry Simons that precipitated the discussion of rules was called not "Rules versus Discretion in Monetary Policy" but "Rules Versus Authority in

Monetary Policy." It was really about *whose* rules—Simons's or the authority's. When people outside the government argue for rules, they are arguing for the imposition of their rules on the authorities. When people inside the government argue against rules, they are arguing for their own rules, which they may not even be able to describe.

What we seek is a set of instruments and objectives that are so much more closely related to each other than to other instruments and objectives that we can draw a line around them and call them macroeconomics. The possibility and difficulty of doing this become clearer if we distinguish between "nominal" macroeconomics and "real" macroeconomics. Nominal macroeconomics consists of the relations between certain instruments and nominal objectives—nominal GNP or the price level. Concern with these nominal objectives does not mean that we are not interested in the real magnitudes—output, employment, and unemployment. It means that in this compartment we are interested in the real magnitudes insofar as they are influenced by the nominal magnitudes. What seems to me the realistic version of this is that we are concerned with the effects on the real magnitudes that result from the instability and unpredictability of the nominal magnitudes. There may be other ways to describe this relationship, but I am not concerned with them here.

With respect to nominal macroeconomics, it does seem possible to identify a limited number of instruments that are distinctly more important than any others and whose macroeconomic effects are much more important than any other effects they have. Thus decisions about the size of the money supply clearly belong in the compartment of nominal macroeconomics, whereas decisions about the B-1 bomber do not, even though producers of B-1 bombers may have propensities to hold money that are different from other people's. One could say that nominal macroeconomic policy consists of the management of the money supply to achieve certain objectives with respect to nominal GNP or the price level— say, stability and predictability.

A problem arises with respect to fiscal policy. We are used to thinking of fiscal and monetary policy as being the instruments of macroeconomics. Whether fiscal policy has any important effect on nominal variables is a disputed question, much less likely to be answered in the affirmative today than thirty years ago. But even if fiscal policy does have an important effect on the nominal variables, it does not necessarily belong in the compartment of nominal macroeconomics. Anything fiscal policy can do about the nominal variables monetary policy may be able to do with fewer other effects, that is, fewer real effects. In that case fiscal policy does not have to be assigned to the nominal compartment, but can be determined in relation to its other effects.

One possibility is that aspects of fiscal policy can be divided between the nominal and the real compartments. It may be that what is important about fiscal policy for the nominal objectives is the short-term variation of fiscal measures whereas what is important for the real objectives is the long-term level and trend. In that case the short-term variations might be put in the nominal compartment and the long-term level and trend in the real compartment.

Of course, there is no necessary reason why the same instrument should not be involved in both compartments. That would complicate decision making, but nothing says it has to be simple. It may, indeed, produce irreconcilable conflicts. Suppose it were true, which I do not believe but can conceive, that satisfactory development of the nominal variables required a large budget deficit but that satisfactory development of the real variables required a large budget surplus. The public wants to hold government securities equal to a constant fraction of nominal GNP as nominal GNP grows, but a high rate of private investment requires that private savings be supplemented by a government surplus. There could then be a difficult choice to be made.

The puzzling questions arise, however, when one thinks about what objectives and instruments belong in the compartment of "real macroeconomics."

The problem is that there seem to be in the real world no single dominant objective and no single dominant instrument related to it. In the nominal world there is a dominant macroobjective, which is predictability. One cannot conceive of a policy with respect to the nominal world that does not aim at predictability. That seems to be the maximum that nominal policy can provide and the minimum it should offer. In the long run, predictable nominal behavior will yield the best real results that nominal behavior can yield. Moreover, even if it might be useful and feasible, it does not seem "right" that the government should follow a policy of misleading the public, which is what would be involved in a policy that did not aim at predictability. This still leaves questions of just what is to be predictable, on what path, and how the predictability is to be achieved, which will be discussed below. But at least one can define in a general way what the objective of nominal macroeconomic policy is. And, as already stated, one can identify an instrument that has a strong comparative advantage in achieving that objective.

In the real macroeconomy there are a number of objectives, none of which seems to dominate all others, and a number of instruments, each of which affects a number of objectives and none of which seems to have a superior relation to any single objective. What we are concerned with here is fiscal policy, or whether there is any such thing. The basic notion of fiscal policy is that there are a few aggregate magnitudes of the budget, or possibly only one, that have effects so important and exceptional that decisions about these aggregates should dominate decisions about their components. This notion is implicit in the federal budget process and in the division between "fiscal policy" and "public finance" in university curricula and elsewhere. The most obvious example is the idea of the size of the deficit or surplus as an overriding consideration to which other policies had to be accommodated. This was, of course, implicit in the idea that balancing the budget was a principle to which decisions about particular expenditures and taxes must conform. It was also implicit in the simpler and more operational version of the "functional finance" rule, which held that there was some deficit or surplus that would be optimum for full employment, and expenditure and revenue decisions had to be adapted to that. Everyone knew that was not literally true and that the optimum size of the deficit depended on the level of expenditures as well as on the composition of both the expenditures and the revenues. But the discussion proceeded as if that could be ignored.

We have passed beyond the idea that the budget-balancing rule was handed down from Mount Sinai, however, and we have also left functional finance behind us. It is now much less clear than it seemed that one can arrive at a decision about the size of deficits or surpluses that is independent of and prior to decisions about the particulars of the budget. We have to ask what objective is to be served by the choice of the size of deficit or surplus. Probably the answer that would most commonly be given to that question today is that the decision has something to do with economic growth. The larger the surplus, the more funds are available for private investment and the higher will be the rate of economic growth. But this provides no unique guide to the size of the surplus or deficit that is so clear and imperative that other budget decisions must be adapted to it. For one thing, the desirable rate of growth is something to be decided. We obviously do not want the maximum possible rate of growth. Economic growth has its costs, and beyond some point more of it is not worth the cost. Moreover, even if we knew what the optimum rate of growth was or what the optimum contribution to growth was, there would be various packages of budgetary policies and other policies that would achieve it. The budget surplus would be only one ingredient in those packages. Thus in the early 1960s there was a "liberal" budget strategy for economic growth, which involved, paradoxically, large budget surpluses, high taxes, especially on the rich, and increasing expenditures for "human capital"—education, training, and labor mobility. This strategy, which was clearest in the writings of James Tobin, was never implemented, probably because the high-tax element was politically impossible to carry through. Today we have a "conservative" budget strategy for economic growth, which involves large budget deficits, tax incentives for private saving, and even greater tax incentives, including in some circumstances negative tax rates, for certain kinds of investment—business plant and equipment. The 1960 policy was a low-interest-rate strategy; the 1980 policy is a high-interest-rate strategy. Probably some desired contribution to growth could be achieved by either of these strategies, but the outcome would differ in important respects, notably in the distribution of income by size and in the size of the government sector.

The point is that even if some given growth goal were accepted as the object of fiscal policy, and even as an objective superior to all others, that would not enable us to say that the budget surplus must be such-and-such and that other budget decisions must be accommodated to that. There would be various policy packages involving different budget surpluses or deficits that would yield the growth result, and a choice among these policy packages would have to be made on the basis of their effect on other objectives. And these other objectives are important—defense, size of government, income distribution, claim of individuals to dispose of their own earned incomes, at least. Moreover, it is unrealistic to think that a goal for economic growth could be sensibly chosen without consideration of the means by which it was to be achieved—whether, for example, by cutting defense or by severe limitation of the ability of income earners to conserve their own income.

What has been said here about the idea that the connection between surpluses and growth provides a precise and overriding answer to the proper size of the surplus applies also to a more recent view of the connection between taxes and growth. This view is simply that taxes should be reduced where they impede growth. There are two problems with this. One is that the analysis is usually partial. Except in the unlikely cases where tax reduction raises the revenue, tax reduction involves, arithmetically, tax increases elsewhere or expenditure decreases or deficit increases. And these consequences will have effects on growth that may make the total policy negative from the standpoint of growth. There will also be effects other than the growth effect, which must be considered in deciding on the merits of the policy.

This discussion helps us to understand the meaning of "supply-side" economics and to see what is valid and what is invalid about it. The relevant distinction is between the nominal economy and the real economy, not between the demand side and the supply side. (I sometimes regret having coined the term "supply side.") The supply-siders reject the use of fiscal policy to affect the nominal variables, notably nominal total income. That is because they think that fiscal policy cannot be used efficiently for that purpose, or because they think that the behavior of nominal income does not affect the real economy. So they believe that fiscal policy should concentrate on the real economy directly. This seems to be a defensible position. The difficulties arise in understanding the relations of fiscal policy to the real economy. There, it seems to me, several mistakes have been made, though not all by all supply-siders:

- Overestimating the "partial" effects of particular tax or expenditure changes on total output or its rate of growth. The partial effects are the effects that would occur if all other taxes, expenditures, and the surplus or deficit were unchanged, which is impossible except under quite unlikely circumstances.
- Neglecting or underestimating the significance of the repercussions of particular tax changes on other elements of the

budget. Most important, this meant neglecting the adverse effect on the growth of output that might result from the deficits that tax reductions would cause.

• Underestimating the importance from the standpoint of the supply of output of the difference among types of taxes and objects of expenditure. There is a tendency to consider all taxes—or in some formulations, all expenditures—equally as a "wedge" between production and the income that is an incentive to produce.

• Neglecting aspects of the real economy other than the supply of output that are legitimate and necessary concerns of economics and economic policy.

What was wrong with supply-side economics was not that it discarded the last remnants of the Keynesian idea of using fiscal policy to manage the nominal economy. It was an unrealistic and oversimplified view of what was entailed in using fiscal policy to manage the real economy.

We have many objectives in the real economy, and many of these objectives must be balanced against one another. That is, we do not want as much growth, or as much income equality, or as little government, or even as much defense as we can get. There are tradeoffs among the various objectives, and the amount of any one that is desirable depends on its cost in terms of the others. Moreover, the amount of any one objective that it is worth giving up in order to get some of another objective will be appraised differently by different people and cannot be determined in any mechanical way. These tradeoffs have to be valued in a political process, and the valuation will change from time to time. The government has a number of instruments, not all in the domain of fiscal policy, that affect the achievement of these objectives. Many of the instruments affect several objectives, and most of the objectives are affected by a variety of instruments.

The upshot of this is that it does not seem possible to make reasonable decisions about any of the big aggregates of the budget—say, the deficit or total spending or total revenues—without regard to the decisions made about the other aggregates or without regard to the components of the aggregates or without regard to several objectives, not only one. If this thought is carried to its logical extreme, it calls for simultaneous decisions with regard to all budgetary instruments and objectives. The decision whether to build the B-1 bomber or the Stealth bomber would affect the income of people in Kansas and therefore would have to be made in the light of what agricultural price support policy is doing to the price of wheat, but that would affect the real incomes of poor families in the Bronx and would have to be decided in the light of the appropriation for aid to families with dependent children, and so on. But that, as we said at the outset, is impossible and also means that there is no such thing as macroeconomic policy.

It is necessary to find some practical level of aggregation at which decisions can be made that would dominate decisions made at lower levels. All that is being suggested here is that the sensible procedure might not permit a prior decision about total deficit or total expenditures or total receipts, or all three of them together. One could imagine a somewhat lower level of aggregation at which the fiscal instruments might be:

> total defense expenditures
> total income assistance expenditures
> total investment expenditures (human and physical capital)
> interest
> other expenditures
> revenues from proportional taxation
> revenues from progressive taxation
> other revenues
> deficit or surplus (by subtraction)

Decisions could be made about these aggregates in terms of their effect on economic growth, national security, income distribution, dominance of government, and consumption by income earners. Once these decisions had been made, decisions at a lower level—navy versus army, education versus dams, and so on— would be adapted to them.

The foregoing is meant as an illustration, not as a proposal. It comes fairly close to the categories in which the public discussion of the first budget resolution in 1982 ran. There was then, however, a tendency for the discussion and decisions to be "tainted" by reference to subordinate details. Moreover, the relation between the instruments and the objectives was much less explicit than it might have been.

The illustration may serve, however, to point up two difficulties. One is the problem of choosing the efficient level of aggregation. It is always possible to say that we could decide on total defense expenditures better if we knew how much was for strategic weapons, and could decide how much to spend for strategic weapons better if we knew how much was for the MX, and how much to spend for the MX better if we knew where it was to be based, and so on. But that way lies frustration and madness. The problem is to choose a level of decision making where the value of the additional information that would be provided by more detail does not equal the cost in loss of ability to weigh the big issues. There is a point at which one cannot see the forest for the trees.

Some presidents have been justly criticized for paying so much attention to the details of the budget that they lose sight of the most important choices. They fall into this error probably not because they want more information in order to decide the basic questions but because of failure to see the basic questions or frustrations in trying to deal with them. Something like that seems to have been happening in the congressional budget process. The new procedure established in 1974 reflected the belief that the previous, decentralized process did not sufficiently focus on the global issues like the size of the deficit or surplus, total expenditures, and total receipts. The new procedure presumably would force the Congress first to concentrate on the big issues and then to conform the details to the decisions on those issues. The budget committees and the two houses in acting on the budget resolutions, however, have become more and more concerned with the details, so that the aggregates are increasingly the consequence of the detailed decisions. This is probably because the connection between the global decisions and the global objectives is not seen to be so clear and compelling that the global decisions dominate the details.

There is thus an administrative management or information management problem of where to draw the line between macroinstruments and macroobjectives and microinstruments and microobjectives. That is a question that every large organization faces. It does not seem to have been systematically studied for the U.S. budget. What is involved, of course, is not the academic question of dividing the college curriculum between fiscal policy and public finance. It is the practical question of getting the decisions made at the right level of government and in relation to the right objectives.

My suggestion above that macropolicy at the fiscal and real

level would include several—say, six or seven—instruments (categories of expenditure and revenue) and a similar number of objectives runs into another difficulty, which is political. The decisions obviously cannot be made by a computer. The relation between the instruments and the objectives is too uncertain, and the relative weight to be given to the several objectives is too much a matter of subjective evaluation. The decisions will have to be made by people and will reflect their estimates and value judgments. The question then is what people will make the decisions and what their biases will be.

It seems clear that if we have a decision process with six or seven instruments, the decisions will have to be made by living government officials—politicians—using their discretion. One can imagine a different procedure. Conceivably there could be a decision now that the budget should be balanced forever, that total expenditures and receipts should be 20 percent of GNP, transfer payments 10 percent of GNP, personal income tax 9 percent of GNP, and a few other numbers. All of this could be incorporated in the Constitution or, by a process of persuasion, made part of a durable national consensus. That would free those decisions from the biases of living, transient politicians. But no one proposes to go that far. Doing so would eliminate the possibility of taking advantage of new information as it becomes available or of responding to changing national preferences. For most of these decisions it would be universally agreed that the loss of information would outweigh the gain from avoiding transient bias. Moreover, one cannot be certain whether the constitutional amendment or moral rule about the budget avoids "bias" in the decisions or only substitutes the biases of dead politicians for those of living ones, or the biases of politicians out of office or going out for those of politicians in office or expecting to come in.

There may, however, be one or two decisions for which the elimination of what I will call contemporary bias (as distinguished from inherited bias) is much more important than adaptation to changing conditions, information, and priorities. The decision about the size of the budget deficit or surplus (the correct decision being assumed to be zero) is frequently considered to fall into this category. There are people who believe that ratio of total government spending to GNP falls into this category (the proper ratio being a little lower than the ratio just reached).

The intent here is to emphasize the need to think about and

try to reach agreement about how various budget decisions are made—at which level of government, by what procedures, in terms of what objectives, for what duration, and subject to what outside constraints. This problem is made exceedingly difficult by many considerations: the budget consists of a number of policy instruments; there are a number of objectives; each objective is affected by several instruments, and many instruments affect several objectives; effects of the instruments on the objectives are hard to estimate; the relative values of the objectives are matters of personal preference, which change from time to time; and the instruments interact with each other, not least because the sources and uses of funds will be equal. But some intermediate practical ground must be sought, both for thinking and for acting, between trying to make all the decisions simultaneously and singling out individual decisions to be made in isolation.

It may be pointed out here that the problem of fixing some decisions for all time, or a very long time, and insulating them from contemporary politics is different in the monetary-nominal realm than in the fiscal-real realm. Possibly in some sense better monetary decisions would be made if they were flexibly adapted from quarter to quarter to changing conditions, information, and preferences. But the dominant objective of policy for the nominal world is not this adaptation but the creation of an environment in which the actors—individuals, business, and governments—can efficiently make their own adaptations. And the most important characteristic of that environment is constancy and predictability. For some aspects of the budget, constancy and predictability are also valuable. But they are not nearly as dominant over the need for adaptation as in the case of monetary policy. Budget policy *is* making decisions about the uses of the real output of the economy, not merely providing a "neutral" stage for making those decisions. To freeze those real decisions for any great length of time would be unrealistic, whereas freezing is the essence of good nominal decisions.

THE TARGETS OF MONETARY POLICY

The preceding discussion has assumed that monetary policy is aimed proximately at some variable in the nominal world—money supply, nominal GNP, the price level—with the expectation, of course, that a beneficial result for the real world will follow. This is to be distinguished from aiming directly at a real variable like the unemployment rate or real output or its rate of growth. Whether this assumption is correct or not is a critical question, which needs to be discussed. I believe that professional opinion is coming increasingly to this view, but there are still dissenters within the economics profession and probably more people outside the profession who still think in the other terms.

The experience of the past fifteen or twenty years seems to support strongly the idea of not aiming at a real target. During most of that period monetary policy has undertaken to achieve some rate of unemployment or has felt obliged to reduce the rate when it significantly exceeded some acceptable level. This policy has contributed to an acceleration of inflation, because the unemployment goal was consistently lower than could be achieved without accelerating inflation. The policy did not for long keep the unemployment rate at the target level, because the inflation rate that would have been necessary for this would have been unacceptable. Policy hovered between being expansive enough to keep unemployment low and being restrictive enough to keep inflation from accelerating. And now we face a painful and perhaps protracted period of unemployment in an effort to regain price-level stability.

Some would disagree with this diagnosis. They would argue that the problem was not in aiming at an unemployment target but in aiming at too ambitious an unemployment target. Economists work with a concept called the nonaccelerating inflation rate of unemployment (NAIRU), which is the lowest unemployment rate that would be experienced if the rate of inflation were stable. If monetary policy aimed to make the actual unemployment rate equal to the NAIRU—restricting when the actual was below NAIRU, and vice versa—there would be no tendency for inflation to accelerate.

The trouble is, of course, that no one knows what the NAIRU is at any moment. We have no way to measure it. All we can say is that NAIRU is the unemployment rate that would prevail if the inflation rate was stable for a considerable period and was expected to stay that way. So there is no reliable way to aim directly at the NAIRU. The best we can do is to aim at stabilizing the inflation rate and watching the NAIRU emerge. Moreover, it is extremely likely that if we try to aim directly at the NAIRU, we will in fact aim at too low a rate. Since no one can be sure

what the NAIRU is, the political temptation will always be strong
to aim at a low unemployment rate, because the inflationary consequences of that will come only after the passage of some time.

Moreover, it seems clear, as already noted, that if the immediate target is a nominal variable, the essential characteristic to be
sought in the nominal variable is predictability. Fundamentally
this is an argument for the predictability of the price level, although, as will be explained shortly, this does not necessarily
mean that monetary policy should aim directly at the predictability
of the price level. Individuals and businesses make decisions and
commitments for the future in terms of dollars and with expectations of what the future real value of the dollar will be. Businesses
and their employees enter into wage contracts in which both parties are estimating what the future value of the dollar will be.
Businesses and their creditors make borrowing, lending, and investing decisions in the light of some expectations about the future
value of the dollar. Uncertainty about the future value of the
dollar is a burden on these decisions and makes investment and
employment less than they would otherwise be. Moreover, if the
actual value of the dollar turns out to be different from what
had been expected, there are disappointments, unexpected
changes in the distribution of income, shortages, and unemployment.

Predictability does not have to mean constancy. The time
of sunrise changes from day to day but is perfectly predictable.
That only means, of course, that there is a constant cycle through
the year. But as a practical matter predictability of the price level
will only be achieved with constancy of either the level or its
rate of change. Moreover, since we are dealing with a predictability
that is to be achieved by policy, there is no reason to make the
predicted pattern more complicated than simple constancy. So I
shall assume that we are considering a monetary policy aimed
at achieving stability in the level or rate of change of a nominal
variable.

A number of questions then arise. The first is, What should
be the nominal variable at which monetary policy should aim?
There are a number of possibilities:

- "the" price level (or "a" price index, there being many)
- nominal GNP
- some measure of the money supply

- the monetary base—bank reserves plus currency in circulation—which limits the supply of money
- the price of gold
- interest rates

The previous discussion might seem to have made it obvious that the price level is the proper target of monetary policy. Predictability of the price level is what we are after as a condition in which economic decisions will yield their best results because expectations about the value of money will come true. So one might think that monetary policy should be directed toward stabilizing the price level or its rate of inflation, with the monetary authority (the Federal Reserve) accelerating or decelerating the growth of the money supply as it considers appropriate for achieving the desired behavior of the price level.

This formulation immediately reveals one critical difficulty with use of the price level as the target. The instruction to the Federal Reserve would be that it should accelerate or decelerate growth of the money supply "as it considers appropriate." But the acceleration or deceleration of growth that is appropriate would not be known objectively and precisely. The Federal Reserve would have to use its discretion in managing the money supply. Moreover, one could not tell after the fact whether departures of the price level from its target path were the result of honest and inevitable errors or showed that the Federal Reserve was not following its instructions. That is, it would be difficult to maintain accountability and check a bias that would probably be in the inflationary direction.

The first four possible targets listed above are ranked in a certain hierarchical order. The price level is the most relevant target—that is, its predictability would yield the most of what we would like to achieve. Controllability and accountability are least, however, if the price level is the target. At the other extreme, the monetary base is the variable most controllable by the Federal Reserve, and the Federal Reserve could most clearly be held responsible for departures from the desired path of the base. But the predictability of the base would contribute least to the efficient operation of the economy because individuals and businesses do not make decisions on the basis of their expectations about the base.

These four targets are causally linked to one another. The

growth of the base controls the growth of the money supply, but with some looseness and uncertainty in the linkage. The growth of the money supply controls the growth of nominal GNP, but with some looseness and uncertainty in the linkage. The growth of nominal GNP controls the rate of inflation, but again with some looseness and uncertainty in the linkage.

If the linkages were tight and well known, the choice among these four targets would make no difference. Targeting on the base would yield the desired behavior of the price level. Targeting on the price level would indicate precisely what had to be done about the base. The choice of the target depends on two factors— the looseness of the linkage and the risk of bias that emerges when accountability is weak. If the linkage is close but the risk of bias great, it may be worthwhile to aim at the base, or the money supply, even at the sacrifice of some relevance. Or some intermediate position might be optimum. The money supply might be a better target than the base, for example, if the link between the base and the money supply was loose while the link between the money supply and the price level was tight.

There are two other reasons, probably less important, why the price level may not be the best target. One is that we mean by the price level the price at which, on the average, goods and services can be bought and sold. The price index may not measure that very well in some circumstances. The main case is that in times of recession, when demand declines, prices are sticky, and it is not true that the volume of goods and services that would be supplied at the quoted prices can be sold at those prices.

A second problem results from what are now called supply shocks. Suppose that the target is 2 percent per year inflation and that real growth nominally goes on at 3 percent per year, so that nominal GNP is rising by 5 percent per year. If there is a temporary interruption of some important supply, such as an oil embargo, so that real growth falls to 1 percent per year, the inflation rate will rise to 4 percent if the growth of nominal GNP remains unchanged. To hold the inflation rate constant at 2 percent would require a very prompt contraction of the growth of nominal GNP, and that would almost certainly cause a sharp contraction of real output. A policy of stabilizing the growth rate of nominal GNP would avoid or moderate the secondary contractions of real output, but would also permit the price level to deviate for a period from the desired path.

There has been a good deal of recent interest in using nominal GNP as a target of monetary policy, and not only for the reason just cited. Nominal GNP is intermediate among the possible goals. It is closer to what we are really interested in—the price level— than the money supply or base money, and it is quite unlikely that the inflation rate could accelerate markedly if the growth rate of nominal GNP were stabilized. At the same time, it is probably more controllable than the price level itself.

The choice among the hierarchy of targets is best looked at as a question of deciding the period to which the targets refer, rather than as a question of choosing one target to the exclusion of the others. That is, there have to be targets for all four variables all the time, and the issue is how frequently, or on what evidence, the targets are to be changed. Suppose, for example, we decide that the monetary base should be the target. How would we decide what the height of the target should be—whether, for example, we should aim at constancy of the monetary base or a 3 percent per year increase? Presumably we would have to go through a thinking process about the relation between the base and the price level. We might say that our basic goal is that the price level should be stable. We estimate that the normal growth of real output is 3 percent per year. Therefore, to keep the price level stable we need a 3 percent per year increase of nominal GNP. We estimate that velocity increases by 1 percent per year, so that to get nominal GNP rising by 3 percent, we need the money supply growing by 2 percent. Finally, we estimate that the money supply rises at the same rate as the monetary base— the "base multiplier" is constant—so that to have the money supply rising by 2 percent per year, the monetary base must rise by 2 percent per year.

Thus the target for the monetary base is derived from a target for the price level, through estimates of real growth, velocity, and the base multiplier. But these estimates are only estimates. They can be wrong in the short run or in the long run. If they are wrong, the desired levels of the four targets will not all be achieved at once. The choice of "the" target is a decision about what will be adapted first if some adaptation is necessary. If the monetary base is "the" target, the other variables will be allowed to deviate from their expected and desired path until strong evidence, probably accumulated over some period of time, shows the need to change the path of the monetary base. If, for example, nominal GNP is "the" target, this would imply, through estimates of velocity and of the base multiplier, targets for the money supply and for base money. But saying that nominal GNP is "the" target implies that if these estimates of velocity and the base multiplier turn out to be incorrect, the base multiplier and the money supply will be adapted in an effort to keep nominal GNP on its path, rather than the other way around.

I have elsewhere suggested one approach to the problem of ordering the targets. We might say that our long-term goal is an inflation rate of 2 percent per year. We could then decide that for a period of, say, five years we would aim at nominal GNP growing by 5 percent per year, on an estimate that real output would grow by 3 percent per year. But we could revise this nominal growth target every five years if there was strong reason to believe that 3 percent was not the normal growth rate of real output. Each year the Federal Reserve would set a target for the growth of the money supply, calculated to achieve the nominal GNP growth target. This involves a forecast of velocity. The Federal Reserve could revise the target rate for money growth each year as necessary to get on the nominal GNP growth path. Moreover, the growth of the monetary base could be more or less continuously adapted to try to achieve the desired growth of the money supply.

A more sophisticated and cautious version of this approach has been suggested by William Fellner. He believes that the relation between the monetary base and nominal GNP can be reasonably well predicted from one business cycle to another. Therefore, he would fix the rate of growth of the monetary base for each entire business cycle to achieve the desired course of nominal GNP over the entire cycle. But he believes that the relation between the monetary base and nominal GNP is not sufficiently predictable during the cycle to justify the attempt to vary the base in an effort to offset cyclical or random fluctuations in the relation. That is, he believes that keeping constant the rate of growth of the monetary base during the period of each business cycle will achieve as much stability of nominal GNP within the cycle as is achievable and will reduce the danger of cumulative errors that might lead to accelerating inflation or deflation.

Again, I am not proposing either of the answers to the question of monetary strategy, but only trying to illustrate what the question is. Although there has been much study of this subject in the past twenty years, there is still disagreement among experts on the targets of monetary policy. Neither can it be said that there is agreement about what the policy of the Federal Reserve now is. Although the Federal Reserve is said to take the growth of the money supply as its target, this leaves a great many uncertainties. The Federal Reserve sets the target for monetary growth each year and sometimes revises the target at the midyear point. But it has not committed itself to any longer-run path with respect to either the price level or nominal GNP, although it is believed to be aiming at something with respect to these two variables. Thus not only do we not know what the money supply targets are beyond the next twelve months (or less), we do not even know what the Federal Reserve will be thinking about or aiming at when it does set the next year's money supply target. Moreover, the annual targets are set in terms of a wide range for the permissible growth of the money supply and also in terms of at least two definitions of the money supply, which often point in different directions. And there is uncertainty about what the policy of the Federal Reserve will be if the actual money supply runs outside the target range. Observers do not know whether such a development foretells action to get down within the target range or signifies a change in the target range. There is still doubt about the most critical question, which is whether the Federal Reserve still has in mind some real targets, such as the unemployment rate.

Because the Federal Reserve has not been more explicit about its strategy, it has not gained the results in predictability and credibility that it undoubtedly sought when it made what it regarded as a major turn to anti-inflationary policy in 1979. It will not be sufficient, however, for the Federal Reserve to clarify its policy, important as that would be. It will be necessary for the policy to be endorsed by the other actors in the making of monetary policy—the administration and the Congress—and to be understood in the private sector.

Only a few words need to be said about two other possible targets that have recently attracted attention. One is to stabilize the price of gold. The rationale for this proposal is the belief that the real price of gold tends to be stable—that is, the price of gold moves in parallel with the price level. If that relation remains constant, stabilizing the price of gold will stabilize the general price level, but the underlying premise about the stability of the relationship is not sufficiently reliable to be the basis of monetary policy. This was the conclusion of a recent examination of the subject by a government commission. This question is analyzed further in Phillip Cagan's *Current Problems of Monetary Policy: Would the Gold Standard Help?*[4]

The other recent, or revived, proposal is that monetary policy should be used to stabilize interest rates. This proposal can only be attributed to confusion and ignorance of history. During World War II and until 1951 we had such a policy in the United States. Experience and argument at that time demonstrated that the policy was a prescription for endless inflation. Inflation tended to raise interest rates, and under the policy the tendency for interest rates to rise had to be countered by expansion of the money supply, which raised inflation further, tending to raise interest rates further and thus requiring more monetary expansion, and so on.

Whatever target is chosen for monetary policy, a decision has to be made about what the rate of growth of the target variable should be. As has already been said several times, the fundamental consideration is that the rate of growth should be predictable. Whether the annual rate of increase of the price level is zero or 10 percent does not in principle seem to be very important if the two rates are equally predictable.

The problem has to be seen in historical perspective. We have been going through fifteen years of accelerating inflation. We have labor contracts, credit contracts, and less formal arrangements that reflect the expectation of a high rate of inflation—say, 8 percent. If monetary policy were to aim now at getting the inflation rate promptly to zero—or to a target for the money supply consistent with that—there would be losses and unemployment for some people in the process. Thus there seems to be a case for stabilizing the inflation rate where it is, and there are supporters of this idea.

But such a policy may not achieve the predictability that is desired. It may be interpreted as signifying that if the inflation rate rises, as a result of errors of policy or exogenous forces, the Federal Reserve will then attempt to stabilize the rate of inflation at its new level. This will lead to the expectation of an inflation rate that continues to ratchet upward, as it has done in the recent

[4] American Enterprise Institute for Public Policy Research, Washington, D.C., and London, 1982.

past. There will be much uncertainty about the rate at which this happens and occasional temporary bouts of disinflation. This would not be the path of predictability that is sought.

So there seems to be a choice between trying to stabilize the high rates of growth of money, nominal GNP, and the price level already achieved and getting back down to a lower level more consistent with price-level stability. This choice depends on the painfulness of getting down and the feasibility of staying up without further escalation. Choosing the policy of getting down opens up the question of the rate at which this is to be done. That is a question largely disregarded in the discussion of monetary stabilization, which tends to focus on the virtue of keeping to a low rate of inflation that has somehow been achieved and to ignore the problem of a transition to that point from a more inflationary one.

There are two main options for this transition—cold turkey and gradualism. Where this choice has been presented, the answer has always been for gradualism. Although there has been no rigorous demonstration that gradualism is the less costly solution, it does seem to be the less risky solution, or at least the solution with less immediate risk. But gradualism, even if it is accepted, is not a precise term and encompasses a considerable range of speeds of disinflation. The importance of this question was highlighted in 1981–1982. There was, at least for a time, a faster deceleration of money growth than many people, including the administration, expected, and a faster deceleration of inflation. This was accompanied by a bigger rise of unemployment than had been expected. But it was not clear whether this was to be considered a desirable course, to be continued, or whether it was an overshooting of the disinflationary process, to be compensated for subsequently by more expansionary policy. This question became acute in the summer of 1982, when unemployment reached 10 percent, and it was not obvious what answer the Federal Reserve gave to it. More explicit discussion of this question and agreement on it, especially between the administration and the Federal Reserve, is needed.

The Principles of Stabilizing Fiscal Policy

I have stated above my belief that, with one exception, fiscal policy should be regarded as dealing with the real economy, rather than with nominal variables and those aspects of real economic behavior that are mainly determined by the nominal variables. The exception was that year-to-year stability in fiscal policy as it affects the nominal variables is desirable. This view is based on the belief that monetary policy could compensate for any effects of fiscal policy on nominal demand and on those variables that are affected by nominal demand if the effects of fiscal policy were predictable and stable.

The general separation between fiscal policy and the management of aggregate nominal demand is, of course, like other suggestions advanced here, put forward as a question deserving study and decision. I shall proceed here, however, on the assumption that this idea is accepted.

The first question that arises is how to describe a policy that stabilized the effect of the budget on the nominal variables, by which I mean nominal demand or nominal GNP. There are two problems here: how to measure the effect of the budget and how to distinguish the effect of the budget on nominal GNP from the effect of nominal GNP on the budget.

With respect to the first problem, one can imagine assigning multipliers for the effect on nominal GNP of each particular tax, expenditure, or means of borrowing—different multipliers for each—and adding up to get a weighted total effect. But while one can imagine that, one cannot do it. We do not know enough to be confident that this weighted multiplier would be a more reliable indicator of the total effect than would some cruder measure, such as the size of the deficit or surplus.

There may be some intermediate practice between trying to assign different multipliers to each expenditure and receipt, on the one hand, and looking only at the deficit or surplus, on the other hand, which would give a better measure of the net effect on aggregate demand. The textbooks suggest, for example, that expenditures for the purchase of goods and services should have a higher weight than transfer payments and tax receipts. My own view is that the gain in precision is not worth the complexity introduced, especially if we are concerned with measuring the change in effect between one year and another within short periods, where the composition of the budget in these terms is not likely to change much. That is, however, an empirical question, which deserves further study.

Even if we are going to use the size of the deficit or surplus as the measure of net effect on aggregate demand, the problem of weights arises in the definition of the budget. Since sources and uses of funds will be equal, for the federal government as for other entities, the notion of a deficit or surplus implies giving a weight of one to some sources and uses and a weight of zero to others. The chief relevance of that at present is the treatment of loan transactions, some of which are officially given a weight of one and included in the budget and others given a weight of zero and called off-budget. Many unofficial observers of budget policy do not accept this and include the off-budget transactions in their conception of the budget and the deficit. For the moment this does not matter much, since with or without the "off-budget" items the deficits are commonly agreed to be "outrageously" high. But the question of definition would become more significant as we approached an acceptable budget position. My preference would be to exclude all loan transactions from the budget, both those that are now included in the budget and those that are "off-budget." I believe that government lending and borrowing are closer to debt transactions than to expenditure transactions. That is, however, also an empirical question, which needs to be studied.

A larger question is how we would define stability of whatever measure we accept as the indicator of aggregate demand effect—presumably the budget deficit or surplus. The economy fluctuates in response to many variables outside the budget, and the deficit or surplus fluctuates in response to such fluctuations of the economy. Fluctuations arising in this way do not reflect changes in the aggregate-demand effect of the budget. There is, I suppose, common agreement that attempting to offset such fluctuations by changing tax rates or expenditure programs is neither necessary nor desirable.

The problem is how to distinguish these passive changes in the budget position from other changes that do actively disturb the aggregate-demand situation. The answer to that is to calculate the budget position (deficit or surplus) as it would be at some standard stable, or steadily growing, condition of the economy and to consider the budget to be in a stable position if this hypothetical deficit or surplus is stable. That is what the notion of balancing the budget (actually, in the first formulation, running a small surplus) at high employment did. There turned out to be serious difficulties with that formulation. First, no one knew what "high employment" was, and second, this formulation assumed away the problem of inflation. Yet the basic idea incorporated there was sound, even though the particular formulation was rather primitive. The idea was that we wanted to stabilize the budget position as it would be under desirable, feasible, and probable conditions of the economy. To aim at stabilizing the budget position under conditions that were not desirable or not feasible or not probable would not yield desired results from any standpoint. The strategy implicit in the idea was that monetary policy would aim at achieving the feasible, desirable aggregate conditions, that fiscal policy could be based on the assumption that the monetary policy would be successful on the average, though not in every year, and that fiscal policy could be directed to achieving its desired results under those targeted conditions and in a way that would at least not disrupt the efforts of monetary policy and might assist them. Thus there would be a complementarity of fiscal and monetary policies. Monetary policy would make the feasible and desirable conditions probable. A fiscal policy that would keep the budget position stable under these probable conditions would at least not interfere with the achievement of this goal of monetary policy and would tend to achieve in actuality whatever were the goals of fiscal policy itself.

The prescription that the budget should be set so as to balance at high employment was, as it turned out, a crude expression of that theory. The original formulation of the Committee for Economic Development, in 1947, recognized the price-level problem, but not the magnitude it would actually take, and offered no formula for handling it. Implicitly, the fiscal policy assumed that the monetary policy would succeed in stabilizing the price level. If monetary policy did not do that—as, of course, it did not—then the fiscal policy would not yield the results its developers sought from it.

As for fiscal policy, the basic proposition is that it should stabilize its outcome—presumably the size of the budget surplus or deficit—as it would be if the economy moved along the path at which monetary policy is aiming. This requires, since fiscal policy has to be planned for several years in advance, that the targets of monetary policy be specified for some years in advance and that these targets be agreed to by both the fiscal authorities and the monetary authority. This relation between fiscal policy and monetary policy requires that the monetary target either be nominal GNP or be translatable into nominal GNP, because the nominal GNP is a necessary ingredient for calculating the revenue and expenditure consequences of tax and expenditure programs. That is, one could not calculate what the revenues, expenditures, and surplus results would be under assumed conditions of the money supply or of the monetary base without first estimating what nominal GNP would be under those monetary conditions.

Of course, this kind of fiscal policy does not assume that monetary policy achieves its targets year by year but only that it does so on the average over a longer period. It is only the recognition that the actual path of the economy will deviate from the target path that requires the calculation of hypothetical budgets and the prescription of budget goals in terms of these hypothetical calculations.

This whole approach to the budget through calculation of hypothetical outcomes has commonly been rejected by "practical" people. They have regarded it as an evasion or gimmick to escape the hard requirements of actually balancing the budget, and they have dismissed the calculations of "high employment" budgets as mere dreaming or fakery. They insist, as a secretary of the Treasury once said, on "balancing the budget, period." This issue will have to be faced. The practical people will have to recognize that "balancing the budget, period" is the least practical of all the possibilities. Budgeting is planning for the future, and while policies can be decided in advance, the outcome of those policies cannot be told in advance. The policy decisions will have to be made on the basis of predictions of their outcomes, which depend on unforeseeable developments in the future state of the economy. The only question is what should be assumed about the future when the decisions are made. The proposition advanced here is that the path of the economy that is the target of monetary policy is both the most probable path and the path that fiscal policy should be most careful not to disturb and therefore the path on which it is most meaningful to stabilize the budget position. This subject requires much more explicit discussion than it has recently had. Nothing could be more obvious than that much current talk about deficits is made meaningless by failure to specify the conditions under which the deficits are assumed to be incurred.

The idea that the budget position should be stable, so as

to avoid disrupting the efforts of monetary policy, does not imply that it should be constant forever. It only means that it should change infrequently and should not change abruptly or unpredictably from year to year. It would not, for example, be inconsistent with deciding that the budget deficit should be gradually reduced as the economy moves along a path to low inflation and high employment and that the deficit should then settle down at a low level—not necessarily zero. Neither would it be inconsistent with a decision, at some later date, that the deficit should settle for some extended period at some larger number or, alternatively, at zero.

Stability of the hypothetical, or target, deficit or surplus would be the contribution of fiscal policy to the stability of aggregate demand and to the effectiveness of monetary policy. The level at which the deficit or surplus is stable would be determined by considerations other than aggregate demand, considerations that presumably change slowly and do not require frequent changes in the overall fiscal target.[5]

Real Fiscal Policy

The preceding discussion narrows the stabilization function of fiscal policy to serving as a rather minor and passive adjunct of monetary policy. Not everyone may accept this "demotion" of fiscal policy. But no one can deny that a major, and possibly dominant, function of fiscal policy is found in another arena— namely, in the allocation of the national output among alternative uses and persons. This is, we are increasingly coming to recognize, as true of the deficit or surplus as it is of expenditures for defense or for aid to families with dependent children. The deficit or surplus is a way of allocating the national output between investment and consumption.

[5] In its 1947 policy statement, *Taxes and the Budget,* the Research and Policy Committee of the Committee for Economic Development recommended that taxes be set so as to yield a moderate surplus and kept there "unless there is a major change in the conditions of national life." This final clause was a Keynesian escape hatch, in case it turned out that at some future time the achievement of high employment would be incompatible with a moderate budget surplus. I am not suggesting that we need a Keynesian escape hatch. I am suggesting that the considerations determining the proper size of the deficit or surplus are not constant forever.

I have considered above whether there is any "macro" aspect to this function of fiscal policy. Are we required, or permitted, to consider each of several thousand microdecisions about the budget in comparison with each of the several thousand other microdecisions? I have answered that question in the negative, on the ground that we do not have the information that would make it possible to answer all the questions simultaneously and that it would not be politically acceptable to do so even if it were possible. We must organize the decisions in the budget according to their degree of importance and generality, with higher-level, more responsible officials making the more general and important decisions and lower-level officials making the lesser decisions within the limits set by the more general decisions. The classification of these decisions and their assignment to levels of government is one of the key issues of budget policy.

A related question is whether there is any "economics" to the real budgetary decisions, however macro or micro those decisions are considered to be. There are two kinds of issues involved in these decisions. One is the issue of values. How much does the society value, for example, efficiency or growth in comparison with equality or justice? A similar question can be asked about the value to be attached to degrees of freedom from national security risks. These are not questions that economists or other social scientists should be expected or trusted to answer, although they do seem quite prepared to offer answers.

The other kind of issue is more instrumental. It is a matter of assessing or predicting the results of actual or proposed policies in terms of the objectives we are interested in. How much difference for the rate of economic growth would result from the difference between balancing the budget and running a deficit of $100 billion a year? How much difference would it make if the top marginal rate of income tax were 30 percent rather than 50 percent? How much more education would result from another $10 billion of federal aid to education, how much additional competence would result from that, and how much additional productivity and national output would result from that additional competence? How much do transfer payments reduce poverty, and how much do they increase dependency?

These are questions on which economists and other social scientists ought, in principle, to be able to throw light. That is, they are not just questions of preferences and tastes, about which disputes and investigations are ruled out. But the fact is that we do not know much about them. The situation can be put more precisely. We do not know nearly as much about these questions as we would like to know, but we know more about many of them than is reflected in public discussion and in the policy-making process.

The 1981 supply-side tax cut is the most obvious example of this situation. It is perfectly true that economists did not know with any precision what the size and timing of the effects of the tax cuts on incentives to work and save would be. Still, the argument made for the tax cut, and probably the reasons that supported it in the minds of many people, implied that these effects would be of a size and speed quite outside the range that economists would have considered probable.

Similar observations, though less clear-cut, can be made about other major fiscal decisions. Economists and other social scientists would probably agree, for example, that they can estimate only crudely and uncertainly the effects of government antipoverty programs on poverty, dependency, and other conditions of national concern. But the popular and political discussion of such programs commonly implies judgments about these effects, positive and negative, that are outside the range within which experts would think the truth lies.

There is little that can be said here about how to make better decisions on the real aspects of fiscal policy. Obviously, we need to learn more. Students of fiscal policy have had an excursion for about fifty years in the field of nominal macroeconomics. It is time now to devote more attention to the real side of things— to the effects of budget decisions on the allocation of the national output. That has already begun, but it needs to be carried much further.

But at best we will learn slowly. We will have to make decisions with inadequate information, and for a long time we will not have much more information than we now have. The problem of government policy will be, as always, what to do when you don't know what to do—when the available information does not point unequivocally to a certain policy as best. There is no specific prescription for handling this problem. The answer lies in the qualities that are generally described as sound judgment and responsibility. There are some rules of thumb that suggest elements of what is required: policy should not change in big leaps unless there are unusual and radical changes in conditions; "try and see" is a good rule; the lessons of experience should be studied; political consensus should be respected, and the squeaking wheel should get the grease; if it ain't broke, don't fix it. To spell out a prescription for sound judgment and responsible behavior is obviously beyond the scope of this paper and the competence of this author. But to recognize what we don't know, and what we must think about, is a step toward better decisions, and it is hoped that this paper is a contribution toward that.

Index